IEG
LEGAL GUIDE
TO SPONSORSHIP

Published by
International Events Group, Inc.
Chicago, Illinois

BY MARY HUTCHINGS REED

Lesa Ukman
Editor

Jon Ukman
Publisher

Mary Hutchings Reed
Author

Ann Heinrichs
Manuscript Editor

Liska and Associates, Inc.
Design

Published by International Events Group, Inc.
213 West Institute Place, Suite 303
Chicago, Illinois 60610 U.S.A.
Tel: 312/944-1727
Fax: 312/944-1897

Jacqueline Moriarty
Special Projects Director

Jim Ryscamp
Assistant Publisher

Jim Andrews
Editorial Director

Jeanette LoCurto
Associate Editor

Special Events Report™
The Official Directory of Festivals, Sports &
Special Events™
IEG Guide to Sponsorship Agencies™
Event Marketing Seminar Series™
IEG Consulting™

Library of Congress Cataloging-in-Publication Data

Reed, Mary Hutchings.
    IEG legal guide to sponsorship.

    Including bibliographical references.
    1. Performing arts sponsorship—Law and legislation—
United States. 2. Promotion of special events—Law and
legislation—United States. 3. Corporate sponsorship—
Law and legislation—United States. I. International
Events Group. II. Title.
KF4290.R44 1989   344.73'097   89-26934
ISBN 0-944807-01-1   347.30497

TABLE OF CONTENTS

INTRODUCTION

Lesa Ukman, executive editor, *Special Events Report*

IEG is proud to publish this guide on the legal concerns of sponsorship. We've watched interest in the industry skyrocket and we recognize the special legal questions that this growth has engendered. Can organizers of a parade sell broadcast exclusivity when the event is held on a public street? Who receives signage when a rock group sponsored by one cola plays a venue sponsored by another? To what extent is a sponsor liable for tragedies at its events?

The IEG Legal Guide to Sponsorship, by Mary Hutchings Reed, a practicing advertising, entertainment and intellectual properties lawyer and partner with Winston & Strawn, Chicago, tackles these and many other issues between sponsors and sponsees. Her approach, accessible to both laypersons and lawyers, encourages sponsors to weigh their level of involvement and urges promoters to realize the full selling potential of their events. Reed defines common sponsorship contract terms and gives sponsor and sponsee an understanding of their obligations and expectations, so that ultimately each can view the other's concerns dispassionately.

From the start, Reed acknowledges that the scope of exclusivity is always the bottom line on a sponsorship contract. Sample contracts follow the first chapter. Reed also presents a sponsorship contract checklist that covers everything from official status and advertising credits to merchandising rights and liabilities.

Agreements regarding an event's proprietary value and trademark use are continuing to evolve as event promoters and sponsors invent new ways to package and exploit properties. Reed prescribes methods for protecting broadcast and recording rights, preventing event theft and determining where logo and trademark rights really rest.

As companies have integrated sponsorship into their overall marketing plans, often as the spur for cross-selling and the hook for broader advertising, off-site promotions add value to events and make the specifics of contractual agreements essential. Reed explains what's legal in ambush marketing and illustrates how events have been effectively pirated outside structured sponsorship agreements. She devotes a significant portion of her text to trademark protection – appreciating that an understanding of these contractual agreements is critical to realizing the promotion value of a sponsorship.

Reed also summarizes sponsorship's legal concerns for non-profit organizations and municipalities, and has compiled a chart outlining state legislation. Cause-related sponsorships have mushroomed and will continue to grow as long as sponsors and promoters find value beyond goodwill. Reed offers advice on what sponsors can claim as charitable contributions and outlines limitations for promoters who claim non-profit status. Municipalities caught in the sponsor frenzy also are facing new legal issues. Reed discusses the First Amendment's protection of access to permits and restrictions on alcohol and tobacco sponsorships, which vary by state.

Illuminating and objectively addressing the legal concerns of event-marketing, Reed makes accessible what can otherwise be daunting and difficult for sponsors and promoters. An industry first, *The IEG Legal Guide to Sponsorship* is a vital document for every sponsorship library.

PREFACE
THE LAWYER'S ROLE

There is a wonderful dynamic of enthusiasm between event promoter and event sponsor, and a shared and less enthusiastic societal attitude about lawyers. How warmly are lawyers to be welcomed to the sponsorship relationship? Won't lawyers muck it up?

Lawyers are paid to think about the unthinkable, to talk about the unspeakable – in short, to think and talk about the day when *the parties won't speak to each other*. This is not to say that we are by nature a negative sort; we are trained to worry. But when we are at our best, we *solve* problems (even those of our own imagination or creation) and find a creative way to do what at first blush "can't be done." In short, lawyers can help save both promoters and sponsors from their own enthusiasm, while actually enabling the parties to keep their distance from the negativism of contemplating worst-case scenarios.

Sponsorship law is fun and it is challenging. It invites a lawyer to think both like a promoter and like a sponsor. It is fast-paced at times and painfully slow at others. It offers the lawyer the opportunity to witness not only the birth of an idea but also its growth into a national tradition.

This book is not meant to substitute for the hiring of lawyers (that is not in our nature). In these chapters, I do not purport to give legal advice – each reader should consult with his or her own lawyer. The sample contracts presented are illustrative only and should not be used without consultation with legal counsel. This information is presented to help the reader make better use of lawyers – to make more informed, effective and cost-efficient use of an expensive service. THE FOREGOING DISCLAIMER IS THE KIND OF THING LAWYERS ARE HIRED TO WRITE. It could have been said with more or longer words or fewer or shorter ones; the point is, something of that nature should be said – and lawyers are hired to say it.

What can lawyers add to the dialogue between promoter and sponsor? I believe lawyers can add their experience, their objectivity, their negotiating ability and their knowledge of areas of the law peculiar to sponsorship.

What we perceive to be the principal legal concerns of sponsor and promoter are discussed in the following chapters. Sample contracts are provided to focus attention on the basic legal relationships among those participating in events. (Some alternative contract provisions are provided in brackets.) The chapters also examine particular problems with respect to trademarks, protecting the proprietary value of an event, liability and not-for-profit organizations. Some special industries and their regulatory problems are addressed in some detail. The appendices reproduce some key laws and legal forms. In addition, a short glossary of legal and industry terms is included for those not familiar with the jargon.

This work is meant to be comprehensive, but the very creative nature of sponsorship dictates that it cannot be exhaustive. Nonetheless, I hope that the reader will find these pages useful in achieving ever more pleasant and rewarding sponsorship relationships.

Mary Hutchings Reed
Winston & Strawn

ACKNOWLEDGMENTS

Many people and experiences contribute on many levels to a work such as this. Here, I can thank only a few. Most importantly, my thanks to Lesa Ukman and Jon Ukman for introducing me to the world of sponsorship and for encouraging me to explore this challenging area of the law. Over the years I have learned much from my former partners in the law firm of Sidley & Austin. My partners Charles E. Lomax, Stephen P. Durchslag (now also with Winston & Strawn) and Philip J. Crihfield have helped me to learn about various aspects of sponsorship law; R. Quincy White, Jr. has guided my drafting style since the beginning of my career – and many of us are still learning from him. My former partners Tom W. Davidson and Robert C. Wootton have contributed their respective insights on communications and tax law. Mary A. Carragher's comments on television contracts, Andrew L. Goldstein's and Maureen B. Collins's work on trademarks and Florise Neville's summary of work-for-hire doctrine contributed significantly to the book's usefulness, and I am grateful for their work. (Parts of the chapter on trademarks was published in another form by Matthew Bender & Company, Inc. in the Spring of 1989 in *Business Torts* and are used in a modified form with permission.) Amy K. Singh, Howard R. Fine and Alan Goldman provided additional research assistance.

My secretary, Diane Roberts, typed nearly every word of this book with speed, skill, patience and good humor, and various members of Sidley & Austin's Word Processing staff, especially Joan Hill and Debbie Ochwat, completed the work under the guidance of Lela Whitted.

Also helpful was the legal research of Sidley & Austin's student interns Caprice Bragg, Douglas A. Coblens, Isaac Corre, Molly Diggins, Peter Etienne, Kenneth Higgins, Kathryn L. Johnson, Sheila B. Kennedy, Stephen King, John Rafkin, Richard Y. Sako, Mark K. Schrupp, Edward M. Snyder, Vimal K. Shah and Christopher B. Wilson. All of our work was, of course, made better by my editor, Ann Heinrichs, whose insights and attention to detail were greatly appreciated. Ann also provided the helpful index.

On a personal level, it is the joy of true love to have a spouse who is supportive of my professional ambitions (and who provides me hours of "free time" while he makes weekend rounds on his internal medicine patients!). I am always indebted to my parents, who provided me with the example of combining, as in sponsorship, hard work and good fun. I am grateful to my father for believing that women, like my mother, can (and should) have careers. I apologize to my mother that this is not the Great American Novel – but maybe next time!

Despite the number of people who in many ways contributed to this work, I take responsibility for all errors and omissions and for every contract that could be just that much better. Such is the challenge of the legal profession.

Mary Hutchings Reed
Winston & Strawn

CHAPTER I:
CONTRACTS

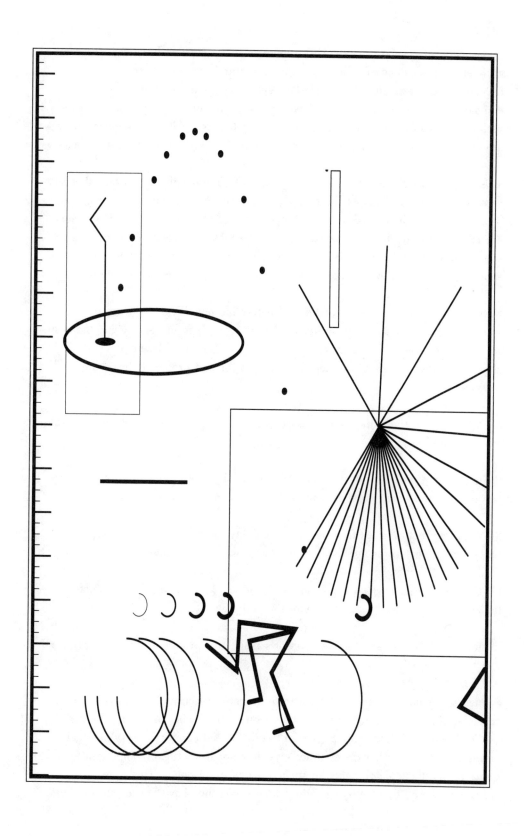

THE REASON FOR SPONSORSHIP CONTRACTS

Sponsorship of special events such as concerts, marathons and contests presents an interesting challenge for promoters, sponsors and participants, as well as for lawyers. What starts out as a simple handshake agreement can become more complex when the lawyers get involved, and while many might want to avoid the verb-less pages of fine type that attorneys often feel compelled to produce, there are important reasons to formalize agreements in a written contract of some sort.

This chapter deals extensively with the variety of contractual relationships that help create a successful event. At the end of the chapter are samples of the major types of contracts used in sponsored events. A number of other event-related contracts are presented throughout the book. Perhaps the most important of these is the sponsorship contract itself. Examining the major points to be covered in the sponsorship contract will illustrate why written contracts generally are desirable.

Often the price tag on a sponsorship will determine how "legal" the written sponsorship agreement will be. But in virtually every form of sponsorship there are some good reasons for putting the agreement in writing with the help of an attorney. In the case of a contract between sponsor and promoter, five main reasons are:

(1) to clarify the rights the sponsor is getting and the promoter is retaining (to sell to someone else);

(2) to preserve the value of the sponsor's exclusivity by avoiding possible conflicts between sponsors and other presenters and suppliers;

(3) to protect both parties from unwanted liability for personal injury, property damage and other problems likely to arise out of any event that draws a crowd;

(4) to protect the sponsor's reputation and trademarks as well as the promoter's trademarks and official logos and symbols; and

(5) to protect the promoter's and sponsor's respective proprietary and other interests in the event.

Sponsorship comes in many different forms – from picking up hall costs for a concert to buying the event itself for television and/or cable broadcast. Terms such as "lead sponsor," "presenting sponsor" and "official supplier" carry no legal meaning other than what the contract says they do. It is critically important to sponsors that their major rights be spelled out in exact detail. This protects promoters as well by identifying clearly what rights they have left to sell to others.

Drafting such a list of sponsor rights is instructive, too. Which commitments each party can make in writing and which are of the "oh-we'll-take-care-of-that" variety can be illuminating rather than merely reflective of personal style.

The value of an event sponsorship is often dependent on the scope of exclusivity. A sponsor could have exclusive sponsorship of the entire event, or be the sole sponsor in a category, or have some veto power regarding other sponsors not compatible with its image. This can become particularly complicated when an event takes place at different sites or is planned as a series. Thus the contract should specifically address the scope of exclusivity and the issue of whether "presenters" or "official suppliers" are allowed. The sponsor may argue that too many names associated with an event dilute the value of its sponsorship; the contract can be used to limit the extent to which a sponsor must share the spotlight. In addition, the contract should address possible conflicts between official event sponsors/suppliers and permanent advertising signage at the site or, worse yet, preexisting official suppliers to the site. For instance, if Pepsi-Cola is the sponsor of an event, it may be embarrassing if the arena served only Coca-Cola. Such snafus can be avoided if the sponsorship contract anticipates the scope of the sponsor's rights and the possible interferences.

Another important reason to have a written contract is that the promoter and the sponsor of an event will each be using the other's trademarks, which are often their most valuable assets. Trademark law requires that a trademark owner police the use of its trademarks to assure the quality of the goods or services sold under them. In addition, most trademark owners want the right to protect their images by controlling how their trademarks are used.

Size and placement of the sponsor's trademarks in relation to others' marks should also be specified with some particularity. This helps to avoid too much clutter. If the promoter of an event develops a unique name or logo that incorporates the sponsor's marks, the sponsor should require approval rights and probably co-ownership. On the other hand, a promoter who has created an event mark that does not include the sponsor's marks will want the contract to recite the promoter's sole ownership of that mark.

Moreover, the organizer of an event may also feel the need to protect itself against the event's being "stolen" by a sponsor. Provisions that prevent a sponsor from sponsoring similar competing events within a certain radius of the event site for a certain period of time break the sponsor's continuity and help to protect the organizer. Such contract provisions are usually heavily negotiated.

Conversely, the sponsor usually feels that it is investing a significant amount of its goodwill in an event in addition to its monetary commitment. In order to protect its investment, the sponsor should have some assurance of the opportunity for continued involvement. That can take the form of a long initial term with options to cancel, a shorter term with options to renew, a right of first refusal or some combination of these. The contracting parties should write and review such clauses carefully to avoid ambiguities.

Having covered the basics – who gets what and who pays how much – the balance of the sponsorship contract will include "what ifs." What if the event is rained or burned out, underdraws, loses key personnel or performing talent, creates a riot or falls victim to some other not-so-unforeseeable "unforeseeable" catastrophe? The contract drafter's job, of course, is to think of the unthinkable and to find an equitable solution. Risk can be allocated depending on the relative fault of the promoter and sponsor or on the ability of the parties to bear the "act of God" or "force majeure" occurrence. Rescheduling might be feasible; a reduction in the sponsorship fee might suffice. Either the promoter or the sponsor (or both) may insure against some risks – such as failure of a talent to perform or failure of broadcasting facilities. A contract can be used to pass what liability the sponsor might have in such cases back to the promoter of the event through an indemnification or hold harmless clause (see Chapter 5).

Some important miscellaneous issues can be covered in some detail in sponsorship contracts. For instance, outlining when and how the sponsorship fee is paid often requires careful drafting. Some sponsorship contracts specify progress payments after certain tasks are completed or third-party commitments obtained. Some involve the use of commercial paper such as letters of credit. A letter of credit basically obligates the bank of the person giving the letter to pay the payee up to a certain amount upon the payee's presentation of certain documents. For example, a letter of credit may be payable upon presentation of an article from a newspaper of general circulation stating that the event took place. The sponsor is thus assured that it pays no money (or perhaps only a very small advance) until the event actually happens. On the other hand, the promoter has an assurance that the money will be there upon completion of the event; moreover, it may be able to borrow operating funds against the letter of credit. Letters of credit and contract terms concerning them should be drafted by attorneys.

Lastly, certain groups and industries operate under peculiar legal or quasi-legal constraints. This may call for special contract clauses to assure that special requirements will be honored. For example, some sponsorships involve amateur athletic governing bodies, and those bodies will want assurances that the promoter and sponsor will not interfere with the amateur status of their members. (A sample of such a clause is included in Appendix A.) Highly regulated industries include the tobacco and alcohol industries, and sponsorship in those industries is subject to numerous state regulations (see Chapter 7).

Below is an informal checklist that may be helpful in drafting a sponsorship contract. The various issues raised in the checklist are addressed in detail in this and other chapters and in the annotations to the sample contracts.

SPONSORSHIP CONTRACT CHECKLIST

Sponsorship Rights

1. Sponsor's Official Status

   As only sponsor?
   As only sponsor in a category?
   Right to veto other sponsors for reasons of incompatibility?
   Any conflicts with official suppliers?
   What about sponsorships at other sites or related events?

2. Signs at the Event

   How many?
   What is the size and placement of sponsor's name relative to others?
   Who pays?
   Distance from others' signs?
   Sign on curtain?
   Billing on marquees?
   Signs on vehicles (sound trucks, courtesy cars, etc.)?
   Any conflicts with permanent signage or arena suppliers?

3. Advertising Credits

   On stationery?
   In name of event?
   On program cover?
   In program advertisement?
   In all advertising?
   In all print advertising only?
   In television billboards?
   On souvenirs (T-shirts, bumper stickers, etc.)?
   In Press releases?

4. Sponsorship Fee

   How paid?
   When paid?
   Secured by letter of credit or escrow?
   Refundable if television ratings are poor?

5. Merchandising Rights

   Can the sponsor sell T-shirts, mugs and similar souvenirs?
   Can the sponsor manufacture its own souvenirs or buy from the promoter at cost?
   Who gets the profit on merchandising efforts?

6. Ownership of Television Rights

   Who owns and controls?

   If the promoter owns, does the sponsor have right of first refusal on available spots?

   Is there an estimated rating and/or a rebate for low ratings?

   Does the sponsor get opening/closing credits or billboards?

   Does the sponsor have rights to use footage of the event for current
       and/or future advertising?

   Will the Promoter get all rights necessary from participants to allow use of clips in
       commercials without further compensation?

7. Public Relations and Personal Appearances

   Can the promoter commit key personnel or talent to personal appearances
       on behalf of the sponsor?

   Can the promoter commit its spokespersons to mention the sponsor's name
       whenever possible?

   Does the sponsor have the right to erect a courtesy tent?

   Can the promoter commit the key personnel participating in an event to attending
       post-event parties in their honor?

   Does the sponsor get free tickets (for key customers, tie-in contests, etc.)?

8. Future Options

   Does the sponsor have the right to renew its sponsorship on the same terms and
       conditions (plus a fixed increase in the price)?

   Does the sponsor have the right of first refusal for subsequent years?

Trademarks

1. Sponsor's quality control
2. Promoter's quality control
3. Ownership of special logos

Liabilities

1. To observers
2. To participants
3. To the site
4. To innocent bystanders
5. For infringement of trademarks
6. For contractual commitments in the event of rain, broadcast interruption,
       force majeure events

COMMON CONTRACT TERMS

A contract is an agreement – a "meeting of the minds" between two parties. Contracts need not be written to be enforceable – in some cases, handshakes will do – but whenever anything valuable is at stake, it is wise to put the essentials in writing. It is perfectly reasonable, for example, for a radio station to provide the music for a spontaneous celebration in honor of a local sports team on nothing more than a phone call. A multimillion dollar concert tour sponsorship is something else, both for the sponsor demanding a return on its investment and for the promoter depending on the sponsorship fee.

Contracts are not merely for the lawyers. Event organizers and sponsors, as well as participants in events, should read their contracts carefully – no matter how foreign the language. Once signed, a written contract is binding; even if not signed, reliance by one party on the other's proposed terms may also be binding.

Of course, the best contracts written by promoters and sponsors are easily read – that is, common English words are used in simple sentences to describe the rights and duties of the parties. However, some common English words, like "good faith," "reasonable" and "best efforts" carry with them some legal meaning and effect at common law. Therefore, they should not be used without an understanding of what they mean. (Common law is the body of precedent that has developed from the decisions by courts in cases, as opposed to the statutory law passed by legislative bodies.) A client should never sign a contract without knowing what the terms mean. Moreover, no matter how plain the English, the law restricts how parties can contract with respect to events like bankruptcy and issues like enforcing personal service contracts and morals clauses. These common words and phrases, used as contract terms, are discussed in the following pages.

"Good Faith"

Many promoters of events like to write contracts that use words like "best efforts" and "good faith." Such terms are vague at best, and courts have had surprisingly little success in defining them precisely. Most American jurisdictions, now read into all contractual relationships an implied duty of good faith and fair dealing.[1] It is this implied duty, rather than explicit clauses, that has been interpreted most often by the courts.

1.
See *Restatement (Second) of Contracts* § 205, U.C.C. 1-203.

The concept of good faith is difficult to define precisely because the words "good faith" appear in the law in a variety of contexts. Here, we deal with the duty of good faith in the context of contract performance under common law. While a precise concept of good faith performance is elusive, one court has said:

> It is a term incapable of exact legislative definition, to the same extent and for the same reasons as are such words as "willful" and "malicious" and "intent," connoting conditions of the mind which may be fathomed, if at all, only in their special factual setting . . . [Good] faith is a juridical tool of remarkable flexibility.[2]

One law professor, in an article discussing "good faith" in general contract law, asserted that:

> good faith is an "excluder." It is a phrase without general meaning or [meanings] of its own and serves to exclude a wide range of heterogeneous forms of bad faith. In a particular context the phrase takes on specific meaning but usually this is only by way of contrast with the specific form of bad faith actually or hypothetically ruled out.[3]

Generally, courts employ a rule called the good faith performance doctrine to effectuate the intentions of the parties. In so doing, courts seek to protect the reasonable expectations of the parties.[4] Good faith performance has been defined as "faithfulness to an agreed common purpose and consistency with the justified expectations of the other party; it excludes a variety of types of conduct characterized as involving [bad faith] because they violate community standards of decency, fairness or reasonableness."[5]

"Faithfulness to a common purpose" requires cooperation by one party to a contract so that the other party will not be deprived of his or her reasonable expectations. Of course, there are various levels of contract performance. Each party may exercise some discretion in its performance of the contract and agrees to exercise that discretion in good faith. It has been said that the doctrine of good faith permits the exercise of such discretion for any purpose reasonably within the contemplation of the parties. Under that analysis, good faith is breached if a party uses its discretion in a way not reasonably contemplated by the party claiming a breach. Therefore, two questions should be asked in determining good faith: (1) What was the purpose of the party in exercising its discretion, and (2) Was that purpose within the reasonable contemplation of the other party? The

2.
In re Heard, 6 B.R. 876, 883 (1980).

3.
Summers, "Good Faith in General Contract Law and the Sales Provisions of the Uniform Commercial Code," 54 Va. L. Rev. 195, 201 (1968).

4.
Burton, "Breach of Contract and the Common Law Duty to Perform in Good Faith," 94 Harv. L. Rev. 369, 371 (1980).

5.
Restatement (Second) of Contracts § 205 comment a.

first is an inquiry as to subjective intent. In contrast, the second is an objective question that assumes a normal or ordinary course of events consistent with a party's expectations.

6.
30 N.Y.2d 34, 330 N.Y.S.2d 329 (1972).

The New York case of *Van Valkenburgh* v. *Hayden Publishing Co.*[6] illustrates an interpretation of a good faith performance clause using the subjective intent/objective expectations test. In *Van Valkenburgh,* a publisher promised the author of two books a royalty on sales and its best efforts to promote the books. Nine years later, the author refused the publisher's request to update the books. The publisher then hired a third person to update the books at a lower royalty, concealed that fact from the original author and sought to sell the updated version to buyers requesting the original. The court found no violation of the implied covenant of good faith, although the diversion of customers to the updated book was held to violate the publisher's express promise to use its best efforts to promote the plaintiff's work. The court said that the publisher, by entering the contract, did not "close off" its right to issue books on the same subject. To phrase the court's opinion in terms of the subjective intent/objective expectations analysis: (1) Had the publisher's subjective purpose been to promote *other* authors' works in accord with its own economic interest, (2) that purpose would not violate the covenant of good faith because, objectively speaking, the parties did not contemplate that the publisher would promote only Van Valkenburgh's work.

Obviously, this standard provides little guidance. Proof of the parties' intentions and the reasonableness of their expectations is amorphous at best. As is obvious from the lack of case law, few litigants would rely solely on the breach of a good faith clause as the basis for a lawsuit; the difficulties of proof would make the cost of enforcement nearly prohibitive. Good faith, then, is a common contract term that allows the parties to leave some issues unresolved so that a contract can be signed. But it could also be seen as an agreement to disagree at some future date, since neither side is likely to enforce a good faith performance clause.

In addition to requiring performance in good faith, a contract may require the parties to negotiate in the future in good faith. Nearly all of the common law concerning negotiation in good faith is based on interpretation of various labor relations statutes that require an employer to bargain collectively in good faith.

7.
Mead Corp. v. *N.L.R.B.*, 697 F.2d 1013 (11th Cir. 1983).

In determining whether a party has refused to bargain in good faith, the party's conduct must be considered in light of all circumstances.[7] Broadly, however, the requirement of "good faith bargaining" imposes an obligation to come to the bargaining table with an open mind and a sincere desire to reach agreement. "Good faith bargaining" necessarily entails the earnest efforts of both sides to resolve a controversy.[8]

In many respects, it is easier to substantively define "bad faith bargaining" than "good faith bargaining." In order to show a lack of good faith, it is necessary to establish facts from which it can be reasonably inferred that a party entered on a course of negotiation and pursued it with desire or intent *not* to enter into an agreement at all.[9] Good faith is rendered impossible where one party has foreclosed in advance any possibility of agreement.[10] For example, rigid adherence to disadvantageous proposals or summary rejection of another party's demands, without apparent serious consideration of them, may provide a basis for inferring bad faith.[11] Typically, courts have held that the content of a proposal supports an inference of intent to frustrate a negotiation where the entire spectrum of the proposal is so consistently and predictably unpalatable to the other party that the proposer should know that agreement is impossible.[12]

It should be noted that adamant insistence on a bargaining position is not itself a refusal to bargain in good faith.[13] In fact, refusal to meet the other party's demands, when based upon facts and sound business judgment, is not inconsistent with good faith negotiation.[14] Because there is a more substantial body of law concerning good faith bargaining, a contract clause requiring good faith bargaining may be enforceable. Here, again, there is little case law outside the labor context.

"Best Efforts"

Contractual clauses requiring the parties to use their "best efforts" to perform, promote or produce a product or an event are also common. Although there is again a surprising absence of case law on the meaning of this not uncommon clause, it is nevertheless apparent that "best efforts" implies more of a duty than good faith.

It is generally thought that "best efforts" imposes a legal duty of performance more demanding than mere competence or due diligence. In the view of one court, "if the duty of best effort is owed, a contract must be performed even at a loss."[15] Other courts have suggested an interpretation of "best efforts" broadly consistent with that statement. For example, in *Bloor* v. *Falstaff Brewing Corp.*,[16] a contract required the buyer (Falstaff) of certain assets of a brewery to pay royalties of fifty cents per barrel for beer sold under the brewery's brand name and required the buyer to use its best efforts to promote and maintain a high volume of sales. The court held that, although Falstaff wasn't required to spend itself into bankruptcy to promote the sale of the plaintiff's product, it was not free to emphasize profit at the

8.
See Duval County School Bd. v. Florida Public Emp. Relations Commission, 353 So. 2d 1244, 1248, (Fla. App. 1978); N.L.R.B. v. DeCorel Corp., 397 F.2d 488, 493 (7th Cir. 1968).

9.
Brotherhood of R.R. Trainmen v. Akron & Barberton R.R. Co., 385 F.2d 581, 597 (D.C. Cir. 1967).

10.
N.L.R.B. v. Westinghouse Air Brake Co., 120 F.2d 1004, 1006 (3d Cir. 1941).

11.
See N.L.R.B. v. Blevins Popcorn Co., 659 F.2d 1173 (D.C. Cir. 1981); N.L.R.B. v. Century Cement Manufacturing Co., 208 F.2d 84 (2d Cir. 1953).

12.
See, e.g., N.L.R.B. v. Mar-Len Cabinets, Inc., 659 F.2d 995 (9th Cir. 1981).

13.
Chevron Oil Co., Standard Oil Co. of Texas Division v. N.L.R.B., 442 F.2d 1067 (5th Cir. 1971).

14.
Yellow Cab Operating Co. v. Taxi-Cab Drivers Local Union No. 889 of Oklahoma City, 35 F. Supp. 403 (D.C. Okla. 1940), rev'd on other grounds, 123 F.2d 262.

15.
In re Heard, 6 B.R. 876, 884 (1980).

16.
601 F.2d 609 (2d Cir.
1979).

expense of volume, but instead was bound to merchandise the beer to the extent of its capabilities.[17] In other words, the "best efforts" clause implied that the parties expected Falstaff to give due consideration to the volume of sales as well as profit.

17.
Id. at 614.

"Best efforts" is not a concept terribly distinct from "good faith." In general, however, a "best efforts" clause contemplates that a party will *do more* than merely profit-maximize. A contract that obligates a party to use its best efforts to promote or perform may require that party to run the risk of financial sacrifice in order to do so. In that way, it requires more of the promisor than good faith.

APPROVAL CLAUSES

Many sponsorship contracts reserve to the sponsor a right of approval over various aspects of the event, such as advertising, participants or other sponsors. Such contracts often state that approval "shall not be unreasonably withheld." Though such clauses are frequently used, there is not much case law on their meaning. Many cases discuss approval rights in general, though, and a brief look at some of them is useful in defining the clause's legal effect and meaning.

Even when the words "unreasonably withheld" are not used, the law interprets an approval clause in a contract in one of two ways. In matters involving operative fitness, mechanical utility or commercial value, judges use an objective, "reasonable person" test. Under this test, any disapproval must be based on reasonable grounds. However, in matters dealing with personal taste, feeling, fancy or judgment, courts use a subjective test, requiring only a party's honest disapproval. In this situation, the party holding the right of approval is the sole judge of his or her satisfaction, as long as he or she disapproves in good faith.[18] A contract may specify which of the two tests – "reasonable person" or good faith – will apply. When an "approval shall not be unreasonably withheld" clause is included in a contract, courts use the "reasonable person" test to determine whether a party's rejection is legitimate. If a sponsor desires greater approval power than the "reasonable person" test affords, it should so specify in the contract, such as by stating that approval may be withheld in the sponsor's sole discretion. In either case, the sponsor must exercise its approval power honestly and in good faith.

The "Reasonable Person" Standard. The "reasonable person" standard applies to contracts involving matters of commercial value or quality, operative fitness or mechanical utility.[19] Under the "reasonable person" test, dissatisfaction cannot be claimed arbitrarily, unreasonably or capriciously.[20] Rather, legitimate reasons must support any claim of dissatisfaction.

For example, in *Meredith Corp.* v. *Design & Lithography Center, Inc.,*[21] the court considered whether a door manufacturing company properly rejected advertising sheets because of color variations within each sheet and among the sheets. The court reasoned that, because performance in most commercial contracts is judged by operative fitness, mechanical utility and commercial value, the "reasonable person" standard was appropriate.[22] The court found that the quality of the printing work could be judged objectively.

The Subjective Standard. If a contract involves matters of personal taste, fancy or judgment, courts employ a subjective test when examining the approval or disapproval of another's performance.[23] Examples include contracts for a portrait,[24]

18.
17 Am. Jur. 2d *Contracts* § 367.

19.
Mattei v. *Hopper*, 330 P.2d 625, 626 (Cal. 1958) [Contract provision requiring acquisition of leases satisfactory to purchaser of shopping center].

20.
Id. at 627.

21.
101 Idaho 391, 614 P.2d 414 (1980).

22.
Id. at 393, 614 P.2d at 416.

23.
Mattei v. *Hopper*, 330 P.2d 625, 627 (Cal. 1958).

24.
See Wolff v. *Smith*, 303 Ill. App. 413, 25 N.E.2d 399 (1940) [Painting not true likeness of father].

25.
See Zaleski v. *Clark*, 44 Conn. 218 (1876) [Facial features disporportionate].

26.
See Haven v. *Russell*, 34 N.Y.S. 292 (1895) [Actor not satisfied with plot].

27.
See Walker v. *Edward Thompson Co.*, 37 App. Div. 536, 56 N.Y.S. 326 (1899).

28.
See Hartman v. *Blackburn*, 7 Pittsb. Legal J. (Pa.) 140 [Appearance of teeth unsatisfactory].

29.
See Brown v. *Foster*, 113 Mass. 136 (1873) [Fit of suit unsatisfactory].

30.
Meredith Corp., 101 Idaho at 393, 614 P.2d at 416.

31.
303 Ill. App. 413, 25 N.E.2d 399 (1940).

32.
Id. at 417, 25 N.E.2d at 403.

33.
Id.

34.
Oakland Raiders, Ltd. v. *National Football League*, 791 F.2d 1356, 1361 (9th Cir. 1986) [Holding that the NFL must exercise rights over franchise moves reasonably and in good faith].

a bust,[25] a script,[26] a journal article,[27] artificial teeth[28] and a suit of clothes.[29] Artwork on sponsored products or publicity stills of key participants also fall within this category.

Where idiosyncratic preferences of the contracting party are the contractual standard, the law requires only a party's honest dissatisfaction to find the contract unperformed.[30] For example, *Wolff* v. *Smith*,[31] involved a contract for the painting of a portrait, with the condition that the defendant be satisfied with the finished work. The court used the subjective test in determining whether the defendant's rejection of the portrait was justified under the contract.[32] The court found that satisfaction with a portrait was a matter of personal taste and that the defendant's honest dissatisfaction with the portrait was sufficient to validate his rejection of performance.[33]

Such powers of approval are not unconstrained, however, and must be exercised within the parameters of the duty of good faith.[34] In this context, good faith requires only that any disapproval be based on honest dissatisfaction and not solely on the desire to avoid contractual duties.[35] In addition, the party rejecting performance must tell the other why he or she is dissatisfied and give the other an opportunity to cure his or her performance, if possible.[36]

"Approval Shall Not Be Unreasonably Withheld" Clauses. When interpreting an "approval shall not be unreasonably withheld" clause, courts look for the meaning actually intended by the contracting parties.[37] The law interprets such a contractual clause as requiring *objective dissatisfaction* with the other party's performance. The objectivity of the dissatisfaction is judged by the "reasonable person" standard. Should a sponsor desire greater control over a promoter's performance, it is free to negotiate that a subjective standard applies.

The case of *Aztec Film Productions, Inc.* v. *Prescott Valley, Inc.*[38] exemplifies the legal interpretation of an "approval shall not be unreasonably withheld" clause. That case involved a contract for the production of a film for use as a sales aid in connection with several real estate developments. The defendant, Prescott Valley, retained a right of approval over the scripts and agreed to a contract provision that its approval would not be unreasonably withheld.[39] Scripts fall within the category wherein courts normally employ the subjective test, requiring only honest dissatisfaction.[40] However, the court held that the "approval shall not be unreasonably withheld" provision required Prescott Valley to be *objectively dissatisfied* with the script.[41] Thus, the court employed the reasonable person standard to determine whether Prescott Valley's rejection of the script was justified. Since the script included unverified factual statements, Prescott Valley's disapproval met that test.

When a contract specifies that "approval shall not be unreasonably withheld," a party must have a legitimate, objectively reasonable justification to reject another party's performance. This is true even for matters where courts traditionally employ a subjective, honest dissatisfaction test. If a party desires a greater degree of control over the other party's performance, it should not agree to an "approval shall not be unreasonably withheld" clause. Instead, to ensure application of the subjective standard, the party should specify that approval may be withheld in its sole discretion. The law still requires, however, that the party exercise its approval power honestly and in good faith.

35.
San Bernardino Valley Water Development Co. v. San Bernardino Valley Municipal Water District, 45 Cal. Rptr. 793, 805, 236 Cal. App. 2d 238, 250 (1965).

36.
Id. at 805, 236 Cal. App. 2d at 250.

37.
See Ard Dr. Pepper Bottling Co. v. Dr. Pepper Co., 202 F.2d 372 (5th Cir. 1953) [Clause was evidence the parties intended an objective standard to apply to performance].

38.
128 Ariz. 402, 626 P.2d 132 (1981).

39.
Id. at 404, 626 P.2d at 134.

40.
See Wolff, 303 Ill. App. at 415-16, 25 N.E.2d at 401-2.

41.
128 Ariz. at 406, 626 P.2d at 136.

OPTIONS AND RIGHTS OF FIRST REFUSAL

Options

Options on a participant's or organizer's future services or on future sponsorship rights, while legal, may be tricky to enforce in the personal services area (see discussion of personal service contracts at page 20), but fairly straightforward where goods are concerned. Generally, to be enforceable, an option must typically contain an offer, a specific time period in which the option must be exercised and valuable consideration given to the person granting the option.

An option contract is essentially one in which a person (the offeror) makes an offer and simultaneously waives the right to revoke the offer during some period of time. A typical option might read: "Offeror hereby grants to Offeree the option to renew this Agreement on the same terms and conditions for an additional one-year period, such option exercisable by offeree on or before 30 days prior to the end of the Term of this Agreement." Such a clause gives the offeree the right to renew the agreement, but only if he or she acts in the specified time period. If the offeree does so, the offeror must perform the agreement for another year; if the offeree does not, the offeror is off the hook.

Perhaps the most important element of an enforceable option is that it is supported by valuable consideration. The mere promise to pay or accept a consideration (money or other thing of value) if the option is exercised is not sufficient – there must be consideration for the option itself.[42]

However, the consideration or fee given by a sponsor for the initial performance or event can also constitute consideration for the option on sponsorship of future events. For instance, in *Lemat Corp.* v. *Barry*,[43] a professional basketball player's salary was held to be sufficient consideration for the renewal option contained in his player contract.

State law should be consulted on whether the future consideration, in the event the option is exercised, needs to be specified in the option itself. California, for instance, has enforced a basketball team's option on a player's services where the contract specified that compensation would be no less than 75 percent of the compensation paid in the main contract. However, California law prohibits the issuance of an injunction for breach of exclusivity provisions of personal services contracts unless the compensation granted is at least $6,000 per year.[44] So enforceability of option contracts in California is subject to that condition. Other states may have similar restrictions.

42.
See Warner Bros. v. *Brodel*, 31 Cal. 2d 766, 192 P.2d 949, *cert. denied*, 335 U.S. 844, *reh'g denied*, 335 U.S. 873 (1948) [The court found that an option contract was distinct from the contract to which it related and that the optionee had parted with special consideration for it].

43.
275 Cal. App. 2d 671, 80 Cal. Rptr. 240 (1969).

44.
Cal. Civ. Code § 3423 (West 1970). For instance, in *Foxx* v. *Williams*, 244 Cal. App. 2d 223, 52 Cal. Rptr. 896

Rights of First Refusal

Closely related to options are rights of first refusal. Either sponsors or promoters may insist on right of first refusal clauses depending on their respective views of the value of the rights to be optioned. First refusal rights let the market decide the price; otherwise, an option price may be fixed at the beginning of an event or relationship. Some contracts use a combination of fixed options and first refusal rights. In such cases, if the option is not exercised, the optionee still retains the right of first refusal. This protects the party that declines the option because it finds the price too high. A typical right of first refusal gives the initial contractor the right to match any offer the other party receives for some period of time. For instance, in *American Broadcasting Companies* v. *Wolf*,[45] the court considered a clause in an employment contract that said, ". . . you agree that you will not accept, in any market for a period of three (3) months following expiration of the extended term of this agreement, any offer of employment as a sportscaster . . . without first giving us, in writing, an opportunity to employ you on substantially similar terms and you agree to enter into an agreement with us on such terms."[46] (Such clauses should specify the time in which the party has to match the offer, and could be limited in scope to matching of monetary terms.) The court in that case noted that it may be difficult to enforce such a right of first refusal in the personal service area. It said:

> *Outside the personal service area, the usual equitable remedy for breach of a first-refusal clause is to order the breaching party to perform the contract with the person possessing the first refusal right. . . . When personal services are involved, this would result in an affirmative injunction ordering the employee to perform services for plaintiff. Such relief . . . cannot be granted.*[47]

In contrast, if the contract were one for the sale of goods, a right of first refusal could be specifically performed and enforced according to its terms.

(1966), comedian Redd Foxx was not enjoined from breaking a recording contract under which he could have earned, but was not *guaranteed*, royalties of $6,000 per year. However, where Olivia Newton-John was guaranteed an advance of $200,000 per year and controlled her recording costs, the court found the $6,000 minimum to have been met and issued an injunction against her recording for another recording company. *MCA Records, Inc.* v. *Newton-John*, 153 Cal. Rptr. 153, 90 Cal. App. 3d 18 (1979). Further, in California the annual guarantee of $6,000 must exist from the outset; injunctive relief will not be available if the employer merely has the option to pay the performer $6,000 a year. *Motown Record Corp.* v. *Brockert*, 160 Cal. App. 3d 123, 207 Cal. Rptr. 574 (1984). (*See also* the discussion of personal service contracts at page 20).

45.
52 N.Y.2d 394, 420 N.E.2d 363 (1981).

46.
Id. at 364.

47.
Id. at 368 n.7.

BANKRUPTCY CLAUSES

48.
11 U.S.C. § 101 *et seq.*

The federal bankruptcy code[48] is designed to allow debtors to make a fresh start and to treat creditors fairly. The code is long and complex. It is relevant to a discussion of contracts because many contracts with sponsors and organizers provide for termination in the event that one party goes bankrupt. (The legal rights of debtor and creditor sponsors and organizers are governed by the bankruptcy code; because the expertise of a specialized attorney is required, they are not dealt with in this book.)

Section 365 of the code specifies that, after the commencement of a bankruptcy proceeding, the trustee of the bankrupt estate may assume or reject any executory contract. (An executory contract for those purposes is one on which performance remains due to some extent on both sides. A note is not usually an executory contract if the only performance that remains is repayment. If performance on one side is completed, the contract is no longer executory.) If, however, the contract was terminated prior to commencement of the bankruptcy proceeding, the trustee does not have this option unless state law provides otherwise.

If there has been a default under the contract, the trustee of the bankrupt party must (1) cure the default (or provide adequate assurance that he or she will cure it), (2) compensate any monetary loss to such party resulting from the default (or provide adequate assurance that he or she will) and (3) provide adequate assurance of future performance. What constitutes "adequate assurance" is determined by the bankruptcy judge on a case-by-case basis.

49.
See In re Pioneer Ford Sales, Inc., 729 F.2d 27 (1st Cir. 1984) [Because Rhode Island law prohibited automobile dealer from assigning its franchise without the manufacturer's consent, trustee in bankruptcy could not assign the franchise without consent, which Ford reasonably withheld].

50.
20 Bankr. 139, 143 (1982).

51.
20 Bankr. at 143.

However, Section 365 does not allow the trustee to choose to assume (1) contracts to make a loan, (2) contracts to extend debt financing or (3) personal service contracts. It is not clear whether contracts between sponsors and event promoters or between trademark licensors and licensees would be considered personal service contracts. A contract with a sponsorship sales agency may well be a personal service contract. The determination is based on whether applicable state law other than bankruptcy law makes the contract nonassignable.[49] Personal service contracts are generally not assignable under state law. In *In the Matter of Bronx-Westchester Mack Corporation*,[50] for example, the court held that a dealership agreement was not personal and thus was assumable, saying: "A distributorship or franchise agreement which does not depend upon a special relationship between the parties is not within the reach of the exception."[51] This leaves room for proof of the nature of the relationship; a mere recitation in a contract that it is personal and not assignable will not necessarily make it nonassumable by the bankruptcy trustee.

On the other hand, in *In re Luce Industries*,[52] the court did not allow the debtor's assignment of a trademark license agreement to a third party because it believed that the third party would not continue the prior approved trade practices. In other words, there was no adequate assurance of future performance. Although the court did not analyze the trademark license as being in the nature of a personal service contract, it did characterize the license as nonassignable.

52.
14 Bankr. 529 (Bankr. S.D.N.Y. 1981).

PERSONAL SERVICE CONTRACTS AND INJUNCTIONS

53.
See J. Light, *California Injunction Statute and the Music Industry: What Price Injunctive Relief?*, 7 Colum. J.L. & Arts 141, 143-45 (1982).

54.
Restatement (Second) of Contracts § 367(1) (1981).

55.
323 So. 2d 163, 164 (La. Ct. App. 1975).

56.
See *Aurthur* v. *Oakes*, 63 F. 310, 317-18 (7th Cir. 1894) [Ordering railroad employees to remain in service of the railroad "is a condition of involuntary servitude" and is contrary to the Constitution].

57.
Freund v. *Washington Square Press*, 34 N.Y.2d 379, 357 N.Y.S.2d 857 (1979) [Damages resulting from publisher's failure to publish author's book too speculative to calculate].

58.
42 Eng. Rep. 687 (1852).

59.
Those seeking the injunctive power of the courts must also satisfy the normal requirements for obtaining injunctions or preliminary injunctions. For injunctions a party must show irreparable harm that is beyond mere financial injury. Preliminary injunctions require, depending on the jurisdiction and

The success of an event or promotion often depends on the personalities scheduled to appear or perform – they help attract the attention of the public and the press. For example, tennis and golf tournaments may not draw significant attendance if they do not showcase famous athletes. But how enforceable are contracts with celebrities? What remedies can an event sponsor seek against a celebrity who does not show up or threatens not to?

Celebrities may have several incentives not to perform. Often entertainers or athletes will realize an increase in their market value while under contract to perform at a lower rate – in effect, they get a "better offer." Or difficulties will arise with promoters or sponsors over other issues such as public relations demands or opponents. Despite his or her signature on a written contract, the celebrity's response to these difficulties may be to suspend performance or accept another engagement. The best solution often is to resolve differences through negotiation. At times, however, it becomes necessary to resort to the courts to hold celebrities responsible for their commitments.

Generally, courts will not compel a person to render personal services against his or her will[53] because of the difficulties involved in monitoring the adequacy of the performance.[54] For instance, in *Fletcher* v. *Rachou*,[55] the court refused to order a country music singer to record more songs as required by the contract. Practically, of course, there is no legal way to force a compelled performance to be a good one. Further, the Thirteenth Amendment outlaws involuntary servitude, and compelled performance, even for a fee, might violate that constitutional provision.[56]

Instead of ordering performance, courts remedy breaches of service contracts with traditional legal contractual remedies – damages for lost expectations, for the costs of reliance or for restitution. To the extent that a party can demonstrate loss of profits, out-of-pocket expenses or the unjust enrichment of the breaching party, the courts resolve most contractual disputes without resort to their equitable powers. Only when traditional legal remedies (money damages) are inadequate will the courts consider imposing an injunction. (The injunction restrains a person from engaging in the enjoined conduct for some period of time.)

Money damages often do not adequately remedy breaches of promotion and sponsorship agreements. The promoters of an event basically want the promotion to occur; they do not want to get involved in a legal battle over damages. Moreover, the speculative nature of many promotions makes calculation of lost profits difficult. The courts will not order money damages when they cannot be determined with reasonable certainty.[57] However, failure to bring about an advertised event can spell doom for a promoter seeking to establish or maintain a reputation in the business, and courts have found limited exceptions to the general rule against enforcement of personal service contracts to remedy such inequities.

Beginning with the renowned English case of *Lumley* v. *Wagner*,[58] courts have provided some relief for those damaged by the refusal of a contracting party to perform. In *Lumley*, although not ordering specific performance, the court enjoined an opera singer from performing with other opera houses after she breached her contract to sing exclusively for the plaintiff. The court said that the prohibitive injunction would provide an adequate remedy for the plaintiff without being overly coercive.

United States courts have adopted the *Lumley* doctrine of ordering prohibitive injunctions when performers breach personal service contracts. Generally, a court may enjoin a breaching party from performing for others only if such services are contracted exclusively, they are "unique and extraordinary," and traditional remedies would be inadequate.[59] For instance, in *King Records, Inc.* v. *Brown*,[60] James Brown was enjoined from recording records with anyone other than plaintiff. The court noted Brown's extensive recordings as well as the nature of his music as evidence of his unique and extraordinary talent.[61]

The policies behind these requirements are sound. Where the services are not novel, the aggrieved party can find a substitute performer and sue the breaching party for the costs involved in procuring the replacement. Persons with unique talents, on the other hand, cannot be easily replaced.

The uniqueness and extraordinary character of services depends on the facts of each case.[62] No clear rules have emerged for determining whether a celebrity's services are unique. Recitation in the contract that the services are unique or extraordinary will not control.[63] Courts make an independent determination of an employee's special value.[64] Nonetheless, most personal service contracts drafted by promoters contain a uniqueness clause.

The scope of the injunction must be limited. For example, an injunction may not preclude employment such that the person is unable to earn a living.[65] The injunction must be tailored so that the employee has a reasonable opportunity to work for employers not in competition with the aggrieved party.

circuit, the moving party to show: (1) a strong likelihood of success on the merits of the case (since the injunction would occur before a trial on the issue of who breached the contract); (2) the possibility (or substantial likelihood) of irreparable injury if the preliminary injunction is not granted; (3) that the equities favor the moving party and (4) that the public interest is advanced by ordering the preliminary injunction. The court may also require the posting of a security bond upon granting a preliminary injunction. *See* Fed. R. Civ. P. 65(c).

60.
252 N.Y.S.2d 988 (1964).

61.
Id. at 990.

62.
California has codified the general rule of unique and extraordinary personal services in Cal. Civ. Code § 3423 (West 1970), requiring the performance to be of a "special, unique, unusual, extraordinary or intellectual character, which gives it peculiar value the loss of which cannot be reasonably or adequately compensated in damages. . . ."

63.
Wilhelmina Models, Inc. v. Abdulmajid, 413 N.Y.S.2d 21 (1979) [Modeling agency's policy of requiring all of its models to sign contracts with recitations of uniqueness dilutes the uniqueness of the defendant model's talent].

64.
Id.

65.
See Restatement (Second) of Contracts § 367 comment c.

66.
American Broadcasting Companies v. Wolf, 438 N.Y.S.2d 482, 487, 420 N.E.2d 363, 368 (1981) [Court would not enjoin sportscaster from working for another television station after the contract with the prior station ended], *aff'g*, 430 N.Y.S.2d 275 (1980).

67.
434 F. Supp. 449 (S.D.N.Y. 1977), *rev'd on other grounds*, 562 F.2d 141 (2d Cir. 1977).

68.
Top-Rank first brought suit in New York Supreme Court to restrain the New York State Athletic Commission from determining the validity of the agreement between Shavers and MSG. Later Top-Rank won an order restraining MSG and Shavers from consummating their deal. This order was enjoined by the Federal District Court until the Second Circuit Court of Appeals reversed the injunction against the state court's action. 562 F.2d at 142-43.

The courts have also limited the extent of an injunction against a breaching employee to the period of the employment contract. When the contract term has expired, the injunction ends as well.[66] However, courts generally disapprove of noncompete clauses.

The case of *Madison Square Garden Boxing, Inc. v. Shavers*[67] exemplifies application of the above principles in the United States. In that case, heavyweight boxer Earnie Shavers agreed with Madison Square Garden Boxing, Inc. (MSG) to box Muhammad Ali in October 1977. After disagreements about the terms of the deal, Shavers signed with rival boxing promoter Top-Rank, Inc. to fight Ali for more money. MSG sued to enjoin Shavers from fighting anyone until he satisfied his obligation to fight Ali under its contract.[68]

After finding that a contract between Shavers and MSG did exist, the court preliminarily enjoined Shavers from fighting until he fought Ali in October. The court determined that a noncompetition clause was implied by the circumstances and that this covenant was not overly harsh or one-sided. In a footnote, the court held Shavers's services to be unquestionably unique and extraordinary.[69] An injunction against Shavers, the court stated, "would not unreasonably burden Shavers" since he was protected by a $100,000 bond posted by MSG in case Shavers ultimately prevailed on the contract claim.[70] He was not unreasonably prevented from earning a living since the injunction lasted only from June 24 until October 11, 1977.

On the issue of irreparable injury the court concluded that MSG's reputation as a promoter would be damaged if Shavers were allowed to walk away from the agreement. Television producers, boxing officials and other media representatives who relied on MSG's promotion of the fight might no longer trust MSG as a promoter. Thus, the court concluded, a preliminary injunction against Shavers was proper.

In California the legislature modified the court's injunctive power by specifying the conditions under which a court may enjoin a person from breaching a personal service contract.[71] California Civil Code § 3423 allows an injunction only if (1) the personal service contract is in writing, (2) the services are of a "special, unique, unusual, extraordinary or intellectual character" and (3) the compensation is $6,000 per year or more. The absence of any one of these conditions precludes the issuance of an injunction against the employee.

The three conditions of § 3423 do not pose significantly more difficulty in obtaining an injunction than the common law conditions in other jurisdictions.

Employment contracts in the entertainment industries are usually written. Most employment contracts easily satisfy the archaic $6,000 minimum annual salary requirement. (See discussion of options at page 16.) The final hurdle is what all jurisdictions require for injunctive relief – that the services be unique and extraordinary.

However, California provides further protection for employees under Section 2855 of its Labor Code.[72] That section prevents the enforcement of a personal service contract against an employee beyond seven years from the beginning of service under the contract, no matter what the contract actually says. The seven-year period is not suspended during any stretches of nonperformance for any reason.[73] The parties may not renew the original contract beyond the seventh year from the beginning of the contract unless the renewal is obtained while the employee is free of any continuing obligations.[74] Moreover, an employee may not waive the seven-year period by agreement or otherwise. Thus, the California Labor Code supports the policy that an employee should, once every seven years, be able to test the market to determine his or her value.

The negative injunction may not be helpful for promoters and sponsors who have short-lived contracts with celebrities. The coercive nature of the injunction is only felt for a short time and the celebrity may choose not to perform. In these cases, the employer may attempt to recover monetary damages resulting from the non-performance if such are demonstrable. The downside, of course, is that few sponsors want to be known as the kind that sue celebrities, and energy spent on litigation might be better spent salvaging the event itself by securing alternative talent.

69.
Madison Square Garden, 434 F. Supp. at 452 n.11.

70.
Id. at 452.

71.
Cal. Civ. Code §§ 526, 3423 (West 1970).

72.
Cal. Lab. Code § 2855 (West Supp. 1988); *see* H. Bushkin and R. Meyer, "Employee Emancipation in California: The Seven-Year Itch under Labor Code Section 2855," 56 Cal. St. B.J. 20 (Jan. 1981).

73.
De Haviland v. *Warner Bros. Pictures*, 67 Cal. App. 2d 225, 153 P.2d 983 (1945) [Court refused to toll 25 weeks of nonperformance by Olivia De Haviland, instead holding that the seven-year period expires exactly seven calendar years after the first performance of services under the contract].

74.
Id.

MORALS CLAUSES

Conduct

Many contracts with celebrities contain a "morals" clause, that is, a clause that allows termination of employment for acts that tend to subject the employee or the employer to ridicule, contempt or scandal, or that reflect unfavorably upon the employer or its products or services. These clauses are enforceable, although the parties may differ on the kind of conduct they proscribe. This section briefly looks at the kinds of conduct prohibited by typical morals clauses.

The basic legal principle, whether or not a contract contains a written morals clause, is that employees have a common-law duty to refrain from acts that are, or are likely to be, prejudicial to their employers' interests. This duty exists regardless of whether it is specifically spelled out in an employment contract. Thus, any misconduct inconsistent with the relationship of employer and employee justifies termination. Furthermore, even misconduct occurring *prior* to the employment, or misconduct *not* exhibiting moral turpitude, may be good cause for discharge of an employee. These principles were illustrated in two rather old cases, *In re Nagel*[75] and *Brown* v. *Dupuy*.[76] In both cases, the employee had set out to organize a business that would compete with his employer's. Neither of the employees had a "morals clause" in his contract; however, both contracts included a clause requiring the employee to devote his entire "time, attention, and abilities to his duties"[77] and to "devote his entire time and attention for, on behalf, and in the interest of the [employer]."[78]

75.
278 F. 105, 109 (2d Cir. 1921).

76.
4 F.2d 367 (7th Cir. 1924).

77.
Id. at 368.

78.
278 F. at 107.

Establishing a competing business is clearly contrary to an employer's best interest; a written morals clause is unnecessary. The need for a written morals clause becomes more critical, however, in more ambiguous situations. A typical morals clause for example, allows termination of the contract:

> *if the employee becomes involved in or has at any time been involved in any act, situation or occurrence, which act, situation, or occurrence tends to subject the employee or employer to any ridicule, contempt, or scandal, or which reflects unfavorably upon the employer or its products or services.*

In such a clause, it doesn't matter whether the conduct is engaged in during the term or not. If during the term some proscribed conduct comes to light that tends to subject either party to public ridicule, there may be an option to terminate. Of course, the terminated talent may argue that conduct that took place many years prior does not currently tend to subject either party to ridicule.

The interesting issues, of course, concern which kinds of conduct violate the clause. In three important cases, the court found that employers justifiably terminated an individual's employment because each employee had breached his respective morals clause by refusing to answer questions during hearings of the Committee on Un-American Activities of the United States House of Representatives. The employees' refusals to answer questions concerning alleged communist infiltration of the motion picture industry resulted in each being held in contempt of Congress (a misdemeanor). Therefore, the court found that one defendant acted without "due regard to public conventions,"[79] that another "offend[ed] against decency [and] morality,"[80] and that the third acted to bring himself "into public disrepute, contempt, scorn and ridicule; [which] conduct tended to and did shock, insult and offend the community and public morals and decency."[81] It therefore appears that a court will find that a misdemeanor violates the type of morals clauses mentioned above.

Some talent agents will attempt to limit the applicability of the typical morals clause only to those cases where the employee has been convicted of a felony. This is, of course, subject to negotiation. Promoters and sponsors might agree to such an amendment and rely on the remainder of the clause to allow termination for broader, more vague transgressions such as committing acts that "tend to reflect unfavorably upon the employer." Thus, while conviction for a misdemeanor may not violate the phrase prohibiting conviction for a felony, it still may violate the phrase prohibiting acts that tend to subject the employee to ridicule, contempt or scandal. However, talent agents object to that broad language as well.

Similarly, writing a contract prohibition against "derogation of the employer's products and/or services or the use of its products and/or services" appears unnecessary (although perhaps desirable to remind the talent of his or her duty). The common-law duty to "conduct [oneself] with such decency and propriety as not to injure the employer in his business"[82] would seem to prohibit such actions. A product spokesperson, for instance, injures the employer's business directly by saying anything negative about the product he or she is employed to promote. Consequently, termination as a result of such conduct should be upheld, regardless of whether the prohibition is reduced to writing.

Contracts for the employment of police officers often contain clauses allowing termination for "conduct unbecoming an officer." A brief review of litigation under such clauses is helpful in evaluating morals clauses pertinent to civilians. Courts have upheld terminations under such clauses as a result of sexual misconduct, including engaging in sexual activity with a prostitute,[83] pimping,[84] wearing women's undergarments in public,[85] engaging in sexual activity with a minor,[86] engaging in

79.
Loew's Inc. v. Cole, 185 F.2d 641, 648 (9th Cir. 1950) cert. denied, 340 U.S. 954 (1951).

80.
Twentieth Century-Fox Film Corp. v. Lardner, 216 F.2d 844, 850 (9th Cir. 1954).

81.
Scott v. RKO Radio Pictures, 240 F.2d 87, 90, 92 (9th Cir. 1957).

82.
Lardner, 216 F.2d at 850.

83.
Civil Service Comm'n v. Livingston, 22 Ariz. App. 183, 525 P.2d 949 (1974), cert. denied, 421 U.S. 951 (1975).

84.
King v. Chicago, 60 Ill. App. 3d 504, 377 N.E.2d 102 (1978).

85.
Etscheid v. Police Bd. of Chicago, 47 Ill. App. 2d 124, 197 N.E.2d 484 (1964).

86.
Miglieri v. Lee, 16 Ill. App. 2d 545, 149 N.E.2d 193 (1958); Perry v. Blair, 64 A.D.2d 870, 407 N.Y.S.2d 371 (1978); Steward v. Leary, 57 Misc. 2d 792, 293 N.Y.S.2d 573 (1968); Faust v. Police Civil Service Comm'n, 22 Pa. 123, 347 A.2d 765 (1975).

87.
In re La Fond, 390
N.W.2d 321 (Minn. App.
1986).

88.
*Corwin v. Village of
Ellenville*, 69 A.D.2d
933, 415 N.Y.S.2d 299
(1979).

89.
*Belli v. Orlando Daily
Newspapers, Inc.*, 389
F.2d 579, 582 (5th Cir.
1967), *cert. denied*, 393
U.S. 825 (1968) [Libel
per se is "any publica-
tion which exposes a
person to distrust,
hatred, contempt, ridi-
cule, obloquy"].

90.
*Getz v. Robert Welch,
Inc.*, 418 U.S. 323, 350
(1974).

91.
*Laboratory of Chroma-
tography v. Eastern Lab.*,
112 A.D.2d 143, 490
N.Y.S.2d 832, 834
(1985) [Statements of
corporate president that
former employees con-
spired to sabotage
employer's business and
form a competing enter-
prise were libel *per se*
because they tended to
expose employees to
public ridicule and dis-
parage them in their
profession].

92.
*Brown & Williamson
Tobacco Co. v. Jacob-
son*, 713 F.2d 262, 267
(7th Cir. 1983) (citing
Prosser, *Handbook of
the Law of Torts* 756-60
(4th ed. 1971)) [Allega-
tions in television editorial that tobacco
company's advertising

sexual activity in a closed municipal pool,[87] and adultery.[88] Conduct unbecoming an officer probably is also conduct unbecoming a corporate spokesperson or a sponsored talent, since both are placed somewhat in the public eye as role models. It therefore may be assumed that similar sexual misconduct would breach a morals clause and the resulting termination probably would be enforceable.

Finally, courts have determined that certain conduct presumptively results in harm similar to the harm that morals clauses seek to prevent. Imputing certain acts to an individual has been found to be slanderous or libelous *per se*; that is, harm to the slandered is presumed.[89] Such defamation automatically results in "impairment of reputation and standing in the community"[90] and "tend[s] to expose [the slandered or libeled party] to public contempt, ridicule, aversion or disgrace, or induce an evil opinion of [him] in the minds of right-thinking persons."[91] The typical morals clause is concerned with these same kinds of harms: subjecting either the employer or employee to any ridicule, contempt or scandal, or reflecting unfavorably upon the employer or employee or the products or services being promoted. Therefore, conduct that creates such ridicule or scandal violates the typical morals clause.

Under common law, it is slander *per se* to impute any of the following four categories of conduct to another: commission of a crime, infliction with a loathsome disease, unchastity (if the slandered is female) and conduct likely to discredit the slandered in his trade or business.[92] A morals clause probably could be enforced against any such conduct.

It may be argued that, in modern times, unchastity does not *per se* create public scandal, contempt or ridicule. Courts recently have held, however, that implying that a person engaged in sex outside of marriage is slander *per se* because adultery is a crime.[93] In addition, one court has said, "A mere accusation of marital discord is libelous."[94] Based on these cases, unchastity, or other sexual misconduct, is likely to be held to breach a morals clause.

In addition, the imputation of certain other specific acts or conduct is slander *per se*. For instance, the imputation of homosexuality[95] has been held libelous *per se*. Imputations of insolvency,[96] intoxication while on duty,[97] possession of LSD[98] and racial or religious intolerance[99] have been held libelous or slanderous *per se*. If the imputation of such conduct is slander, then the conduct itself is likely to violate the typical morals clause.

Remedies

What remedies can an event organizer seek for breach of a morals clause?

The usual award in a lawsuit for a breach of contract is damages. Through monetary awards, the courts seek to make the wronged parties whole – to provide restitution or to compensate them for their reliance. While awarding damages is effective in most situations, compensation of this sort is often inappropriate for cases involving employment of entertainers or uniquely talented persons. This is because it is exceedingly difficult to determine the loss incurred by a sponsor when a performer violates a morals clause. In these cases, the courts may hold that the plaintiff has been injured, but that no compensatory remedy will be granted since none can be adequately fashioned to fit the injury.

When a damage award is inappropriate, a court will sometimes grant an equitable remedy such as an injunction or other order. However, as previously discussed, personal service contracts may not be specifically enforced by injunctions. Coercing an individual to perform violates the Thirteenth Amendment of the U.S. Constitution, which prohibits all forms of involuntary servitude. Thus, the negative injunction discussed in this chapter in the context of personal service contracts is probably the most viable remedy (pages 20-23).

The underlying policy reasons for allowing the negative injunction apply in a breach of morals clause case even though the performer is not working for an actual competitor. Negative injunctions are necessary because, "If the time shall ever come when a court of equity must stand helplessly by while unique and unusual . . . performers may be induced to breach contracts with impunity, except for damages, as a jury may see fit to award at some distant date, corporations will find their business hampered by intolerable conditions."[100] In one old case, Harry Rogers Theatrical Enterprises had a five-year contract, beginning in 1923, with a performer named Comstock. Shubert Theatrical Corporation tried to negotiate a deal with Rogers whereby Comstock would be released from his contract so that he could do a musical show for Shubert. When the proposal fell through, Comstock left Rogers to do the musical with Shubert anyway. The court held that the personality of Comstock was so unusual and unique that the only effective remedy for Rogers was a negative injunction preventing Comstock from doing the musical show for Shubert.

The Harry Rogers case indicates that, in determining whether to invoke a negative injunction, the court will focus on whether the negative injunction will remedy the

strategy was to attract young smokers by likening cigarette use to illicit pleasures such as marijuana use, alcohol use, and sex, held slander *per se* because statements were likely to discredit the company in its trade or business]; *Sodowy* v. *Sony Corp. of Am.*, 496 F. Supp. 1071 (S.D.N.Y. 1980) [Statements that plaintiff was alcoholic and took bribes in his business held slander *per se* because they tended to disparage him in his trade]; *Lady Windsor Hairdressers, Inc.* v. *Calvo*, 35 Misc. 2d 739, 231 N.Y.S.2d 221, 223 (N.Y. Sup. 1962) [Statements to plaintiff's daughter that plaintiff was "phony," a "cheat," "two-faced" and a "trouble-maker" held not slander *per se* because they were not uttered in relation to plaintiff's business or trade].

93.
Guccione v. *Hustler Magazine, Inc.*, 632 F. Supp. 313, 316-17 (S.D.N.Y. 1986), *rev'd on other grounds*, 800 F.2d 298 (2d Cir. 1986), *cert. denied*, 107 S. Ct. 1303 (1987).

94.
See Thacky v. *Patterson*, 157 F.2d 614, 615 (D.C. Cir. 1946).

95.
Mazart v. *State*, 109 Misc. 2d 1092, 441 N.Y.S.2d 600 (N.Y. Ct. Cl. 1981).

96.
Maytag Co. v. Meadows Mfg. Co., 45 F.2d 299 (7th Cir.), *cert. denied,* 283 U.S. 843 (1930).

harm, not on whether the performer is directly working for an actual competitor of the original sponsor. Without injunctive relief, the sponsor's ability to create a particular image through a highly visible personality is greatly undermined.

97.
Rutman v. Geidel, 67 A.D.2d 662, 411 N.Y.S.2d 961 (1979).

When neither damages nor negative injunctions are appropriate, rescission may be the only option available to the sponsor. (Rescission only gives the organizer back its initial payment, if any, to the talent.) However, organizers and sponsors should seriously consider the potentially adverse effect that enforcement of a morals clause will have on future efforts to contract with celebrities. As a practical matter, plaintiffs rarely seek to enforce morals clauses in the courts.

98.
Levine v. Kiss, 47 A.D.2d 544, 363 N.Y.S.2d 101 (1975).

99.
Sweeney v. Schenectady Union Publishing Co., 122 F.2d 288 (2d Cir.), *aff'd by an even decision*, 316 U.S. 642 (1941).

100.
Harry Rogers Theatrical Enterprises v. Comstock, 232 N.Y.S. 1 (1928).

CONTRACTING SPONSORSHIP SALES AGENCIES

Sometimes an event is represented by a sales agency whose job it is to solicit sponsors and suppliers. Written contracts are particularly important in establishing such relationships because of the unique problems inherent in an agency relationship.

The most critical thing about appointing an agency is to define the scope of the agency, that is, to specify the ways in which the agent is empowered to act for the principal. Normally the event organizer will appoint a sales agency to negotiate sponsorship packages, but final acceptance of a proposal remains with the organizer. Thus the contract must specify that the agency is not authorized to enter agreements for the event organizer or to represent to third parties that it is so authorized. This is particularly important because an agency may have "apparent authority." In *Clark Advertising Agency, Inc.* v. *Tice*,[101] the court held an advertising contract to be valid because the comptroller and the vice-president of an automobile dealership association had the apparent authority to bind the association. The court defined apparent authority as the authority that "exists whenever a principal manifests to a third person that an officer or agent may act in its behalf, and the third person in good faith believes that the authority exists. When that third person reasonably relies upon the apparent authority to his detriment, the principal is estopped to deny the authority."[102]

One authority on advertising agencies states that the legal nature of the relationship between an advertising agency and an advertiser has been adjudicated in comparatively few cases; he speculates that this is because advertising agencies wish to avoid litigation in order to preserve their images.[103] He notes that, despite the language appointing an advertising agency, the agency may still act as an independent contractor with respect to third parties. The specifics of each such relationship must be examined individually to determine whether an agency relationship in fact exists. For instance, an agency representing an event may order brochures or videotapes or other materials for use in presenting the event to potential sponsors. These could be ordered by the agency as agent for the principal (the client); alternatively, the costs may be included in the agency's fees and the agency could order them as an independent contractor for its own use and at its own expense. In the first instance, if the agency fails to pay the supplier, the principal may be liable. In the second case, the principal would not have liability.

The language the parties use in expressing their relationship is not determinative. It has been held instead that the intention to form an agency relationship must be clear from the conduct of the parties, regardless of the words used to describe a relationship.[104]

101.
490 F.2d 834 (5th Cir. 1974).

102.
Id. at 836.

103.
Rosden, *The Law of Advertising*, section 1.04, pp. 1-11 (Matthew Bender, New York, 1988).

104.
Goodway Marketing v. *Faulkner Advertising Associates, Inc.*, 545 F. Supp. 263, 267 (E.D. Pa. 1982).

An agent owes certain legal duties to the principal. For instance, in soliciting business, a sales agency typically represents, either directly or indirectly, that it possesses a high degree of specialized skill. Thus, it is obligated to exercise that skill in serving its client.[105]

105.
Rosden, *supra*, note 103, at section 1.07, pp. 1-35.

Recently, some advertisers have sued their advertising and marketing agencies when advertising programs they designed failed to reach expected levels of success. For instance, the manufacturers of a cold-water detergent called Delicare sued their New York advertising agency when that new product failed to achieve the market share the agency had predicted for it. The agency allegedly had convinced the manufacturer to spend some $18,000,000 in advertising the new product based on its market research, which projected that a 45 to 52 percent market share would result from that level of spending. The suit was settled for an undisclosed amount, but understandably news of the suit made many in the industry nervous.

A similar case was brought by a fast-food chicken restaurant chain against a promotional agency when its promotion failed to achieve the desired result of increased breakfast traffic. The chain claimed that the promotional agency failed to do adequate research and analysis before presenting a program which increased frequency among breakfast customers but failed to generate new customers. The chain already had very high frequency among users. That case was pending at publication, but raises additional questions concerning how much responsibility a sales promotion agency should have when programs do not generate the hoped for results.

106.
CCMS Publ. Co., Inc. v. Dooley-Maloof, Inc., 645 F.2d 33(10th Cir. 1981).

Obviously, a sales agency would be well advised to specifically disclaim any expected degree of success in locating sponsors for an event. Often, however, that disclaimer is at odds with attempts to garner the business in the first place.

107.
United Roasters, Inc. v. Colgate-Palmolive Co., 649 F.2d 985, 990 (4th Cir. 1981) [When Colgate ceased advertising and manufacturing "Bambeanos" it deprived the creators of the product of the right to sell a going concern or to develop the business].

Having undertaken a representation, a sales agency is required to attempt to market the event. For instance, an advertising representative has been held liable to a medical journal for breach of contract in not using its best efforts to procure advertisers for the journal after representing that the full time of the principal would be spent on the business.[106] Stopping all promotional efforts has also been held to violate a contractual obligation to advertise and promote sales of a product,[107] but precisely how much effort must be spent is a question of fact.[108]

108.
Triple-A-Baseball Club Assoc. v. Northeastern Baseball, Inc., 832 F.2d 214 (1st Cir. 1987).

It goes almost without saying that agencies owe their clients the duties of loyalty and nondisclosure, yet it is wise to specify in a written contract the scope of these duties. In particular, an agreement should address the agency's representation of other events that may be competitive. One expert believes it is "axiomatic" that an agency cannot serve two competing advertising clients. For instance, in one case the court held that a sales agent breached its contractual obligation to a client by representing competing journals.[109] It said, "[the defendants were] advertising sales agents of [the plaintiff] and owed it the duty of not acting for others whose interests conflicted with those of [the plaintiff]."[110] The difficult issue, of course, is whether two events are competing. Therefore, it is wise to specify whether the agency may take on the representation of other events and also to specify the parameters governing other representations, such as proximity in geographic location, time or kind of event. In addition, if an agency represents an event, it may be prudent to prohibit it from also representing participants in the event.

Further, the sales agency's duty of loyalty should be spelled out in a promise not to appropriate the event for itself, that is, not to create and organize a competing event (with or without the same sponsors it obtains for its client's event).

A written confidentiality clause is also useful, even though the agency probably has an implied duty not to disclose proprietary information it learns about its clients.[111] A written clause helps avoid any question about what is and what is not a trade secret or other proprietary information subject to the duty of confidentiality.

One of the more difficult problems in working out the details of a sales agency relationship is figuring out how and under what circumstances the agency should be compensated. For instance, an agency may be compensated only for sponsorship opportunities it brings to the organizer, or it may be deemed to have an interest in all sponsorships that are finally negotiated, regardless of whether the initial contact with the sponsor was made by the organizer or the agency. If the compensation scheme is in some way based on whether the lead for the sponsorship came from the organizer or the agency, there are likely to be more problems than if some simpler method is used (unless the parties agree at the outset as to which leads belong to each of them). An exclusive relationship, in which the agency makes all the contacts and negotiates all of the sponsorships, is not only simpler to administer but also has some advantages in terms of developing a comprehensive approach to the sponsorship package.

Another important issue in the sales agency relationship arises when the agency has negotiated a one-year deal that includes options to be exercised after the sales agency relationship itself has terminated. Even if a sponsor does not have renewal options, it may end up sponsoring an event for more than one year. The agency would argue that it should be compensated even after the agency is terminated because it made the initial contact or negotiated the original deal. A written agency contract should be specific on this point.

109.
CCMS Publ. Co., 645 F.2d 33.

110.
Id. at 37.

111.
Rosden, *supra*, note 103, at section 1.07, pp. 1-45.

Compensation is often a percentage of sponsorship fees procured for the event. The scale might decline for renewals, which require less work by the agency. A unique problem is raised when the sponsorship "fee" is not all in the form of cash. In that case, some method must be found for valuing in-kind contributions. Some objective, verifiable reference should be used, such as wholesale or list prices. "Fair market value" is not a good valuation method because it is subject to dispute. Alternatively, the parties could agree to cap the fee that the organizer will pay the agency for in-kind contributions. In any event, if an organizer does not have the cash to compensate the agency for an in-kind deal, it can always reject a proposal.

SAMPLE TITLE OR LEAD
SPONSORSHIP AGREEMENT

[handwritten margin notes: Rules; Fixed & Replace; Sponsor - PFIZER; Organizer - Tennis Events; EVENT NAME - The PFIZER National Corporate Tennis CHALLENGE; Florida; Florida; PFIZR]

THIS AGREEMENT ("Agreement") is made and entered into as of the (*number*) day of (*month*), (*year*), by and between Organizer ("Organizer"), a corporation organized under the laws of the State of (*state name*), and Sponsor ("Sponsor"), a corporation organized under the laws of the State of (*state name*).

Recitals

WHEREAS, Organizer has the ~~exclusive~~ right to organize and conduct a (*type*) event which is to be held (*when*) in (*city, state*) and to be known as ("*Event Name*") (the "Event"); and *[handwritten: PNCTC]*

WHEREAS, Sponsor has determined to provide financial support for the Event in exchange for certain promotional rights to be provided by Organizer; *[handwritten: PFizer]*

NOW, THEREFORE, in consideration of the mutual agreements and promises contained herein, the parties hereto agree as follows:

These introductory paragraphs basically describe in the broadest terms the intentions of the parties. Often they contain "sell copy."

1. Official Status. Organizer grants to Sponsor the exclusive right during the Term of this Agreement to use the Organizer's Trademarks as described herein in advertising and promoting Sponsor's Products [Services] as defined herein and to refer to such Products [Services] as the "Official [*product or service category*]" of the Event.

This is the basic right granted the Sponsor by the Organizer. The rest of the Agreement explains in detail the full scope of the specific sponsorship rights granted.

2. Advertising and Promotion. (a) Subject to Organizer's rights of approval as described in this Agreement, Sponsor shall have the right to use the Organizer's Trademarks [Service marks] in advertising and promotional activities as it deems desirable during the Term of this Agreement.

This subsection lets the Sponsor know that while it has discretion over the type of promotional activities to undertake, the Organizer will have some approval.

[handwritten margin note: Asterisk This]

(b) Organizer shall [use its best efforts to] provide the following rights to Sponsor during the Term of this Agreement:

(i) the right to sell Products [Services] at the Site of the Event;

This right may need to be described in greater detail, depending on the nature of the Event and the arena and whether there will be an official concessionaire. (It's obviously easier for a Sponsor to have a truck at an outdoor festival than to arrange a concession stand at an existing arena.)

(ii) the right to have banners [or curtains] on center stage [or at the entrance], such banners to be provided by Sponsor [Organizer] and to be of a size and design chosen by Sponsor [Organizer] and placed in accordance with Sponsor's [Organizer's] directions;

Control of signage in terms of design, cost and placement is important to both the Sponsor and Organizer and is negotiable.

(iii) the right to have (*number*) additional signs at locations specified by Organizer [Sponsor] and at a distance of at least (*number of feet*) from other signage, such signs to be provided by Sponsor [Organizer];

This subparagraph focuses on the "clutter" from other sponsors' and suppliers' signs that may interfere with the value of the sponsorship. From the Organizer's point of view, promising a certain number and spacing of signs is much too specific, could tie the Organizer's hands unnecessarily and shows a lack of trust by the Sponsor, etc. On the other hand, it helps the Sponsor to clarify what it is getting.

(iv) the right to signage on all courtesy vehicles, if any, used by Organizer in connection with the Event;

Courtesy vehicles are just roving publicity; this clause is added to reinforce the Sponsor's Title sponsorship.

(v) the right to credit as follows in all print advertising [of a size larger than (*square inches*)] [placed by Organizer] in connection with the Event; "(*Sponsor's Event*)";

The credit will be determined by whether the Sponsor is a Title Sponsor, a Major Supplier or a Presenter. Examples of title or lead sponsorship are: "Coors International Bike Classic," "Benson & Hedges Command Performance Riverblues," "Davis Cup by NEC." The Organizer however, can control only its own placements. In other advertising (e.g., by local presenters), it may retain contractual rights to approve credits, but it should not be ultimately responsible to the Title Sponsor for third party actions. In addition, the size of the ad may determine whether there is room for nontitle sponsors.

(vi) the right to have Sponsor's Trademarks [Service marks] on stationery, business cards and other brochures used by Organizer in connection with the promotion of the Event;

Sponsor's total involvement in the Event is reinforced by such uses of its Trademarks.

(vii) the right to have Sponsor's name and/or Trademarks [Service marks] on [*(number) % of all units of each type of*] all official merchandise authorized by Organizer;

This is a provision used when the Sponsor has title sponsorship of the Event and the muscle to require all – or in the alternative, a percentage – of the Event Related Merchandise to bear the Sponsor's name or Trademarks.

(viii) the right to be named in all press releases issued by Organizer;

Being named in press releases is standard; the most complete agreements will include this clause "just to be sure."

(ix) the right to sell or give away promotional merchandise in connection with advertising or promoting the Event, but only in compliance with Paragraph 8 of this Agreement;

Merchandising rights are dealt with in detail in a separate paragraph.

(x) the right to purchase advertising spots on network, cable or other television broadcasts of the Event licensed by Organizer [to the extent permitted in Organizer's broadcast license agreement];

This probably should be a "best efforts" clause since the Organizer does not always control the broadcast. For some events, a number of spots will be included "free" in the Sponsorship Fee. If the Organizer has already licensed the broadcast, it can be more specific about the rights available.

(xi) the right to opening and closing audio and video billboards in all television coverage, to the extent permitted by the station licensed by Organizer to cover the Event;

This, too, should be "best efforts" unless the Organizer is producing the coverage. Billboards are the opening and closing announcements.

(xii) the right to one page of advertising in the official program authorized by Organizer;

This is, of course, optional and could be specific as to location of the page, i.e., inside front cover, and as to whether it is black-and-white or color.

(xiii) the right to use film clips (not to exceed (number) minutes in length) of past events [of this type] organized by Organizer for advertising and promotion, subject to Organizer's prior approval;

Usually clips of up to three minutes are allowed, which is more than adequate for use in 30- and 60-second commercials. It is the Organizer's responsibility to make sure the clips can be used commercially without violating the copyright, right of privacy or other right of any person; otherwise it could not grant this right in good faith.

(xiv) to use film clips (not to exceed (number) minutes in length) of this Event for purposes of advertising Sponsor's involvement with the Event; and

The difference between this subparagraph and (xii) is that this allows for some use of the most current coverage even after the Event if the Term extends beyond the Event date.

(xv) the right to erect a courtesy tent [or host a similar area] at the site of the Event at a location designated by Organizer.

Courtesy tents and areas are common perks of sponsorship; the location is important, but because it involves logistical issues, the Organizer should retain control (unless the site is well known to both and a specific area can be defined).

3. Sponsorship Fee. In consideration of the full performance by Organizer of all of its obligations hereunder and of all rights granted hereunder to Sponsor, Sponsor shall pay to Organizer the total sum of $_____, payable as follows:

$_____ *on or before (date)*
$_____ *on or before (date)*
$_____ *on or before (date)*
$_____ *on or before (date)*
$_____ *on or before (date)*

[by irrevocable letter of credit drawn on and confirmed by a U.S. bank acceptable to Organizer, which letter of credit shall be automatically payable on sight on and after (*date*) if accompanied by an article from a newspaper of general circulation reporting that the Event took place. Sponsor shall furnish said letter of credit to Organizer within 14 days after the execution of this Agreement and it shall expire at the close of business in (*city*) on (*date*)].

The Sponsorship Fee here is paid out in installments as progress is made toward the Event. The schedule is determined by the Organizer's cash needs and the Sponsor's fiscal prudence. Some Sponsors require the right to approve the budget and fund the Organizer against the budget (plus a stated overage). In the alternative, a letter of credit, while it has carrying costs, insulates the Sponsor from loss if the Event does not take place and should provide the Organizer with access to cash because the Organizer may be able to borrow against it.

4. Rebate of Sponsorship Fee. (a) If the Organizer does not secure television coverage or if the rating described in subparagraph (b) hereof is not achieved, then Organizer shall rebate to Sponsor $_____ within (*number*) days after the Event takes place.

If television coverage justifies the amount of the Sponsorship Fee, it seems appropriate to reduce that fee if television coverage is less than expected. However, Organizers will object strenuously to this provision since it shifts the risk of lack of viewer interest to them. One way to insure widespread coverage (if not audience) is to write this paragraph in terms of the number of stations carrying ("clearing") the Event.

(b) Organizer shall use its best efforts to assure that the television coverage of the Event will achieve a (*number*) rating according to (*rating service*).

Realistically, this can only be a "best efforts" clause. The preceding paragraph gives it teeth. A rating service such as Nielsen should be agreed upon. While the Organizer can't guarantee ratings, its promotional activities greatly affect the size of the television audience. Moreover, with respect to new events, the Sponsor may be unwilling to commit the largest dollars without an estimate of audience. This creates in effect a sliding scale. By reducing the Sponsor's risk, new Events and new Organizers are more likely to find sponsors.

5. Option to Renew. Organizer hereby grants to Sponsor the right to renew its Official Sponsorship hereunder on the same terms and conditions as contained herein (except that the Sponsorship Fee described in Paragraph 3 shall be $_____ and shall be paid on a mutually agreeable schedule similar to the one set forth in Paragraph 3 and the Rebate described in Paragraph 4 shall be $_____). Sponsor shall exercise said option, if at all, by giving Organizer written notice thereof within (*number*) days prior to the expiration of the Term of this Agreement. In the event that Sponsor does not exercise such option, the exclusivity described in Paragraph 6 shall nonetheless continue for a period of (*number of months or years*) or the completion of (*number*) events similar to the Event hereunder, whichever comes first.

The right to renew is important to Sponsors. In exchange for taking the risk, they get a fixed increase in the Sponsorship Fee. Organizers should try to limit the right to renewal to a few years; if an Event really takes off, the increased value will not be recognized because of the locked-in renewal fee. If the option to renew is limited, the Sponsor should ask for a right of first refusal to match subsequent offers.

Here, if a Sponsor does not renew, it nonetheless gets competitive protection for some period of time in order to avoid a competitor's usurping the Sponsor's goodwill in the Event. Some would argue, however, that when the Sponsor drops a sponsorship, it should not preclude the Organizer from pursuing all possible Sponsorship sources.

6. Exclusivity. Organizer represents and warrants that it will not authorize any seller of any product [service] competitive to the Products [Services] or antithetical or incompatible with the Products [Services] to be an Official Sponsor or Supplier or to be associated in any way with the Event [(including on-site signage and concessions)]. Sponsor shall have the right to approve all other Sponsors and Suppliers. [If Organizer proposes a potential Sponsor or Supplier which makes goods [offers services] competitive to those of Sponsor but proposes to promote goods [services] which are not competitive to any product [or service] made by Sponsor, then Sponsor will not unreasonably withhold its approval of said sponsor or supplier.]

Competitive protection is critical and Title Sponsors should try to retain approval over all other sponsors, presenters and suppliers. The impact of antithetical co-sponsors (for instance, antacids and pizza parlors) should be considered. Some companies are closely associated with other branded products and need to avoid the embarrassment of being associated with the wrong group – e.g., McDonald's will want to exclude Pepsi from the list of suppliers and sponsors. Some Organizers will suggest handling such situations through a general "mutual goodwill" or "corporate morals clause," which can accomplish the same thing. This paragraph also raises the issue of permanent signage and concessionaires at the site of the Event.

There is also an issue to be resolved if a Company competitive to the Sponsor offers to supply a product not competitive to Sponsor's; here, the Sponsor retains approval rights, which it agrees not to exercise unreasonably.

7. Trademarks. (a) Sponsor's trademarks [service marks], label designs, product identifications, artwork and other symbols and devices associated with Sponsor Products [Services] ("Sponsor's Trademarks") [("Sponsor's Service Marks")] are and shall remain Sponsor's property and Sponsor shall take all steps reasonably necessary to protect such Sponsor's Trademarks [Service Marks] through federal U.S. registrations and foreign registrations as it deems desirable and through reasonable prosecution of infringements. Organizer is hereby authorized to use Sponsor's Trademarks [Service Marks] in advertising and promoting the Event during the Term of this Agreement provided Sponsor shall have the right to approve all [the format of] such uses in writing in advance. [Organizer shall submit materials to Sponsor in writing and if Sponsor does not approve or reject such materials in writing within (*number*) business days after receipt thereof, then

Sponsor shall be deemed to have approved such materials.] The right to use Sponsor's Trademarks is nonexclusive, nonassignable and nontransferable. All uses by Organizer of Sponsor's Trademarks shall inure solely to the benefit of Sponsor.

(b) Organizer's trademarks [service marks], designs, artwork and other symbols and devices associated with the Event ("Organizer's Trademarks") [("Organizer's Servicemarks")] are and shall remain Organizer's property and Organizer shall take all steps reasonably necessary to protect Organizer's Trademarks [Service Marks] through federal U.S. registration and foreign registration as it deems desirable and through reasonable prosecutions of infringements. Sponsor is hereby authorized to use Organizer's Trademarks [Service Marks] in advertising and promoting the Products [Services] during the Term of the Agreement, provided Organizer shall have the right to approve all [the format of] such uses in writing in advance. [Sponsor shall submit materials to Organizer in writing and if Organizer does not approve or reject such materials in writing within (*number*) business days after receipt thereof, then Organizer shall be deemed to have approved such materials.] The right to use Organizer's Trademarks [Service Marks] is nonexclusive, nonassignable and nontransferable. All uses by Sponsor of Organizer's Trademarks [Service Marks] shall inure solely to the benefit of Organizer.

As described in more detail in Chapter 2, one who allows another to use its trademark must control the quality of the goods and services offered under the mark. Paragraphs 7(a) and 7(b) address that issue. The mechanism for having approval be deemed given is designed to allow both sides to move ahead expeditiously. Some trademark owners never agree to such mechanisms. Despite the fact that each party is using the other's trademarks, the goodwill and other benefits thereof inure to the trademark owner's benefit; the other will never have more interest in them than what the Agreement provides – a mere license to use in accordance with the Agreement.

(c) Organizer shall not manufacture or sell, or license the manufacture and/or sale of, any promotional or other merchandise which bears Sponsor's Trademarks [Service Marks] without Sponsor's prior written consent. Sponsor shall have the right to manufacture and/or sell promotional or other merchandise which bears Organizer's Trademarks only in accordance with Paragraph 8.

The Sponsor should retain a veto over the use of its Trademarks on merchandise, particularly because it may already be involved in exclusive relationships not related to the Event.

8. Merchandising. (a) Organizer represents and warrants that all merchandise authorized by it to bear the Organizer's Trademarks [Service Marks] or to be associated with the Event ("Event Related Merchandise") shall be of high standard and of such style, appearance and quality as to suit the best exploitation of the Event and shall be free from product defects and shall be merchantable and suited for its intended purpose. Organizer shall indemnify and hold harmless Sponsor and Sponsor's officers, directors, employees, successors and assigns from any claims, damages, liabilities, losses, government procedures, costs and expenses, including reasonable attorneys' fees and costs of suit, arising out of the failure of this warranty. All Event Related Merchandise which also bears Sponsor's Trademarks [Service Marks] shall include appropriate notice of any applicable trademark, service mark or copyright relating to Organizer's Trademarks [Service Marks] or Sponsor's Trademarks [Service Marks]. Each party shall reasonably determine what constitutes appropriate notice for its respective Trademarks [Service Marks] and copyrights.

Event Related Merchandise, especially that which bears the Sponsor's Trademarks, will reflect on the Sponsor and therefore should be of high quality (see Chapter 2). As producers of licensed merchandise, both the Organizer and the Sponsor can have liability (see Chapter 5). The warranty and indemnity here are fairly standard and perhaps redundant because of the general indemnity in paragraph 11. The Organizer may wish to limit the indemnity to the limits of its applicable insurance.

(b) Sponsor shall have the right in connection with its advertising and promotion of the Products [Services] during the Term to produce and sell Event Related Merchandise provided it also bears Sponsor's Trademarks [Service Marks]. Such merchandise shall be subject to Organizer's approval, which shall not be unreasonably withheld.

This gives the Sponsor the right to produce its own Event Related Merchandise with both the Event's and the Sponsor's Trademarks.

(c) If Sponsor desires to sell Event Related Merchandise for which Organizer has authorized a licensee, and Sponsor desires to purchase such merchandise from such licensee, then Organizer shall require such licensee to sell such merchandise to Sponsor without Organizer's royalty thereon. Organizer and such licensee shall inform Sponsor in a statement signed by one of each of their respective officers of the amount of Organizer's royalty thereon.

Sometimes it is easier for the Sponsor to buy the Organizer's officially licensed merchandise. In that case, the licensee's price includes a royalty payable to the Organizer. Since arguably the Sponsor has already paid for the right to sell Event Related Merchandise, this subparagraph attempts to avoid double payment by the Sponsor to the Organizer.

(d) If Sponsor manufactures or causes to be manufactured its own Event Related Merchandise, Sponsor represents and warrants that such merchandise shall be free from defects and merchantable and fit for its particular purpose. Sponsor shall indemnify and hold harmless Organizer and Organizer's officers, directors, employees, successors and assigns from any claims, damages, liabilities, losses, government proceedings, costs and expenses, including reasonable attorneys' fees and costs of suit, arising out of the failure of this warranty.

This is the converse of Organizer's warranty in subparagraph 8(a). If the Organizer succeeds in limiting its warranty to the limits of applicable insurance, then this clause should also be so limited.

(e) In any agreement between Sponsor and any third party relating to the manufacture, distribution or promotion of Sponsor's Event Related Merchandise or otherwise relating to the Event, under which obligations or liabilities in excess of $5,000 in the aggregate may be incurred, Sponsor agrees that such agreement will contain a clause substantially similar to the following:

[Third party] will look solely to [Sponsor] for performance and for payment and satisfaction of any obligation or claim arising out of or in connection with this Agreement, and [Third Party] hereby covenants that it will not assert any claim against or look to Sponsor or any officer, director, employee or representative of Sponsor for satisfaction of any such obligation or claim.

This is designed to insulate the Organizer from any substantial claims by third parties that contract with the Sponsor. It is standard in many trademark licenses. The Sponsor may request a similar clause in its favor.

9. Warranties. (a) Organizer represents and warrants that:

(i) it has the full right and legal authority to enter into and fully perform this Agreement in accordance with its terms without violating the rights of any other person;

(ii) Organizer's Trademarks [Service Marks] do not infringe the trademarks or trade names or other rights of any other person;

(iii) it has all government licenses, permits or other authorizations necessary to conduct the Event as contemplated under this Agreement.

(iv) it will comply with all applicable laws, regulations and ordinances pertaining to the promotion and conduct of the Event.

(b) Sponsor represents and warrants that:

(i) it has the full right and legal authority to enter into and fully perform this Agreement in accordance with its terms without violating the rights of any other person;

(ii) Sponsor's Trademarks [Service Marks] do not infringe the trademarks or trade names of any other person;

(iii) it has all government licenses, permits or other authorization necessary to conduct its business.

These warranties are fairly straightforward and standard. The trademark warranty in (ii) may not apply for certain events like the Olympic and Pan Am Games, where ownership and control of the relevant trademarks is extremely complicated and the Organizer's warranties are typically limited.

10. Indemnity. (a) Each party will indemnify, defend and hold harmless the other, its parent, subsidiary and affiliated corporations and their respective directors, officers, employees, agents, successors and assigns, from and against any and all claims, damages, liabilities, losses, government proceedings and costs and expenses, including reasonable attorneys' fees and costs of suit, arising out of any alleged or actual breach of this Agreement or the inaccuracy of any warranty or representation made by it or any act or omission by it in the performance of this Agreement or the purposes hereof.

(b) Each party will give the other prompt written notice of any claim or suit possibly coming within the purview of any indemnity set forth in this Agreement. Upon the written request of an indemnitee, the indemnitor will assume the defense of any such claim, demand, action or proceeding. The indemnitee shall also have the right to provide its own defense at its own expense, provided the indemnitee shall not settle any claim without the indemnitor's consent unless it is willing to release the indemnitor from its obligation of indemnity hereunder. Termination of this Agreement shall not affect the continuing obligation of each of the parties under this Paragraph and Paragraph 11.

The indemnity here is a broad one, mutual and fairly standard. Each party is responsible for the liabilities and expenses incurred by the other as a result of that party's conduct under the Agreement or its breach of the Agreement. Again, it could be limited on both sides to the amount of applicable insurance (see Chapter 5). The party to be indemnified can provide its own counsel, but can't settle a suit (because the indemnitor has to pay).

11. Insurance. Each party hereunder shall obtain and maintain at its own expense, during the term of this Agreement and for a period of (*number*) years following the Event, a standard Comprehensive General Liability Policy written by a United States insurance company in the face amount of $_____, which policy shall (i) specifically cover such party's incidental contractual obligations; (ii) provide standard product liability protection and (iii) list the other as a named insured. Such insurance shall be in a form reasonably acceptable to counsel for the other and shall require the insurer to give the other at least 30 days' prior written notice of any modification or cancellation. Each party shall provide the other with such evidence of coverage as may be reasonably acceptable to the other within 30 days following the execution of this Agreement.

The coverage and limits of insurance are very important. Standard comprehensive insurance in the amount of $1,000,000 each occurrence/$3,000,000 aggregate is not unusual. In the alternative to insurance carried post-event, a "claims arising" policy might be acceptable (see Chapter 5).

12. Term and Termination. (a) This Agreement shall become effective on the date first above written and shall expire on (*date*), unless terminated earlier or renewed pursuant to the terms hereof (the "Term").

This paragraph describes the Term. It would be rare for a Sponsor to be irrevocably committed for more than 2 to 3 years, although the Sponsor might have rights of first refusal and/or an option to renew. However, it is fairly common for a sponsor to commit to a 2 or 3 year term in order to be certain of some continuity and to assure the Organizer of recovery of start-up costs.

(b) Without prejudice to any other rights or remedies that Organizer may have, Organizer may terminate this Agreement immediately by delivery of notice to Sponsor at any time if any of the following events shall occur:

(1) Sponsor shall fail to comply with Paragraph 7 hereof in any respect and fail to cure the same within (*number*) days of receipt of notice of such failure;

Because trademark rights are so fragile and a licensor has a duty to control its licensee, the failure to abide by the requirements of the trademark approval paragraph can lead to termination if the breach is not cured in a relatively short period of time.

(2) Sponsor shall (i) make an assignment for the benefit of creditors, (ii) be adjudicated bankrupt, (iii) file a voluntary petition in bankruptcy or a voluntary petition or an answer seeking reorganization, arrangement, readjustment of its debts or for any other relief under Title 11 of the United States Code or any successor or other federal or state insolvency law ("Bankruptcy Law"), (iv) have filed against it an involuntary petition in bankruptcy or seeking reorganization, arrangement, readjustment of its debts or for any other relief under any Bankruptcy Law, which petition is not discharged within 30 days or (v) shall apply for or permit the appointment of a receiver or trustee for its assets;

Termination in the event of insolvency or bankruptcy may not be effective under the Bankruptcy Code, except perhaps in personal service contracts (see Chapter 1). If a sponsor is insecure about an Organizer's ability to perform, it should utilize specific performance criteria, e.g., raising other sponsorship money, so that termination can be based on default.

(3) Sponsor shall default under any provision of this Agreement and shall have failed to cure such default within 30 days after it received written notice of such default from Organizer; or

An opportunity to correct the event of default is fairly standard.

(4) any of the representations or warranties made by Sponsor in this Agreement shall prove to be untrue or inaccurate in any material respect.

If the warranties of a party aren't true, the basic understandings and assumptions of the parties before entering into the contract are false and thus grounds for termination.

(c) Without prejudice to any other rights or remedies that Sponsor may have, Sponsor may terminate this Agreement immediately by delivery of notice to Organizer if at any time (i) Organizer shall fail to comply with Paragraph 7 hereof in any respect and fails to cure the same within (*number*) days of receipt of notice of such failure; (ii) any of the events described in subparagraph (3) above shall occur with respect to Organizer; (iii) Organizer shall default under any provision of this Agreement and shall have failed to cure such default within 30 days after it shall receive written notice of such default from Sponsor or (iv) any of the representations or warranties made by Organizer in this Agreement shall prove to be untrue or inaccurate in any material respect.

This subparagraph parallels subparagraph (b) and allows the Sponsor to terminate in similar circumstances.

13. Cancellation and Preemption. In the event that the Event does not take place, in whole or in part, due to any Act of God or force majeure, including without limitation, weather, fire, flood, strike, labor dispute or similar cause beyond the control of the parties, then Sponsor shall be entitled to an immediate refund of the Sponsorship Fee [or a pro rata portion thereof if the Event took place only in part]. In the event of preemption of television coverage, Sponsor shall be entitled to the rebate described in Paragraph 4, except that if network television coverage were planned and if only one national network preempted a substantial portion of the relevant time period Sponsor shall not be entitled to a rebate (except as allowed in Paragraph 4). Organizer will provide adequate rain, cancellation and preemption insurance to cover its obligations hereunder.

This paragraph requires the Organizer to provide rain, cancellation and other insurance necessary to make the Sponsor whole if the Event or the television coverage doesn't take place. For a fuller discussion of this problem, see Chapter 5. Network preemption does not trigger this paragraph unless more than one network preempts the coverage, the idea being that unless the other two national networks preempt the time, the network carrying the Event should not preempt the time. However, one network's preemption may affect the ratings guarantee under paragraph 4.

14. Arbitration. The parties agree that any dispute between them arising out of, based upon or relating to this Agreement shall be resolved exclusively by arbitration conducted in accordance with the Commercial Rules then in effect of the American Arbitration Association. Such arbitration shall be held in (*city*). Judgment upon the award rendered shall be final and nonappealable and may be entered in any court having jurisdiction. Each party shall bear its own expenses arising out of any such proceeding, except that the fees and costs of any arbitrator(s) shall be borne equally by the parties. Notwithstanding the obligations set forth in this Paragraph, each party shall be permitted to seek equitable relief from a court having jurisdiction to prevent the unauthorized use or misuse of their respective Trademarks [Servicemarks].

Whether the parties desire arbitration is up to them, as is the site of the arbitration. (Hawaii in January is often hopefully suggested!) However, this clause exempts trademark disputes from the arbitration mechanism and allows either party to seek injunctive relief, which often is a speedier process.

15. Miscellany. (a) *Confidentiality.* The parties hereto agree to maintain in confidence the terms and conditions of this Agreement except to the extent that a proposed disclosure of any specific terms or conditions hereof by either party is authorized in advance by the other party.

Confidentiality, particularly with respect to the Sponsorship Fee, may be important to the Sponsor and helpful in negotiations with other promoters.

(b) *No Joint Venture or Partnership.* This Agreement shall not be deemed to create a joint venture, partnership, principal-agent, employer-employee or similar relationship between Organizer and Sponsor.

This is a standard clause meant to establish that neither party can act for or bind the other.

(c) *Invalidity.* The determination that any provision of this Agreement is invalid or unenforceable shall not invalidate this Agreement, all of said provisions being inserted conditionally on their being considered legally valid, and this Agreement shall be construed and performed in all respects as if such invalid or unenforceable provision(s) were omitted.

If any provision of this Agreement becomes illegal, that portion would be struck and the Agreement would continue. In some industries, it is standard to draft a clause here that instead says, for instance, that if it becomes illegal to advertise alcoholic beverages or tobacco products, the Agreement shall be null and void in its entirety.

(d) *Notices.* All notices required or permitted to be made under this Agreement shall be in writing and shall be deemed to have been duly given when delivered or sent by prepaid certified or registered mail or telex:

If to Sponsor, to: _____ address _____

If to Organizer, to: _____ address _____

or such other address as either party may designate in writing to the other party for this purpose.

This is boilerplate.

(e) *Governing Law [and Consent to Jurisdiction].* This Agreement is subject to and shall be construed in accordance with the laws of the State of (*state name*) [and Sponsor [Organizer] consents to jurisdiction in the state and federal courts located in (*city, state*) and hereby waives personal service. Sponsor [Organizer] hereby appoints the ambassador and any consul or vice consul from (*foreign country*) as its agent for the receipt of process hereunder.]

Rarely does the law to govern paragraph create significant differences. While some parties insist on specifying a venue where suits may be brought, the normal compromise is silence on the issue. However, with respect to foreign companies, consent to jurisdiction and waiver of personal service may simplify any lawsuits and is frequently negotiated.

(f) *Non-Assignment.* Neither party shall assign this Agreement without the prior written approval of the other party, except that Sponsor may assign this Agreement to any entity which acquires substantially all of its assets.

Since promotions are rather personal, it makes sense to prevent assignment by either party, although the Sponsor should provide for the possibility of a corporate takeover.

(g) *Complete Agreement.* This Agreement represents the entire agreement between the parties and supersedes all other agreements, if any, express or implied, whether written or oral. Organizer has made and makes no representations of any kind except those specifically set forth herein.

While boilerplate, this paragraph is useful to the Organizer because it disclaims any representations as to the success of the Event unless, as in some instances television ratings, the level of success is explicitly stated.

(h) *Binding Agreement.* This Agreement shall be binding upon the parties, their successors and assigns.

If the Agreement is assigned (with the consent of the parties) it binds their successors and assigns.

IN WITNESS WHEREOF, the parties have executed this Agreement on the date first above written.

Organizer

By: _____

Title: _____

Sponsor

By: _____

Title: _____

SAMPLE SHORT FORM
SPONSORSHIP LETTER AGREEMENT

Sponsor
Address
City/State/Zip

Dear _____ :

This will confirm the terms and conditions on which (*name of Sponsor*) ("you")
have agreed to sponsor the (*name of Event*) (the "Event") organized by (*name of
Organizer*) ("us").

1. We shall use our best efforts to conduct and promote (*describe*). [We will use
our best efforts to cause the Event, date and place to be sanctioned by (*name of
Sanctioning Organization if any*). The failure of the Event to be sanctioned shall
not, however, void this Agreement.]

2. We hereby grant you the right to be [an] [the] official Sponsor of the Event. You
shall have the right to use the name of the Event [and the name of (*trademark*)] as
well as the names and likenesses of participants in advertising prior to and for
_____ months after the Event in connection with your sponsorship, provided the
names of participants are not used as an endorsement of any product or service.
All such materials are subject to our prior written approval, which shall not be
unreasonably withheld.

3. We shall use our best efforts to provide you with [signage at the Event, etc.].

4. We shall provide you with _____ free tickets. ; *Pro Am clinic*

5. We shall give you credit as [a] sponsor in all advertising and promotional
materials prepared by us in the following form: "_____."

6. If we produce a videotape of the Event for home distribution or broadcast or
other use, we will use our best efforts to provide you with sponsorship credit
therein.

7. In consideration of all rights granted you hereunder, you will pay us
$_____, payable _____ .

8. We shall provide a comprehensive general liability insurance covering the participants and the crowd in the face amount of $_____ and shall cause you to be named as an insured thereon.

9. You recognize that we own all rights to the Event and you agree not to sponsor a similar event within (*number*) miles of (*site*) for a period of (*number of months or years*) from the date of the Event.

10. We shall have the right to use your trademarks in advertising and promoting the Event, including on any merchandise authorized by us in connection with the Event. Any merchandise produced by us shall be of high quality consistent with your outstanding public image and you shall have the right to approve the same in writing in advance, provided such approval shall not be unreasonably withheld.

11. Each party represents and warrants that it is free to enter into this Agreement without violating the rights of any person, that its trademarks do not infringe the trademarks or trade names of any person and that it will comply with all laws and regulations pertinent to its business.

12. In the event that the Event does not take place due to any cause beyond the reasonable control of the parties, this Agreement shall terminate and our only obligation shall be to return to you the fee paid us hereunder less any direct out-of-pocket expenses incurred by us prior to the date of termination.

13. This Agreement does not constitute a partnership or joint venture or principal-agent relationship between us. This Agreement may not be assigned by either party. It shall be governed by the laws of the State of (*state*). It is complete and represents the entire agreement between the parties.

If this accurately sets forth our Agreement, please sign below and return a copy to me.

Sincerely,

Event Organizer

By: _____

Agreed and Accepted this _____ day of _____, 19_____

_____
Sponsor

SAMPLE SUPPLIER AGREEMENT

THIS AGREEMENT (this "Agreement") is made and entered into as of the (*number*) day of (*month*), (*year*), by and between Organizer ("Organizer"), a corporation organized under the laws of the State of (*state name*), and Supplier ("Supplier"), a corporation organized under the laws of the State of (*state name*).

Recitals

WHEREAS, Organizer has the exclusive right to organize and conduct a (*type*) event which is to be held (*when*) in (*city, state*) and to be known as ("*Event Name*") (the "Event"); and

WHEREAS, Supplier has determined to provide in-kind support for the Event in exchange for certain promotional rights to be provided by Organizer;

NOW, THEREFORE, in consideration of the mutual agreements and promises contained herein, the parties hereto agree as follows:

These introductory paragraphs basically describe in the broadest terms the intentions of the parties. Often they contain "sell copy."

1. Official Supplier Status. Organizer grants to Supplier the exclusive right during the Term of this Agreement to use the Organizer's Trademarks as described herein in advertising and promoting Supplier's Products [Services] as defined herein and to refer to such Products [Services] as an "Official Supplier of [*product or service category*]" to the Event.

This is the basic right granted the Supplier by the Organizer. The rest of the Agreement explains in detail the full scope of the specific rights granted and the obligations of the Supplier. Not all rights described in this Agreement would be given to every supplier.

2. Advertising and Promotion. (a) Subject to Organizer's rights of approval as described herein, Supplier shall have the right to use the Organizer's Trademarks in advertising and promotional activities only in connection with advertising its Official Supplier status.

This subsection lets the Supplier know that while it has discretion over the type of promotional activities to undertake, the Organizer will have some approval.

(b) Organizer shall [use its best efforts to] provide the following rights to Supplier during the Term of this Agreement:

(i) the right to sell Products [Services] at the Site of the Event;

This right may need to be described in greater detail, depending on the nature of the event and the arena and whether there will be an official concessionaire. (It's obviously easier for a Supplier to have a truck at an outdoor festival than to arrange a concession stand at an existing arena.)

(ii) (*number*) signs at locations specified by Organizer [Supplier] and at a distance of at least (*number of feet*) from other signage, such signs to be provided by Supplier [Organizer];

This subparagraph focuses on the "clutter" from other signs that may interfere with the value of the sponsorship. From the Organizer's point of view, the promising of a certain number and spacing of signs is much too specific, could tie the Organizer's hands unnecessarily and shows a lack of trust by the Supplier, etc. On the other hand, it helps the Supplier to clarify what it is getting.

(iii) credit as follows in all print advertising [of a size larger than (*number of square inches*)] [placed by Organizer] in connection with the Event: "Supplier, an Official Supplier of _____ to the Event";

The Organizer can control only its own placements. In other advertising (e.g., by other local presenters), it may retain contractual rights to approve credits, but it should not be ultimately responsible for third-party actions.

(iv) the right to be named in all press releases issued by Organizer;

Being named in press releases is standard; the most complete agreements will include this clause "just to be sure."

(v) the right to purchase advertising spots on network, cable or other television broadcasts of the Event licensed by Organizer after any Official Sponsor has made its purchases;

This probably should be a "best efforts" clause since the Organizer does not always control the broadcaster.

(vi) the right to use film clips (not to exceed (*number*) minutes in length) of past events [of this type] organized by Organizer for advertising and promotion, subject to Organizer's prior approval.

Usually clips of up to three minutes are allowed, which is more than adequate for 30- and 60-second commercials. It is the Organizer's responsibility to make sure the clips can be used commercially without violating the copyright, right of privacy or other right of any party.

(vii) to use film clips (not to exceed (*number*) minutes in length) of this Event for purposes of advertising Supplier's involvement with the Event; and

The difference between this subparagraph and (vi) is that this allows for some post-Event use of the most current coverage during the Term.

(viii) the right to erect a courtesy tent [or host a similar area] at the site of the Event at a location designated by Organizer.

Courtesy tents and areas are common perks of sponsorship; location is important but because it presents logistical problems, the Organizer should retain control (unless the site is well known to both and a specific area can be defined).

3. Contribution. (a) In consideration of the full performance by Organizer of all of its obligations hereunder and of all rights granted hereunder to Supplier, Supplier shall provide Organizer with the following products ("Products"), delivered to Organizer on the dates and at the locations specified:

Product _____
                            quantity, description

Delivery Date _____
                            date

Location _____
                            (address)

The details here are important so that both sides are clear on what is being promised.

(b) At Supplier's expense, Supplier shall deliver the Products to, and store such Products at, Organizer's location. [Any Products furnished for the purpose of athletic competition or preparation shall meet the standards, if any, of the appropriate governing body having jurisdiction over the relevant sporting event.]

The storage expenses may be negotiable. The bracketed warranty is standard for events such as boxing matches; the Organizer may wish to specify a specific sanctioning body.

(c) Supplier agrees to provide service personnel on an "on call" basis to assist in the delivery, installation, repair, maintenance and removal of the Products, in a number mutually agreed upon between the parties. All of Supplier's personnel shall be subject to Organizer's security and personnel policies and practices.

If the Supplier provides personnel, the Organizer needs to maintain security and should be able to enforce policies such as dress codes, no-smoking areas, etc.

(d) During the Term of this Agreement, Supplier agrees to carry workers' compensation and employer's liability insurance, in such amounts as may be required by law, for any personnel Supplier may utilize for the delivery, installation, maintenance, repair and removal of the Products.

The Supplier must maintain insurance on its employees, even while they are working on the Organizer's premises.

(e) Organizer represents and warrants that to the extent storage of the Products is under the control and/or supervision of Organizer, Organizer will assume all risk of loss and will provide adequate insurance to cover their replacement and will further store the Products safely and securely in a manner which will not cause the Products to become defective or not merchantable or fit for their intended purpose.

The Supplier should insist on a paragraph like this one, especially if it is supplying Products like foods, which can spoil if improperly handled. The Organizer could also ask the Supplier to give it storage instructions so that liability could be turned back on the Supplier.

4. Option to Renew. Organizer hereby grants to Supplier the right to renew its Official Suppliership hereunder annually on the same terms and conditions as contained herein (except that the Contribution described in Paragraph 3 shall be increased by (*number*) % of units). Supplier shall exercise said option, if at all, by giving Organizer written notice thereof within (*number*) days prior to the expiration of the Term of this Agreement. In the event that Supplier does not exercise such option, the exclusivity described in Paragraph 5 shall nonetheless continue for a period of (*number of months or years*) [or the completion of (*number*) events similar to the Event hereunder, whichever comes first].

The right to renew is important to the official Supplier. In exchange for taking the risk, it gets a fixed increase in the Suppliership Fee. Organizers should try to limit the right to renewal to a few years; if an Event really takes off, the increased value will not be recognized because of the locked-in renewal fee. If the option to renew is limited, the Supplier should ask for a right of first refusal to match subsequent offers.

Here, if a Supplier does not renew, it nonetheless gets competitive protection for some period of time in order to avoid a competitor's usurping the Supplier's goodwill in the Event.

5. Exclusivity. Organizer represents and warrants that it will not authorize any seller of any product [service] competitive to the Products [Services] or antithetical or incompatible with the Products [Services] to be an Official Sponsor or Supplier or to be associated in any way with the Event [including on-site signage and concessions]. [Organizer shall consult with Supplier concerning other Official Suppliers or Sponsors.]

Competitive protection is critical and Suppliers should try to retain approval over other sponsors, presenters and suppliers. The impact of antithetical Suppliers (for instance, antacids and pizza parlors) should be considered as well as the impact of incompatible suppliers – e.g., McDonald's is so closely associated with Coca-Cola that Pepsi-Cola would be an incompatible supplier. This paragraph also raises the issue of permanent signage and concessionaires at the site of an event.

6. Trademarks. (a) Supplier's trademarks [service marks], label designs, product identifications, artwork and other symbols and devices associated with Supplier Products [Services] ("Supplier's Trademarks" [Supplier's Service Marks"]) are and shall remain Supplier's property, and Supplier shall take all steps reasonably necessary to protect such Supplier's Trademarks [Service Marks] through U.S.

federal registrations and foreign registrations as it deems desirable and through reasonable prosecution of infringements. Organizer is hereby authorized to use Supplier's Trademarks [Service Marks] in advertising and promoting the Event during the Term of this Agreement, provided Supplier shall have the right to approve all [the format of] such uses in writing in advance. [Organizer shall submit materials to Supplier in writing and if Supplier does not approve or reject such materials in writing within (number) business days after receipt thereof, then Supplier shall be deemed to have approved such materials.] The right to use Supplier's Trademarks [Service Marks] is nonexclusive, nonassignable and nontransferable. All uses by Organizer of Supplier's Trademarks shall inure solely to the benefit of Supplier.

(b) Organizer's trademarks [service marks], designs, artwork and other symbols and devices associated with the Event ("Organizer's Trademarks") [("Organizer's Service Marks")] are and shall remain Organizer's property and Organizer shall take all steps reasonably necessary to protect Organizer's Trademarks [Service Marks] through U.S. federal registrations and foreign registrations as it deems desirable and through reasonable prosecution of infringements. Supplier is hereby authorized to use Organizer's Trademarks [Service Marks] in advertising and promoting the Products [Services] during the Term of this Agreement, provided Organizer shall have the right to approve all [the format of] such uses in writing in advance. [Supplier shall submit materials to Organizer in writing and if Organizer does not approve or reject such materials in writing within (number) business days after receipt thereof, then Organizer shall be deemed to have approved such materials.] The right to use Organizer's Trademarks [Service Marks] is nonexclusive, nonassignable and nontransferable. All uses by Supplier of Organizer's Trademarks [Service Marks] shall inure solely to the benefit of Organizer.

As described in more detail in Chapter 2, one who allows another to use its trademark or service mark must control the quality of the goods and services offered under the mark. Paragraphs 6(a) and 6(b) address that issue. The mechanism for having approval be deemed given is designed to allow both sides to move ahead expeditiously. Some trademark owners never agree to such mechanisms. Despite the fact that each party is using the other's trademarks, the goodwill and other benefits thereof inure to the trademark owner's benefit; the other will never have more interest in them than what the Agreement provides – a mere license to use in accordance with the Agreement.

(c) Organizer shall not manufacture or sell, or license the manufacture and/or sale, of any promotional or other merchandise which bears Supplier's Trademarks without Supplier's prior written consent. Supplier shall have the right to manufacture and/or sell promotional or other merchandise which bears Organizer's Trademarks only in accordance with Paragraph 8.

The Supplier should retain a veto over the use of its Trademarks on merchandise, particularly because it may already be involved in exclusive relationships not related to the Event.

7. Warranties. (a) Organizer represents and warrants that:

(i) it has the full right and legal authority to enter into and fully perform this Agreement in accordance with its terms without violating the rights of any other person;

(ii) Organizer's Trademarks Service Marks do not infringe the trademarks or trade names or other rights of any other person;

(iii) it has all government licenses, permits or other authorizations necessary to conduct the Event as contemplated under this Agreement;

(iv) it will comply with all applicable laws, regulations and ordinances pertaining to the promotion and conduct of the Event.

(b) Supplier represents and warrants that:

(i) it has the full right and legal authority to enter into and fully perform this Agreement in accordance with its terms without violating the rights of any other person;

(ii) Supplier's Trademarks Service Marks do not infringe the trademarks or trade names of any other person;

(iii) it has all government licenses, permits or other authorizations necessary to conduct its business;

(iv) all Products furnished by Supplier shall be of high quality and shall be free from product defects and shall be merchantable and suited for their intended purpose.

These warranties are fairly straightforward and standard. The trademark warranty in (ii) may not apply for certain events like the Olympic and Pan Am Games, where ownership and control of the relevant trademarks is extremely complicated.

8. Indemnity. (a) Each party will indemnify, defend and hold harmless the other, its parent, subsidiary and affiliated corporations and their respective directors, officers, employees, agents, successors and assigns, from and against any and all claims, damages, liabilities, losses, government proceedings and costs and expenses, including reasonable attorneys' fees and costs of suit, arising out of any alleged or actual breach of this Agreement or the inaccuracy of any warranty or representation made by the other or any act or omission by the other in the performance of this Agreement or the purposes hereof.

(b) Each party will give the other prompt written notice of any claim or suit possibly coming within the purview of any indemnity set forth in this Agreement. Upon the written request of an indemnitee, the indemnitor will assume the defense of any such claim, demand, action or proceeding. The indemnitee shall also have the right to provide its own defense at its own expense, provided the indemnitee shall not settle any claim without the indemnitor's consent unless it is willing to release the indemnitor from its obligation of indemnity hereunder. Termination of this Agreement shall not affect the continuing obligation of each of the parties under this Paragraph and Paragraph 9.

The indemnity here is a broad one, mutual and fairly standard. Each party is responsible for the liabilities and expenses incurred by the other as a result of its conduct under the Agreement or its breach of the Agreement. Again, it could be limited on both sides to the amount of applicable insurance (see Chapter 5). The party to be indemnified can provide its own counsel, but can't settle a suit (because the indemnitor has to pay).

9. Insurance. Each party hereunder shall obtain and maintain at its own expense, during the term of this Agreement and for a period of (*number*) years following the Event, a standard Comprehensive General Liability Policy written by a United States insurance company in the face amount of $_____, which policy shall

(i) specifically cover such party's contractual liabilities; (ii) provide standard product liability protection and (iii) list the other as a named insured. Such insurance shall be in a form reasonably acceptable to counsel for the other and shall require the insurer to give the other at least 30 days' prior written notice of any modification or cancellation. Each party shall provide the other with such evidence of coverage as may be reasonably acceptable to the other within 30 days following the execution of this Agreement.

The limits and coverage of insurance is very important. Standard comprehensive insurance in the amount of $1,000,000 each occurrence/$3,000,000 aggregate is not unusual. "Claims arising" insurance could be substituted for the insurance after Termination (see Chapter 5).

10. Term and Termination. (a) This Agreement shall become effective on the date first above written and shall expire on (*date*), unless terminated earlier or renewed pursuant to the terms hereof (the "Term").

This paragraph describes the Term. It would be rare for a Supplier to be irrevocably committed for more than 2 to 3 years, although it might want rights to continue to supply the Event thereafter under a right of first refusal.

(b) Without prejudice to any other rights or remedies that Organizer may have, Organizer may terminate this Agreement immediately by delivery of notice to Supplier at any time if any of the following events shall occur:

(1) Supplier shall fail to comply with Paragraph 6 hereof in any respect and fail to cure the same within (*number*) days of receipt of notice of such failure;

Because trademark rights are so fragile and a licensor has a duty to control its licensee, the failure to abide by the requirements of the trademark approval paragraph can lead to termination if a cure is not effectuated in a relatively short period of time.

(2) Supplier shall (i) make an assignment for the benefit of creditors, (ii) be adjudicated bankrupt, (iii) file a voluntary petition in bankruptcy or a voluntary petition or an answer seeking reorganization, arrangement, readjustment of its debts or for any other relief under Title 11 of the United States Code or any successor or other federal or state insolvency law ("Bankruptcy Law"), (iv) have filed against

it an involuntary petition in bankruptcy or seeking reorganization, arrangement, readjustment of its debts or for any other relief under any Bankruptcy Law, which petition is not discharged within 30 days or (v) shall apply for or permit the appointment of a receiver or trustee for its assets;

Termination in the event of insolvency or bankruptcy may not be effective under the Bankruptcy Code (see Chapter 1). If the Organizer is insecure about the Supplier's ability to perform, it should utilize specific performance criteria so that termination can be based on default.

(3) Supplier shall default under any provision of this Agreement and shall have failed to cure such default within 30 days after it received written notice of such default from Organizer; or

An opportunity to correct the event of default is fairly standard.

(4) Any of the representations or warranties made by Supplier in this Agreement shall prove to be untrue or inaccurate in any material respect.

If the warranties of a party aren't true, the basic understanding and assumption of the parties before entering the contract are false and thus grounds for termination.

(c) Without prejudice to any other rights or remedies that Supplier may have, Supplier may terminate this Agreement immediately by delivery of notice to Organizer if at any time (i) Organizer shall fail to comply with Paragraph 6 hereof in any respect and fails to cure the same within (number) days of receipt of notice of such failure; (ii) any of the events described in subparagraph (2) above shall occur with respect to Organizer; (iii) Organizer shall default under any provision of this Agreement and shall have failed to cure such default within 30 days after it shall receive written notice of such default from Supplier or (iv) any of the representations or warranties made by Organizer in this Agreement shall prove to be untrue or inaccurate in any material respect.

This subparagraph parallels subparagraph (b) and allows the Supplier to terminate in similar circumstances. If the Supplier is insecure about the Organizer's ability to perform, it could utilize performance criteria such as the Organizer's raising a set amount of official sponsorship/suppliership money.

11. Cancellation and Preemption. In the event that the Event does not take place, in whole or in part, due to any Act of God or force majeure, including, without limitation, weather, fire, flood, strike, labor dispute or similar cause beyond the control of the parties, then Supplier shall be entitled to an immediate refund of the value (as measured by supplier's cost) of all Products contributed by Supplier [or a pro rata portion of the value of the Products used in the Event if the Event took place only in part]. Organizer will provide adequate rain, cancellation and preemption insurance to cover its obligations hereunder.

This paragraph requires the Organizer to provide rain, cancellation and other insurance necessary to make the Supplier whole if the Event does not take place. For a fuller discussion of this problem, see Chapter 5.

12. Arbitration. The parties agree that any dispute between them arising out of, based upon or relating to this Agreement shall be resolved exclusively by arbitration conducted in accordance with the Commercial Rules of the American Arbitration Association then in effect. Such arbitration shall be held in (*city*). Judgment upon the award rendered shall be final and nonappealable and may be entered in any court having jurisdiction. Each party shall bear its own expenses arising out of any such proceeding, except that the fees and costs of any arbitrator(s) shall be borne equally by the parties. Notwithstanding the obligations set forth in this Paragraph, each party shall be permitted to seek equitable relief from a court having jurisdiction to prevent the unauthorized use or misuse of their respective Trademarks.

Whether the parties desire arbitration is up to them, as is the site of the arbitration. However, this clause exempts trademark disputes from the arbitration mechanism and allows either party to seek injunctive relief, which often is a speedier process.

13. Miscellany. (a) *Confidentiality.* The parties hereto agree to maintain in confidence the terms and conditions of this Agreement except to the extent that a proposed disclosure of any specific terms or conditions hereof by either party is authorized in advance by the other party.

Confidentiality, particularly with respect to the Contribution, may be important to the Supplier and helpful in negotiations with other promoters.

(b) *No Joint Venture or Partnership*. This Agreement shall not be deemed to create a joint venture, partnership, principal-agent, employer-employee or similar relationship between Organizer and Supplier.

This is a standard clause meant to establish that neither party can act for or bind the other.

(c) *Invalidity*. The determination that any provision of this Agreement is invalid or unenforceable shall not invalidate this Agreement, all of said provisions being inserted conditionally on their being considered legally valid, and this Agreement shall be construed and performed in all respects as if such invalid or unenforceable provision(s) were omitted.

If any provision of this Agreement becomes illegal, that portion would be struck and the agreement would continue. In some industries, it is standard to draft a clause here that instead says, for instance, that if it becomes illegal to advertise alcoholic beverages or tobacco products, the Agreement shall be null and void in its entirety.

(d) *Notices*. All notices required or permitted to be made under this Agreement shall be in writing and shall be deemed to have been duly given when delivered or sent by prepaid certified or registered mail or telex:

If to Organizer, to: _____ *address* _____

If to Supplier, to: _____ *address* _____

or such other address as either party may designate in writing to the other party for this purpose.

This is boilerplate.

(e) *Governing Law [and Consent to Jurisdiction]*. This Agreement is subject to and shall be construed in accordance with the laws of the State of (*state name*) [and Supplier [Organizer] consents to jurisdiction in the state and federal courts located in (*city, state*) and hereby waives personal service. Supplier [Organizer] hereby appoints the ambassador and any consul or vice consul from (*foreign country*) as its agent for the receipt of process hereunder].

Rarely does the law to govern paragraph create significant differences. While some parties insist on specifying a venue where suits may be brought, the normal compromise is silence on the issue. However, with respect to foreign companies, consent to jurisdiction and waiver of "personal service" may simplify any lawsuits and is frequently required by the U.S. party. ("Personal service" is the means by which a party is served with notice of a lawsuit.)

(f) *Non-Assignment.* Neither party shall assign this Agreement without the prior written approval of the other party, except that Supplier may assign this Agreement to any entity which acquires substantially all of its assets.

Since promotions are rather personal, it makes sense to prevent assignment by either party, although the Supplier should provide for the possibility of a corporate takeover.

(g) *Complete Agreement.* This Agreement represents the entire agreement between the parties and supersedes all other agreements, if any, express or implied, whether written or oral. Organizer has made and makes no representations of any kind except those specifically set forth herein.

While boilerplate, this paragraph is useful to the Organizer because it disclaims any representations as to the success of the Event unless the level of success is explicitly stated, such as in minimum attendance, etc.

(h) *Binding Agreement.* This Agreement shall be binding upon the parties, their successors and assigns.

If the Agreement is assigned (with the consent of the parties) it binds their successors and assigns.

IN WITNESS WHEREOF, the parties have executed this Agreement on the date first above written.

Organizer

By: _____

Title: _____

Supplier

By: _____

Title: _____

SAMPLE LOCAL ORGANIZER/
PROMOTER AGREEMENT

Effective (*date*), (*NATIONAL ORGANIZER*) ("NATIONAL"), a (*state*) corporation with its principal place of business in (*place*), and LOCAL PROMOTER ("LOCAL"), an individual with a place of business at (*address*), agree as follows:

I Background

1.0 NATIONAL is the owner of the "NATIONAL" service mark which denotes the source of a unique (*describe event*). NATIONAL also has the expertise and capabilities to market, manage, produce and publicize a series of NATIONAL events known as "the NATIONAL Tour."

1.1 LOCAL has obtained all necessary governmental permits to stage a NATIONAL event in (*city*) and has the capability to obtain such permits in future years. In addition, LOCAL has certain expertise and capabilities in the management and production of special events.

1.2 NATIONAL desires to license to LOCAL certain rights to use the NATIONAL SERVICE MARK and LOCAL desires to acquire those rights.

The situation here is that the National Organizer of an event that has several regional sites (a "touring" event) needs a Local Promoter, largely for political reasons, as well as the need to be on-site for a good part of the planning. The economics of such arrangements vary widely. This agreement may be generous to the Local Promoter; it presumes a relatively new event.

II Definitions

2.0 "SERVICE MARK" means the NATIONAL name, mark, and any other words or symbols which designate the NATIONAL Tour and which are either a registered service mark or trademark owed by NATIONAL or in which NATIONAL has a statutory or common-law proprietary interest.

2.1 "NATIONAL TOUR" means all NATIONAL events, including an event in (*city*), which are either staged by NATIONAL or licensed by NATIONAL in any calendar year.

2.2 "PRELIMINARY EVENTS" means all events, races, contests, shows or other forms of entertainment held in conjunction with a NATIONAL event whether staged before or after the NATIONAL event.

2.3 "(*City*)" means the area within (*number*) miles of (*city*).

2.4 "LICENSE INCOME" means income in the form of cash or goods or services converted to cash by LOCAL or other considerations received by LOCAL as a result of the use of the SERVICE MARK in (*city*).

2.5 "NATIONAL SPONSORSHIP" means sponsorship of NATIONAL TOUR events which allows the use of the SERVICE MARK in (*city*) and other areas of the country. The title sponsorship of each NATIONAL TOUR event shall be considered a NATIONAL SPONSORSHIP.

2.6 "NATIONAL LICENSING" means licenses which allow the use of the SERVICE MARK in connection with the marketing, advertising and promotion of products or services in (*city*) and other areas of the country.

2.7 "LOCAL SPONSORSHIP" means sponsorships of NATIONAL events within (*city*) only and includes no rights outside of (*city*).

2.8 "LOCAL LICENSING" means licensing of the SERVICE MARK for use in the marketing, advertising and promotion of products or services within (*city*) only and includes no rights outside of (*city*).

These definitions will, of course, vary depending on the event, but these samples should be useful in structuring these kinds of agreements. Of course, the definition of National and Local Sponsorships can be tricky.

III Grant of License

3.0 NATIONAL, subject to the reservations contained in Paragraph IV, grants to LOCAL an exclusive license to use the SERVICE MARK in connection with the advertising or promotion of events, services and products in (*city*) and to engage in LOCAL LICENSING and to authorize LOCAL SPONSORS.

The Local Organizer should control local sponsorships and licensing.

IV Reservations

4.0 NATIONAL reserves the following rights:

(a) To license use of the SERVICE MARK in connection with other NATIONAL TOUR events outside of (*city*);

(b) To sell NATIONAL SPONSORSHIPS in (*city*);

(c) To sell NATIONAL LICENSING in (*city*).

Here the National Promoter controls national advertising and sponsorship.

V Enforcement of Service Mark

5.0 In its discretion, NATIONAL in its own name (or also in LOCAL's name), will bring and prosecute suits and claims at its expense when reasonably necessary to prevent unlicensed persons from using the SERVICE MARK. After recouping its expenses, one-half of any recovery from such suits and claims shall be paid to LOCAL by NATIONAL promptly upon receipt thereof.

The National Organizer, which owns the Service Mark for the Event, should police infringements. Because infringements affect the profits of the Local Organizer as well as the National, it is appropriate that the Local share some percentage of the recovery, after expenses.

VI Sale Priorities

6.0 NATIONAL shall have the exclusive right to sell both NATIONAL SPONSORSHIPS and NATIONAL LICENSING.

The National Organizer sells national rights. Again, the primary issue is determining which are National and which are Local Sponsorships.

6.1 LOCAL may sell NATIONAL SPONSORSHIPS with the consent of NATIONAL. For any such sponsorship sold a commission of (*number*) percent (_____%) shall be retained by LOCAL.

If the Local Organizer were to sell a national Sponsor, it should get a commission. Twenty percent is not uncommon; more might be appropriate.

6.2 LOCAL may sell LOCAL SPONSORSHIPS and LOCAL LICENSING after consultation with NATIONAL. Such arrangements may not be competitive to any NATIONAL SPONSORSHIPS or NATIONAL LICENSING. LOCAL shall give NATIONAL reasonable notice of its intention to enter into any such arrangement, including a copy of the contract, which NATIONAL shall hold confidential. LOCAL shall pay NATIONAL any expenses it incurs in administrating LOCAL SPONSORSHIPS or LOCAL LICENSING sold by LOCAL, provided such expenses have been approved in advance in writing by LOCAL.

The Local Organizer's sale of Local Sponsorships obviously cannot conflict with the National Sponsorship. If the National is to service such Sponsorships, the National should be reimbursed for its services, but the Local should agree in advance to the amount of the reimbursement therefor.

VII Responsibilities
7.0 NATIONAL shall be solely responsible, financially and administratively, for the following with regard to the NATIONAL TOUR:

(a) Organization, direction and production;

(b) Development and conceptualization, including rules, regulations, standards and promotions;

(c) Marketing NATIONAL SPONSORSHIPS and NATIONAL LICENSING;

(d) Development and marketing of souvenir and promotional items;

(e) Providing minimum funding as described on Exhibit A, payable (*state how*);

(f) Providing technical support [including scoreboards and other structures and facilities which are uniform to NATIONAL TOUR events] as described on Exhibit B;

(g) Providing consulting support and week-of-event on-site support as needed;

(h) Producing the NATIONAL TOUR program.

This paragraph should specify the obligations of the National Organizer in as much detail as possible. The Exhibits would be added as necessary.

7.2 LOCAL shall have the following responsibilities with regard to the NATIONAL TOUR event in (*city*):

(a) Producing a high quality NATIONAL race which is at least substantially similar in quality and presentation to (*specify*);

(b) In its discretion, produce PRELIMINARY EVENTS which are of equal or better quality than similar events staged in (*other cities*);

(c) Provide an adequate office staff to handle inquiries and other local NATIONAL event matters on a year-round basis;

(d) Provide local copy and sell local advertisements for the NATIONAL TOUR program;

(e) Provide all necessary municipal permits;

(f) Provide adequate food and drink concessions at the site of the NATIONAL TOUR in (*city*).

This paragraph should specify the obligations of the Local Promoter in as much detail as possible.

VIII Broadcast Rights

8.0 NATIONAL owns any and all right, title and interest in television, cable and radio telecast, videotapes, films and all other rights of the NATIONAL TOUR, including the (*city*) event. In the event that NATIONAL desires to include the (*city*) event in a television program or to license the inclusion of the (*city*) event in another's program, then NATIONAL shall negotiate with LOCAL in good faith prior to any such authorization by NATIONAL with respect to the compensation to be paid LOCAL.

Compensation to the Local Promoter for television coverage can be handled a number of ways. This paragraph presumes very good faith between the parties, since it requires only negotiation. If there is to be negotiation, it should occur prior to the National Organizer's entering into any agreement for television coverage of the Event.

IX Income to Local

9.0 LOCAL shall be entitled to the following compensation in connection with the (*city*) event: [specify] ["LICENSE INCOME"]

The Local Organizer here might specify that it will get income from ancillary events that it may plan at its own expense and from food and drink concessions. In addition, the Local Organizer may get a portion of the profits on the sale of souvenir items sold by the National as well as retain the proceeds of Local Sponsorship.

9.1 In (*year*), LOCAL shall be guaranteed by NATIONAL a minimum annual income of $_____.

If the event is a new one, the Local Organizer may well demand compensation for its time, regardless of the success of the event.

9.2 If LOCAL's first report shows less than $_____ income in (*year*), NATIONAL shall pay to LOCAL under paragraph 9.1 the difference between the income stated and $_____.

This paragraph specifies the performance mechanism for the guarantee of Paragraph 9.1.

X Royalties

10.0 LOCAL shall pay no royalties on LICENSE INCOME below $_____ per calendar year.

This reinforces a guaranteed fee to the Local Organizer for a new event.

10.1 If LOCAL's INCOME equals or exceeds $_____ in a calendar year, it shall pay NATIONAL _____ percent (_____%) of its LICENSE INCOME for that year as royalties.

The Local Organizer here is permitted to make a certain level of income before the National Organizer takes a royalty, but note that this Paragraph provides a royalty on the entire income, not just the income in excess of a specified minimum.

10.2 For purposes of this section, the term LICENSE INCOME shall include money or goods valued at retail received by LOCAL, but only if such goods or services are converted to cash by LOCAL.

While goods should be valued if they become cash in the hands of the Local Organizer, there may be instances where goods are used to present the event or are given to participants (e.g., T-shirts given to or beverages consumed by participants in a marathon) and it seems unfair to require the Local Organizer to pay the National Organizer a percentage of such contributions.

10.3 LOCAL shall make two written reports to NATIONAL: thirty (30) days after the (*city*) event date, and within thirty (30) days after the following December 31. The reports shall state LOCAL's income from the event for the period on an itemized basis and shall be accompanied for any royalty payments which are due and payable by reason of the report.

Reports are a method of accountability. This paragraph could be more specific with respect to the form and content of the report. On the other hand, reports do not substitute for performance.

10.4 LOCAL agrees to keep records showing the total amount of LICENSE INCOME it receives under this Agreement in sufficient detail to determine the royalties payable. LOCAL further agrees to permit its books and records to be examined by NATIONAL from time to time to permit the verification of the reports provided for in the section, provided NATIONAL gives LOCAL reasonable advance written notice of such inspection.

This kind of audit clause is standard.

XI Assignment

11.0 The rights and licenses granted by NATIONAL in this agreement are personal to LOCAL and may not be assigned or otherwise transferred without the written consent of NATIONAL. Any attempted assignment or transfer without such consent shall be void and automatically terminate all rights of LOCAL under this Agreement.

This is standard: the relationship between the National Organizer and the Local Sponsor is usually very personal.

XII Covenant Not to Compete

12.0 During the term of this Agreement and for a period of (*number*) years after termination LOCAL agrees not to produce, stage, market, or in any way facilitate an event in (*city*), either in its own name or with others, which competes with or is similar to NATIONAL TOUR events. The foregoing will become ineffective only if NATIONAL, INC. notifies LOCAL in writing that it no longer intends to produce or have produced a NATIONAL TOUR event in (*city*) or if NATIONAL has defaulted under the Agreement.

A clause like this helps to protect the National Organizer from theft by the Local Organizer. However, if the National Organizer discontinues the event either nationally or in the local area, or otherwise defaults in the performance of the Agreement, the Local Organizer is free to organize a similar event, subject to whatever trademark rights the National Organizer might assert (see Chapter 2 on trademark abandonment). The Local Organizer may demand some form of reciprocity in this paragraph, i.e., the National cannot continue the event with a different local organizer as long as the Local Organizer is willing to work.

XIII Protection of Service Mark

13.0 LOCAL will use the SERVICE MARK only in accordance with the guidelines developed by NATIONAL for protection of the SERVICE MARK. Any continuing or deliberate violation of these guidelines or other action by LOCAL which jeopardizes the NATIONAL SERVICE MARK is a violation of this Agreement and will automatically terminate LOCAL's rights hereunder.

The National Organizer should establish guidelines for the use of its marks. The Local Organizer should not be terminated for inadvertent failures to comply with those guidelines, only continuing or deliberate failures to protect the marks.

XIV Indemnity

14.0 NATIONAL and LOCAL each will hold the other harmless against all liabilities, demands, damages, expenses or losses arising from the acts or omissions of the other. Each party represents and warrants that it maintains comprehensive general liability insurance in the amount of $_____ written by a U.S. company and that it will name the other as an additional insured thereon. Each party will provide the other with a certificate of such insurance within _____ days after execution of this Agreement.

The indemnities here are mutual. They could be more specific in terms of procedure, as in other forms in this book. In any event, each side should require the indemnity to be backed by insurance unless the other is a substantial company.

XV Term and Termination/Options

15.0 The term of this Agreement shall be for (*number*) years(s) beginning (*date*) and ending (*date*) unless terminated earlier or renewed pursuant to its terms.

15.1 LOCAL shall have (*number*) successive one-year options to renew this Agreement. To exercise its option, LOCAL must notify NATIONAL in writing of its desire to continue the Agreement on or before (*date*) of each year.

The Local Organizer should want options on future events to protect its investment in the first years. Presumably experience makes it easier (and more profitable) in future years.

15.2 NATIONAL shall have the option to cancel or discontinue its NATIONAL TOUR event in (*city*). In the event that it exercises this option, NATIONAL shall notify LOCAL of its decision in writing on or before (*number*) days preceding the date when such event would have taken place.

The National Organizer is not required to continue the event – that would be nearly impossible to enforce – but it is required to give the Local some advance notice. It should be noted that the Local can continue the event on its own under this Agreement if the National discontinues the event. Alternatively, a "liquidated damages" or one-time payment by National to Local could be specified to compensate Local for its initial risk-taking.

15.3 If either party shall, at any time, default in its obligations under this Agreement and shall fail to remedy any such default within thirty (30) days after written notice thereof, the other party may, at its option, terminate this Agreement and the license granted herein by written notice to the defaulting party.

A default in a material obligation here is grounds for termination. Other grounds might include trademark infringement or misuse. See Chapter 1 on bankruptcy and insolvency as events of termination.

XVI Choice of Law

16.0 This agreement shall be governed in all respects by the laws of the State of (*state*).

Boilerplate.

XVII Arbitration

17.0 Any dispute which arises under this contract shall be settled by arbitration as follows:

(a) The dispute shall first be submitted to (*person*) in any such form as he desires and thereafter decided by him.

(b) If (*person*) is unavailable or refuses to decide the dispute within 30 days after its submission to him, it shall be submitted for settlement by arbitration in (*usually a neutral city*) in accordance with the applicable rules of the American Arbitration Association.

(c) The decision of either (*person*) or an arbitration under subsection (ii) hereof shall be binding.

The mechanics of arbitration of disputes can be specified in detail. Here, the parties have agreed up front to an arbitrator.

NATIONAL, INC. _____

LOCAL _____

SAMPLE FOOD VENDOR
SIMPLE LETTER AGREEMENT

Name
Address
City/State/Zip

Dear _____:

We are pleased that you will be participating as a vendor in the (*Name of Event*) on (*date*). This letter will confirm the terms of your participation; your location is listed below.

We will assist you in securing any necessary permits for the conduct of your business at the (*event*), but it is your sole responsibility to have all necessary licenses and permits and to comply with all laws and regulations pertinent to your business. You must also carry adequate insurance against all public liability claims as described below, and you will indemnify and hold us harmless from any claims and costs, including reasonable attorneys' fees, incurred as a result of any personal injury or property damage claim by anyone.

During the (*event*), you may use our trademark, (*Trademark*), and our logos in advertising in accordance with our reasonable instructions. Upon our request, you will provide us samples of your advertising.

We wish you every success at the (*event*). Please acknowledge your agreement to these terms of your participation by signing below and returning a copy to me.

Sincerely,

Organizer

By: _____

Agreed and Accepted this _____ day of _____, 19__.

Vendor

By: _____

Location: _____

Insurance: _____

SAMPLE CONCERT TOUR
SPONSORSHIP AGREEMENT

THIS AGREEMENT is entered into between Sponsor ("Sponsor"), a (*state*) corporation with its principal place of business at (*address*), and (*corporate name*), a (*state*) corporation with its principal place of business at (*address*) ("Corporation"), for the performing services of (*name of performer*), (*name of performer*) and (*name of performer*) ("Performers"). In consideration of the covenants set forth herein and for other good and valuable consideration, the parties agree as follows:

This agreement presumes the performers are incorporated, i.e., the Corporation owns all rights to their performing services and to their personae.

Recitals

WHEREAS, Sponsor desires to sponsor a tour of concert appearances by Performers performing as (*Name of Band*) and to utilize the names, likenesses, individual and collective personalities and appearances of Performers in television, print, radio and similar advertising and promotional media in connection therewith; and

WHEREAS, Corporation desires to provide Performers' services, names and likenesses and trade name of (*Name of Band*) on the terms and conditions set forth in this Agreement;

NOW, THEREFORE, in consideration of the terms and conditions set forth herein, it is agreed:

The recitals simply summarize the purpose of the agreement.

1. Territory: (a) The Territory will be (*list countries*).

(b) In addition to the Territory described above, Corporation hereby grants to Sponsor for a period of one (1) year commencing upon the date of this Agreement, the option to enter into good faith negotiations to sponsor a tour by Performers in (*list additional countries*) following the Tour hereunder, such option exercisable at Sponsor's sole election and discretion and said negotiations to be completed no later than one (1) year from the date of this Agreement.

The territory is, of course, important, particularly in light of the Sponsor's marketing objectives. Here, the requirement to negotiate in good faith is quite loose (see discussion of good faith negotiation at page 8). Alternatively, this could be drafted as a right of first refusal (see discussion of contract options at page 16).

2. Duration of Agreement: Corporation shall cause Performers to perform at a series of musical concerts in the Territory commencing (*date*) and continuing until (*date*) (the "Tour"). This Agreement shall commence and be effective upon its execution by all the parties and shall continue until the later of (i) the final concert of the Tour, or (ii) upon completion of (*number*) concerts within the Territory. In determining the number of concerts to be performed by Performers, the parties agree that the same shall include (*number*) concerts in market of (*population*) or more; (*number*) concerts in markets of (*population*) or more and (*number*) in all other markets. The concert schedule shall be mutually agreed upon within (*number*) days after the execution of this Agreement.

Ideally, this paragraph would list the specific markets on the Tour, which would aid the Sponsor in evaluating the worth of the event financially and in terms of its marketing objectives. This paragraph settles for specifying the size of population centers, which is a rough approximation of exposure.

3. Exclusivity and Non-Compete: Corporation warrants and represents that during the Tour, and for a period of (*number of months*) thereafter, Corporation shall not authorize or provide Performers' services or permit the use of Performers' names, likenesses or endorsements in connection with the advertising, promotion or sale of any products competitive to those of Sponsor or of any other sponsor, including without limitation (*list products*). Corporation represents and warrants that Performers have not heretofore rendered such services directly or indirectly in commercials or advertisements on behalf of any person, firm or corporation which manufactures, distributes or sells such products.

The extent of the non-compete, both as to product category and duration, is critical. Depending on the product category (e.g., snack food), specificity can be useful if the list of products is complete enough. The Sponsor may also want assurance that the Performers won't endorse antithetical products.

4. Control of Concerts: Corporation shall organize a Tour of the highest quality and shall cause Performers to perform to the best of their ability. Corporation shall have sole control over all artistic matters pertaining to the Tour, but shall consult with Sponsor with respect to, and give due regard to, Sponsor's marketing objectives.

Artistic control is something most Performers will require. The Sponsor should be thoroughly familiar with the Performers' act before entering the sponsorship relationship.

5. Advance Concert Information: Corporation shall notify Sponsor, at least (*number*) days prior to the commencement of the Tour, of the following:

(a) A full schedule of concert dates and locations for the Tour;

(b) The name, address and phone number of each local promoter for each concert;

(c) The hall capacity of each concert location and, upon request, and when reasonably possible, the status of ticket sales with respect to each concert in advance of the date of the concert; and

(d) The date tickets for any concert on the Tour are scheduled to go on sale to the general public. With respect to the date ticket sales are to begin, Corporation shall give notice to Sponsor of such date no less than thirty (30) days prior to such date.

(e) Corporation shall ensure the availability of the information required in this clause by requiring the same in any agreement entered into between Corporation and the concert promoter.

The information called for in this paragraph allows the Sponsor to plan and implement its local promotional programs.

6. Concert Advertising and Promotional "Credit": Subject to local restrictions, Corporation shall cause substantially all of the concert tickets, posters, flyers, programs, and television, radio and print advertisements to prominently include the words "SPONSOR PRESENTS (*Name of Band/Tour*)" in a manner to be mutually agreed upon by Sponsor and Corporation. Corporation warrants that when used in conjunction with a local concert promoter, Sponsor's name will appear first and in a size and type at least equal to the size and type of the local promoter's name. Corporation shall cause the foregoing to be included in any agreement between Corporation and the local promoter. Corporation shall also cause the local promoter to abide by the provisions of Paragraph 3 hereof and to include the same in their agreements with the site.

Billing, of course, is what sponsorship is all about. The Corporation must pass these responsibilities on because the local promoter will be placing much of the advertising.

7. Concert Advertising: Corporation shall use its best efforts to advertise and promote the Tour and each concert. Within (*number*) days after each concert, Corporation shall provide Sponsor with a true and accurate copy of the promoter's ticket reconciliation as provided to Corporation and with a statement of all advertising run on behalf of the concert, including the identity of television and radio stations and newspapers, the number and size of insertions and the length of spots. Corporation shall provide Sponsor with copies of the foregoing (broadcast commercials may be in script form). Corporation shall contractually require each local promoter to comply with the terms of this Paragraph.

The information required here gives the Sponsor the chance to evaluate the impact of the sponsorship in terms of leveraged advertising dollars.

8. Sponsorship Activities: Subject to the prior written approval of Corporation, which shall not be unreasonably withheld, Sponsor shall have the right to utilize the names, photographs, likenesses, facsimile signatures and biographical information concerning Performers, the name (*Name of Band*), the Name of Performers' Tour, any logos associated with the Tour and the names of any local Tour sponsor and/or promoter, in any and all media in connection with each concert and the Tour without territorial, time, use or other restriction of any kind except as set forth in this Agreement. Without limiting the generality of the foregoing:

1) Without additional compensation, Sponsor shall have the right to use the foregoing to create and broadcast during the Term television and radio commercials and to use brief segments of hit songs and video recordings of hit songs of Performers in connection therewith (provided the rights thereto are owned or controlled by Corporation or Performers, and provided further that Corporation shall use its best efforts to obtain such rights from the owners thereof without charge to Sponsor). [To the extent any fees become due on account of the use thereof under any applicable collective bargaining agreement, the Sponsorship Fee shall be credited against the same and pension and welfare contributions shall be paid by Sponsor at scale.]

Sponsor should try to get the use of hit songs and music videos for free during the Term. Some sponsors have also negotiated for the separate performing services of the

Performers in commercials, e.g., Michael Jackson provided new services in commercials for Pepsi-Cola at the time of his "Victory Tour." If Performers are members of SAG or AFTRA, session and use fees may become due. The sponsorship fee can be applied against those fees, but pension and welfare (P&W) contributions must be made separately. The Performers may insist that they be "paid" at double scale. Compared to the sponsorship fee, P&W will be a minor expense. In the alternative, if the talent is incorporated, it could be made liable for the P&W since the Corporation technically is the Performers' employer.

2) Corporation shall cause Performers to appear in at least one press conference to be held by Sponsor prior to the Tour at a location and time chosen by Sponsor after consultation with Corporation. Sponsor shall reimburse Corporation for all of Performers' first class travel and accommodations and living expenses if such press conference takes place at a place other than *(Performers' home)* or some other place where Performers are not required to be for personal or professional reasons.

A press conference is the Sponsor's first opportunity to generate some publicity with respect to its sponsorship and the Sponsor is reasonable to expect the Performers to attend.

3) Corporation shall cause Performers to agree that they will use Sponsor's products [where practical during all public appearances] [exclusively] during the Term of this Agreement and, if appropriate, while on stage during each concert, and that they will cause the road crew to utilize Sponsor's products and to wear T-shirts, sweatshirts, jackets, caps and other apparel items bearing Sponsor's name and product logos. Sponsor shall provide products and such wearing apparel as it deems appropriate.

Obviously, the Sponsor wants as much association with the Performers as possible. Some performers will not agree to use the product (as in the case of alcoholic beverages, for instance) or will not use them exclusively, just publicly. At any rate, this paragraph should prohibit the Performers' use of competitive products.

9. Tour Merchandise: (a) The parties agree that all Tour merchandise, including, but not limited to, T-shirts, posters, sweatshirts, caps and Tour programs ("Tour Merchandise"), sold by Corporation or anyone authorized by Corporation or Performers, shall prominently include the words "SPONSOR PRESENTS" in a manner to be mutually agreed upon between the parties. Further, Corporation agrees to include for Sponsor, at no additional charge, a full-page, [four-color] advertisement on the back cover of the Tour program book the layout and text of which shall be conceived and provided by Sponsor. All profits derived from the sale and distribution of all Tour merchandise shall be solely the property of Corporation and Performers and their affiliates, licensees or distributors. Corporation agrees to ensure full performance of this clause by causing the provisions hereof to be included in any agreements between Corporation or Performers or their designees and any product merchandising company manufacturing, distributing, promoting and/or selling such items.

Again, Sponsors want the broadest possible association with the Tour; Performers and novelty manufacturers, on the other hand, might find the inclusion of a commercial logo unaesthetic. Here, the parties mutually agree as to the manner of use. Other solutions are to require a percentage of each type of merchandise to bear the Sponsor's logo, or to put the Sponsor's logo only on the back of T-shirts and other wearing apparel. The placement of the Tour program advertising page should be specified; here, it is the back cover.

(b) Sponsor may utilize Tour Merchandise, as described herein, for its own marketing and promotional purposes. It is, however, expressly understood and agreed that Sponsor shall not offer such Tour Merchandise for sale to the general public, with the exception of contest give-aways, radio contests, free or self-liquidating premiums with purchase of Sponsor's products and other like promotions. Performers grant Sponsor the right to manufacture, or cause to be manufactured, such Tour Merchandise. If Sponsor desires to purchase such Tour Merchandise from Corporation or Performers, or persons authorized by them, Corporation and Performers hereby waive their royalty thereon.

Sponsor should have the right to sell Tour Merchandise bearing its logos. If it buys such merchandise from the Corporation, it shouldn't have to pay twice, i.e., the Corporation should be asked to waive its royalty since it is also getting a hefty sponsorship fee. There should, however, be some restrictions on sale of the Tour Merchandise by Sponsor in order to protect the Corporation's market. Usually, the Sponsor is interested only in the kind of promotional uses set forth in the paragraph.

10. Signage: Subject to local commitments and restrictions at each concert location, Corporation guarantees that Sponsor's signage shall be prominently displayed at each concert. The location of such signage within each respective concert location shall be mutually agreed upon in advance between Sponsor and Corporation, taking into consideration the local commitments of the venue and, where necessary, the local promoter. Sponsor shall design and supply such signage, including drapes or other signage for the stage.

Sponsor should insist on some degree of control over the number and placement of signs. On-stage signage seems a must; however, some Performers will insist on control for aesthetic reasons.

11. Sponsor's Tour Coordinator: Sponsor shall appoint a Tour Coordinator who shall have the right to accompany Performers at Sponsor's expense throughout the Tour. Corporation shall, and shall cause Performers to, cooperate with such Tour Coordinator, who shall have primary responsibility for implementing Sponsor's sponsorship program.

The Tour Coordinator is on the road and has the responsibility for attending to all the details of Sponsor's sponsorship.

12. Concert Tickets: (a) *Availability to Sponsor*: Sponsor shall receive from Corporation a minimum of fifty (50) free prime location tickets per concert. Such tickets shall be provided to Sponsor prior to the sale of any tickets for such concert to the general public. Corporation's and Performers' management will use their best efforts to ensure that these tickets are delivered to Sponsor a minimum of thirty (30) days prior to each concert.

Free tickets are an obvious benefit of sponsorship. In some instances, specifying the row, or box, is better than the vague "prime" description. The Sponsor may want to specify a greater number of tickets for certain cities, such as where the corporation is headquartered.

(b) *Additional Tickets.* Sponsor shall have the right to purchase up to two hundred (200) additional seats for each concert of the Tour. Sponsor shall notify Corporation of the number of tickets so requested for a concert at least (*number*) days prior to any concert date, or prior to tickets going on sale for the particular concert, whichever date shall come first. Sponsor shall pay full price, as noted on the ticket, for such tickets at the time of purchase. The seat location shall be the best available as of the date Sponsor notifies Corporation of its intent to purchase tickets, unless local law or regulation prohibits such an arrangement.

The right to purchase tickets at face value is also important to the Sponsor in effectively marketing the event. This paragraph could alternatively be written to require Corporation to offer the tickets to Sponsor prior to placing them on sale.

(c) *"Backstage Pass" Requirements.* Corporation agrees to provide Sponsor with a reasonable number of "All Access" laminated Tour passes. Designation of persons to receive such passes shall be determined by Sponsor [and Corporation] prior to the start of the Tour.

A backstage pass might be used for VIPs or for promotional contest winners or for Sponsor's Tour Coordinator. It might be better for Sponsor to solely designate the persons to receive the passes, but the Performers obviously have an interest in who is allowed backstage.

13. Hospitality: At its expense, Sponsor may host a party or a hospitality suite for its key executives, key accounts, promotional contest winners or similar invited guests at the site of each concert. Corporation will use its best efforts to cause Performers to attend each such party or suite and to sign autographs and/or pose for pictures with such guests.

The extent of the Performers' obligation to attend parties, etc., is subject to negotiation.

14. Record Company Activities: Corporation shall use its best efforts to cause (*Name of Record Company*) to coordinate with it and Sponsor to provide promotional support to the Tour.

This paragraph could be elaborately detailed (e.g., providing how many free records the Record Company will give the Sponsor for promotional purposes). However, unless the Performers directly control the Record Company, it will all be under the heading of "best efforts" (see the discussion of "best efforts" at page 11). Both the Record Company and the Sponsor have an interest in promoting the Tour; the point of negotiation is how and in what manner the Record Company will mention Sponsor's name.

15. Fees and Payments: (a) Sponsor shall pay to Corporation the sum of $_____ for all rights granted herein. The above described fee shall be payable as follows:

(1) $_____ shall be paid by Sponsor upon execution this Agreement by all parties;

(2) $_____ shall be paid by Sponsor upon the commencement of the Tour; and

(3) $_____ shall be paid by Sponsor within ten (10) days after complete performance of all obligations of Corporation hereunder.

In the alternative, a certain amount could be paid after the completion of each concert.

(b) Corporation represents and warrants that Performers are in its employ and that it shall discharge all obligations of an employer to its employees, including, without limitation, the payment of any withholding, social security or other taxes.

Technically, the Performers are employed by the Corporation, which is responsible for any taxes due on the sponsorship fee and for any amounts to be paid the Performers, including Performers' withholding and social security obligations.

16. Breach and Morals: In addition to any rights or remedies available to Sponsor, if Performers shall be charged with the commission of any act which is an offense involving moral turpitude under federal, state or local laws, or should Performers commit any act which would reasonably and objectively bring Sponsor or its products into disrepute, contempt, scandal or ridicule at any time during the Tour, or if Corporation or Performers shall fail to perform their respective duties and liabilities required of them hereunder, then Sponsor shall be entitled to:

(a) Terminate this Agreement after giving Performers ten (10) days' notice to cure such offense, act or failure to perform. If Performers fail to cure such offense, act or failure to perform within such ten (10) day period, Sponsor shall no longer be responsible for any fees or payments due hereunder; and

(b) Receive a refund of that percentage of any fees received by Performers hereunder as the number of concerts remaining in the Tour bears to the total number of concerts in the Tour.

The "morals clause" is always the subject of intense negotiation, particularly with respect to the vagueness of activities that may be deemed to bring the Sponsor's products into disrepute. For a concert series, the remedy of quitting the sponsorship is probably the best the Sponsor can do (see discussion of morals clauses at page 24). Refund here is tied to the number of concerts remaining, which treats all venues equally. The Sponsor may desire a schedule of fees and refunds, depending on how secure it feels with the Performers.

17. Death or Disability of Performers/Cancellation: If, in the event of the death or disability of one or more of the Performers, or in the event the Tour is cancelled, Sponsor shall be entitled to:

(a) Terminate this Agreement immediately without liability and without any further responsibility for the payment of any fees or payments hereunder; and

(b) Receive a refund of that percentage of any fees received by Performers hereunder as the number of concerts remaining in the Tour bears to the total number of concerts in the Tour.

The Sponsor might want to define the circumstances under which the Tour can be cancelled, but because of the personal service nature of the Tour, the Sponsor probably will not have any very viable remedies in the event of breach (see discussion of personal services contracts at page 20).

18. Representations and Warranties: Each party represents and warrants that each has the power and authority to enter into this Agreement, to grant the rights granted herein and to perform the duties and obligations described herein. Each party further warrants and represents that it shall not take any action which might prevent the exercise by the other party hereto of its rights granted hereunder nor shall either take any action which may encumber the rights granted to the other.

Boilerplate, but here more important because of the corporate structure of the Performers.

19. Permits and Licenses: Corporation shall be fully responsible for and acquire or cause local concert promoters to acquire, at their sole cost and expense, all licenses, permits, authorizations and insurance which may be required under federal, state or local law or regulations in order to legally conduct each concert of the Tour and the activities contemplated hereunder, including, but not limited to, licenses from performing rights organizations and any payments or royalties required to be made; provided, however, that Sponsor shall be responsible for any royalties due and owing any performing rights organization as a result of Sponsor's television and radio commercials and in-store presentations, if any.

The Corporation (the Performers) is (are) responsible for payment of ASCAP and BMI fees due as a result of each concert. However, the Sponsor is responsible for television and other of its advertising uses (see Chapter 4).

20. Indemnity and Insurance: (a) Corporation hereby agrees to indemnify, defend and hold Sponsor, its officers, directors, agents, representatives, shareholders and employees harmless from and against any and all claims, suits, expenses, damages or other liabilities, including reasonable attorneys' fees and court costs, arising out of the breach by Corporation or Performers of any of the representations or warranties made by either of them in this Agreement and any personal injury or property damages arising out of or in connection with an individual's attendance at a concert featuring the performance of Performers. Corporation shall obtain and maintain, at its sole expense, commencing at least five (5) days prior to the commencement of the Tour, general and public liability insurance, naming Sponsor as an additional insured party, from a qualified U.S. insurance carrier acceptable to Sponsor in the amount of at least Five Million Dollars ($5,000,000) for personal injury and Five Million Dollars ($5,000,000) for property damage. Such insurance shall be noncancellable during the term hereof. Prior to the commencement of the Tour, Corporation shall provide Sponsor with a copy of each such policy described above and shall give Sponsor thirty (30) days' advance written notice of any change therein.

(b) Sponsor hereby agrees to indemnify, defend and hold Corporation and its officers, directors, agents, representatives, shareholders and employees and Performers harmless from and against any and all claims, suits, expenses, damages or other liabilities, including reasonable attorneys' fees and court costs, arising out of the breach by Sponsor of any of the representations or warranties made by Sponsor in this Agreement.

Each party indemnifies the other from liability arising out of their respective breaches of the agreement. Insurance backs up the Corporation's obligation, since the greatest exposure is at each concert (see discussion of insurance in Chapter 5).

21. Notices: Notices by either party to the other shall be given by registered or certified mail, return receipt requested, or by telegram with proof of delivery, all charges prepaid. All statements and notices hereunder shall be given as follows:

To Sponsor: (name and address of Sponsor)

with a copy to: (name and address of Sponsor's attorney)

To Corporation: (name and address of Corporation)

with a copy to: (name and address of Corporation's attorney)

Boilerplate

22. Right of First Refusal: Sponsor is hereby granted a first right of refusal to become either a "primary" or "sole" sponsor, as those terms are understood in the television and radio broadcast industries, of any radio, network television, syndicated television or cable television special featuring principally the performance(s) of Performers which may be filmed, videotaped, recorded, created, developed, piloted or aired during the Tour. Sponsor shall have ten (10) business days from written receipt of all relevant details and financial information regarding such special to enter into good faith negotiations to accomplish such a sponsorship.

If the Tour is recorded for a television special, the Sponsor should have the right to purchase the advertising time in "good faith" negotiations. Alternatively, this could be written as a right to match any sponsorship offer made for the same advertising time. (See discussions of good faith at page 8 and of options at page 16.)

23. Construction: This Agreement shall be construed under the laws of the State of (name). Each party hereto acknowledges that this Agreement is entered into within the jurisdiction of (state) and that the courts of the State of (state) shall have jurisdiction over any and all claims, controversies, disputes and disagreements arising out of this Agreement or the breach thereof.

Boilerplate

24. Force Majeure: Neither party shall be liable for any failure of or delay in the performance of their respective obligations under this Agreement to the extent such failure or delay is due to circumstances beyond its reasonable control, including, without limitation, Acts of God or acts of a public enemy, fires, floods, wars, civil disturbances, sabotage, accidents, insurrections, blockades, embargoes, storms, explosions, labor disputes and/or acts of any governmental body, nor shall any such failure or delay give the other party the right to terminate this Agreement. Each party shall use its best efforts to minimize the duration and consequences of any failure of or delay in performance resulting from such force majeure.

Boilerplate. However, there may be situations where the delay is projected to be long enough that the Sponsor would want to terminate.

25. Entire Agreement: This Agreement constitutes the complete Agreement between the parties on the subject matter hereof, and all prior or contemporaneous agreements of the parties, whether oral or written, shall be deemed merged herein. This Agreement may not be modified or amended except by an instrument in writing duly executed by the party to be charged. The failure of either party to enforce any of said party's rights under this Agreement shall not be deemed a continuing waiver and said party may, within such time as provided by applicable law, enforce any and all such rights. This Agreement shall be binding upon the parties hereto, their successors and assigns.

Boilerplate.

Name of Sponsor

By:_____

   Its:_____

Name of Corporation

*By:*_____

*Its:*_____

Personal Guarantee

In order to induce Sponsor to enter into the foregoing Agreement with Performers, each of the undersigned jointly and severally hereby guarantees the performance of all of Corporation's obligations thereunder insofar as the personal services or rights of each of the undersigned are required to completely perform the Agreement.

Performer:_____

Performer:_____

Performer:_____

SAMPLE HOTEL SITE AGREEMENT

THIS AGREEMENT made as of the (*number*) day of (*month*) (*year*) by and between Organizer ("Organizer") a (*state*) corporation with a principal place of business at (*address*) and Hotel, a (*state*) corporation with a principal place of business at (*address*) ("Hotel").

Witnesseth

WHEREAS, Organizer desires to promote, either by itself or with others, a (*type*) event ("Event") at Hotel's facility in (*place*) on (*date*) [or a date agreeable to Organizer and Hotel]; and

WHEREAS, Hotel desires that such Event take place at Hotel's facility;

NOW, THEREFORE, in consideration of the premises, and of other good and valuable consideration, the receipt of which is hereby acknowledged, the parties agree as follows:

These introductory paragraphs explain the intentions of the parties. Sponsors do not have a particular interest in this agreement except to know that the Organizer has acquired all necessary rights.

1. Organizer will use its best efforts to promote the Event at Hotel on (*date*). Organizer will provide the Event as described herein and Hotel shall provide the site of the Event (the "Site").

There is a variety of ways for an Organizer and a Hotel site to work together. Tourist hotels featuring casinos are the most likely to participate in an agreement of this sort.

2. Hotel shall have the following rights:

(a) to collect and retain all proceeds from admissions to [training sessions] [rehearsals] at the Site;

If there are to be rehearsals, or, in the case of athletic events, practice sessions, the Hotel might be permitted to charge admission and retain the proceeds.

(b) to collect and retain all proceeds from the sale at the Site of novelties, promotional materials, souvenirs and any and all similar products and services. Hotel shall have the right to sell food and beverages and retain the revenues from such sales.

The Hotel here is the beneficiary of concession sales, including novelties and souvenir programs. This point, of course is negotiable. The Organizer should at a minimum request a percentage.

3. Hotel shall be solely responsible for and agrees to provide the following without cost to Organizer:

(a) a facility at the Site of the Event fully set up for the first-class presentation and network-quality live television broadcast of [*describe Event*] together with all staff, ushers, internal and external security, tickets, ticket takers and ticket sellers, [a stage and stage decorations], [dressing rooms with food and beverage as required for the use of the participants], [and similar equipment and personnel for the preparation for and presentation of the Event];

The Hotel here undertakes to provide a significant amount of operational support. While lighting for television may seem too minor to be included in a contract, adequate lighting for network quality broadcasts is expensive and may be a direct, out-of-pocket expense for the Hotel.

(b) all officials' fees and expenses of referees, judges, attending physicians, the announcer and other officials at the Event;

For athletic events, the Hotel in this Agreement provides the officials.

(c) press room and credentials for VIPs, the press and officials and related expenses;

Although the Hotel provides the press room (and can take the opportunity to show off its catering service), the Organizer should consider retaining control over the issuance of press credentials.

(d) (*number*) hotel rooms and (*number*) ([*one*] *or* [*two*])-bedroom Hotel suites for (*name personnel*) for a period of (*number*) days prior to the Event, provided that the occupants shall pay their own phone and incidental expenses and Hotel shall require the occupants to post a charge card or other security for such expenses;

If the Event is taking place at a Hotel, the Organizer and key participants will want to stay there. It is expected that they will stay free. To avoid hard feelings, it is best for occupants to post credit cards for incidental expenses (including alcohol); the Organizer should require the Hotel to do this so that the Hotel can't come back to the Organizer for payment of these expenses, which can add up.

(e) food and nonalcoholic beverages as follows:

RFB ("room-food-beverage") is not an uncommon obligation of the Hotel, but the Hotel may want to issue coupons for particular restaurants or specify a daily dollar amount.

(f) insurance for the Site and crowd.

Insurance protecting the Site from physical damage and covering the safety of participants is the Hotel's responsibility under this Agreement.

4. Organizer shall be solely responsible for establishing the prices for all live gate admissions to the Event. [Hotel shall be solely responsible for establishing ticket prices for admission to the training sessions.] Hotel shall also be free to show the live television broadcast of the Event in other places on its premises without further payment to Organizer only if such Event is broadcast on a free basis or on a cable or subscription service to which Hotel subscribes and the Event is otherwise sold out.

Since the Organizer gets the live gate, it sets the ticket price, just as the Hotel does for the rehearsal or practice sessions, if any. Any other showings in the Hotel affect the live gate, so here they are limited.

5. Organizer agrees to provide the following:

(a) the services of all the participants appearing in the Event, including their services for promotional purposes;

The Organizer provides the Event: here, key personnel who will participate in the Event.

(b) payment of all taxes in connection with the Event including but not limited to those levied on the television revenues and those levied on live gate receipts received by Organizer but not those levied on the sale of promotional items and other concessions by Hotel;

The Organizer agrees to pay taxes on its revenues.

(c) all fees contractually due to the participants or their managers, agents or representatives participating in the Event and their transportation;

The Organizer is responsible for paying the participants it provides.

(d) all necessary licenses, [sanction fees] and permits for the Event which are required from state and municipal authorities [and athletic commissions];

The Organizer will get all necessary permits.

(e) all expenses for television staging and broadcast of the Event, except for lighting necessary for a network quality broadcast of the Event, which will be provided by Hotel.

The Organizer provides the television coverage, which often means selling the rights to a network or buying time and doing its own promotion. Again, note that the expense of lighting suitable for creating network-quality coverage is passed to the Hotel.

6. Organizer will enter into a contract for the television broadcast of the Event by free, cable or subscription television, but if the television broadcaster does not broadcast the Event for any reason beyond the control of Organizer, Organizer shall not be in breach of this Agreement, which will remain in full force and effect. Organizer will use its best efforts to obtain the agreement of the television broadcaster to provide (1) a broadcast lead-in to the effect that the program originates "From (*full name*) Hotel in (*place*)"; (2) a reasonable number of audio IDs of Hotel by the commentator; and (3) exemption of Hotel's permanent signage and Hotel's logo and name on (*the stage*) from the prohibition against commercial

matter inserted by Organizer in the production. Organizer's inability to obtain any of the foregoing concessions shall not be grounds for termination of this Agreement.

If the Organizer fails to obtain television broadcast of the Event, the agreement can be terminated by the Hotel for breach. However, this is not a very sophisticated clause: it doesn't specify whether the coverage must be network, must be aired in 85 percent of the country or must be of any particular duration (although "broadcast of the Event" could easily be interpreted to mean "in its entirety," since that is clearly the intention of the parties).

The Organizer may have no real bargaining power to obtain the coverage promised, and so the contract provides that failure of these promises is not a breach or grounds for termination. If the Organizer buys time and produces its own coverage, then these promises should be absolute.

The networks usually try to avoid any signage that is in effect a free commercial (unless the Sponsor has also purchased a significant amount of time on the broadcast).

7. As basic compensation for all rights granted to it hereunder, Hotel shall pay to Organizer $_____, payable by cashier's check delivered to Organizer the date of each Event. In addition, Organizer shall have the right to collect and retain all proceeds from the sale of live gate admissions to the Event.

The ability of an event to draw patronage to the Hotel – usually for gambling – makes the event worth money to the Site. Here, the Site is actually willing to pay the Organizer to put the event at its facility – in addition to bearing the expense of the in-kind contribution made under paragraph 3. If the amount is large, a letter of credit rather than a cashier's check might make sense from both points of view.

8. Organizer shall provide Hotel with (*number*) complimentary tickets to the Event (*specify location*).

Complimentary tickets are standard.

9. Hotel and Organizer shall cooperate with each other in the promotion of the Event. Organizer shall provide Hotel with reasonable amounts of promotional

material concerning the participants, including such photographs and biographies as Organizer may possess. Hotel shall have the right to use the name and logo of Organizer and the names, likenesses and biographical materials concerning the participants in advertising and promotional material in any and all media for purposes only of promoting the Event but not as an endorsement of any product or service. All such material shall be approved by Organizer in writing in advance of distribution, which approval shall not be unreasonably withheld. Organizer shall have the right to use Hotel's name and logo in advertising and promotional materials in any and all media for purposes only of promoting the Event but not as an endorsement of any product or service, provided, however, that all such material shall be approved in writing in advance of distribution, which approval shall not be unreasonably withheld. For purposes of this paragraph, materials shall be deemed approved if the party required to approve such materials does not approve or disapprove such materials within three days after receipt thereof. For Organizer, (*name*) and (*name*) shall be authorized to give such approvals; for Hotel, (*name*) and (*name*) shall be authorized to give such approvals.

Organizer will provide the Hotel with promotional material that it has available (but notice there is no affirmative representation that the Organizer has any material at all!). Both Organizer and Hotel have the right to approve each other's advertising which includes the other's trademarks (see Chapter 2), but agree not to act unreasonably (see discussion of approval clauses at page 13). The "deemed approved" mechanism allows each party to stick to its timetable.

10. All ancillary rights in connection with the Event, including, without limitation, stage advertising and all radio, television (home, theater, closed-circuit, live, delayed, free and pay), motion picture and similar rights shall be and remain the sole and exclusive property of Organizer, and Hotel shall have no right to share in any revenues to be derived from the exploitation of such ancillary rights. All rights not explicitly granted to Hotel are expressly reserved to Organizer.

All rights of any kind not specifically and explicitly given to the Hotel are, and remain, the Organizer's property.

11. Organizer warrants and represents that it has or will obtain the full right and authority to grant to Hotel all rights granted to it hereunder with respect to the Event hereunder, including, without limitation, executed contracts with the participants to be provided by Organizer hereunder.

This is a standard warranty. In part, it requires the Organizer to get promotional rights from participants.

12. Each party shall hold the other party harmless from any and all claims, actions, costs and liabilities, including reasonable attorneys' fees, arising out of the negligent conduct or omission of its employees or agents, or out of the conditions of the facility under its respective control or out of the breach of any of its obligations hereunder. Hotel agrees to name Organizer as an additional insured on Hotel's liability insurance coverage.

This is a standard mutual indemnity clause. The next paragraph provides that the Organizer will also provide insurance to Hotel.

In addition, Organizer agrees to obtain and maintain, at its sole expense, insurance issued by a major U.S. insurance carrier, which insurance shall be maintained until completion of the Event hereunder. Such insurance coverage shall include:

(a) Workers' Compensation and Occupational Disease (if required by federal or state statute).

(b) Comprehensive General Liability, including personal injury and contractual liability.

(c) Such other insurance as may be required by state law or any applicable sanctioning body.

A Certificate of Insurance with an endorsement designating Hotel as an additional beneficiary (insured) thereof in form and substance reasonably satisfactory to Hotel shall be delivered to Hotel prior to the date of the Event.

The Organizer is required to provide certain kinds of insurance (athletic commissions may require additional coverages) and to name the Hotel as a beneficiary of such insurance.

13. This Agreement sets forth the entire understanding between the parties with respect to the subject matter hereof, and incorporates and supersedes any and all

prior or contemporaneous understandings with respect thereto. Neither party has made or relied upon any promises, understandings or representations other than those set forth herein.

This is boilerplate, but here also disclaims that any representations as to the success of the Event have been made.

14. If the Event shall fail to take place for any reason other than Hotel's or Organizer's breach of this Agreement or a reason described in Paragraph 15 hereof, this Agreement shall be deemed null and void and Organizer shall forthwith return any sums paid to it by Hotel as an advance and neither party shall have any further rights, liabilities or obligations to the other with respect to such Event. Both parties shall be solely responsible for their own expenses for such Event. If such Event is postponed to a rescheduled date for any reason other than Hotel's or Organizer's breach of this Agreement, Hotel and Organizer shall mutually agree on a rescheduled date within 3 months from the date of the Event hereunder and Hotel shall provide the Site for such Event on such rescheduled date, upon the same terms and conditions as provided herein. If Hotel and Organizer cannot agree on a mutually acceptable rescheduled date, then this Agreement shall be null and void as to such Event. If the Event fails to take place because one of the main participants in the Event refuses to participate for a reason not described in Paragraph 15 hereof, Hotel may, at its option, renegotiate the fee paid to Organizer under Paragraph 7 hereof for such Event or terminate this Agreement with respect to such Event if a mutually agreeable fee cannot be negotiated within 15 days of receiving notice of such participant's refusal.

Paragraphs 14 and 15 should be read together. Basically, the Hotel gets its money back if the Event fails to take place for a reason beyond the control of either party (except in circumstances described in paragraph 15) but the Hotel is not reimbursed for any expenses. Essentially, both parties share the risk that something – like failure to obtain necessary permits or sanctions – will interfere with the Event.

15. Notwithstanding anything to the contrary contained herein, if (i) a licensed physician certifies that one of the participants is mentally or physically disabled to such an extent that he/she cannot participate in the complete Event as scheduled, and/or (ii) Hotel's facilities are materially and substantially damaged by fire, flood or other calamity, or if Hotel is otherwise unable to provide Organizer with the necessary facilities by reason of any strike, labor controversy, civil tumult,

governmental ordinance, court order, administrative ruling, or other cause beyond Hotel's reasonable control, so as to render it impossible or impracticable for Organizer or Hotel to conduct the Event on the date scheduled hereunder, Organizer shall elect either (a) to cancel such Event date, or (b) to postpone such Event date. Organizer and Hotel shall each immediately give the other written notice of the occurrence of any of said events which it has encountered, specifying therein the nature of such event and the probable duration of the same and the party's recommendation regarding cancellation or postponement of such Event. If Organizer elects to postpone the Event, Hotel and Organizer shall mutually agree on a rescheduled date within 3 months of the original date, and if such agreement cannot be reached within 15 days of notice of any occurrence described herein, the effect thereof shall be to relieve and discharge each of the parties hereto of any and all obligation hereunder to the other with respect to such cancelled or postponed Event, provided, however, Organizer shall forthwith return any and all sums paid to it by Hotel as advances for the Event.

If a participant is incapacitated or the Hotel is substantially damaged, the Event may be cancelled or postponed, in the Organizer's discretion. Again, the parties are to agree on another date no more than three months after the scheduled date; if they fail to agree, the Agreement becomes null and void. The Hotel would get back any advance payment but is responsible for its own out-of-pocket expenses.

16. All advertising, promotions and press releases for the Events published by Organizer or Hotel shall read substantially as follows: (*specify*).

Here, the Hotel may require joint credit such as "A JOINT PRODUCTION OF ORGANIZER AND HOTEL."

17. Any notices required or desired hereunder shall be in writing and delivered or sent postage prepaid by certified or registered mail, return receipt requested, or by prepaid telegraph to the parties at their addresses set forth above (or such other addresses as the parties may otherwise designate in writing). The date of delivery, mailing or delivery to the telegraph office shall be deemed to constitute the date of any such notice. A copy of all notices shall be sent to: (*name/address/city*) _____ .

This is boilerplate.

18. This Agreement may not be altered, amended or discharged except by a subsequent writing signed by both parties.

This is boilerplate.

19. Each party recognizes that the rights granted hereunder are personal, valuable and unique and that a breach of any of the material provisions hereof will cause the other irreparable harm which may not be adequately compensated at law and each shall be entitled to equitable relief, including, without limitation, a preliminary injunction, to prevent such breach in addition to whatever actual damages may be had at law.

This allows each party to seek an injunction, in addition to damages, in the event of breach of the Agreement by the other.

20. Nothing herein shall cause either party to be deemed the agent, representative, partner or joint venturer of the other and neither party shall be authorized to bind the other in any manner nor shall either party represent itself to others to have such authority.

This is boilerplate and is designed to prevent one party from purporting to bind the other.

IN WITNESS WHEREOF, the parties have executed this Agreement on the date first above written.

ORGANIZER

By:_____

HOTEL

By:_____

SAMPLE PROGRAM AGREEMENT

AGREEMENT, made as of the (*number*) day of (*month*), (*year*), by and between (*Organizer*), a (*state name*) corporation with its place of business at (*address*) ("Organizer") and Program Company, a (*state name*) corporation with its principal place of business at (*address*) ("Company").

Witnesseth:

WHEREAS, Organizer represents and warrants that it has the exclusive worldwide rights to the (*describe event*) known as (*name of event*) (the "Event") to take place at the (*name of site*) in (*city, state*) (the "Site") on (*date*), including the rights to use in any media the name, likeness and biographical material of the participants and the sponsors of the Event, for the purpose of advertising and promoting the Event, and that Organizer solely has the exclusive rights to market souvenir programs ("Programs") for the Event at the Site of the live Event [and at closed circuit television locations, if any] and otherwise; and

WHEREAS, Company desires to produce the Programs, including design and layout functions, and to set advertising rates and sell advertising space in the Programs, and to sell the Programs at the Site of the Event [and at closed circuit television locations, if any]; and

WHEREAS, Organizer desires to appoint Company to perform these services and to grant to Company the rights hereinafter set forth;

NOW, THEREFORE, for good and valuable consideration, the receipt of which is hereby acknowledged, the parties agree as follows:

These are introductory paragraphs that express the basic intent of the parties. The complexity of the agreement to follow will, of course, depend on the size of the Event and the profit to be made by selling Programs.

1. Company's Responsibilities

Company will: (a) Produce and deliver a Program as described herein on or before (*date prior to Event*). If Company fails to produce a satisfactory Program by that date, Organizer may terminate this Agreement without liability of any kind to Company, and Organizer may substitute a new party in Company's place;

Obviously time is of the essence in this provision of the agreement. There is a tension between making the date close enough to the date of the Event to be timely and far enough away to allow replacement of the Company if necessary.

(b) Be solely responsible for collecting all funds due for advertisements which appear in the Program, and issue a three-part invoice to all advertisers with one copy sent to the advertiser, one copy sent to Organizer and one copy retained by Company;

Because this program deal gives a share of profits to the Organizer, this allows the Organizer to keep tabs on one important source of revenue advertising.

(c) Handle all design, layout and production functions for the Program;

Basic production of the program is the Company's responsibility.

(d) Negotiate and be responsible for paying all reasonable printing charges for the Programs;

Basic cost of the programs is Company's responsibility. "Reasonable" here is meant to prevent the Company's subsidiary from doing the printing at an exorbitant cost, since the profits are being split with the Organizer. In a fancier contract, the Company could be required to get competitive bids.

(e) Be solely responsible for obtaining from locations other than the Site permission to sell the Programs at such locations and for establishing and implementing the procedure for Program sales at the Site and other locations before, during and after the Event;

It is presumed here that the Company may sell programs at the Site and not through an official or arena-based concessionaire. However, at remote sites or other locations, the selling arrangements must be made by the Company.

(f) Be solely responsible for pricing and distributing Programs [and collecting money from closed circuit television outlets];

This clause lets the Company price the program. In a joint-profit deal, this might be subject to the Organizer's approval. In this contract, the Guarantee protects the Organizer.

(g) Provide insurance adequate to cover the loss or destruction of the Programs before their sale with Organizer named as co-beneficiary of the policy;

This insures that the Organizer will at least get its Guarantee and that advertisers can be repaid.

(h) Not sell advertising to sellers of products or services competitive to the Official Sponsors and Official Suppliers of the Event.

Some competitive protection for official sponsors and suppliers is justified to avoid interference with the value of the event to its supporters.

2. The Programs

(a) Company shall provide without cost or charge to Organizer:

(i) one complimentary whole page advertisement on the inside front cover for the [Title Sponsor];

(ii) one editorial page of promotional copy for the [Title Sponsor];

(iii) one editorial page of promotional copy for [all Official Suppliers]; and

(iv) one editorial page of promotional copy for Organizer.

It is not uncommon for the Organizer to want to reserve pages to be given to the Title Sponsor as part of the sponsorship package.

(b) Company may retain one whole page for an advertisement in which it may sell its prior programs. All other advertising shall be paid for by third parties except with Organizer's prior approval.

Companies that specialize in program production and sales also sell old programs. This paragraph gives the Company a free page; since the Organizer has an interest

*in the profits, it should approve other freebies and be the beneficiary of any trade-
outs. The Company may want to specify a separate method of accounting for trade-
outs, since they usually benefit the Event rather than the Company.*

(c) It is anticipated the Program will be 4-color, no less than 20 pages.

This language could be mandatory, and probably should be if there is no Guarantee.

3. Organizer's Rights and Responsibilities

(a) Organizer may inspect and audit Company's books and records relating to the
Program at any time during business hours at Company's above address upon
reasonable notice to Company.

*An audit clause is standard. Some provide that if there is a difference of more than
5 percent in favor of the Organizer, the Organizer will pay the costs of the audit.*

(b) Organizer shall have the right in its sole discretion to approve prior to
production of the Program all Program editorial copy, layout and advertising.

*Editorial approval should help to protect the Organizer from embarrassing situations.
On the other hand, approval of editorial content could lead to liability for
defamation, etc., so a disclaimer is necessary (see paragraph 6).*

(c) Organizer shall not grant any other party the rights granted Company
hereunder.

There will be only one official program.

4. Payment of Expenses and Division of Income

(a) Company will retain *(number)*% of the Net Revenues from the sale of the
Programs and advertising therein, after deduction of vendor commission (not to
exceed *(number)*%), taxes, shipping charges, printing costs, writer/ photo fees,
advertising commissions (not to exceed *(number)*%) and other reasonable,
documented out-of-pocket expenses. Expenses, exclusive of commissions and
applicable taxes, will not exceed $_____ without Organizer's prior written
approval.

Any compensation scheme in which revenues are awarded after deduction of costs requires careful scrutiny. Here the Organizer has protected itself by specifying maximum commission (at standard rates and ultimately by putting a cap on expenses other than commissions and taxes).

(b) Company will pay Organizer a Guarantee against the percentage stated in (a) of $_____ upon execution of this Agreement (the "Guarantee").

Here the Organizer has required a guaranteed payment.

(c) Company will issue statements and payments to Organizer every 30 days following the Event, with a final reconciliation no later than 120 days after the Event.

Since the Organizer gets one-half the remaining inventory 60 days after the event (see Paragraph 5), this paragraph serves to sever the relationship and duty to account at a generous 120 days past the Event.

(d) Organizer in its discretion will give Company (*number*) tickets to the Event.

Tickets might be a perk requested by the Company and might be useful in helping it make sales.

5. Unsold Programs

Company will deliver to Organizer one-half of any unsold Programs within 60 days following the Event, and thereafter Company shall have no right to further reprint the Programs. Both parties may sell their remaining Programs for their own account.

Under this scheme, the Organizer gets half the post-Event inventory. Therefore there will be no further need for the Company to account to the Organizer – each can dispose of its half of the stock for its own account.

6. Program Content

(a) Company represents that the Program will spotlight all participants specified by Organizer through stories and photographs with an equal emphasis. All editorial is subject to Organizer's approval.

The program content can be controversial if the event features key personalities, as in a boxing match, tennis tournament or music concert. This paragraph requires the Company to give "equal time" to each key participant specified by the Organizer.

(b) Notwithstanding Organizer's approval, Company hereby represents and warrants that the Program and all elements thereof (except for [advertisements and] materials supplied by Organizer) will be Company's sole work and will not infringe the copyright, privacy or other right of any person and will not be libelous or obscene.

Even though the Organizer retains some approval, ultimate responsibility for the copy lies with Company. The Company should attempt to exclude third-party advertisements from the warranty.

7. Indemnification

Each party shall indemnify and hold the other party and its respective officers, agents, directors and employees harmless from any and all losses, claims, liabilities, damages, costs and expenses, including reasonable attorneys' fees and court costs, resulting from the conduct of its employees or agents under this Agreement or its breach of this Agreement or any representation or warranty contained herein. Company shall provide Organizer with evidence of insurance written by a U.S. company covering the foregoing which names Organizer as a named-insured and has limits not less than $_____/$_____.

This paragraph provides a standard mutual indemnity backed up, in the Company's case, by insurance. It is presumed here that the Organizer has few obligations under the agreement that would require specific insurance, and that the Organizer has comprehensive general liability insurance. This paragraph could be modified accordingly.

8. Independent Contractor

Company agrees and acknowledges that it is acting as an independent contractor under this Agreement and not as an agent for Organizer. Company shall have no authority to, and shall not, incur any obligations of any kind in the names of, or for the account of, Organizer. Company will not act in any way which would give the impression that it has the power or authority to bind Organizer in any respect whatsoever.

It is particularly important with respect to the producer of the official Program that there be an acknowledgment of the fact that Organizer and Company are not joint venturers.

9. Termination

This Agreement shall be in full force and effect through the date of the Event and until such time as all bills are paid, revenues collected and income is paid to the parties; however, either party may cancel this Agreement upon five (5) days' written notice to the other party if the other materially breaches this Agreement and fails to cure such breach within five (5) days after receiving written notice of such breach.

A more complicated termination clause could be used covering other events triggering termination; here a simple clause is used because programs are usually on a tight time frame and many events of termination are irrelevant.

10. Delay

If the Event is postponed to another date within six months of the originally scheduled date, Company shall have the same rights as provided herein for the rescheduled Event. If the Event is not so rescheduled, then this Agreement will terminate and Organizer's only liability to Company shall be to repay the Guarantee.

In the event of delay of the Event, the Company has the right for some period of time to redo the program for the rescheduled date. If the event is not rescheduled, the Organizer will return the Guarantee. Some in the position of Company would ask for reimbursement of at least one-half of its out-of-pocket cost as of the date of termination.

11. Credits and Artwork

The Programs will refer to the Event as "*(give official name of Event with presentation credits, if any).*"

To keep sponsors, presenters and suppliers happy, the official program should refer to them properly.

12. Entire Understanding

This Agreement sets forth the entire understanding between the parties with respect to the subject matter hereof, and incorporates and supersedes any and all prior or contemporary understandings with respect thereto. No representations have been made which are not explicitly set forth herein.

This is boilerplate. The disclaimer of representations is important to the Organizer in case the Company takes a loss (i.e., the Guarantee is too high).

13. Amendments

This Agreement may not be altered or amended or discharged except by subsequent writing signed by both parties.

This is boilerplate.

14. Notices

Any notices required or desired hereunder shall be in writing and deemed given when delivered or sent postage prepaid by registered mail, return receipt requested, addressed as first set forth above or as hereafter specified in writing by the parties.

This is boilerplate.

Organizer: _____

Company: _____

SAMPLE SPONSORSHIP SALES
AGENCY LETTER AGREEMENT

(Organizer's Letterhead)

Agency
Address
City/State/Zip

Dear _____:

This is to confirm that we have appointed (*Agency*) ("Agency") our exclusive representative for the purposes of securing and negotiating agreements with corporate sponsors for a (*describe event*) entitled (*name*) (the "Event") to be organized and promoted by (*Organizer*) ("us"). The Event will take place on (*date*).

This sentence is the basic appointment of the Agency as the exclusive sales representative.

It is understood and agreed that the terms of any offer received by Agency shall be transmitted to us and we reserve the sole and exclusive right to accept or reject such offer(s), which we will do within a reasonable time after receipt thereof. The Term of this Agreement shall commence upon execution of this Agreement and end (date) unless extended in accordance with the terms hereof.

The ultimate right to accept or reject corporate sponsors belongs to the Organizer. These sentences give the Organizer a reasonable time in which to respond. The Term of the contract might be several years, in order to protect the Agency's effort in securing initial sponsors. A right to renew might be negotiated by Agency.

In the event we reject any such sponsorship offer solicited or negotiated by Agency and subsequently agree to such sponsorship offer within one hundred twenty (120) days of the initial rejection thereof upon the same or similar terms and conditions as that originally proposed by Agency (and/or such sponsor, as the case may be) then the same shall be deemed incorporated hereunder and Agency shall be entitled to its commission with respect to such sponsorship.

This paragraph is designed to protect the Agency from the Organizer's cutting it out by initially rejecting an offer and subsequently accepting it after the Term of the contract.

As to any sponsorship agreement accepted by us, Agency shall issue appropriate invoices to such sponsor, collect all funds advanced, loaned, paid or otherwise payable to us or on our behalf, deduct Agency's commission and remit the balance to us within ten (10) days of Agency's receipt of same. With each such payment Agency shall render a statement in sufficient detail to show all funds received, the computation of commissions due Agency and the balance due us.

This paragraph may be written to require payment to the Organizer, which in turn will pay the Agency its commission. One way to make both sides feel secure is to ask the corporate sponsor to cut two checks.

In the event Agency successfully negotiates a sponsorship agreement, we shall pay to Agency a commission equal to (*number*) percent (_____%) of the gross compensation paid and/or payable to us or on our behalf arising from or otherwise related to each such sponsorship agreement for the entire term of such sponsorship agreement and any renewals, extensions, amendments, modifications or substitutions thereof. Agency shall be solely responsible for its expenses in connection with its representation of us hereunder.

A standard fee is 15 percent. This paragraph also contemplates that the Agency will get such a commission on all subsequent renewals and extension of the sponsorship agreement, regardless of the termination of the Agency agreement. Many organizers would insist on a declining percentage after termination of the Agency agreement.

If any sponsorship fee is paid not in cash but in goods, then Agency shall be entitled to (*number*)% of wholesale price of the goods contributed by the sponsor.

The parties should agree on a method for valuing in-kind contributions. It may be possible for the Agency and Organizer to agree on the amount of Agency's cash commission at the time of Organizer's acceptance of an in-kind sponsor.

Agency shall not be entitled to compensation in connection with the following sponsorships: (*list preexisting sponsors*).

The Organizer should not pay Agency for sponsors it already had on its own.

If Agency fails to present to us at least $_____ in *bona fide* sponsorship offers before (*date*) this Agreement shall automatically terminate and we shall be free to appoint a new sales representative. Agency shall be entitled only to its commission for sponsorship accepted by Organizer as of (*date*) including renewals and extensions thereof.

This paragraph allows the Organizer to quit a nonproductive Agency. It could be written in terms of firm contracts rather than offers, but the Agency might worry that the Organizer would be capricious in accepting/rejecting offers. Even if terminated, this Agreement will allow the Agency to continue to earn commissions.

Agency shall not solicit any (*list categories of products that would be unacceptable to Organizer*).

The Organizer may wish to exclude certain categories of potential sponsors, i.e., tobacco companies.

It is understood and agreed that this Agreement does not and shall not be construed as or constitute an agency, partnership or joint venture between Agency and us and that Agency shall be deemed to be independent contractor in all respects.

Boilerplate.

This Agreement shall be construed and governed under and in accordance with the laws of the State of (*name*).

Boilerplate.

Notices by any party to the other hereunder shall be given by certified or registered mail, return receipt requested, or by telegram with proof of delivery or by personal delivery, all prepaid. All statements, payments and notices shall be given at the respective addresses of Agency and Organizer hereunder as set forth in the first page of this Agreement unless written notice of change of address is given pursuant to the terms of this paragraph. Courtesy copies of any notice to Agency shall be sent to (*attorney's name*). Courtesy copies of any notices sent to us shall be sent to (*attorney's name*). Notice shall be deemed effective forty-eight (48) hours after posting of mailed notices and sending of telegrams or upon hand receipt thereof, except that notices of change of address shall be effective when received.

Boilerplate.

If this accurately sets forth our Agreement, please sign below and return a copy to us.

Very truly yours,

Organizer

By:_____

Accepted and Agreed:

Agency

By:_____

CHAPTER 2:
TRADEMARKS AND COPYRIGHTS

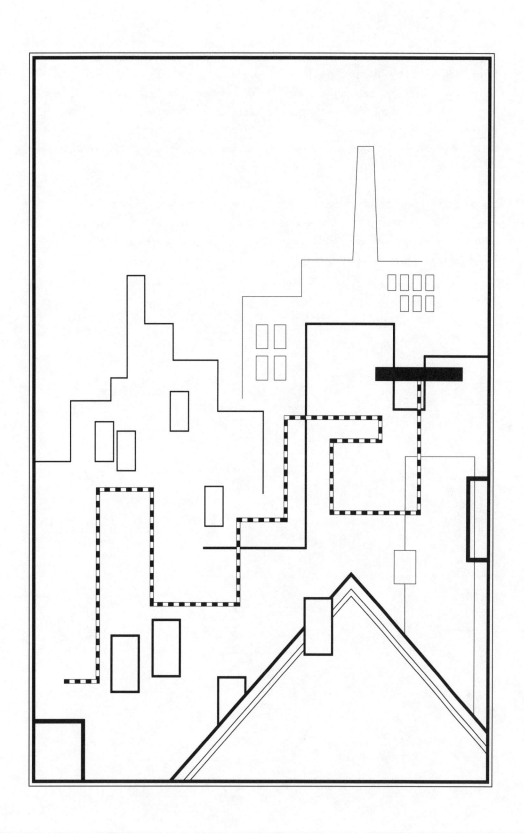

TRADEMARKS AND COPYRIGHTS

Sponsors of special events often are consumer product service companies that seek to promote their brand name products through association with the event. Brand names are, of course, extremely valuable. For example, you can buy cornflakes in a black-and-white "generic" package, but KELLOGG'S cornflakes are somehow different. Clearly, the brand name adds value; perhaps in some cases, it *creates* value. An ordinary product with a fancy name may have snob appeal far in excess of its worth, simply because of the trademark it bears.

Similarly, an event organizer may create a generic event – a 10K race, for instance – but a fanciful trademark can make it more interesting and expand merchandising opportunities. This chapter focuses on trademarks and other intellectual property rights of interest to event organizers and sponsors.

TRADEMARKS

A trademark is a word or symbol used in connection with goods to distinguish them from those of others. It has been said that a trademark answers the question "Who are you?" rather than "What are you?"[1] Thus the trademark distinguishes one product from all other products that answer the second question in the same way, e.g., PREAKNESS horse race.

1.
J. Thomas McCarthy, *Trademarks and Unfair Competition*, § 3.2, p. 88 (The Lawyers Cooperative Publishing Co., Rochester, New York, 1986) [hereinafter McCarthy].

Trademarks (including service marks) can be strong, entitled to a wide scope of protection against similar uses, or weak, entitled to protection only in a narrow field. Fanciful, completely arbitrary trademarks are the strongest; some examples are EXXON, KODAK, and POLAROID. BUMBERSHOOT and HOOP-D-DO are good examples of fanciful event names. At the other end of the spectrum are "descriptive marks." These are marks so descriptive of some product quality or characteristic that they may not serve to distinguish one product from another, e.g., MUSICFEST. Generic words such as "FESTIVAL" cannot be trademarks because they can never distinguish one producer's goods from all goods of that type.

To be protectable, descriptive marks require "secondary meaning," that is, public recognition as distinguishing one source's products from another's.[2] Secondary meaning can be proven by (1) the amount and manner of advertising, (2) the volume of sales, (3) the length and manner of use, (4) direct consumer testimony or (5) consumer surveys.[3]

2.
McCarthy, §15.2(c), p. 661.

3.
See Union Carbide Corp. v. Ever-Ready, Inc., 531 F.2d 366, 380 (7th Cir. 1976), *cert. denied*, 429 U.S. 830 (1976) [EVEREADY for batteries had developed secondary meaning].

However, even if a trademark is descriptive, anyone may use the descriptive part of it in a purely descriptive manner, that is, in its common, ordinary meaning. A classic example involved Clairol's use of the trademark HAIR COLOR SO NATURAL ONLY HER HAIRDRESSER KNOWS FOR SURE. A court held that a competitor could truthfully describe its product with the claim ONLY YOU AND YOUR HAIRDRESSER KNOW WHERE NATURE STOPPED AND ROUX BEGAN.[4] Thus, if an event organizer owned a somewhat descriptive mark like FIRSTNIGHT for a New Year's festival, others are probably free to invite the public to enjoy the "First Night of the Year" with them at a different event, as long as the event itself is not called FIRSTNIGHT.

4.
Roux Labs., Inc. v. *Clairol, Inc.*, 427 F.2d 823, 824 (C.C.P.A. 1970).

The problem with some event marks is that they are so descriptive that they may in fact be generic. Consider marks like FOOD FEST, ART EXPO and MUSIC FESTIVAL. All use common words in their ordinary senses. Each would need a good deal of advertising in order to develop secondary meaning; indeed, they might be incapable of ever achieving secondary meaning. WORLD'S FAIR is descriptive in the same way; however, it may become a trademark because of the amount of advertising and public exposure it receives.

Louisiana World Exposition, Inc., the non-profit sponsor of the 1984 World's Fair, was successful in preventing a defendant from merchandising goods that were deceptively similar to its "official" products. The court in *Louisiana World Exposition, Inc.* v. *R. Gordon-Logue, Jr.*[5] found that the defendant would not have undertaken to sell the products unless the fair was in the process of realization. In essence, the merchandise had value only because the public associated it with the well-publicized fair. The Louisiana court explained that, while some might argue that WORLD'S FAIR is generic, the term had acquired secondary meaning. (Truly generic terms can never acquire secondary meaning but descriptive terms – even very descriptive ones – can.) It cited a 1939 case in which the New York courts had enjoined publication of the unlicensed ILLUSTRATED FAIR NEWS and WORLD'S FAIR NEWS as likely to deceive consumers.[6] The New York court had also found that wide publicity for the 1939 World's Fair had given the mark secondary meaning.

In 1939, the New York legislature attempted to resolve any question concerning the generic nature of the WORLD'S FAIR mark by passing a statute explicitly protecting the words. Since most major international expositions (world fairs) in this country take place as a result of city and state cooperation, organizers of such events should consider requesting similar statutory protection for their marks at the same time that other aspects of funding, such as establishing a World's Fair Authority or a tax, are negotiated and legislated.

It should also be noted that misspelling an otherwise descriptive word will not exempt it from the secondary meaning requirement. The word SAFE-T-BALL, for instance, has been held descriptive.[7] Similarly, foreign language versions of descriptive English words must show secondary meaning if they are likewise descriptive in the relevant language. For example, PIZZE FRITE was held not registrable because it was the Italian equivalent of the descriptive term "fried buns."[8] Geographic descriptions are also weak. With the exception of events steeped in history – such as THE KENTUCKY DERBY – marks that combine geography with descriptive words will not become strong marks no matter how much advertising is behind them.

Acquisition

Trademark rights arise through use. United States trademark law has been somewhat unique in that there has been no way to reserve a trademark prior to its use in commerce. In essence, because a trademark represented the goodwill of a business, until there was a business, the trademark had no significance to the public and thus no protection. This created some unique problems for event

5.
221 U.S.P.Q. 589 (E.D. La. 1983).

6.
New York World's Fair 1939, Inc. v. *World's Fair News, Inc.*, 163 Misc. 661, 297 N.Y.S. 923 (Sup. Ct. 1937), *aff'd*, 10 N.Y.S. 2d 56 (App. Div. 1939).

7.
See Clark v. *K-Mart*, 473 F. Supp. 1299, 1301 (W.D. Pa. 1979) [SAFE-T-BALL was descriptive and had not achieved secondary meaning].

8.
In re Zazzara, 156 U.S.P.Q. 348 (T.T.A.B. 1967).

organizers because of the difficulty of showing use of a mark while the event was still in the planning stages. This problem is largely resolved as of November 16, 1989, by amendments to the Lanham Act, the federal trademark law.

The new law allows the filing of an application for a trademark upon a statement of use of the mark or an "intent to use" the mark within a specified time period. This change enables an applicant to determine whether a trademark may be federally registered before committing substantial resources to the use of the mark.

Under the amended law, an "intent-to-use" applicant is required to file a statement of use. The applicant must present information showing an intent to put the trademark into use within six months after a Notice of Allowance has been issued. (Before this notice is issued, the mark has been examined by the Patent and Trademark Office and has passed the opposition process. The statement of use includes a "good faith" clause, designed to ensure that the applicant's intention to use the mark within the specified time period is in fact *bona fide*).

The initial six-month period is automatically extended for another six months upon submission of an affidavit stating the applicant's continued intent to use the mark in commerce. Any further extensions, however, are granted only if the applicant shows "good cause" for the extension. The extensions for "good cause" may not, however, exceed a total of 24 months. In other words, the applicant has up to three years from the date of the Notice of Allowance to make use of the mark. Throughout the extension periods, however, the applicant is also required to demonstrate a continual *bona fide* intention to use the mark.

These amendments make it easier for event organizers to claim trademarks.

Until a mark is federally registered, the first to use it in a geographic area has superior rights to it. If a second party adopts in good faith the same mark as the original user, though in a remote area, the second (junior) user may continue to use it and in fact may enjoin the senior user in its territory.[9] Whether or not a user occupies a geographic market is a question of fact, determined by weighing a variety of factors, including the volume of sales and number of customers in the area. For event organizers, the burden of showing prior use in a remote geographic area might be a matter of showing reputation in that area.

It has been held that a senior user with a national reputation can prevent a junior user in a remote area even if it does *not* do business in that area. For instance, the Paris restaurant MAXIM'S could prevent another restaurant in New York from using the name MAXIM'S since the Paris restaurant was well known in

9.
See Hanover Star Milling Co. v. Metcalf, 240 U.S. 403 (1916); *United Drug Co. v. Theodore Rectanus Co.,* 248 U.S. 90 (1918).

10.
Vaudable v. *Montmartre, Inc.*, 20 Misc. 2d 757, 193 N.Y.S. 2d 332 (Sup. Ct. 1959). *See also Lincoln Restaurant Corp.* v. *Wolfies Rest., Inc.*, 291 F.2d 302 (2d Cir. 1961), *cert. denied*, 368 U.S 889 (1961) [Miami restaurant named WOLFIE's could enjoin a Brooklyn restaurant of the same name and style since many of the Miami restaurant's customers were from Brooklyn].

New York.[10] Today it is not uncommon for an event's reputation to be regional or national. Therefore, owners of strong marks for local or regional events may well be able to enjoin others from using the same or similar marks in remote areas if their events have been widely publicized.

Under the amended Lanham Act, once a mark is used and registered, the registrant obtains nationwide "constructive use" priority, dating back to the date of its application. This constructive use seniority is not enforceable against any person who either (1) used or applied to register a mark prior to the date of the other registrant's application or (2) obtained an earlier "effective filing date" by obtaining a registration based upon a foreign registration.

Federal Registration

11.
15 U.S.C. §1051.

The easiest way to assure national rights in a mark is to register it under the federal trademark statute (the Lanham Act.)[11] Registration provides constructive notice of a claim of ownership of a mark – after registration, a junior user cannot adopt the same mark in good faith because he or she is charged with notice of the

12.
15 U.S.C. §1072.

registered mark.[12] Registration is *prima facie* evidence of ownership, right to exclusive use and validity of the mark's registration.[13] After registration, the

13.
15 U.S.C. §1056(b).

trademark owner may use the symbol or the words "Registered in the U.S. Patent and Trademark Office" or "Reg. U.S. Pat. Off."[14] (Prior to registration, persons who want to claim trademark or service mark rights may use "Tm" or "Sm,"

14.
15 U.S.C. §1111.

respectively.) Once a mark is federally registered, the owner has access to federal court to protect it from infringement, regardless of the dollar amount in controversy. However, while registration gives national rights to a mark, it does not preempt a senior user that used the mark in a given area prior to a junior user's registration. Moreover, the registrant cannot enforce its rights where it is not using the mark; an injunction against another user in a given area would not be issued until the registrant was ready to enter that market.

The registration process is a relatively easy one. The application must

(1) specify the applicant's name and address;

(2) state the dates of first use in commerce and first use in interstate commerce (or state the intent to use under the new law);

(3) include a drawing of the mark;

(4) include five specimens showing how the mark is used (they can be the same);

(5) state the goods or services (and classes) on which the mark is used;

(6) include a sworn statement that the applicant is not aware of any uses of a mark confusingly similar to its own; and

(7) pay the required filing fee.[15]

15.
15 U.S.C. §1051.

The Trademark Examiner reviews the application to determine if the mark is eligible for registration. Then the examiner reviews existing registrations and applications to determine that the mark does not so resemble a previously registered mark as to be likely to cause confusion, mistake or deception. If it does not, the mark is published in the Trademark Office's Official Gazette, and anyone who believes he or she would be injured by the issuance of the registration may oppose it. If after 30 days there is no opposition, the registration is issued and the mark is entered on the Principal Register. If there is an opposition, the parties present their evidence and arguments to the Trademark Trial and Appeal Board, which makes a decision. Appeals may be taken from the Board's decisions to the federal courts.[16] A sample application for federal trademark registration is found in Appendix B.

16.
15 U.S.C. §1071.

In a rare case, a trademark registration may be issued even though there is a similar mark on the Principal Register. The Lanham Act explicitly provides:

> *That when the Commissioner determines that confusion, mistake, or deception is not likely to result from the continued use by more than one person of the same or similar marks under conditions and limitations as to the mode or place of use of the marks or the goods in connection with which such marks are used, concurrent registrations may be issued to such persons when they have become entitled to use such marks as a result of their concurrent lawful use in commerce prior to (i) the earliest of the filing dates of the applications pending or of any registration issued under this chapter [references to prior trademark acts omitted].*[17]

17.
15 U.S.C. §1052(d).

Under that part of the statute, concurrent use is most frequently allowed when there is a geographic separation between the uses of two marks. The geographic limitations on use are the responsibility of the Commissioner of Patents and Trademarks. The first to register obtains national rights, subject only to areas in which the concurrent user has established rights.

18.
15 U.S.C. §1058(a).

19.
Id.

20.
15 U.S.C. §1059.

The initial term of a federal trademark registration was up to 20 years.[18] Trademarks issued after November 16, 1989 have a 10-year term. However, a registration expires at the end of 6 years if the registrant has not submitted an affidavit that its mark is still in use.[19] No further affidavits after this initial one are required. The registration is renewable for additional consecutive terms as long as the mark is in use.[20]

State Registration Systems

The Lanham Act does not preempt state laws. In fact, most states have their own trademark registration systems. These are useful for purely local businesses that are not in interstate commerce. The promoter of a purely local event may wish to obtain a state registration for its possible deterrent effect and for the notice it provides to others in the state. In the alternative, the organizer may choose to rely on its common-law rights.

TRADEMARK INFRINGEMENT ISSUES

The test for trademark infringement is whether there is a "likelihood of confusion." Confusion may arise because the marks are similar in sight, sound and meaning, or because they are used on similar goods. In determining whether there is a likelihood of confusion, courts consider a variety of factors. These may include the strength of the mark, the proximity of the products and the intent of the junior user.

Likelihood of Confusion

Trademark infringement occurs when an identical or similar mark is used on an identical or related product in a manner that creates a likelihood of confusion as to the source of that product. The statutory test for infringement of a federally registered trademark is whether the infringing mark is "likely to cause confusion or to cause mistake or to deceive."[21]

The "likelihood" that confusion will occur has been interpreted to mean something akin to the "probability" that it will occur. Something more than a mere possibility of confusion must exist, although *actual* confusion is not required.[22] Evidence of actual confusion is, however, highly relevant in determining whether the marks are "likely" to be confused.

The "confusion" that the public may suffer is a confusion as to the source of the products bearing the marks. The consumer need not think that the goods themselves are the same, merely that the goods come from the same source. If consumers are likely to be confused as to the sponsorship or affiliation of the goods, this, too, will constitute infringement. (See discussion of ambush marketing at page 159.)

Who must be likely to be confused? Generally, the potential purchasers of the two products are the relevant group. The public may also be confused as to the source of a product even when there isn't a competing product. For instance, the sale of cloth emblems featuring professional hockey team insignia was held to cause confusion and constitute infringement in *Boston Professional Hockey Association* v. *Dallas Cap & Emblem Mfg.*, Inc.[23] because "the defendant duplicated the protected trademarks and sold them to the public knowing that the public would identify them as being the [plaintiff's] trademarks."[24]

How many people must be likely to be confused? The Lanham Act does not identify any requisite number, and most courts refer only to an "appreciable number." Two particular infringement findings were supported by evidence of potential confusion among 8.5 percent and 57 percent of consumers, respectively.[25]

21.
15 U.S.C. §1114(1)(a).

22.
See W.E. Basset Co. v. Revlon, Inc., 435 F.2d 656 (2d Cir. 1970) [holding evidence of actual confusion difficult to obtain and not necessary].

23.
510 F.2d 1004 (5th Cir. 1975), cert. denied, 423 U.S. 868 (1975), reh'g denied, 423 U.S. 991 (1975), on remand, 597 F.2d 71 (5th Cir. 1979).

24.
Id. at 1012.

25.
See Grotrian, Helffrich, Schiltz, Th. Steinweg Nacht v. Steinway & Sons, 365 F. Supp. 707 (S.D.N.Y. 1973), modified, 523 F.2d 1331 (2d Cir. 1975) [8.5 percent of consumers were confused by use of STEINWEG]; National Football League Properties, Inc. v. New Jersey Giants, Inc., 229 U.S.P.Q. 785 (D.N.J. 1986) [57 percent of persons surveyed confused NEW YORK GIANTS and NEW JERSEY GIANTS].

The typical confusion that results from trademark infringement is that the purchaser of the junior user's goods is misled into believing that the senior user is the source of the product. "Reverse confusion" occurs when the junior user of a mark, often a large company, floods the market with advertising and promotion of its product under a mark similar to that of a senior user. As a result, purchasers may be misled into believing that the junior user is the source of the senior user's product.

Likelihood of confusion may be shown by (1) evidence of actual confusion, (2) survey evidence or (3) a judicial comparison of the marks and the circumstances in which they are used. The burden of proving likelihood of confusion is on the plaintiff. However, many courts have held that any doubt regarding the issue of confusion will be resolved in favor of the senior user.

Likelihood of confusion is generally regarded as a question of fact. Because the determination of whether two marks are likely to be confused is so dependent on the facts of each given case, the value of precedent is limited. However, as discussed below, prior decisions provide useful guidelines.

Confusingly Similar Marks

The use of an identical mark on identical goods presents a simple case of trademark infringement. However, a trademark need not be exactly or literally copied in order to be an infringement. A "colorable imitation" of a mark is as much an infringement as is the use of the mark in its identical form. The United States Supreme Court has long observed that "what degree of resemblance is necessary to constitute an infringement is incapable of exact definition."[26]

A mere side-by-side comparison of two marks is not sufficient. Rather, they must be viewed in the context in which consumers view them in their entirety. It is well established, however, that some component parts of a mark may be considered more salient than others. Those dominant features may be accorded greater weight, while similarities based on descriptive or generic terms are accorded lesser weight.

The factors to be considered in deciding whether or not one mark infringes another are variable, and no single one is, in itself, determinative. Four criteria are often used to evaluate the likelihood of confusion:

(1) the degree of similarity between the designation and the trademark or trade name in (a) appearance, (b) pronunciation of the words used, (c) verbal translations of the pictures or designs involved, or (d) suggestion;

26.
McLean v. Fleming, 16 U.S. 245 (1878).

27.
Restatement of Torts, §729(b).

28.
Esso, Inc. v. Standard Oil Co., 98 F.2d 1 (8th Cir. 1938).

29.
Dr. Ing. h.c.F. Porsche AG v. Zim, 481 F. Supp. 1247, 208 U.S.P.Q. 440 (N.D. Tex. 1979).
30.
Columbia Pictures Industries v. Miller, 211 U.S.P.Q. 816 (T.T.A.B. 1981).

(2) the intent of the actor in adopting the designation;

(3) the relation in use and manner of marketing between the goods and services;

(4) the degree of care likely to be exercised by purchasers.[27]

The "sight/sound/meaning" trilogy is commonly used as the basis for evaluating the similarity of marks.

Sight. Similarities in sight are apparent in a simple "eyeball" comparison. A court must rely on its own visual analysis to determine whether the "overall impressions" created by the marks bear enough resemblance to cause consumer confusion. Visual similarities are of obvious importance when the marks at issue are design marks or trade dress. They are also important when the marks are letters or coined words that may have little significance to the consumer apart from their appearance.

Sound. Marks may also be found confusingly similar on the basis of phonetic similarity. S.O. and ESSO, for example, were found to be confusingly similar because, although visually dissimilar, they sound exactly the same when spoken.[28] Similarities in sound are, of course, capable of objective measurement through phonetic analysis. However, courts will not necessarily hold the consumer to proper pronunciation of a trademark, particularly when the mark is comprised of a foreign word or a proper name. Most courts will look to the way the public is "likely" to pronounce the mark.

Examples of marks found to be confusingly similar based at least in part on phonetic similarity include PORSCHE and PORSHA,[29] CLOTHES ENCOUNTERS and CLOSE ENCOUNTERS[30] and SEIKO and SEYCOS.[31] Marks found not to be confusingly similar despite some alleged phonetic similarities include HOUR AFTER HOUR and SHOWER TO SHOWER,[32] SLEEKCRAFT and SLICKCRAFT[33] and WUV'S and LOVE'S.[34]

Meaning. Even if two marks look and sound different, they may still be considered confusingly similar if they share a common meaning. The marks CYCLONE and TORNADO for chain-link fencing were held to be confusingly similar trademarks despite their obvious visual and phonetic differences.[35] A picture mark that conveys the same meaning as a word mark may also create confusion. For example, a picture of John Philip Sousa and his name were treated as "interchangeable for infringement purposes."[36] Other marks found to be confusingly similar based on their common meaning are PLEDGE and PROMISE,[37] ROACH MOTEL and ROACH INN[38] and KIND TOUCH and GENTLE TOUCH.[39]

31.
Kabushiki Kaisha Hattori Tokeiten v. Scutto, 228 U.S.P.Q. 461 (T.T.A.B. 1985).

32.
Johnson & Johnson v. Colgate-Palmolive Co., 503 F. Supp. 209 (E.D. Pa. 1980).

33.
AMF, Inc. v. Sleekcraft Boats. 599 F.2d 341 (9th Cir. 1979).

34.
Wuv's International, Inc. v. Love's Enterprises, Inc., 208 U.S.P.Q. 736 (D.C. Colo. 1980).

35.
Hancock v. American Steel & Wire Co., 40 C.C.P.A. 931, 203 F.2d 737 (1953).

36.
Instrumentalist Co. v. Marine Corps League, 509 F. Supp. 323 (N.D. Ill. 1981), aff'd, 694 F.2d 145 (7th Cir. 1982).

37.
S.C. Johnson & Son, Inc. v. Drop Dead Co., Inc., 210 F. Supp. 816, 135 U.S.P.Q. 292 (S.D. Cal. 1962).

38.
American Home Products Corp. v. Johnson Chemical Co., 589 F.2d 103 (2d Cir. 1978).

39.
Andrew Jergens Co. v. Sween Corp., 229 U.S.P.Q. 394 (T.T.A.B. 1986).

40.
In re Lar Mor International, Inc., 221 U.S.P.Q. 180 (T.T.A.B. 1983) [TRES JOLIE does not so resemble BIEN JOLIE for women's clothing as to cause confusion].

41.
Re Maclin-Zimmer-McGill Tobacco Co., 49 App. D.C. 181, 262 F. 635 (1920).

42.
Re AGE Bodegas Unidas, S.A., 192 U.S.P.Q. 326 (T.T.A.B. 1976). *See also Re L'Oreal S.A.*, 222 U.S.P.Q. 925 (T.T.A.B. 1984) [The meaning of the marks HI FASHION SAMPLER and HAUTE MODE are similar, but differences in appearance and sound prevent them from being confusingly similar].

43.
See Re Hub Distributing, Inc., 218 U.S.P.Q. 284, 285, (T.T.A.B. 1983) [The Trademark Trial and Appeal Board refused registration to EL SOL for T-shirts and footwear on the grounds that it would cause confusion with prior registrant's SUN for footwear. The Board noted that the article EL put the term in the Spanish language. The Board further stated that the term was a "direct foreign language equivalent of the linguistic portion of the mark of the cited registration"].

To determine whether a mark containing a foreign word is confusingly similar, the mark is translated into its English equivalent.[40] Thus, marks like EL GALLO and THE ROOSTER[41] and SIGLO and CENTURY[42] have been found confusingly similar. However, this rule applies only where the mark would connote its English equivalent to Americans familiar with that foreign language.[43]

House Marks

It has been argued that if a mark is to be considered in its entirety, the addition of a house mark should suffice to distinguish two otherwise confusingly similar marks. A house mark is an overall corporate identity that is associated with a variety of brand-name products. KELLOGG'S is an example of a strong house mark.[44] The addition of a house mark does not offer immunity; however, it is a factor to be considered in comparing the overall similarity of the marks.[45]

Intent to Infringe

It is not necessary for a defendant to have acted maliciously or willfully for infringement to be found. Courts have held, however, that if the defendant *intended* to trade on goodwill of the plaintiff, that intent may serve as evidence that confusion is likely to occur. In other words, if the junior user intended to mislead consumers, it may be presumed that he or she was successful.

Sophistication of the Buyer

When determining the relevant population likely to be confused by the marks, courts will most often look to the "typical buyer exercising ordinary caution." This standard includes the "ignorant" and the "credulous."

However, the greater the value of an article, the more careful the typical consumer can be expected to be. The expertise and level of education or sophistication of the consumer may also elevate the standard of care. Where the buyer is a "professional" or "commercial" one, the standard will be that of the "ordinary discriminating purchaser."

The kind of product, its cost, the conditions of purchase and the expertise of the typical purchaser are all important factors in determining whether the sophistication of the buyer can eliminate the likelihood of confusion that would otherwise exist in the marketplace.

Related but Non-Competing Goods

The classic case of trademark infringement occurs when the same or a similar mark is used on a product directly competitive to the plaintiff's. However, the law does not require a trademark owner to prove direct competition between the products. Infringement can exist if the goods are related and there is a likelihood that consumers will believe the product bearing the infringing mark is related to or connected with the trademark owner. Related goods are those goods that would be reasonably thought by the buying public to come from the same source if sold under the same mark. The confusion generated by the use of an infringing mark on non-competing goods is not only confusion as to source, but also confusion as to affiliation with the trademark owner. For instance, in *Dallas Cowboy Cheerleaders, Inc.* v. *Pussycat Cinema, Ltd.*,[46] the court found that the public could believe the NFL football team was somehow associated with a sex film because the stars of the film wore uniforms similar to those of the Dallas Cowboys' cheerleaders.

Strength of Mark

The strength of a trademark will determine the scope of protection it receives. A weak mark will be entitled to protection only against uses of similar marks on similar goods or services. Conversely, a strong mark is entitled to greater protection where the goods are non-competing.

Proximity of Products

In evaluating the proximity of products, courts consider whether a product is the same "type" or "species" as another. For example, many different types of clothing have been found to be "related" goods, as have different types of food. Souvenir merchandise like caps, T-shirts, jackets and bags are probably related goods for purposes of trademark infringement analysis. Goods may also be found to be related if they are "complementary" or likely to be used together, such as bread and cheese.

In addition, courts will consider the "channels of trade" in which similar marks pass. For example, where a mark is used only on goods sold to commercial users, for example, it is not likely to be confused with a mark used on goods sold only at the retail level. Similarly, expensive goods often travel in different channels of trade than their less expensive counterparts.

Bridging the Gap

The concept of "bridging the gap" protects the senior user's interest in preserving reasonable avenues of future expansion into related fields. This interest is balanced against the public interest in preventing the senior user from precluding others from entering unrelated markets in which it has no interest. Courts have required various degrees of immediacy of expansion when applying this factor.

44.
General Mills, Inc. v. *Kellogg Co.*, 824 F.2d 622, 627 (8th Cir. 1987) [GENERAL MILLS OATMEAL RAISIN CRISP cereal did not infringe KELLOGG's APPLE RAISIN CRISP cereal. Over the plaintiff's contention that consumers pay little attention to house marks, the court found that "both parties are widely recognized in the food industry and that both have appended their house marks in a sufficiently prominent manner so that consumers would likely distinguish between the two products' sources. . . "].
But see Elizabeth Taylor Cosmetics v. *Annick Goutal, S.A.R.L.*, 673 F. Supp. 1238 (S.D.N.Y. 1987). [ELIZABETH TAYLOR'S PASSION was enjoined from being marketed in "first-tier" stores in which PASSION was sold].

45.
T&T Manufacturing Co. v. *A.T. Cross Co.*, 449 F. Supp. 813 (D.R.I. 1978), aff'd, 587 F.2d 533 (lst Cir. 1978), *cert. denied*, *A.T. Cross Co.* v. *Quill Co., Inc.*, 441 U.S. 908, 60 L. Ed. 2d 377, 199 S. Ct. 2000 (1979), *on remand, Quill Co., Inc.* v. *A.T. Cross Co.*, 477 A.2d 939 [The display of a house mark is relevant to likelihood of confusion, but does not necessarily excuse infringement. It may bear on the question of intent in unfair competition cases].

46.
604 F.2d 200 (2d Cir. 1979).

47.
*National Lampoon, Inc.
v. American Broadcasting Cos., Inc.*, 376 F.
Supp. 733, 750 (S.D.N.Y.
1974). ["The law recognizes that the consequences of trademark
infringement, or passing
off, and unfair competition generally, are by
their nature not fully
compensable by money
damages." Two television programs, one entitled NATIONAL
LAMPOON and the
other either LAMPOUN
or ABC LAMPOON,
were held to be confusingly similar].

48.
*General Foods Corp. v.
Borden, Inc.*, 191
U.S.P.Q. 674 (N.D. Ill.
1976)]. [COUNTRY
PRIZE for beverages
was held to be confusingly similar to plaintiff's
mark COUNTRY TIME
for a similar product].

49.
*Visa International v.
Bankcard Holders of
America*, 211 U.S.P.Q.
28, 39 (N.D. Cal. 1981).
[Use of the VISA trademark and accompanying
design were preliminarily
enjoined as an infringement of the plaintiff's
registered marks. The
court said, "Loss of business is not the test of
irreparable injury in
motions for preliminary
injunctions against the
use of a trademark. The
fact that plaintiff has
had the symbol of its
reputation placed in the
hands of another is
irreparable injury"].

50.
15 U.S.C. §1116.

51.
McCarthy, §30.15,
p. 483.

Choosing a Mark

Avoiding infringement can be relatively simple. In choosing a trademark, an event organizer should first look for as fanciful a mark as will still meet marketing and communications needs. Then the organizer should consult an attorney who specializes in trademark law (sometimes subsumed under the rubric of intellectual property law). The attorney will conduct a search of the trademark registrations in the U.S. Patent and Trademark Office, the state registries and various unregistered trade names. This can be done through on-line computerized database services and/or through commercial services. The attorney will then review the search for possible conflicts and render an opinion on the availability of the proposed mark. If the organizer wishes, the attorney can also prepare the registration application.

Enforcement, Remedies and John Doe Orders

The traditional remedy for trademark infringement is an injunction, but monetary damages are also available. Under general equitable principles, an injunction is only appropriate where monetary recovery is inadequate. In the case of trademark infringement, an injunction is almost always necessary to prevent a continuing wrong.[47] Thus, while monetary recovery is also available to compensate for lost sales and profits,[48] the traditional remedy for trademark infringement is injunctive relief in order to protect against the loss of goodwill, which is "difficult to identify with precision."[49] This remedy is codified in the Lanham Act, which states that courts "shall have the power to grant injunctions, according to the principles of equity and upon such terms as the court may deem reasonable."[50]

Because of the nature of the harm caused by trademark infringement – both to the owner of the mark and to the public – preliminary relief is often sought. A leading trademark authority has identified five basic criteria for the issuance of a preliminary injunction:

(1) Can plaintiff show a probability of success at the ultimate trial on the merits?

(2) Can plaintiff show that he will suffer "irreparable injury" pending a full trial on the merits?

(3) Will a preliminary injunction preserve the "status quo" which preceded the dispute?

(4) Do the hardships balance in favor of plaintiff?

(5) Is a preliminary injunction necessary to protect third parties?[51]

Each federal appellate court has expressed its test for preliminary relief in a trademark infringement case slightly differently. Attorneys should refer to the law of their respective jurisdictions for the exact proof requirements.

The key to winning injunctive relief is a finding of a likelihood of confusion on the part of the consuming public. Consistent with the likelihood-of-confusion test, actual confusion need not be shown in order to establish a likelihood of success on the merits.[52] Any evidence of actual confusion is, of course, highly relevant to the determination of the likelihood of confusion and thus to the probability of success on the merits. Because of the nature of the injury, irreparable harm is often presumed if the requisite showing of likelihood of confusion is made. Loss of control over the quality of goods sold under a mark[50] and loss of licensing opportunities[54] constitute irreparable harm.

An injunction is an extremely flexible remedy; it can be tailored to fit the facts and equities of a given case. Where geographically remote uses are involved, the scope of the injunction may be limited to the geographic area in which confusion is likely to occur.[55] An injunction can also be structured to lessen the hardship to the defendant by allowing the use of existing trademarked stock.[56] An injunction may also be fashioned so as to permit the use of a trademark but to limit the manner in which it may be used[57] or to require that the mark be accompanied by a disclaimer.[58]

The Federal Rules of Civil Procedure provide that an injunction is enforceable against any parties to the litigation, as well as their agents and employees.[59] Third parties who are contributory infringers, even though innocent infringers, may also be bound by the injunction.[60] Violations of an injunction against trademark infringement are punishable through contempt proceedings.[61]

Trademark owners are sometimes entitled to *ex parte* relief (without the defendant being present or having an opportunity to respond) and to relief against unnamed, perhaps unknown, defendants called "John Does." The availability of this relief is extremely important to promoters of events such as concerts, which may only last a day or two.[62]

Ex parte orders, while issued sparingly by courts, are particularly useful in counterfeiting cases. In a leading case, *In the Matter of Vuitton et Fils S.A.*,[63] Vuitton was held to be entitled to an *ex parte* temporary restraining order against a counterfeiter of its expensive and distinctive leather goods because of the immediate and irreparable injury Vuitton would suffer from the infringement. Moreover, Vuitton satisfied the court that notice to the counterfeiter should not be

52.
Tisch Hotels, Inc. v. Americana, Inc., 350 F.2d 609 (7th Cir. 1965) [Use of AMERICANA on Chicago motel likely to cause confusion with identical mark on Miami Beach hotel].

53.
A.J. Canfield Co. v. Vess Beverages, 796 F.2d 903, (7th Cir. 1986).

54.
Frisch's Restaurants, Inc. v. Elby's Big Boy of Steubenville, Inc., 670 F.2d 642 (6th Cir. 1982), *cert. denied*, 74 L. Ed. 2d 182, 103 S. Ct. 231 [The defendant was enjoined from using BOYBIG for restaurants in Ohio].

55.
Bass Buster, Inc. v. Gapen Mfg. Co., Inc., 420 F. Supp. 144 (W.D. Mo. 1976) [Injunction was limited to the trademark owner's actual market area penetration].

56.
Minnesota Mining & Mfg. Co. v. 3M Electric Corp., 184 U.S.P.Q. 470 (S.D. Fla. 1974) [The defendant was given 100 days to stop using infringing signs and posters and nine months to change its corporate name].

57.
Volkswagenwerk A.G. v. Rickard, 181 U.S.P.Q. 611 (5th Cir. 1974 [The court allowed a garage to advertise that it serviced Volkswagen products but not to use BUG or VW].

58.
Franklin Mint Corp. v. Franklin Mint, Ltd., 178 U.S.P.Q. 176 (E.D. Pa. 1973) [A British corporation was required to disclaim any association with an American company with a similar name].

59.
Fed. R. Civ. P. 65(d).

60.
15 U.S.C. §1114(2).

61.
15 U.S.C. §1116; 18 U.S.C. §401(3).

62.
See Comment, *Rock Performers and the 'John Doe' Temporary Restraining Order: Dressing Down the T-Shirt Pirates*, 16 J. Marshall L. Rev. 101 (1982).

63.
606 F.2d 1 (2nd Cir. 1979).

64.
Id. at 2.

65.
Moon Records v. Various John Does, 217 U.S.P.Q. 46, 48 (N.D. Ill. 1981).

66.
See also Joel v. Various John Does, 499 F. Supp. 791 (E.D. Wisc. 1980) [Billy Joel and exclusive T-shirt licensee were entitled to *ex parte* seizure orders against John Doe infringers outside the Milwaukee arena where he was scheduled to appear].

required. Vuitton alleged that there was a network of counterfeiters and that, upon notice of a lawsuit, one counterfeiter would transfer its inventory to another for cash. The court cited Vuitton's brief:

> . . . *[I]n most Vuitton cases defendants maintain few, if any, records. The now too familiar refrain from a "caught counterfeiter" is "I bought only a few pieces from a man I never saw before and whom I have never seen again. All my business was in cash. I do not know how to locate the man from whom I bought and I cannot remember the identity of the person to whom I sold."*
> . . . *If after Vuitton has identified a counterfeiter with an inventory of fake merchandise, that counterfeiter is permitted to dispose of that merchandise with relative impunity after he learns of the imminence of litigation but before he is enjoined from doing so. Vuitton's trademark enforcement program will be stymied and the community of counterfeiters will be permitted to continue to play its "shell game" at great expense and damage to Vuitton.*[64]

Ex parte orders are also useful to event promoters who anticipate the sale of unauthorized T-shirts and souvenirs at or around the event. Rock concert promoters have been particularly successful in obtaining temporary restraining and seizure orders against T-shirt bootleggers. In a case involving the musical group Rush, the court explained that the seizure order authorizes the federal marshall to seize and impound:

> *all infringing merchandise which any defendant (after lawful service of a true copy of this order and the complaint filed in this case) attempts to sell or holds out for sale in the vicinity of the International Amphitheater, Chicago, Illinois, on or about February 26, 27, 28 and March 1, 1981.*[65]

Typically, the plaintiff's attorney will accompany the marshall and identify defendants. The infringers are handed a copy of the complaint and the order and are issued a receipt for their goods. The defendants are told of the court date (usually the next available court date following the event) at which they may appear and protest the seizure. To protect the defendants, the plaintiff is required to post a bond to benefit any John Doe wrongfully restrained by the marshall.[66]

Often *ex parte* orders are sought on an emergency basis. At least one court, while granting the temporary *ex parte* relief sought, chastised the plaintiff's attorneys for not bringing the petition for relief earlier. The court in *Brockum International, Inc. v. Various John Does*[67] said:

> *The Who and its souvenir hawkers knew they were going to be here over two months ago. They could have filed their lawsuit at that time and requested an orderly placement on the calendar a week or two in advance of the concert date. In future cases of this type I will look for good reasons why such a procedure was not utilized before I hear one of these cases on an emergency rush-rush basis.*

Moreover, the court there declined to issue a national order, saying that such matters should be handled on a local basis. Therefore, part of planning any multi-site event should include a program for obtaining *ex parte* restraining orders in each jurisdiction in which the event will take place.

It should also be noted that John Doe orders must be sought judiciously. In *Winterland Concessions Co. v. Trela*,[68] the defendant alleged that the authorized T-shirt company violated the antitrust laws by employing John Doe orders in a manner designed to drive him out of business. The allegations were:

> *that Winterland purposely delayed filing actions until the day before a licensor's scheduled performance and then repeatedly dismissed such actions against Trela after the concert was over and the market value for his products had been severely reduced. Trela claims that Winterland's purpose in proceeding in this manner was to avoid an adjudication on the merits of its property rights while simultaneously eliminating Trela as a competitor during performances.*[69]

While generally use of the courts to vindicate rights is privileged, initiating "sham litigation" is not. If allegations similar to those in *Winterland* are even facially supported, a court may not dismiss the claim but rather require a trial, which can be long and costly.

Despite the general acceptance of *ex parte* relief as discussed above, a few courts are not favorably disposed to grant such petitions. The District Court in Washington, D.C. denied the NFL's request for a John Doe order, saying:

67.
551 F. Supp. 1054, 1055 (E.D. Wisc. 1982).

68.
735 F.2d 257 (7th Cir. 1984).

69.
Id. at 263.

*Even on the surface, the order requested by plaintiff would appear
to invite catastrophe. It promises a nightmare of jurisdictional
flaws, deprivations of due process, and windfall litigation that
could ensue for years to come.*[70]

70.
*National Football League
Properties, Inc. v. Conig-
lio,* 554 F. Supp. 1224
(D.D.C. 1983).

The court rejected the same argument that had been made by the plaintiff in
Vuitton:

*Contrary to that decision, it appears to this Court that the injury
plaintiff has alleged here definitely is not reparable only by means
of a TRO. By plaintiff's own contention, once notice of this lawsuit
is given to one infringer, word will spread immediately to others,
who will thereupon disappear, and merchandise will be concealed,
shipments will be halted, and goods will be transported out of the
jurisdiction. It seems to the Court that this is precisely the result
that plaintiff is seeking here through a restraining order, and it can
be accomplished merely by service of a complaint. In the
alternative, if plaintiff prefers to make an example of the
"professional infringers" and "vendors of 'bootleg' merchandise"
that it alleges have flooded the streets of Washington, it can allow
them to prosper, continue to gather information about their
activities (using the elaborate system of investigators and "Knockout
Report Forms" that plaintiff proudly describes in its papers, and
which it evidently used at the last Super Bowl), and then
retroactively sue for the profits earned. In other words, the injury
plaintiff has claimed is, by its own statements, clearly not
irreparable.*

Even assuming, arguendo, *that plaintiff has shown irreparable
injury and the likelihood of success on the merits, the third and
fourth considerations for preliminary injunctive relief strongly
vitiate against plaintiff. The harm that may come to the defendants
and "other parties interested in the proceedings" from the issuance
of the order requested by plaintiffs is potentially enormous. As
already noted, the order would burden the already overworked
Marshall's Service, which would be sent scuttling through Washington as messenger for the NFL. The order would open small
businesses and street vendors throughout the city to the threat of
forcible confiscation, which, when implemented, could result in the
taking of legitimate and authorized merchandise at the time when
it was most marketable. It could also result in physical outbreaks*

*and other substantial disruptions of the city's commerce, completely
contrary to the "public interest." Surely plaintiff must jest when it
contends that all of this would be a "minimal inconvenience" to
defendants and would serve to "aid the efforts of the Police
Department of the District of Columbia to exercise crowd control."
If anything, it would cause great inconvenience and increase public
disruptions at some of the District's busiest interchanges.*[71]

Thus, attorneys must consider the predisposition of the local courts prior to
advising promoters to seek John Doe orders.

A plaintiff in an infringement action may seek monetary as well as injunctive relief.
This recovery may take the form of the defendant's profits, the plaintiff's actual
damages, reasonable attorneys' fees, court costs and punitive damages. Under the
Lanham Act, a successful plaintiff is entitled to recover (1) defendant's profits,
(2) any damages sustained by the plaintiff, and (3) the costs of the action.[72]

However, the award is not mandatory; the act further states:

*If the court shall find that the amount of the recovery based on
profits is either inadequate or excessive the court may in its
discretion enter judgments for such sum as the court shall find to
be just, according to the circumstances of the case.*[73]

Thus, monetary recovery is subject to the principles of equity. Both under the
Lanham Act and at common law, equitable principles have been employed to deny
monetary relief where injunctive relief will satisfy the equities of the case.[74] Most
courts require something more than mere infringement before any monetary
recovery will be awarded.[75]

Just what constitutes that "something more" is unclear. McCarthy, while referring
to the case law on monetary recovery as a "confusing melange," has identified
several factors that a court may balance:

(1) whether defendant was willful, negligent or innocent

(2) whether plaintiff suffered losses in any provable amount

(3) whether there is proof of actual confusion of some customers

(4) whether defendant realized profit from its infringing actions.[76]

71.
Id. at 1226.

72.
15 U.S.C. §1117.

73.
Id.

74.
McCarthy, §30.24(b),
p. 495.

75.
*See Champion Spark
Plug Co.* v. *Sanders*, 331
U.S. 125, 130, 67 S. Ct.
1136, 1139, 91 L. Ed.
1336 (1947) [Under the
Trademark Act of 1905,
"the character of con-
duct giving rise to the
unfair competition is relevant to the remedy
which should be
afforded"].

76.
McCarthy, §30.24(b),
p. 495.

Quality Control and Licensing

Merchandising is one of the most important areas of trademark law for event organizers. Typically, both event organizers and sponsors produce signs, brochures, advertising and merchandise bearing their own and the other's trademarks. Because trademarks act as indicators to the public of the quality of the goods or services sold under them, trademark owners must be careful when others are allowed to use their marks.

The basic rule is that a trademark owner must maintain control over the quality of the goods and services offered under the mark. This assures the public of the trademark owner's approval of the product or service – that is, that the quality of the product or service is the same as that associated with the trademark.

77.
Stockpot, Inc. v. Stock Pot Restaurant, Inc., 220 U.S.P.Q. 52, 59 (T.T.A.B. 1983), *aff'd*, 737 F.2d 1576 (Fed. Cir. 1984).

One of the key issues (and one of the main areas for negotiation between the parties) is often the issue of how much quality control the trademark licensor needs to exert. Not enough control will lead to abandonment; too much can choke the licensee's creativity or inhibit its ability to do business.

78.
See McCarthy, §18.17, p. 639.

As one court has noted, there "has been an almost hopeless inconsistency in the decisions in defining how much quality control is needed to satisfy the requirements of the law."[77] A recognized expert in the trademark field has grouped the quality control decisions into three useful categories:

79.
See General Motors Corp. v. Gibson Chemical & Oil, 786 F.2d 105, 110 (2d Cir. 1986).

(1) the majority view that *actual control* over the licensee is required despite the presence or lack of contractual provisions

(2) the view that reliance upon the *licensee's own quality control* is sufficient

80.
See, e.g., Haymaker Sports, Inc. v. Turian, 581 F.2d 257 (C.C.P.A. 1978) [Licensors were mere holders of title of mark for debt repayment purposes and had no interest in quality of goods]; *Mason Tackle Co. v. Victor United Inc.*, 216 U.S.P.Q. 197, 201 (C.D. Cal. 1982) [After lump sum payment received, no incentive to set up and police quality control system]; *Robinson Co. v. Plastics Research and Development*, 264 F. Supp. 852 (W.D. Ark. 1967) [License lacking any quality control provision held invalid].

(3) the position that *contractual provisions* for control are sufficient.[78]

However, the majority view is the one that most often should govern sponsorship relationships. As one court stated, "The critical question in determining whether a licensing program is controlled sufficiently by the licensor to protect his mark is whether the licensees' operations are policed adequately to guarantee the quality of the products sold under the mark."[79]

In cases where abandonment was found due to insufficient control, generally there was no actual quality control being exercised, there was no written license containing quality control provisions and the licensor had no interest in the quality of the goods being sold under the mark.[80]

Thus, trademark licensors should retain contractual quality control and should exercise it in order to avoid any questions with respect to naked licensing. Merchandise licenses should provide manufacturing specifications and/or the opportunity for the licensor to approve prototypes. The licensee should be required to provide the licensor with samples and the opportunity to inspect its premises. (See sample exclusive trademark license at page 139).

Termination of an Event and Trademark Abandonment

An interesting question arises when an event dies, for example, when the sponsor or organizer announces that the event will no longer be held. What happens to the trademark? Can the organizer sell it? Can a third party adopt the mark for free by creating a new corporation or filing an application for state or federal registration?

A trademark may be abandoned voluntarily or involuntarily. Voluntary abandonment occurs when the trademark owner expressly states its intent to abandon the mark and, thereafter, ceases use of the mark. Abandonment may also occur involuntarily.

Under the Lanham Act, a federally registered mark is deemed abandoned

(a) when its use has been discontinued with intent not to resume. Intent not to resume may be inferred from circumstances. Non-use for two consecutive years shall be *prima facie* abandonment.

(b) when any course of conduct of the registrant, including acts of omission as well as commission, causes the mark to lose its significance as an indication of origin.[81]

81.
15 U.S.C. §1127.

To prove abandonment of a trademark, one must present evidence of non-use of the mark for a period of time, as well as the owner's intent not to resume use.[82] Because abandonment results in forfeiture of property rights, the evidence must be substantial.[83] Courts have held that intent not to resume use may be found where the mark has lost its significance as an indication of origin. The mark may be deemed abandoned where substantial changes in the product or in the mark itself have resulted in a different commercial impression. Some courts have also stated that failure to prosecute offenders may lead to abandonment.

82.
Saratoga Vichy Spring Co. v. Lehman, 625 F.2d 1037, 1043 (2d Cir. 1980).

83.
Id. at 1044.

As noted above, the Lanham Act provides that non-use for two consecutive years constitutes *prima facie* abandonment. In *Silverman* v. CBS, Inc.[84] ("*Silverman II*"), a playwright came up with an idea to create a musical based on the popular show "Amos 'n' Andy" and requested from CBS, the trademark holder, a license to use the AMOS 'N' ANDY mark. CBS refused. The playwright then brought suit, seeking a

84.
666 F. Supp. 575 (S.D.N.Y. 1987).

85.
Id. at 578.

86.
Saratoga Vichy, 625 F.2d at 1043.

87.
Silverman v. CBS, Inc., 632 F. Supp. 1344, 1357 (S.D.N.Y. 1986) ("*Silverman I*"), citing McCarthy, §17.4, pp. 776-77.

88.
Silverman II, 666 F. Supp. at 578, 580.

89.
See Exxon Corp. v. Humble Exploration Co., 695 F.2d 96, 217 U.S.P.Q. 1200 (5th Cir. 1983), *reh'g denied*, 701 F.2d 173 (5th Cir. 1983), *on remand*, 592 F. Supp. 1226, 224 U.S.P.Q. 234 (N.D. Tex. 1984).

90.
15 U.S.C. §1127(a).

91.
Silverman I, 632 F. Supp. at 1357.

92.
557 F. Supp. 178 (S.D.N.Y. 1983).

93.
Id. at 183.

94.
Id.

declaration that the mark was abandoned. The court found that plaintiff had established non-use by showing CBS's very limited use of the mark for the previous two decades.[85] However, according to the Second Circuit, "prima facie abandonment" as used in the statute "means no more than a rebuttable presumption of abandonment."[86] Thus, temporary suspension of the use of the mark would not constitute abandonment if the non-use were the result of circumstances beyond the owner's control or if intent to resume were proven.[87] CBS was able to rebut the presumption of non-use and shift the burden of persuasion back to the plaintiff by showing that it had continued to license limited use of the show, had considered resuming use, had registered for or renewed copyrights in the shows and had challenged infringing uses of the mark.[88]

In unusual circumstances, a trademark may be formally abandoned. This may be done for tax purposes. In such cases the owner must prove its intent not to resume use of the mark as well as actual cessation of use.[89]

In some cases, however, the intent not to resume use is not expressly stated, and the trademark owner does not want to relinquish use of the mark. It may be that an event organizer is still hopeful of gaining sponsors or restructuring the event in the future. The Lanham Act provides that intent may be inferred from the circumstances.[90] Self-serving statements of an intent to resume use of the mark will not prevail over objective evidence of abandonment.[91] Generally, the court will look to the nature of the product or service in evaluating the intent to resume use. Thus, even if a musical group disbands and the individuals appear to have no present intent to continue performing, the group's name can still be protected. For instance, in *Kingsmen v. K-Tel Intern Ltd.*,[92] a group of five musicians who had been members of the "Kingsmen" band successfully sued to restrain sale of an album containing the band's former lead vocalist's re-recording of a group song. The court appeared to focus on the band's effort to continue to get benefits from previously recorded works, not on the band's intent to resume performance under its old name.[93] As the *Kingsmen* court noted, the group has "no more abandoned their right to protect the name of Kingsmen than have the Beatles, The Supremes or any other group that has disbanded . . . but continues to collect royalties from the sale of previously recorded material."[94] Apparently, under the *Kingsmen* rationale, continued sales of postcards, buttons, books or other memorabilia about a group or an event would provide evidence that the trademark has not been abandoned.

However, it is fairly well established that, where no present intent to market the trademark product is found, minimal sales are insufficient to protect trademark rights. As the court put it, "trademark rights are not created by sporadic, casual, and nominal shipment of goods bearing a mark."[95] The *La Societe* principle also applies to services. One court found that giving over twenty cooking classes to almost 5,000 students in seven cities was sufficient to disprove non-use and intent to abandon the use of a cooking school's educational services trademark.[96] The court said the school's use of the trademark was not "sporadic, casual or transitory' as would warrant cancellation."

The continued existence of goodwill may be important in rebutting an abandonment claim.[97] The name of an event may still be remembered by the public for some time after the event no longer exists. For example, the Trademark Trial and Appeal Board found that the mark RAMBLER for automobiles had not been abandoned because a "considerable reservoir of goodwill in the mark Rambler" still inured to American Motors Corporation as a result of the number of such vehicles still on the road.[98]

Depending on the length of time an event was known under a given mark, an organizer may retain rights in the mark long after it is no longer being run. This means that the organizer may have a valuable asset to sell; it might also mean that entrepreneurs are not always safe if they try to resume or pick up old marks. Organizers should not hastily announce their abandonment of a mark if there is any hope for revival – for a new sponsorship or for a sale to a new organizer. In the absence of a public announcement of abandonment, it would take some time for the trademark to be lost. In the meantime, third parties might be found that would prefer to buy the mark rather than to incur the costs of litigation to prove abandonment.

95.
La Societe Anonyme des Parfums Le Galion v. Jean Patou, Inc., 495 F.2d 1265, 1272 (2d Cir. 1974).

96.
Le Cordon Bleu, S.A. v. BPC Pub. Ltd., 451 F. Supp. 63, 71 (S.D.N.Y. 1978).

97.
Id. at 71.

98.
American Motors Corp. v. Action-Age, Inc., 178 U.S.P.Q. 377, 378 (T.T.A.B. 1973).

STATUTORY MARKS

99.
36 U.S.C. §380.

The words "Olympic," "Olympiad" and "Citius Altius Fortius," the familiar five interlocking rings and other symbols of the International Olympic Committee and the United States Olympic Committee function like trademarks but are actually protected by federal statute.[99] (The statute is reproduced in Appendix F.) The United States Olympic Committee has the sole right by statute to authorize contributions and suppliers of goods or services to use the International and U.S. Olympic symbols in advertising.

100.
483 U.S. 522, 107 S.Ct. 2971, 97 L.Ed.2d 427 (1987).

This protection is arguably different than that given normal trademarks. The U.S. Supreme Court ruled in *San Francisco Arts & Athletics, Inc. v. United States Olympic Committee*[100] that the committee did not need to show confusion in order to be entitled to an injunction against a special event called the Gay Olympics. The U.S. Olympic Committee prevailed over the Gay Olympics's argument that it was exercising its First Amendment rights. The word "Olympics" may not be used if the ultimate purpose is for trade or to promote some other exhibition. However, the word may be used in some contexts. For instance, protestors were free to publish "Stop the Olympic Prison" posters during the Lake Placid Olympics.[101]

101.
See *Stop the Olympic Prison v. United States Olympic Committee*, 489 F. Supp. 1112 (S.D.N.Y. 1980).

Despite the super-trademark protection afforded the Olympics by statute, advertisers and promoters may find creative ways to cash in on the goodwill associated with Olympic events. (See discussion of ambush marketing at page 159.)

SAMPLE EXCLUSIVE TRADEMARK LICENSE AGREEMENT

Agreement made as of this (*number*) day of (*month, year*), between Trademark Owner ("Licensor"), and (*name of merchandise manufacturer*) ("Licensee").

WHEREAS, Licensee is engaged in the development, manufacture, distribution and sale of consumer products, including, without limitation, (*list products*), and wishes to use the Trademark in connection therewith; and

WHEREAS, Licensor wishes to provide Licensee the rights, as herein defined, to use the trademark (*Trademark*) (the "Trademark") in connection with Licensee's products as defined herein;

The introductory paragraphs express the intentions of the parties.

NOW, THEREFORE, it is agreed:

1. Definitions
The following terms shall have the meanings set forth in this Paragraph:

(a) "Trademark" means the trademark (*Trademark*) and (*Trademark plus design*) which Licensor has registered in the U.S. Patent and Trademark Office and which bear Registration Nos. (*number*) and (*number*), respectively.

The Trademarks should be defined to include both federal registrations and rights at common law. Trademarks need not be registered to be protected; confining the definition to registrations is too restrictive. This agreement could be used for service mark licenses as well.

(b) "Licensed Product" means the following products: (*list*)

The Licensed Products must be defined with particularity. If the category is "photography," can the photographs be poster size? Similarly, the category "clothing" is obviously too broad. The Licensor also must be aware of limitations imposed by prior licenses and should inquire as to preexisting licenses.

(c) "License Year" means each twelve (12) month period beginning on the date of execution of this Agreement.

License Year is a useful definition for accounting purposes.

(d) "License Quarter" means each three (3) month period beginning on the date of execution of this Agreement.

License Quarter also is a useful defined term pertinent to royalty payments.

(e) "Territory" means (*specify*).

The Territory should be listed by state or country.

(f) "Net Sales" means the gross invoice price of Licensed Product sold by Licensee, less only quantity discounts; but no deductions shall be made for cash, freight or advertising allowances or other discounts, returns or uncollectible accounts. No costs of manufacture, sale, distribution or exploitation of the Licensed Product shall be deducted. Net Sales shall include all Licensed Products distributed by Licensee including those Licensed Products not billed, such as free introductory offers and samples, in which case Net Sales shall be based upon the usual billing price for such Licensed Products as if sold.

The definition of Net Sales is one of the most critical terms in any trademark license agreement, since royalties are based on a percentage of Net Sales. Here the deductions are limited to quantity discounts. Cash, freight or advertising allowances are not deducted since these sales terms primarily benefit the Licensee, which has the use of the collected cash immediately. Other discounts, including returns and uncollectibles, are not deducted since the Licensee is in the best position to control the quality of the product (and hence customer return levels) and to assess the creditworthiness of its customers. The reason for using a gross price and for not deducting manufacturing costs is to avoid disputes over accounting methods. Free samples count here in Net Sales at the usual price, although a certain number of free samples could be agreed upon and not included.

2. License

Licensee is hereby granted the right and license to use the Trademarks during the term of this Agreement solely in connection with the promotion, sale, advertising and marketing of the Licensed Products in the Territory.

This is the basic grant and it is exclusive, although limited to the Territory.

3. Term

The term of this Agreement shall commence upon execution of this Agreement and shall continue thereafter until terminated in accordance with the termination provisions set forth in Paragraphs 4 or 7.

The term here is tied to the payment of annual minimum royalties. In the alternative, it could be a fixed number of years.

4. Royalties

(A) Licensee shall pay Licensor the following royalties in United States dollars on each item sold: (*number*) percent of the price at which that item is sold by Licensee (*i.e.*, the wholesale price), said royalties to be paid within thirty (30) days of the end of each License Quarter.

(B) In each License Year hereof, Licensee guarantees to Licensor that Licensor will earn royalties of ($_____). If at the end of a License Year, Licensee has not earned ($_____), this Agreement shall terminate sixty (60) days after said License Year unless Licensee has paid to Licensor the difference between ($_____) and royalties actually received by Licensor during said License Year.

(C) Licensee shall deliver to Licensor without charge (*number*) of each Licensed Product. These Licensed Products will be royalty-free.

The royalties here consist of an annual guarantee against which a percentage of Net Sales is paid. The annual guarantee serves to keep the Licensee motivated and gives the Licensor the assurance that it can get the rights back if the Licensee's performance is inadequate.

5. Periodic Statements; Records and Inspection

Within thirty (30) days following the end of each License Quarter, Licensee shall furnish Licensor complete statements, certified as accurate by an officer of Licensee, fully describing gross sales, number, description and actual selling price of all Licensed Products sold or distributed by Licensee during such quarter, identified by product number. In addition, within sixty (60) days following the end of each License Year, Licensee shall furnish Licensor a report certified as accurate by the then independent public accountants employed by Licensee fully describing the same information for such License Year. Licensee shall maintain, and shall make available to Licensor, or its representatives, for inspection, copying and audit, at reasonable times and during normal business hours, records and accounts of all information relevant to a determination of royalties due Licensor hereunder. Licensor shall have the right to take a physical inventory to verify any statements. Any such verification by Licensor shall be conducted at its own expense, and upon prior written notice to Licensee. Receipt or acceptance by Licensor of any statements furnished pursuant to this Agreement or any sums paid hereunder shall not preclude Licensor from questioning the correctness thereof at any time, and if any inconsistencies or mistakes are discovered in such statements or payments, they shall be immediately rectified and the appropriate payments made by Licensee. Licensee shall take all steps necessary to guarantee Licensor's access to any of the records, inventory or other material subject to inspection by Licensor under this paragraph which are in the possession of any third party.

The right to receive accounting statements helps the Licensor to enforce its contractual rights to royalties. The right to inspect is standard. A Licensee might seek to restrict inspections to one or two per year.

6. Approval Right

Licensor shall have a right of prior approval over all materials which bear or refer to the Trademark (including the Licensed Product, and all packaging, promotional materials and advertisements) that either are used or are authorized for use by Licensee. All such materials shall be submitted to Licensor for its approval prior to the production, use, execution or implementation thereof.

Trademark Licensor must maintain quality control over products sold under the marks.

7. Termination

This Agreement may be terminated by the parties as follows:

(a) By Licensor in the event:

(i) Licensee fails to pay any of the sums provided for in Paragraph 4;

(ii) Licensee breaches or defaults in the performance of any other material provision hereof, including, but not limited to, Licensee's obligations under Paragraph 6;

(iii) Licensee makes any assignment of assets or business for the benefit of creditors, a trustee or receiver is appointed to conduct Licensee's business or affairs, Licensee is adjudicated to be voluntarily or involuntarily bankrupt or Licensee admits in writing its inability to pay its debts generally as they become due.

Termination by Licensor shall be effective: under subsection (i), upon written notice to Licensee; under subsection (ii), upon thirty (30) days' written notice to Licensee following the breach or default in question, provided that if Licensee cures the default under subsections (i) or (ii) within thirty (30) days, this Agreement shall continue in effect; and under (iii), immediately upon the event taking place.

This paragraph gives the Licensee a chance to cure any breach of the agreement, but a shorter cure period is appropriate where the Trademark is concerned. On whether insolvency or bankruptcy can be effective as an event of termination, see Chapter 1.

(b) By Licensee:

(i) upon the breach or default by Licensor in the performance of any material provision hereof. Termination by Licensee shall be effective upon thirty (30) days' written notice to Licensor following the breach or default in question, provided that if Licensor cures the same within such thirty (30) day period, this Agreement shall continue in effect.

This gives the Licensee the right to terminate if the Licensor defaults in any manner. Usually, this would come into play if the Trademark was held to infringe a third party's mark or if the Licensor breached the exclusivity provisions.

8. Rights Upon Termination or Expiration of Agreement

Upon the termination of this Agreement for any reason, the License granted in Paragraph 2 shall cease; provided that Licensee, for a period not to exceed three months thereafter and subject to a monthly accounting and payment of applicable royalties, may continue to use the Trademark solely in connection with the sale and distribution of finished goods produced, and goods in process prior to such termination or expiration, provided Licensee shall not sell or dispose of any Licensed Products if termination is based on failure of Licensee to affix any notice to Licensed Products, cartons, containers, packing, advertising, promotional or display material or because Licensee departed from material approved by Licensor as provided in Paragraph 6. Notwithstanding any other provision of this Agreement, all sums accrued or owed to Licensor through the date of termination or expiration (which for the purpose of this Paragraph shall include royalties on all sales and distribution of the Licensed Product through such date) shall be due and payable within thirty (30) days. Following such termination or expiration Licensee shall:

(a) deliver to Licensor a statement detailing the nature, location and quantities of finished goods and goods in process (Licensor having the right, at its own expense, to conduct a physical inventory thereof); and

(b) execute, acknowledge and deliver to Licensor such waivers, assignments or other documents as Licensor deems necessary or desirable to establish the relinquishment by Licensee of any continuing right to the use of the Trademark.

Licensee acknowledges that its failure (except as otherwise provided herein) to cease the manufacture, sale or distribution or any Licensed Product on the termination or expiration hereof will result in irreparable damage to the Licensor not wholly compensable in damages and Licensee agrees that, in the event of such failure, Licensor shall be entitled to whatever relief the law deems fair and equitable, including without limitation injunctive relief.

Unless termination occurs due to failure to observe trademark protection formalities, this paragraph allows the sell-off of inventory and goods in process for a period of time after termination. It also requires that a statement of inventory be provided to the Licensor for control purposes. The consent-to-injunction paragraph does not provide additional remedies as much as it removes the Licensee's defenses if the Licensor seeks an injunction.

9. Manufacture and Distribution
(a) During the Term of this license, Licensee will diligently and continuously manufacture (or cause to be manufactured) and sell the Licensed Product and will make and maintain adequate arrangements for the distribution of the Licensed Product in all available markets throughout the world.

The duty to diligently market the Licensed Products is difficult to enforce; the annual minimum guarantee gives it teeth (see Paragraph 4).

(b) Licensee shall not use the Licensed Product for combination sales, as self-liquidating or free giveaways or for any similar method of merchandising without the prior written consent of Licensor. Licensee will not permit the use of the Licensed Product as a premium except with the prior written consent of Licensor.

The method of sale may be important to the Licensor. Consignment sales would create accounting headaches for the Licensor. Some Licensors do not approve of low-end methods of distribution and consider use as a self-liquidator not desirable.

(c) All Licensed Products shall be of high standard and of such style, appearance and quality so as to reflect well upon Licensee and Licensor.

Quality control is critical.

(d) The license herein granted is conditioned upon Licensee's full and complete compliance with the notice and other provisions of the copyright law of the United States. Licensee agrees to cause to appear on or within each Licensed Product, on each carton, container and/or packing or wrapping material bearing the Trademark, and on or within all advertising, promotional or display material bearing the Trademark, appropriate notice of any applicable trademark, service mark or copyright and any other appropriate notice desired by Licensor, and Licensee shall do everything reasonably necessary to maintain such trademark, service mark, copyright or other right. Each and every tag, label, imprint or other device containing any such notice and all advertising, promotional or display material bearing the Trademark shall be submitted by Licensee to Licensor for its written approval prior to use by the Licensee. Licensor reserves the right to make changes in its notice requirements at any time by sufficient written notice to Licensee of not less than forty-five (45) days.

If as a result of Licensee's activities hereunder, Licensee acquires any copyrights, trademarks, equities, titles or any rights in or with respect to the Licensed Products, or any of them, Licensee shall, in the event of termination of this Agreement, assign and transfer all such rights to Licensor without additional consideration.

Copyright and trademark notices should comply with applicable laws and regulations. The Licensee cannot acquire any separate interest in the Trademarks by virtue of its use and this paragraph so states.

Licensee shall not undertake any billboard, radio, television or motion picture advertising in connection with the Licensed Product without the prior written consent of Licensor.

All advertising for the Products must also be approved by the Licensor, again in order to protect the Trademark.

A token shipment interstate, with prior approval of all artwork and labeling by Licensor, must occur within the first two months of the first license year hereof for purposes of forming a basis for trademark registration of the Trademark for the Licensed Product hereunder. Licensee shall supply the following information to Licensor as soon as such information is available.

When and to whom Licensee's first sale of goods under this Agreement is made;

When such goods are first shipped in interstate commerce;

How they were sent, i.e., truck, rail, air.

The token shipment was to establish trademark rights in the Trademark for the new product. The information was used to file a federal application for the class of goods pertaining to the Product. As of November, 1989, token shipments no longer are necessary in order to file a federal application for trademark registration.

10. Exclusivity
Licensor shall not license or permit the use of the Trademark in connection with any products competitive to the Licensed Products hereunder.

The scope of exclusivity is important and should be defined with some specificity.

11. Acknowledgements of Ownership; Limitations on Use
This Agreement shall not create on Licensee's behalf any right, title or interest in or to the Trademark, other than the exclusive license and right to use the same in the manner provided in Paragraph 2. Licensee acknowledges that its right to use, or to authorize others to use, such Trademark shall be limited by the terms of this Agreement, including, but not limited to, the scope of the license granted in Paragraph 2, and Licensor's rights of approval provided for in Paragraph 6.

Licensee here recognizes Licensor's ownership of the Trademarks, which eliminates some of Licensee's defenses in the event of infringement.

12. Indemnification; Insurance

Licensee hereby indemnifies and agrees to hold Licensor harmless against all claims, liabilities, damages and expenses (including expenses of litigation and attorneys' fees) asserted against or incurred by it arising in whole or in part out of Licensee's activities hereunder, including, but not limited to, (a) any patent, process, method or device used or licensed by Licensee, (b) alleged defects in the Licensed Product, (c) Licensee's agreements, policies or activities relating to the manufacture, sale, distribution or advertising of the Licensed Product, (d) alleged violations of any applicable law or regulation relating to manufacture, sale or distribution of Licensed Product and/or (e) alleged acts of piracy, plagiarism, infringement, libel or invasion of privacy. Licensee shall notify Licensor in writing of any infringements or imitations of the Trademark similar to those hereunder. Licensee shall have the right to bring an action at its own expense on account of any such infringements or imitations. Licensor, if it so desires, may commence or prosecute any claims or suits in its own name or in the name of Licensee or join Licensee as a party thereto. The proceeds of any such action by Licensor or Licensee in excess of documented expenses shall be deemed to be Net Sales under this Agreement. Licensee shall obtain and maintain, at its own expense, during the Term of this Agreement and for a period of six (6) years following its termination or expiration, a standard Comprehensive General Liability Insurance Policy written by a United States Company in the face amount of two million dollars ($2,000,000) which specifically covers Licensee's contractual obligations under this Agreement, provides standard products' liability, and lists Licensor as a named insured. Such policy shall be in a form reasonably acceptable to counsel for Licensor, and shall require the insurer to give Licensor at least thirty (30) days prior written notice of any modification or cancellation. Licensee shall provide Licensor a copy of such policy (or such other evidence of coverage as may be acceptable to Licensor's counsel) within forty-five (45) days following the execution of this Agreement.

On the liability of trademark licensors, see Chapter 5.

13. Representations and Warranties

Licensee represents and warrants that:

(a) It has the unencumbered right and authority to execute and perform this Agreement;

Boilerplate.

(b) All agreements entered into by Licensee with third parties, and all policies administered by Licensee regarding the manufacture, sale, distribution, promotion or advertising of the Licensed Product, in all respects shall conform to and shall be consistent with the rights of Licensor hereunder, and

Boilerplate.

Licensee shall include the following clause in all agreements with third parties which relate to the Licensed Product or to the use of the Name and Character under which obligations or liability in excess of $25,000 may be incurred:

[Third party] will look solely to [Licensee] for performance of, and for payment and/or satisfaction of any obligation or claim arising out of, or in connection with, this Agreement and hereby covenants that it will not assert any claim against, nor look to or for satisfaction of, any such obligation or claim.

This paragraph seeks to prevent the Licensee from causing a third party to rely on Licensor's credit. The dollar amount, of course, depends on the nature of the business and the Licensee's net worth.

(c) All applicable laws and regulations relating or pertaining to the manufacture, sale, distribution, promotion, advertising and use of the Licensed Product shall be complied with in all respects.

Boilerplate.

Licensor represents and warrants that:

(a) It is the owner of U.S. Trademark Registration Nos. (*number*) (*Trademark*) and (*number*) (*Trademark*), but Licensor does not otherwise warrant that said registrations will survive any challenge or that third parties may not validly claim superior rights.

Boilerplate; the proviso could be negotiated out, since one would expect an established trademark owner to know of any problems.

(b) It has the unencumbered right and authority to execute and perform this Agreement.

Boilerplate.

14. Correspondence

All payments, correspondence and any notice required or permitted to be given under this Agreement by either of the parties hereto shall be given by registered or certified mail, postage prepaid, addressed to the party to be notified at the following address:

If to Licensee to: _____

_____

If to Licensor to: _____

_____

or to such other address as may be furnished in writing to the notifying party.

Boilerplate.

15. Remedies

Licensor and Licensee acknowledge that either party's breach of any of the terms, conditions, warranties or representations in this Agreement may result in immediate damage to the other, and that in such event the aggrieved party may seek whatever remedies may be available to it in a court of law or equity.

Boilerplate.

16. Relationship of Parties

Nothing herein shall be deemed to constitute a partnership or a joint venture between the parties hereto, nor shall anything herein be deemed to constitute either party hereto the agent of the other.

Boilerplate.

17. Assignment

Neither this Agreement nor any rights hereunder shall be assignable by Licensee, in whole or in part, without the prior written consent of the Licensor. Licensee shall not sublicense nor franchise any of the rights granted Licensee hereunder without Licensor's prior written consent.

The prohibition on assignment helps to maintain and enforce the quality control provisions.

18. Miscellaneous

This Agreement:

(a) Contains the entire agreement of the parties hereto and no provisions of this Agreement may be changed or modified except in writing, signed by the parties hereto. There are no representations, warranties, promises or undertakings other than those contained in this Agreement. The failure or delay of either party in enforcing any of its rights under this Agreement shall not be deemed a continuing waiver or a modification thereof, and either party may, within the time provided by applicable law, commence appropriate legal proceedings to enforce any or all such rights.

Boilerplate.

(b) May be executed in any number of counterparts, each of which shall be deemed to be an original and all of which together shall constitute one and the same instrument.

Boilerplate.

(c) Shall be construed and governed in accordance with the laws of the State of (*name*).

Boilerplate.

IN WITNESS WHEREOF, the parties have caused this Agreement to be executed as of the day and year first above written.

Licensor

By: _____

Licensee

By: _____

COPYRIGHTS

Under the U.S. Constitution, Congress has the power to pass statutes that grant authors and inventors the exclusive rights to their writings and inventions in order to promote the public good. Congress has developed schemes of copyright and patent protection in pursuit of that constitutional goal.

102.
17 U.S.C. §101 *et seq.*

Copyright is a federal system that gives a bundle of rights to authors of works fixed in a tangible medium of expression.[102] Protection extends to literary works, musical works, dramatic works, compilations, computer programs, choreographic works, graphic works, sculptural works, audio-visual works – in short, any creative work that is fixed in a manner that can be perceived by the human eye or through machines. However, copyright does not extend to ideas, methods, processes, formulae or mere facts.

The rights of copyright are (1) the right to reproduce the work, (2) the right to perform the work publicly, (3) the right to display the work publicly, (4) the right to create new works based on or derived from the work and (5) the right to initially distribute the work. These rights are separable; they can be licensed or transferred individually.

103.
17 U.S.C. §101.

The copyright issues that sponsors and event organizers most frequently encounter are related to ownership of television and radio rights, video recording rights (see Chapter 4), public performance of music, event graphics (logos) and publicity releases. The graphic logo may be subject to copyright protection in addition to trademark protection and is valuable as a licensable property. The copyrights in written publicity releases and photographs may have less value. However, the copyright in audio-visual coverage of an event may be extremely valuable; protecting it may be an important way of protecting the proprietary value of an entire event (see Chapter 3).

104.
17 U.S.C. §101 provides in part that a "work made for hire" is:
(1) a work prepared by an employee within the scope of his or her employment; or
(2) a work specially ordered or commissioned for use as a contribution to a collective work, as a part of a motion picture or other audio-visual work, as a translation, as a supplementary work, as a compilation, as an instructional text, as a test, as answer material for a test, or as an atlas, if the parties expressly agree in a written instrument signed by them that the work shall be considered a work made for hire.

Ownership and Work for Hire

While event organizers and sponsors generally own the copyrights in work created by their permanent employees, they need to protect themselves with written contracts when using copyrightable material from outside suppliers. These include photographers, film producers, graphic designers, and premium suppliers.

Copyright in a work exists from the moment of creation. Ordinarily, the author of a work is the copyright owner. However, work that an employee creates in the course of his or her employment belongs to the employer as "work for hire."[103] In addition, the work of an independent contractor or someone specifically commissioned to create a work is "work for hire" if the contractor has agreed in writing that it is work for hire and if the work falls into one of nine special categories, including contributions to audio-visual works.[104]

Until the U.S. Supreme Court ruled in a case in mid-1989, there was some disagreement among the courts concerning work for hire performed by independent contractors. The confusion stemmed from the fact that the copyright law does not define "employee" or "scope of employment." Some courts held that if an independent contractor met common-law tests for an employee, the work could be work for hire regardless of whether it fell into one of the nine categories specified in subsection (2) or whether there was a written agreement. Congress may have left "employee" undefined with the intent that the courts would use the same agency principles relating to the master-servant doctrine that were used under the 1909 Copyright Act (the approach finally taken by the Supreme Court).[105] Courts have applied such principles to find that some works, even though commissioned, do not meet the tests of subsection (2), and yet are work for hire under subsection (1). (See below for further discussion of independent contractors.)

Permanent Employees. In the absence of a writing to the contrary, a work is work for hire if it was prepared by a permanent employee acting within the scope of his or her employment.

For instance, in *Brunswick Beacon, Inc.* v. *Schock-Hopchas Publishing Co.*,[106] the plaintiff filed a copyright infringement action against another newspaper that had copied three of its advertisements. Plaintiff's permanent employees had designed and created the layout for the advertisers' products. The court held that the copyrights vested in the plaintiff (the employer), and that the defendant had infringed the plaintiff's rights even though the advertisers had given permission to use the advertisements.

Similarly, in *Marshall* v. *Miles Laboratories, Inc., et al.*,[107] one of the defendant's former employees sought a court order affirming his copyright interest in an article he had written with another Miles employee. The court granted the defendants' motion for summary judgment. Plaintiff Marshall was an employee while the work was being prepared, and the research he used to complete the article had been done by another Miles employee, with whom he had frequently discussed the article. "The mere fact that preparations were done outside [the] employee's office or normal working hours [did] not, [however], remove such preparations from the scope of employment."[108] Rather, the court concluded that the employer-employee relationship "was the direct cause of the preparation of the article"[109] and that the copyright vested in the employer. Normally, then, sponsors and organizers can expect to own the copyrights in works prepared by their permanent employees.

Volunteers. The work of unpaid volunteers can also be work for hire. At least one court has found the existence of an employer-employee relationship where the "employee" volunteered his services and the "employer" never directly exercised its right to control the volunteer's work.

105.
See H.R. Res. No. 1733, 94th Cong., 2d Sess. 121, reprinted in 1976 U.S. Code Cong. & Admin. News 5736; *see also* 1 M. Nimmer, *Nimmer on Copyright* 5.03[B], 5-12.1 to 5-13 (1986).

106.
810 F.2d 410 (4th Cir. 1987).

107.
647 F. Supp. 1326 (N.D. Ind. 1986).

108.
Id. at 1330.

109.
Id. at 1331.

110.
566 F. Supp. 137
(S.D.N.Y. 1983).

In *Town of Clarkstown* v. *Reeder, et al.*,[110] the town had established a Youth Court to enable the town's youth to participate in a quasi-judicial forum and act as judges and lawyers. The lawsuit arose after a Youth Court executive board member (a volunteer) claimed that he owned the copyright in the group's *Manual*, which he had helped to draft. Relying on the work-for-hire doctrine, the court held that the town owned the copyright. At all times, the town maintained direct control over the volunteer's "expression of his own thoughts" and had the "implicit" power to control and supervise his work, which was done in conjunction with his activities as an executive board member of the Youth Court.[111] In that capacity, although he did most of the writing, the Manual was a "compilation of ideas, suggestions and outlines extracted from [several individuals]."[112] Thus, the town, as the employer, was the author for copyright purposes.

111.
Id. at 141, 142.

112.
Id. at 142.

Sponsors and organizers should not rely on the work-for-hire doctrine when dealing with volunteers. By far the safer course is to ask them to agree in writing that the copyrights in their contributions belong to the organizer.

Independent Contractors. Some courts have also found the existence of an employer-employee relationship where the party who performs the work is ordinarily viewed as an independent contractor. Courts have found the contractor to be an "employee" where the "employer" has the right to direct and supervise the manner in which the worker performs the work. Thus, for purposes of the copyright law, a contractor may become a temporary or transitory employee. For instance, in *Aldon Accessories, Ltd.* v. *Spiegel, Inc.*,[113] the plaintiff successfully sued a defendant for copyright infringement of its unicorn statuettes. The plaintiff had hired artists in Japan and Taiwan to develop the statuettes. The defendant manufactured its own similar statuettes. The defendant argued that, since the artists were not the plaintiff's regular employees, subsection (1) of the work-for-hire doctrine did not apply. The court concluded that one of the plaintiff's principals had actively supervised and directed the artists as they created the statuettes. Thus, although the principal did not use sketching pens and sculpturing tools, he worked with the artists at critical stages of the process by *telling* them what to do. Therefore, the statuettes were work for hire.

113.
738 F.2d 548 (2d Cir. 1984), *cert. denied*, 469 U.S. 982 (1984).

114.
621 F. Supp. 916
(E.D.N.Y. 1985).

Similarly, in *Iris Arc* v. *S.S. Sarna, Inc.*,[114] the plaintiff sought to preliminarily enjoin defendants from manufacturing and marketing crystal sculptures that allegedly infringed the plaintiff's copyrights in certain crystal figurines. The defendants argued that, since the designer who created the works was an independent contractor, he could not fall within the definition of subsection (1). Relying on the *Aldon* case, the court concluded that the plaintiff-employer, not the contractor, owned the copyrights and issued an injunction. The court said that the designer was an employee – he had his own office on the plaintiff's premises and had worked closely with the plaintiff's employees through all stages of the creative process, from initial conception until completion.

Finally, in *Peregrine* v. *Lauren Corporation*,[115] the plaintiff, a professional photographer, sued an advertising agency after it refused to pay for his services because it thought the fee was excessive. The plaintiff sought and received a copyright registration in order to encourage the agency to pay. The agency had hired the plaintiff to take pictures for an advertising brochure. The court found that while the plaintiff may have made suggestions at the shooting sessions, the defendant could have vetoed the plaintiff's ideas. The court said the parties' "mutual intent" was that title would vest in the defendant.

115.
601 F. Supp. 828 (D. Colo. 1985).

Two recent cases have construed work for hire by independent contractors more literally. In both instances the courts concluded that, in order to be work for hire, the work of an independent contractor *must* be one of the nine types specified in subsection (2) *and* there must be a written agreement.

In *Easter Seal Society* v. *Playboy Enterprises*,[116] the court held that a public television station owned the videotape of a Mardi Gras-style parade that it made at the request of the Easter Seal Society. The Society used a portion of the tape in its telethon. The public television station used other parts of the videotape as "file" tape or "stock footage." It also licensed a Canadian film producer to use some of the footage in a movie. Subsequently, the movie, *Candy, The Stripper*, was seen on cable TV by New Orleans residents who recognized themselves and demanded that the Easter Seal Society stop the producer from further distributing the film. The Easter Seal Society sued the television station for copyright infringement, claiming the work was work for hire for the Society. The Court of Appeals disagreed. It found that the station was an independent contractor and that there was no writing acknowledging that the station intended its work to be work for hire.

116.
815 F.2d 323 (5th Cir. 1987).

A literal reading of the work-for-hire definition was similarly applied in *Community for Creative Non-Violence* v. *Reid*.[117] A sculpture commissioned by the community activist group was found not to be work for hire because sculpture is not one of the nine categories specified in subsection (2) and there was no written agreement. The U.S. Supreme Court applied agency principles to determine that the sculptor was not an employee of CCNV and affirmed the lower court's holding. It said the following factors should be considered: the hiring party's right to control the manner and means by which the product is accomplished; the skill required, the source of the instrumentalities and the tools; the location of the work; the duration

117.
846 F.2d 1485 (D.C. Cir. 1988), aff'd _____ U.S. _____ (1989)

of the relationship between the parties; whether additional projects can be assigned; the discretion of the hired party over when and how long to work; the method of payment; the hired party's role in hiring and paying assistants; whether the work is part of the regular business of the hiring party; whether the hiring party is a business; the provision of employee benefits and the tax treatment of the hired party.[118]

118.
Community for Creative Non-Violence v. Reid, ____ U.S. ____ (1989).

These cases suggest that organizers and sponsors should not rely on proof of control and supervision to establish ownership of copyrights. They should require written agreements from photographers, film producers, graphic designers, premium and souvenir merchandisers and all other creative suppliers. Conversely, independent contractors who work for event organizers or sponsors cannot safely rely on their status as a guarantee of copyright ownership unless this is specified in writing.

119.
523 F. Supp. 21 (S.D.N.Y. 1981).

Co-authorship. As an alternative, a court may find that a temporary worker co-authored a work with the employer. For instance, in *Mr. B. Textiles Inc.* v. *Wood Crest Fabrics, Inc.,*[119] the plaintiff sought a preliminary injunction to prevent the defendant from selling certain fabrics that allegedly infringed its copyrighted fabric. The plaintiff had hired a designer on a temporary basis to help it create a fabric design. Throughout the project, the designer had worked extensively with the plaintiff's permanent employee. In resolving the preliminary issue of whether the plaintiff owned the copyright, the court held that the plaintiff's interest, as a co-author, was sufficient to maintain the lawsuit. Since the plaintiff's permanent employee had worked closely with the designer and both had made significant contributions, each had helped to create the work. Thus, due to the employer-employee relationship, the plaintiff-employer was a co-author with the designer. Joint owners of copyright each have the right to exploit the work, provided the joint owner pays a share of profits to the other owner.

120.
846 F.2d 1485 (D.C. Cir. 1988).

The court in *Community for Creative Non-Violence* v. *Reid*[120] suggested that joint authorship might vest partial copyright ownership in a buyer of creative works from an independent contractor if the work-for-hire doctrine does not apply. There, the plaintiff had conceived the idea for a sculpture and designed and made its base. The sculptor contributed sculpted human figures. The court did not decide the issue, however, since it needed more facts than those proved at trial.

Fixation, Notice and Registration

Since copyright in a work exists from the moment of creation, one may place a notice of copyright on it as soon as the work is fixed. No formal process is required to secure copyright protection. Once a work is publicly distributed, it should bear the statutorily specified notice of copyright: ["©" or "copyright" or "copr."] [year of first publication] [name of copyright claimant].[121] The notice should appear on copies of a work in a manner likely to give reasonable notice to others of the claim of copyright.[122] The U.S. Copyright Office has published guides for the location of the notice for different types of works.[123] For instance, the required notice on audio-visual works should be (1) with or near the title, (2) with the cast and other credits or (3) at or immediately following the beginning or the end of a work, so that it appears whenever the work is shown in its entirety.[124] On graphic works such as T-shirts, the notice may be sewn or otherwise attached durably by means of a label on the front or back of the shirt; it may also be affixed directly, for instance, by incorporating it in the graphic.[125] The Copyright Office's suggestions for placement of notice are reproduced in Appendix C.

Registration of copyright is not a prerequisite to protection, but it is a prerequisite to bringing a lawsuit.[126] Registering a work is a relatively simple process. The applicant must submit two copies of the work as published (one if unpublished), a nominal filing fee and a short application. The forms are available from the U.S. Copyright Office, and two samples are reproduced in Appendix D. A portion of the Copyright Revision Act of 1976 is reproduced in Appendix E.

Infringement

In order to prove infringement of copyright, the copyright owner must show access to the copyrighted work and substantial similarity. For instance, the court in *Sid & Marty Krofft Television Productions, Inc.* v. *McDonald's Corporation*[127] found that cartoon characters created by an advertising agency for a client infringed the rights of a production company in its H. R. Pufnstuf characters. The advertising agency had tried to obtain a license to use the characters but negotiations failed. It then created its own McDonaldland characters, which the court found to be substantially similar to the Pufnstuf ones. Clearly, the agency had access to the preexisting work.

Proving access is important because, unlike the patent laws, the copyright law does not protect against independent creation of even an identical work. Instead, it seeks to prevent *copying*. Theoretically, two people could write exactly the same book or song, but unless one author *copied* the other's work, there would be no infringement. Showing access is essential to showing copying, but access can also be inferred from similarities that are very substantial; the presumption is that copying must have taken place, consciously or unconsciously.

Similarities that derive from the nature of the work are not sufficient to establish substantial similarity or an inference of copying. For example, in *Alexander* v. *Haley*,[128] the novel *Roots* was held not to infringe a book called *Jubilee* even though

121.
17 U.S.C. §401(b).

122.
17 U.S.C. §401(c).

123.
See 37 C.F.R. §201.20(c).

124.
37 C.F.R. §201.20(h).

125.
37 C.F.R. §201.20(i)(2).

126.
17 U.S.C. §411.

127.
562 F.2d §1157 (9th Cir. 1977).

128.
460 F. Supp. 40 (S.D.N.Y. 1978).

both were epics about slaves. Similarities arising out of historical fact, folk customs and similar themes and settings do not show copying; such similarities are to be expected because of the nature of the subject matter. On the other hand, an element can be so unique that copying might be found if there were some possibility of access. For instance, George Harrison was found to have subconsciously infringed the popular 1962 song "He's So Fine" with his 1970 hit "My Sweet Lord" in *Bright Tunes Music* v. *Harrisongs Music, Ltd.*,[129] largely because of a unique trill and proof of the popularity of the earlier song. Such cases are rare but worth noting.

129.
420 F. Supp. §177 (S.D.N.Y. 1976).

One of the most viable defenses to a claim of infringement is the doctrine of fair use. The copyright statute provides:

Sec. 107. Limitations on Exclusive Rights: Fair Use

Notwithstanding the provisions of section 106, the fair use of a copyrighted work, including such use by reproduction in copies or phonorecords or by any other means specified by that section, for purposes such as criticism, comment, news reporting, teaching (including multiple copies for classroom use), scholarship, or research, is not an infringement of copyright. In determining whether the use made of work in any particular case is a fair use the factors to be considered shall include:

(1) the purpose and character of the use, including whether such use is of a commercial nature or is for nonprofit educational purposes;

(2) the nature of the copyrighted work;

(3) the amount and substantiality of the portion used in relation to the copyrighted work as a whole; and

(4) the effect of the use upon the potential market for or value of the copyrighted work.

In the commercial context, however, the scope of fair use is somewhat narrow. The most valuable copyrightable properties usually are television and graphics rights, and with the exception of the news privilege (see Chapter 3) fair use is unlikely to come into play.

AMBUSH MARKETING

"Ambush marketing" refers to certain activities by companies that, though not official sponsors, nonetheless attempt to capitalize on the popularity of certain events. The *Wall Street Journal* described the practice during the 1988 winter Olympics: "[C]ompanies 'ambush' the official sponsors by associating themselves with the Games indirectly; they buy commercial time during Olympic broadcasts or support individual teams or athletes – all at a fraction of the official sponsors' costs."[130] Another form of ambush is to give away tickets to a popular event, such as the World Series, in a sweepstakes or other contest. Such activities, cleverly conducted, are generally legal. Nonetheless, many organizations, particularly in professional sports, are quite litigious. Although case precedent to date suggests that a preliminary injunction in most ambush cases will be denied, the cost of defending such actions should be carefully weighed against the expected benefits and the costs of official sponsorship.

Why is ambush marketing legal? *When* is it legal? First, it must be remembered that commercial speech is protected by the First Amendment. A trademark owner may not prevent any and all uses of its mark; there are certain limitations on and exemptions from the scope of trademark protection. For instance, one may use another's trademark to state truthfully that one services goods bearing the trademark of another, e.g., "foreign car service for Volkswagens and Porsches."[131] In addition, one may use another's trademark in comparative advertising campaigns. Also, as previously discussed, one may use another's trademark if the mark is purely descriptive, e.g., "It's a joy."[132] It is often a short step from these clearly protected uses to an aggressive ambush campaign that is closer to the legal limits.

In the most obvious ambush described by *The Wall Street Journal*, the competitor has validly licensed trademarks that are closely associated with the main event. Any ads referring to the main event are literally true, and any "noise" the ads create in terms of consumer confusion is difficult to measure and even more difficult to object to, given that the competitor is also supporting a good cause. For instance, in 1988 SEAGRAM'S COOLERS sent more than 500 family members of U.S. athletes to the summer Olympic Games in Seoul. The program was not officially sponsored by the United States Olympic Committee. Instead, Seagram arranged it through agreements with 23 National Governing Bodies of medal events.

Most of the time, the ambush marketer has not done anything affirmative that would give rise to a cause of action. An example might be a manufacturer's advertising that it will donate $1.00 to the U.S. Olympic Committee for every three

130.
"Ambush Marketing Is Becoming Popular Event at Olympic Games," *The Wall Street Journal*, February 8, 1988, p. 25, col. 4.

131.
See Volkswagenwerk Aktiengesellschaft v. Church, 411 F.2d 350 (9th Cir. 1969).

132.
See Jean Patou, Inc. v. Jacqueline Cochran, Inc., 312 F.2d 125 (2d Cir. 1963).

products purchased. As long as official symbols are not used, one may argue that the manufacturer is free to make the gift and to advertise that it will. Another example is the creation of a graphic that relates to a popular event but carefully avoids any use of a protected mark. For instance, in 1988 a T-shirt manufacturer designed a "Body & Seoul" graphic in honor of "The Summer Games."

A legal cause of action might be shown for trademark infringement, however, if an ambush is so close as to cause confusion, mistake or deception[133] or to falsely describe or represent goods or services.[134] Unfair competition or misappropriation might also be available common law remedies if the goodwill of the event has been usurped.

Some companies have succeeded in using others' trademarks on their own products because no confusion, mistake or deception was found. For instance, in *University of Pittsburgh* v. *Champion Products, Inc.*,[135] the court refused to enjoin the sale of T-shirts, sweatshirts and other athletic soft goods bearing the marks "Pitt" and the panther mascot, both registered trademarks of the University of Pittsburgh. The court held that, while consumers purchased these products to associate themselves with the university and its highly successful sports program, there was no evidence that Champion intended or created any confusion about its association or affiliation with the university. Champion had maintained high quality and distinguished its own name throughout its marketing of these products.

With respect to sports team and event insignia, however, most courts have found otherwise. For instance, in *National Football League Properties, Inc.* v. *Wichita Falls Sportswear, Inc.*,[136] the court said the sale of replica NFL jerseys was likely to confuse purchasers as to their sponsorship by NFL and member clubs. That view is the predominant one.

Similarly, a company may benefit from the goodwill associated with an event, yet not incur liability as long as it avoids a likelihood of confusion. Whether such confusion exists, though, is often difficult to determine. Consider a hypothetical situation in which a company offers tickets to the World Series in an "Octoberfest" festival. The company does not flash a "World Series" headline or name its promotion "World Series Octoberfest." But it does prominently describe the prize, using the words "World Series." How else is it to announce its prize truthfully? Surely, the fact that the prize is attractive is beneficial to the company. But has the company deprived the official sponsor or the organizer of the event of its goodwill?

133.
15 U.S.C. §1114 (1982).

134.
15 U.S.C. §1125 (1982).

135.
566 F. Supp. 711 (W.D. Pa. 1983).

136.
532 F. Supp. 651 (W.D. Wash. 1982).

To say that the organizer could charge the company for the right to offer validly purchased World Series tickets as prizes is circular and begs the question. Such an argument also ignores the fact that the First Amendment protects commercial speech, at least to the extent that such speech is not false, deceptive, disparaging or misleading.[137]

Terms like "World Series," "Super Bowl" and "Indy 500" are very close to being the generics for the events – the public recognizes them as the names of one-of-a-kind events. To use those words to describe a prize does not *necessarily* lead to consumer confusion as to source, sponsorship or affiliation – such confusion being the touchstone of trademark infringement.

One way that some advertisers have attempted to dispel the possibility of confusion is to use a disclaimer, such as "Not Endorsed or Sponsored by _____." In fact, for many years the courts favored the use of disclaimers in trademark infringement cases. For example, in *National Football League* v. *Governor of Delaware*,[138] the court required the state to place a disclaimer on tickets, advertising and other materials for its football lottery game, indicating that the contest was not affiliated with the NFL. Participants in the game chose the weekly winners of professional football games, and the back of each ticket bore the legend "The 'Scoreboard Lottery' is sponsored solely by the Delaware State Lottery."

A disclaimer was deemed necessary to eliminate confusion as to sponsorship, even though the state had not affirmatively suggested sponsorship or approval by the NFL. The court recognized that the lottery was intended to generate profit from the popularity of NFL football but said this case was "difficult to distinguish from the multitude of charter bus companies who generate profit from servicing those of plaintiff's fans who want to go to the stadium or, indeed, the sidewalk popcorn salesman who services the crowd as it surges toward the gate."[139]

The court said that the lottery did not utilize the NFL service marks "for the purpose of identifying, as opposed to describing, the service which it offers."[140] Thus, Delaware could truthfully describe its football lottery to the public, provided that any advertising did not create the impression among the relevant segment of the public that a connection with the NFL existed. If such an impression were created, even without any affirmative action by the defendant, then the defendant would have "a duty to take affirmative steps to avoid a mistaken impression which is likely to arise from a truthful description of the service even though it does not literally suggest a connection."[141] Thus, the disclaimer was required.

137.
Friedman v. *Rogers*, 440 U.S. 1, *reh'g denied*, 441 U.S. 917 (1979) [State ban on optometrists advertising and using trade names rather than personal name of optometrist upheld because of possibility of deception. Recognized that trademarks and trade names are commercial speech]; *Bolger* v. *Young's Drug Products Corp.*, 463 U.S. 60 (1983) [Advertising pamphlets of contraceptives manufacturer are entitled to First Amendment protection and could not be banned]; *Lamar Outdoor Advertising, Inc.* v. *Mississippi State Tax Commission*, 701 F.2d 314 (5th Cir. 1983), *cert. denied sub nom. Dunagin* v. *Oxford*, 467 U.S. 1259 (1984) [Liquor advertising is commercial speech entitled to First Amendment protection].

138.
435 F. Supp. 1372 (D.Del. 1977).

139.
Id. at 1378.

140.
Id. at 1380.

141.
Id.

142.
832 F.2d 1311 (2d Cir.
1987).

143.
832 F.2d 1317 (2d Cir.
1987).

144.
756 F.2d 1535 (11th Cir.
1986).

145.
510 F.2d 1004 (5th Cir.),
cert. denied, 423 U.S.
868 (1975).

146.
832 F.2d 1325 (2d Cir.
1987).

Under the logic of this case, many ambush marketers are in a strong position. However, it should be noted that in three recent Second Circuit trademark infringement cases, disclaimers appear to have lost some of their previous appeal as a cure for confusion. For instance, in *Home Box Office, Inc.* v. *Showtime/ The Movie Channel, Inc.*,[142] the defendant Showtime used a headline "SHOWTIME & HBO. It's Not Either/Or Anymore." The District Court had approved the use of disclaimers stating that HBO and Showtime were unrelated pay television services. On appeal, the Second Circuit noted that Showtime had not submitted any evidence to show that the disclaimers would actually alleviate the confusion generated by the original slogan and, therefore, required the defendant to produce such evidence on remand. In *Charles of the Ritz Group Ltd.* v. *Quality King Distributors, Inc.*,[143] the Second Circuit also retreated from earlier opinions that had characterized disclaimers as a favored way of alleviating customer confusion. There, the defendants had tried to save their perfume advertising – "If you like Opium, you'll Love Omni" – by proposing variations on express language indicating that the two were from different manufacturers. The appellate court affirmed rejection of their proposals, stating that the defendants had failed to produce any evidence that the disclaimer would reduce confusion.

The Eleventh Circuit also weakened the argument for disclaimers in *University of Georgia Athletic Ass'n* v. *Laite*.[144] The appellate court upheld an injunction barring a wholesaler from marketing the novelty beer "Battlin Bulldog" in red and black cans depicting an English bulldog similar to the University of Georgia mascot. The court said that the use of school colors and the bulldog mascot suggested authorization, sponsorship or approval by the university and was likely to confuse consumers. While the defendant had placed a disclaimer on the cans, the court held this ineffective because the words were inconspicuous and "nearly invisible" in six-packs. The court relied on *Boston Professional Hockey Ass'n* v. *Dallas Cup & Emblem Mfg.*[145] That reliance is confusing, however, since *Boston Hockey* involved patches bearing exact duplications of National Hockey League clubs' insignia. *Laite*, by contrast, involved an imitation of a mark rather than a duplication. Nevertheless, the holding seems to imply that where a confusion of association triggers product sales, a disclaimer may not suffice to remedy that confusion.

None of these cases expressly precludes the use of disclaimers in trademark infringement or false advertising cases. In *Softex Polymer Corp.* v. *Fortex Industries, Inc.*,[146] the Second Circuit affirmed the use of a court-ordered disclaimer, despite an apparent lack of evidence that the disclaimer would dispel confusion. The appeals court said that the lower court had not abused its discretion in concluding that the risk of confusion, which it found to be minimal, could be cured by a disclaimer. (Plaintiff used FORTIFLEX on plastic resin; the defendant, a rubber manufacturer, used it on its animal feeding and agricultural product line.)

While this recent criticism of disclaimers undermines *Governor of Delaware*, these cases are distinguishable from cases where trademarks are not used. Three involved actual uses of another's trademark. In *Laite*, the beer wholesaler was apparently attempting to confuse football fans by closely modeling his product after the university colors and mascot. In a case where another's trademark is not used in a dominant manner, one might be able to show that a disclaimer is more likely to be effective.

Another genre of ambush marketing is the congratulatory sort: "Best of Luck in the Final Four," "Congratulations to the World Champion Chicago Bears," "Cubs Will Shine in '89: Happy Opening Day." Such advertising gets closer to the line, but on a one-time basis it is unlikely to result in a substantial lawsuit. While the law is not clear, insofar as corporations have free speech rights they should be free to offer their congratulations as long as they do not imply that the congratulated team endorses their products.

The success of such one-time ambushes is similar to the situation presented in *National Football League Properties, Inc.* v. *Coniglio*.[147] The NFL sought a temporary restraining order to prevent the sale of unauthorized souvenir merchandise in the District of Columbia. Apparently the excitement of the Washington Redskins' Super Bowl appearance had created a huge demand for products bearing the team's insignia. The court, however, refused to grant the team an injunction, noting that if the NFL could demonstrate injury it could sue in the future to recover damages. The court believed a restraining order might hamper legitimate merchants as well as infringers.

This appears to strengthen the hand for congratulatory ambush marketing since any damage to the recipient will be almost impossible to prove, particularly if the advertisement is on a one-time basis. Moreover, sports organizations may be reluctant to sue a company that has offered public congratulations and may employ some of its members as spokespersons.

147.
554 F. Supp. 1224 (D.D.C. 1983).

The following guidelines for legal ambush marketing might be useful to the non-sponsor:

(1) Tie in with a related organization (i.e., a particular team, a player or a special or handicapped version of the same event).

(2) Avoid use of official symbols and trademarks of the main event.

(3) Do not use the main event's name in the headline of your ads or in the name of your promotion.

(4) Keep the period of ambush short to minimize any serious damage (it takes time to prepare and fight a lawsuit, even a preliminary injunction).

(5) If there may be a possibility of confusion, consider using a disclaimer such as, "Not affiliated with the _____." However, consider seriously whether use of such a disclaimer admits the possibility of confusion.

(6) Where possible, use clearly geographic rather than trademark-type names. Example: "You'll win tickets to the professional football game between Chicago and Washington."

(7) Congratulatory ads should not contain additional "sell" copy and should be one-time only.

The following is a digest of trademark cases brought by organized sports and other professional organizations.

DIGEST OF TRADEMARK CASES

Marathon Cases

Boston Athletic Association v. *Sullivan*, (No. 88-1352, 1st Cir. January 27, 1989). The court held that shirts imprinted with the logos 1987 MARATHON and HOPKIN- TON- BOSTON contained a sufficient reference to the BOSTON MARATHON trademark to create a likelihood of confusion as to both goods and sponsorship. Although the defendant tried to argue that BOSTON MARATHON had become generic, he introduced no evidence concerning the primary significance, of the mark to the public. The court noted that the defendant had made no effort to distinguish his products or to disclose their lack of sponsorship by the Boston Athletic Association. It also said that the meaning of the two marks was identical. The court said, "Given the undisputed facts that (1) defendants intentionally referred to the Boston Marathon on its shirts, and (2) purchasers were likely to buy shirts precisely because of that reference, we think it fair to presume that purchasers are likely to be confused about the shirt's source or sponsorship. We presume that, at the least, a sufficient number of purchasers would be likely to assume – mistakenly – that defendant's shirts had some connection with the official sponsors of the Boston Marathon. In the absence of any evidence that effectively rebuts this presumption of a 'likelihood of confusion,' we hold that plaintiffs are entitled to enjoin the manufacture and sale of defendants' shirts."

NFL Cases

National Football League Properties, Inc. v. *New Jersey Giants, Inc.*, 637 F. Supp. 507, 229 U.S.P.Q. 785 (D.N.J. 1986): Defendant was permanently enjoined from marketing souvenir merchandise bearing the mark NEW JERSEY GIANTS. Following the relocation of the New York Giants football team from various New York City stadia to the Meadowlands Sports Complex in East Rutherford, New Jersey, defendant incorporated the name New Jersey Giants and began manufactur- ing and selling T-shirts and other souvenir merchandise bearing the New Jersey Giants' logo. The New York Giants football team had strenuously avoided any change from their traditional name despite their relocation to a New Jersey site for home games. (They "eschew a New Jersey identification as resolutely as a vampire eschews the cross.") In entering the injunction, the court noted the likelihood of confusion among purchasers of football souvenirs, the bad faith of the defendants and the loss of the quality control that NFL Properties sought to maintain.

National Football League v. *Cousin Hugo's, Inc.*, 600 F. Supp. 84 (E.D. Mo. 1984): Preliminary injunction was granted to prevent several bar owners in St. Louis from intercepting satellite transmissions of broadcast NFL games. The local contests had been blacked out in the St. Louis area in accordance with the NFL contract, which required a sellout 72 hours in advance before allowing local broadcasts. The court noted that, given the strong likelihood of success of the NFL's copyright infringement claim, a preliminary injunction was justified.

National Football League Properties, Inc. v. *Coniglio,* 554 F. Supp. 1224, 223 U.S.P.Q. 6 (D.D.C. 1983): Temporary restraining order to prevent the distribution and sale of unlicensed souvenir merchandise bearing registered trademarks of NFL Properties was denied by District Court. This request was apparently in response to a flood of souvenir sales in the Washington, D.C. area following the Washington Redskins' 1983 Super Bowl victory. However, the NFL could not demonstrate the likelihood of irreparable harm due to the defendants' actions. If unlicensed sales did occur, the court noted, the NFL could file a complaint at that time. The court was unimpressed by the NFL's plea to empower the U.S. Marshall Service and "duly-authorized security representatives of the plaintiff" to confiscate any suspect merchandise for sale within the District of Columbia.

National Football League Properties, Inc. v. *Wichita Falls Sportswear, Inc.,* 532 F. Supp. 651, 215 U.S.P.Q. 175 (W.D. Wash. 1982): Football jersey manufacturer was preliminarily enjoined from producing jerseys with the name, emblem and colors of NFL member teams without a license from plaintiff. This injunction was modified to allow limited sales if a required disclaimer stating "Not authorized or sponsored by the NFL" was placed on all replica jerseys. Defendant subsequently violated this partial injunction.

The court held that defendant's overall conduct established an intent to create confusion in the minds of consumers over NFL authorization. "This is not a case of someone legitimately trying to compete in the jersey market, but of an entity calculatedly operating to deceive." In the face of this bad faith, the court ordered a full injunction prohibiting defendant's manufacture and sale of not only replica jerseys in the full, official colors of any NFL member club, but also jerseys that used the dominant team color of an NFL member club. The injunction did, however, permit the limited sale of non-NFL replica jerseys to high schools, colleges and other organizations that shared a nickname and a dominant team color with an NFL member club.

Dallas Cowboy Cheerleaders v. *Pussycat Cinema, Ltd.,* 604 F.2d 200 (2d Cir. 1979): Preliminary injunction preventing defendants, a New York-based film producer and movie theater, from distributing or exhibiting the film *Debbie Does Dallas* was affirmed on appeal. The movie, according to the Second Circuit, was a gross and revolting sex film depicting an actress dressed in a uniform similar to that of the Dallas Cowboy Cheerleaders and performing various sex acts. The court held that the uniform consisting of a combination of white boots, white shorts, blue blouse and white star-studded vest was an arbitrary design making an otherwise functional costume trademarkable.

National Football League v. *Governor of State of Delaware*, 435 F. Supp. 1372, 195 U.S.P.Q. 803 (D. Del. 1977): Suit was over Delaware state lottery game based on NFL games, and listing teams by city, not by name or emblem. The court recognized that the lottery intended to profit from the popularity of NFL football but found this case "difficult to distinguish from the multitude of charter bus companies who generate profit from servicing those of plaintiffs' fans who want to go to the stadium or, indeed, the sidewalk popcorn salesman who services the crowd as it surges toward the gate." Use of NFL schedules, scores and public popularity by the lottery held not to be misappropriation. As for trademark infringement and unfair competition claims, the lottery "does not utilize the NFL name or any of plaintiff's registered service marks for the purpose of *identifying*, as opposed to *describing*, the service which it offers." One cannot advertise one's services in a manner that creates the impression that a connection exists between such services and the holder of a registered mark. One has an affirmative duty to avoid a mistaken impression suggesting such a connection. "Apparently, in this day and age when professional sports team franchise . . . a wide range of . . . products, a substantial number of people believe, if not told otherwise, that one cannot conduct an enterprise of this kind without NFL approval. . . . [T]he ultimate result of their promotion of the Delaware Lottery is significant public confusion and the loss to the NFL of control of its public image." Monetary relief was held inappropriate, so the court ordered lottery to disclaim association with or authorization by the NFL.

National Football League Properties, Inc. v. *Consumer Enterprises*, 26 Ill. App. 3d 814, 327 N.E.2d 242, 180 U.S.P.Q. 90, *cert. denied*, 423 U.S. 1018 (1975): NFL sued manufacturer of patches depicting NFL team emblems, names and colors and obtained order prohibiting manufacture of the patches.

National Football League Properties, Inc. v. *Dallas Cap & Emblem Mfg.*, 26 Ill. App. 3d 280, 327 N.E.2d 247, 185 U.S.P.Q. 554 (1975): NFL sued manufacturer of patches depicting NFL team names, emblems and colors and obtained order prohibiting manufacture of the patches.

NHL Cases
In re National Novice Hockey League, Inc., 222 U.S.P.Q. 638 (T.T.A.B. 1984): The Trademark Board refused to register the marks "National Novice Hockey League" and "NNHL" due to the likelihood of confusion with the National Hockey League.

Although the NNHL was in no way affiliated with professional hockey, the Board noted that the similarity in the names and the initials tended to imply an association or sponsorship. The NHL, however, had not raised any objection nor commented officially on the matter.

Boston Professional Hockey Ass'n v. Dallas Cap & Emblem Mfg., 510 F.2d 1004 (5th Cir.), *cert. denied*, 423 U.S. 868 (1975): Defendant, after unsuccessfully negotiating for an exclusive license, continued to manufacture duplications of professional hockey team symbols on an embroidered emblem for sale to the public, without a license from the NHL. On appeal, the Fifth Circuit reversed the limited injunction and disclaimer required by the District Court and instead entered a full injunction against unauthorized production or sale of the team patches. As the court stated, "words which indicate it was not authorized by the trademark owner are insufficient to remedy the illegal confusion. Only a prohibition of the unauthorized use will sufficiently remedy the wrong." The court was persuaded by three points: (1) the major commercial value of the emblems was derived from the efforts of the plaintiffs, (2) defendant had previously sought and would have asserted, if obtained, an exclusive license and (3) in the general business of team sports, the sale of a reproduction of a trademark is an accepted use of such team symbols.

Boston Professional Hockey Ass'n v. Reliable Knitting Works, Inc., 178 U.S.P.Q. 274 (E.D. Wisc. 1973): A preliminary injunction was entered barring defendant from manufacturing, selling, advertising or distributing knit caps displaying the word BRUINS or the circled letter "B." Hats bearing such marks had a high likelihood of confusing consumers about the Boston hockey team's approval of such merchandise and diluted the club's goodwill. Defendant was not barred, however, from manufacturing or selling knit caps in the team colors of the Boston team, or from placing the word "Boston" or a design of a hockey player on the caps, unless plaintiff could demonstrate that a secondary meaning ("public association") associating its team with such hats had been established.

Professional Basketball Cases

American Basketball Ass'n v. AMF Voit, Inc., 358 F. Supp. 981 (S.D.N.Y.), *aff'd*, 487 F.2d 1393 (2d Cir. 1973), *cert. denied*, 416 U.S. 986 (1974): Preliminary and permanent injunctions to prevent sporting goods company from manufacturing for sale a red-white-and-blue basketball in the pattern used by the ABA denied by the District Court. The ABA had adopted the multicolored ball in order to distinguish itself from the older, more established NBA. The ball was considered more appealing to women and more attractive on color TV broadcasts. A trademark for the design was sought and granted. The court held, however, that the colors were merely a decoration or embellishment and did not constitute a distinctive design. Furthermore, the ABA had not established a secondary meaning in the ball nor conducted the kind of extensive quality control over the product that would tend to justify injunctive relief.

In re National Basketball Ass'n, 180 U.S.P.Q. 480 (T.T.A.B. 1973): Application by the MBA to register the mark DRIBBLE AND SHOOT was denied. The phrases as applied to a series of children's basketball skill contests was determined to be merely a descriptive name of the activities involved and, thus, not protectable by trademark.

Golf Cases

United States Golf Ass'n v. *St. Andrew's Systems, Data Max, Inc.*, 749 F.2d 1028, 224 U.S.P.Q. 646 (3d Cir. 1984): Amateur golf organization sought to enjoin computer company from using its mathematical formula for "handicapping" golfers. The formula was held to be "functional" rather than merely an identifying feature and thus not protectable by trademark laws.

Augusta National, Inc. v. *Northwestern Mutual Life Insurance*, 193 U.S.P.Q. 210 (S.D. Ga. 1976): Owners of mark THE MASTERS for the Masters Golf Tournament successfully prevented use of the mark in the Ladies' Masters at Moss Creek Plantation under §43(a) of the Lanham Act, and state unfair competition, trademark and dilution theories.

Professional Golfers of America v. *Bankers Life & Casualty Co.*, 514 F.2d 665, 186 U.S.P.Q. 447 (5th Cir. 1975): Defendant was enjoined from displaying the initials "PGA" on its clubhouse and golf courses after plaintiff golf association persuaded the court that such use of a collective service mark falsely suggested an affiliation and constituted unfair competition and trademark infringement. Plaintiff had housed its national headquarters in defendant's facilities for ten years. However, the PGA subsequently terminated the arrangement and vacated the premises. Bankers Life continued to display "PGA" initials, however, claiming a limited license to do so.

Sailing Cases

America's Cup Properties Inc. v. *America's Cup Club Inc.*, 8 U.S.P.Q. 2d 2025 (S.D. Cal. 1988): America's Cup Properties, a corporation organized for the purpose of holding and enforcing the AMERICA'S CUP trademarks, and Sail America, a not-for-profit corporation managing the trademarks for the San Diego Yacht Club's defense of the 1988 America's Cup races, were entitled to a preliminary injunction against the defendant's use of the trademarks on clothing and other items in violation of the Lanham Act and the California Business and Professional Code's prohibition on unfair competition and trademark infringement.

College Football Cases

University of Georgia Athletic Ass'n v. Laite, 756 F.2d 1535, 225 U.S.P.Q. 1122 (11th Cir. 1985): Beer wholesaler was enjoined from marketing BATTLIN' BULLDOG beer in red-and-black cans depicting an English bulldog similar to the mascot of the University of Georgia football team. The court held that a sufficient likelihood of confusion existed to satisfy the requirements of the Lanham Act. Such confusion, the court held, need not relate only to the product, but rather to the public's knowledge that the trademark, which triggers the sale of the product, originated with the University of Georgia. The disclaimer on each can denying any affiliation with the university was held to be ineffective because it did not stand out sufficiently and "was practically invisible when grouped in six-packs."

University of Pittsburgh v. Champion Products, Inc., 566 F. Supp. 711 (W.D. Pa. 1983): District Court denied the University of Pittsburgh's plea for an injunction against the manufacturer of sweatshirts, T-shirts and other athletic soft goods to bar the commercial marketing of products bearing the PITT logo. Defendant had sold such products in the Pittsburgh area for over forty years. The university, however, had recently acquired a popular reputation due to its success in building a nationally powerful football program. The court held that plaintiff was not entitled to relief from trademark infringement because no likelihood of confusion existed between defendant's products and the university. The insignia had not acquired a secondary meaning, and defendant's use of the insignia was functional in nature.

Olympics Cases

San Francisco Arts & Athletics, Inc. v. United States Olympic Committee, 107 S. Ct. 2971 (1987): Supreme Court upheld injunction preventing San Francisco organization from using the phrase GAY OLYMPICS to promote athletic contests among homosexual competitors. The Amateur Sports Act of 1978 granted the U.S.O.C. the exclusive right to license the use of the word "Olympic" and the Olympic symbols. The court held that the term Olympic had acquired value and secondary meaning as a result of the efforts of the U.S.O.C. and, thus, Congress's actions were a constitutionally valid protection of its legitimate property right. The protection granted the U.S.O.C. was broader than traditional Lanham Act trademark protection, however, since no likelihood of confusion was required to demonstrate infringement of the property right. The petitioner's equal protection claim failed as well because while the U.S.O.C. was a federally chartered private corporation; it was not a governmental entity and therefore not covered by the Fifth Amendment.

United States Olympic Committee v. *Intelicense Corp.* 737 F.2d 263, 222 U.S.P.Q. 766 (2d Cir.), cert. denied, 469 U.S. 982 (1984): Swiss Corporation's commercial marketing of pictograms bearing the Olympic rings without the consent of the U.S.O.C. held to be an infringement of the trademark granted by the Amateur Sports Act, 26 U.S.C. §380. Defendant was, therefore, enjoined from all further sales in the United States despite license from International Olympic Committee.

United States Olympic Committee v. *Olymp-Herrenwasche-fabriken Bezner GmbH & Co.*, 224 U.S.P.Q. 497 (T.T.A.B. 1984): German sportswear manufacturer's application for registration of the mark OLYMP to be placed on shirts, blouses and collars was denied by the Trademark Board due to the likelihood of confusion of these products with the athletic uniforms and equipment bearing the registered mark of the U.S.O.C., "OLYMPIC." In sustaining the U.S.O.C.'s objections to the "OLYMP" mark, however, the board noted that this denial was based on traditional Lanham Act confusion grounds and should not be seen as an expansion of the limited exclusive right to "OLYMPIC" and the Olympic rings granted by the Amateur Sports Act.

United States Olympic Committee v. *Union Sport Apparel*, 220 U.S.P.Q. 526 (E.D. Va. 1983): Sportswear manufacturer was enjoined under §380 of the Amateur Sports Act from marketing clothing bearing a logo of three interlocking rings and the letters U.S.A. The court held that defendant had adopted these marks for the purpose of taking advantage of the goodwill created by the U.S.O.C. and thus infringed the trademark established by Congress through the Amateur Sports Act.

United States Olympic Committee v. *International Federation of Bodybuilders.* 219 U.S.P.Q. 353 (D.D.C. 1982): Defendants, editors of several bodybuilding magazines and distributors of various health and bodybuilding products, were permanently enjoined from using a 7-ring symbol similar to Olympic interlocking ring symbol, or any other colorable imitation, in their magazines or for the purposes of advertising various products. In addition, the board barred defendants from using for promotional purposes the terms OLYMPIC, OLYMPIA or OLYMPIAN. The term MR. OLYMPIA, used to refer to the winner of a professional bodybuilding contest, was allowed to stand. The board noted that §380 of the Amateur Sports Act provided broader protection than traditional trademark infringement and was more akin to an antidilution statute. Thus, the likelihood of confusion or conscious association was not required as under the Lanham Act. Simply a mistaken or deceptive impression of sponsorship or approval was enough to justify injunctive relief.

Stop the Olympic Prison v. *United States Olympic Committee*, 489 F. Supp. 1112, 207 U.S.P.Q. 237 (S.D.N.Y. 1980): The court declined to enjoin the printing and distribution of a poster protesting the conversion of the Lake Placid Olympic village into a state prison. Although the poster depicted the Olympic rings, the court held that no violation of the Amateur Sports Act had occurred since the poster was political rather than commercial in nature. No trademark infringement could be demonstrated in the absence of confusion, dilution or false or misleading statements.

First Amendment Cases

Friedman v. *Rogers*, 440 U.S. 1, *reh'g denied*, 441 U.S. 917 (1979): State ban on optometrists' advertising and using trade names rather than personal name of optometrist was upheld because of possibility of deception. The court recognized that trademarks and trade names are commercial speech.

Bolger v. *Young's Drug Products Corp.*, 463 U.S. 60 (1983): Advertising pamphlets of contraceptives manufacturer are entitled to First Amendment protection and could not be banned.

Lamar Outdoor Advertising, Inc. v. *Mississippi State Tax Commission*, 701 F.2d 314 (5th Cir. 1983), *cert. denied sub nom. Dunagin* v. *Oxford*, 467 U.S. 1259 (1984): Liquor advertising is commercial speech entitled to First Amendment protection.

Oklahoma Telecaster's Association v. *Crisp*, 699 F.2d 490 (10th Cir. 1983), *rev'd other grounds sub nom. Capital Cities Cable, Inc.* v. *Crisp*, 467 U.S. 691 (1984): Advertising of alcoholic beverages is commercial speech entitled to some degree of protection under the First Amendment.

Posadas de Puerto Rico Associates v. *Tourism Co. of Puerto Rico*, 106 S. Ct. 2968 (1986): Advertising by casino is commercial speech entitled to limited First Amendment protection as long as it concerns a lawful activity and is not misleading or fraudulent.

CHAPTER 3:
PROTECTING THE PROPRIETARY
VALUE OF EVENTS

TELEVISING PUBLIC EVENTS

Part of what an event promoter has to sell are television and radio broadcast rights. Obviously, the exclusive broadcast rights to events like the Superbowl are worth millions. They can be sold as a whole or broken up – live and delayed, U.S. and foreign, English language and Spanish language, and so on. Home video and CD technology have added new market segments. When exclusive rights can be guaranteed to one or more purchasers, the promoter can maximize its revenues from this bundle of rights.

However, some events are not easily contained or controlled. Unlike a Superbowl game, which takes place in a single confined area, marathons and parades take place on public streets. How can the promoter sell exclusive rights to broadcast or videotape the event? How can the promoter prevent others from filming the same event? Very few cases have considered this problem, and the case that directly raised the issue did not reach a substantive result.

Copyright

Production Contractors, Inc. v. *WGN Continental Broadcasting Co.*[1] vividly demonstrates that promoters cannot rely on copyright theory to protect events that take place on public streets. Copyright theory might apply when an event is private, but for parades and marathons, promoters must seek legal protection under other theories. *Production Contractors* arose when Chicago television station WGN announced that it would cover the 1985 McDonald's Chicago Christmas Parade in its entirety. Production Contractors had sold the exclusive rights to televise the parade to another Chicago station, WLS. Production Contractors sued WGN, alleging copyright infringement and unfair competition. The court refused to protect the organizer's economic interest in the parade, even though several legal theories were available.

The federal District Court for the Northern District of Illinois first found that there was no case support for Production Contractor's assertion that the production and promotion of a parade was a work of authorship subject to copyright protection. The Court cited the late Professor Melville Nimmer, who stated in his treatise, "If a live broadcast is not based upon a work of authorship, as in the case of a sporting event, a parade, etc., then no statutory copyright infringement would result from its reproduction."[2] The court added:

> the idea of a Christmas parade is a common one, relatively simple
> and contains no original creative authorship. Therefore, the parade
> itself, including its production and promotion, is not a work of
> authorship entitled to copyright protection.[3]

The court also relied on two cases that are not particularly on point: *Morrissey* v. *Procter & Gamble*[4] and *Noble* v. *Columbia Broadcasting System.*[5] Both cases rest

1.
622 F. Supp. 1500 (N.D. Ill. 1985).

2.
1 M. Nimmer, *Nimmer on Copyright* § 2.03[B] n.33 (1988).

3.
622 F. Supp. at 1503.

4.
379 F.2d 675, 678 (1st Cir. 1967) [rules for a sweepstakes consumer contest not protected by copyright].

on the essential notion that ideas are not protectable. In *Morrissey*, the court noted there was a limited number of ways to express the rules of a contest; in *Noble*, the court refused to protect the mere idea for a program. While the idea of a parade is not protectable, there are numerous ways to "express" the parade: floats are individually protectable; the arrangement of units arguably is a copyrightable arrangement, and each parade is likely to differ from others in its participants and ordering. (The court in *Production Contractors* recognized that the decorative floats to appear in the parade were copyrightable as original works of authorship – presumably graphic or sculptural works – but held that since there had been no registration, the copyright claim could not be heard.)

The plaintiff in *Production Contractors* argued that the compilation of the various elements and the flow of the parade was protectable, but the court failed to consider that argument fully, focusing instead on the non-copyrightability of parades. (For reasons discussed below, the court may have rejected the compilation or arrangement argument even if it had considered it.) Yet as a compilation or arrangement of various elements, a parade should be copyrightable subject matter. The Copyright Revision Act of 1976[6] specifically extends copyright protection to compilations and arrangements. It defines a compilation as "a work formed by the collection and assembling of preexisting materials or of data that are selected, coordinated, or arranged in such a way that the resulting work as a whole constitutes an original work of authorship."[7] Thus, even if every single element in a compilation or arrangement is not individually protectable, the work, taken as a whole, is copyrightable subject matter.[8] If the other requirements for copyright (such as fixation) had been observed (or *could* have been observed), the court in *Production Contractors* could have extended copyright protection to the parade's organizers for their compilation or arrangement.

As discussed in Chapter 2, copyright registration is a prerequisite for instituting a legal action for copyright protection, but it is not a prerequisite to protection, which exists from the moment of creation (fixation).[9] To assert a copyright claim in the parade as a compilation, Production Contractors would have to have fixed the arrangement in a tangible medium of expression prior to its taking place. Because the court failed to fully consider the compilation argument for copyright protection, it impliedly left open the issue of whether a description of a parade would be a fixation sufficient to support a claim of copyright.

The court in *Production Contractors* recognized that a telecast of a parade is protectable if it is fixed in a tangible medium of expression. Specifically, the court referred to the legislative history of the Copyright Revision Act of 1976, which refers to the fixation of live events, such as sporting events, by filming or videotaping. The Notes of the Committee on the Judiciary state that the activities of

5.
270 F.2d 938 (D.C. Cir. 1959) [idea for a television program consisting of spontaneous, unrehearsed, fictitious courtroom drama was not an original work of authorship].

6.
17 U.S.C. 101 *et seq.*

7.
Id.

8.
For example, the compilation and arrangement of names and phone numbers – public domain information – has been held to be protectable under copyright law. *Leon v. Pacific Telephone and Telegraph Co.*, 91 F.2d 484 (9th Cir. 1937); *Southwestern Bell Telephone Co. v. Nationwide Independent Directory Service*, 371 F. Supp. 900 (W.D. Ark. 1974); *see also Southern Tel. & Tel. v. Associated Telephone Directories*, 756 F.2d 801 (8th Cir. 1985) [Compilation of Atlanta Yellow Pages protected]. When a compilation involves subjective judgment and selectivity in choosing items for inclusion, the rationale for protecting the effort involved is even stronger. *Schroeder v. William Morrow & Co.*, 566 F.2d 3 (7th Cir. 1977) [catalogue of garden suppliers, the types of supplies covered by each, prices, delivery periods and other information infringed by use of names and addresses only].

9.
17 U.S.C. 102, 411.

10.
Committee on the
Judiciary, H.R. Rep. No.
94-1476, 17 U.S.C.A.
§102 (West 1977),
Historical Note, p. 14.

the cameramen and director in "choosing which of their electronic images are sent out to the public and in what order . . . constitute authorship."[10] assuming those activities have been fixed in some tangible medium, they are a copyrightable work. The court concluded:

11.
622 F. Supp. at 1503.

> *This passage of legislative history suggests that the live telecast of a parade is copyrightable because the telecast is a work of authorship which is fixed simultaneously with its transmission.*[11]

12.
17 U.S.C. § 411(b).

Thus, live television programs gain protection when they are simultaneously videotaped.[12] In covering a news event, a television station may obtain a copyright in its presentation of the event – the words its on-camera broadcaster uses, the camera angles, etc. If such a presentation is spontaneous – not scripted – there is nothing to copyright before the camera rolls. The problem, of course, is that since copyright exists in the fixation, both WLS and WGN would own copyrights in their separate videotapings – their fixations. Both would have their own scripts and narrators as well as their own camera angles. In fact, even if Production Contractors had registered a WLS script, copyright infringement would not necessarily be found in WGN's unique broadcast. Some parades are in fact televised by two or more broadcasters. Tradition, more than economics or legal theory, may govern these situations, but it is worth noting that sometimes sponsors would rather have more coverage than less, even if promoters earn less money as a result.

In *Production Contractors*, the court rightly found that, prior to the date of the event, the organizers had not fixed a work subject to copyright protection. However, the judge left open the possibility that, in the case of a parade, a written description of the floats, the order of the parade units or some other written description of the parade are fixations that could be protectable by copyright. How particular would such a description have to be? Could floats be described in words or would they have to be in sketches or detailed building plans? Does one describe a marching band by name or by position of each musician? The court did not elaborate because it seemed convinced that parades were not copyrightable until they took place; indeed, one could easily conclude that the very imprecision of written descriptions of parades makes copyright an inappropriate vehicle for protecting them. Moreover, for some events that take place on public streets, written descriptions would be unworkable, unless, for instance, a map of a marathon route were a sufficient description. While there is no doubt that scripts are copyrightable, it can be argued that a description of a parade or a race is only a prediction of what is expected. The spontaneity of the event is itself at odds with the notion of fixation. It makes little sense to enjoin a third party from infringing a mere prediction on copyright grounds.

The problems described above are unique to events that take place on public streets. Live sports events are not scripted in advance in order to achieve exclusive copyright protection. Copyright does not exist in a football game until the cameras roll and the announcers comment. As the judge in *Production Contractors* recognized, the number of different copyrightable works possible in one football game is limited only by the number of camera positions available. In private arenas, however, the organizers of football games control the number of camera positions. For instance, in *Pittsburgh Athletic Co.* v. *KQV Broadcasting Co.*[13] the court addressed the simultaneous live broadcasts of the Pittsburgh Pirates games – one authorized and one not – under misappropriation and unfair competition theories rather than copyright. The court enjoined a radio station from broadcasting baseball games live from a leased location overlooking the ball park. The court in *Production Contractors*, however, exercised its discretion and dismissed the state unfair competition claims because of its dismissal of the federal copyright claim.

13.
24 F. Supp. 490 (W.D. Pa. 1938).

Misappropriation

Time, effort and money go into the organization of a parade or similar event. Organizers must obtain the participation of various persons, design a plan for the event and obtain cooperation from relevant government authorities. For instance, marathon organizers might guarantee appearance money to star athletes, and parade organizers might pay transportation expenses for special units. At the very least, parade organizers have probably paid a permit fee to the local government for the privilege of parading on the public streets. While the organizers may be willing to have private individuals witness it for free and describe it to their friends, they might be able to sell exclusive rights to broadcast it at a substantial profit. Misappropriation is a legal theory well suited to protection of events made public by their organizers. The burden of proof under misappropriation is fairly simple: the organizer need only show (1) ownership of the event (creation or sponsorship, regardless of fixation) and (2) unauthorized activity by the defendant.

The classic misappropriation case is *International News Service* v. *The Associated Press*.[14] There, AP sought an injunction against INS, which copied AP news from bulletin boards and early editions of AP newspapers and obtained AP news through various employees, and sold it, sometimes rewritten, to its own customers. Copyright protection was not sought; rather, AP argued that INS's conduct constituted piracy, a form of unfair trade. INS argued that, by posting news on bulletin boards for all to see, the plaintiff "no longer has the right to control the use to be made of it, that when it reaches the light of day it becomes the common possession of all to whom it is accessible . . . ."[15] The court said the fault in that reasoning was in applying a test that applied to the public but not to competitors.

14.
248 U.S. 215 (1918).

15.
Id. at 239.

Transmitting the news for a commercial purpose was essentially different than the right of an individual to gratuitously pass on the news of the day. The court said:

> *In doing this defendant, by its very act, admits that it is taking material that has been acquired by complainant as the result of organization and the expenditure of labor, skill, and money and which is saleable by complainant for money, and that defendant in appropriating it and selling it as its own is endeavoring to reap where it has not sown, and by disposing of it to newspapers that are competitors of complainant's members is appropriating to itself the harvest of those who have sown.*[16]

16.
Id. at 239-40

The argument that AP had spent its money for something "too fugitive or evanescent to be the subject of property"[17] was rejected by the court, which said it sought to do equity:

17.
Id. at 240.

> *. . . where the question is one of unfair competition, if that which complainant has acquired fairly at substantial cost may be sold fairly at substantial profit, a competitor who is misappropriating it for the purpose of disposing of it to his own profit and to the disadvantage of complainant cannot be heard to say that it is too fugitive or evanescent to be regarded as property.*[18]

18.
Id.

Similarly, courts have protected the effort involved in developing and publishing stock indexes.[19] In each case, even though no copyright claim could be made, the courts recognized that effort had gone into the creation of certain information. While the information was in the public domain, the defendant could not avoid the effort of gathering it for itself.

19.
Board of Trade of City of Chicago v. Dow Jones, 456 N.E.2d 84 (N.D. Ill. 1983).

This was essentially the rationale in *Pittsburgh Athletic Co.* v. *KQV Broadcasting Co.*[20] There, the court, relying on *INS* v. *AP*, said:

20.
24 F. Supp. 490 (W.D. Pa. 1938).

> *The plaintiff and the defendant are using baseball news as material for profit. The Athletic Company has, at great expense, acquired and maintains a baseball park, pays the players who participate in the game, and have, as we view it, a legitimate right to capitalize on the news value of their games by selling exclusive broadcasting rights to companies which value them as affording advertising mediums for their merchandise. This right the defendant interferes with when it uses its broadcasting facilities for giving out the identical news obtained by its paid observers stationed at points outside Forbes Field for the purpose of securing information which*

it cannot otherwise acquire. This, in our judgment, amounts to unfair competition and is a violation of the property rights of the plaintiffs. For it is our opinion that the Pittsburgh Athletic Company, by reason of its control of the park, and its restriction of the dissemination of the news therefrom, has a property right in such news, and the right to control the use thereof for a reasonable time following the games.[21]

Protecting public events through application of the misappropriation doctrine makes more sense than through copyright theory. Because there is no copyright in the unscripted live event itself until it takes place (because there is no fixation), there is no preemption problem under the federal copyright law.[22] However, since the outcome of litigation is always uncertain, promoters should consider practical ways of protecting the proprietary value of their events.

Practical Considerations

The obvious way to make an otherwise public event private is to make the climax of the event private. For example, organizers of a marathon might rent an arena for the finish line. No television broadcaster would spend several hours televising an event if it could not televise the finish. Likewise, the promoter who rents a baseball field or similar stadium can control the media's access to that arena. Access for news coverage might be limited to broadcast only of short clips or after a specified delay. If the contractual terms of news access are violated, the promoter has a relatively easy time proving damages – the official broadcaster's rights fee or the authorized clip fee indicates what the value of the event was in the marketplace.[23]

A promoter might also use local ordinances to privatize an event. Many municipalities issue parade as well as movie-filming permits, and the differences are worth investigating. In some cities, for instance, a parade permit allows the organizer to use the street – curb to curb. A movie-filming permit, on the other hand, may allow use of the sidewalks as well. During the period of the permit, the organizer should be able to determine who uses the sidewalk. This may limit non-official broadcasters to rooftops (if they can gain access) and other undesirable locations along the route. If the terms of a permit do not contemplate filming rights (and they usually do not), a promoter might consider bargaining with the municipal authorities for precisely that right. While such an approach might get legally complicated, it seems worth the chance. With the municipality's authority supporting the promoter's exclusive right to broadcast the event, the promoter might be able to discourage non-authorized broadcasters without litigation.

21.
Id. at 492.

22.
17 U.S.C. § 301; see *New York World's Fair 1964-1965 Corporation* v. *Colourpicture Publishers, Inc.,* 141 U.S.P.Q. 939 (N.Y. Sup. Ct. 1964) [Organizers of World's Fair could enjoin unauthorized sales of postcards of the Fair; even if buildings were in public domain, the Fair organizers had a valuable property right in the event as a whole and in its licensing programs].

23.
See *New Boston Television, Inc.* v. *Entertainment Sports Programming,* 1981 Copyright L. Dec. (CCH) § 25,293 at 16, 625, 16, 627 (D. Mass. 1981) [Court enjoined ESPN from taping games off the air for purpose of broadcasting clips and rejected fair use defense, stating "Evidence of plaintiff's revenues from the three major networks lends further credence to their claim that defendant's use deprives them of substantial revenue to which they are entitled as the owners of the copyright to these materials"].

PREVENTING EVENT THEFT

Protecting Event Ideas

Ideas are not protectable, no matter how unique, clever or blockbuster. Inventions, of course, are patentable, but the idea of a midnight run on New Year's Eve is not patentable and not protectable. How can an organizer of an event be certain a competitor or even its own client or a current sponsor won't "steal" the idea and cut the organizer out next year? The cautious event owner will plan ahead to avoid such unhappy surprises.

Since ideas are not protectable, anyone can enter the competitive arena with the same idea and try to do it better. The event owner thus should focus its attention on making it more difficult for a competitor to enter the market. And yes, there are legal ways to make it hard for a Johnny-come-lately: (1) choosing a trademark that is as attractive as the event itself, (2) establishing long-term contracts with as many key players or participants as possible and (3) by contract, prohibiting sponsors (or organizers) from sponsoring (or organizing) a similar event within a given geographic area for some period of time.

Choosing a Distinctive Trademark

Trademarks can represent an enormous amount of goodwill, as one can readily appreciate by looking at the cornflakes, bleach, cola or cream-filled chocolate cookie markets. So, too, events and festivals benefit from names that are more distinctive than foodfest, art fair, jazz festival or 5K race. THE GREAT AMERICAN RAT RACE is an excellent example of a trademark that adds to the event – participating in that event is different than running in any other footrace. Even if the corporate sponsor wanted to bypass the promoter and conduct another Great American Rat Race, it couldn't. There can be only one Great American Rat Race. The trademark owner, by creating a unique trademark, has also created a barrier to entry in its market. Even identical events will always be imitations in the minds of consumers.

Many organizers make the classic mistake of naming an event descriptively. While that helps consumers understand immediately the nature of the event, descriptive marks, like New York Marathon, are weak. It would take many years of effort to establish any trademark rights in such a name, if indeed it could ever be done.

Having chosen a distinctive event name, promoters would be wise to invest in federal (and perhaps state) trademark registrations (see Chapter 2). It should be noted, too, that where a sponsor has created an event, it owns the trademark and can take the event elsewhere at will, absent any contractual restrictions to the contrary.

Establishing Long-Term Contracts

If there are key players in an event, having them under contract gives the organizer some protection. However, reliance on long-term contracts is fraught with potential problems, including the reluctance of most individuals to be bound for long periods of time. Events that require the use of public parks and other spaces are also unlikely to get long-term commitments from municipalities; in addition, they often face annual permit systems. (In some cities, the lottery system of awarding event permits for certain venues would seem to preclude any long-term security for organizers of events at such venues; see Chapter 8). In most cities, "politics is politics" and the city can always find a way to dump a promoter, even one with a long-term contract. There is no substitute for political goodwill.

For certain kinds of events, an option on the winner's services for the next year can provide a critical element for a successful event and thus discourage a competitor. To be enforceable, the option should state a price, that is, a minimum fee for the following year's appearance (it can be negotiated upwards). There are also some limitations on enforcement of personal service contracts that make this mechanism less than foolproof (see Chapter 1).

Covenants Not to Compete

There are literally thousands of cases concerning the validity of an individual's covenant not to compete. In general, these covenants must state limits in time, scope and geographic location. While it is tempting to refer to that body of law with respect to the validity of clauses that prohibit a corporate sponsor from conducting an event similar to an organizer's, it is unnecessary. In negotiations between a corporation and an organizer, the decision makers are presumed to be sophisticated and capable of bargaining for a rational restriction. Here, since neither party is an individual person, the right to earn a living is not at stake. Therefore, a clause like the following should be enforceable:

> *Sponsor represents and warrants that for a period of two years after termination or expiration of this Agreement it will not directly or indirectly conduct, sponsor, present, supply or otherwise be associated with an event substantively similar to [Event Name] anywhere in [the United States].*

It might be that only regional protection is appropriate or only one year's protection is justified. The organizer should consider what limitations are appropriate in light of the nature of the event, its draw, its hoped-for reputation, the sponsorship fee, and so on. The scope of the covenant is of course negotiable, and if the negotiation takes place at the beginning of the sponsorship relationship, the organizer is more likely to be successful in getting the kind of protection it deems necessary or desirable.

In the absence of defensive measures by the organizer, the sponsor is free to drop the organizer and the organizer's event. And, keep in mind that there may be times when dropping an irresponsible or unsuccessful organizer is the only rational business decision. In such a case, if the organizer has not fully performed its obligations, preventing the sponsor from trying again may be unfair. Adding an introductory proviso to the sample clause above may give the sponsor some relief:

> *". . . provided Organizer has fully complied with the terms and conditions of this Agreement . . ."*

Such a proviso would at least give the sponsor some opportunity to argue that the organizer failed to conduct a successful event because it did not comply with the agreement, and that therefore the sponsor is free to conduct its own similar event.

It may also be that an organizer has performed so well that the event has outgrown the organizer's capabilities. The sponsor may want to continue its affiliation but bring in a new, bigger organization. In such a case, it might be appropriate for the organizer to seek an ongoing royalty interest in the event. If the organizer owns the trademark, it can retain a financial interest through a trademark license. If the sponsor owns the trademark, the organizer's negotiation will be more difficult, but a continuing financial interest could nonetheless be justified.

It should also be noted that there are cases where it is appropriate for the sponsor to restrict the organizer from promoting events similar to the sponsor's. Clauses similar to the ones described above would be appropriate.

CHAPTER 4:
RECORDING, VIDEOTAPING AND
TELEVISING EVENTS

RECORDING, VIDEOTAPING AND TELEVISING EVENTS

There are obviously many ways to exploit the commercial value of an event in both live and delayed media. In order to fully exploit broadcast rights, organizers need to be aware of legal constraints imposed on the various media. Before broadcasting or recording an event, particular care needs to be taken to be sure all the necessary rights are in place. These include the rights of spectators and participants (whether or not they are celebrities), since most states recognize individual privacy rights, and those of other rights holders (such as the owners of copyrighted music). In addition, there are some special Federal Communications Commission rules regarding television that require attention.

BACKGROUND

The right of privacy – or the right to be left alone – was first articulated in a law review article and later developed by Prosser, who identified four separate privacy rights: (1) the right to be free from intrusion on one's seclusion; (2) the right to be free from public disclosure of private, embarrassing facts; (3) the right to be free from false statements and (4) the right to control the commercial appropriation of one's name and likeness.[1] The fourth right may be in issue if footage of spectators or participants is used in a film, video or commercial.

1.
Prosser *Privacy*, 48 Calif. L. Rev. 383 (1960).

The flip side of privacy is publicity, a right recognized by the U.S. Supreme Court only as recently as 1976. Celebrities certainly have publicity rights; performers and participants probably have publicity rights, and even spectators could assert such rights when their likenesses are used for a commercial purpose.

The first right of publicity case decided by the U.S. Supreme Court was in essence a misappropriation case (see discussion in Chapter 3). In *Zacchini v. Scripps-Howard Broadcasting Co.*,[2] the court held that a television station invaded the right of publicity of a human cannonball. The plaintiff performed a fifteen-second act at the county fair in which he was shot from a cannon. The television station showed the entire act on the evening news. Zacchini sued, alleging unlawful appropriation of his professional property. The court reasoned that

2.
433 U.S. 562 (1976).

> *the State's interest in permitting a "right of publicity" is in protecting the proprietary interests of the individual in his act in part to encourage such entertainment. [footnote omitted]. . . . [T]he State's interest is closely analogous to the goals of patent and copyright law, focusing on the right of the individual to reap the reward of his endeavors . . . .*[3]

3.
Id. at 573.

The court's language in *Zacchini* sounds like classic misappropriation theory, focusing on the economic value of control over broadcasting the event. The court said:

> *The broadcast of a film of petitioner's entire act poses a substantial threat to the economic value of that performance. As the Ohio court recognized, this act is the product of petitioner's own talents and energy, the end result of much time, effort and expense. Much of its economic value lies in the "right of exclusive control over the publicity given to his performance;" if the public can see the act free on television, it will be less willing to pay to see it at the fair. The effect of a public broadcast of the performance is similar to preventing petitioner from charging an admission fee.*[4]

4.
Id. at 575-76.

5.
Id. at 576.

6.
Id. at 576 n.12.

7.
229 F.2d 481 (3d Cir. 1956).

8.
Id. at 487.

9.
The following states have codified the right of privacy: California, Cal. Civ. Code § 3344 (West Supp. 1989); Florida, Fla. Stat. Ann. § 540.08 (West 1982); Kentucky, Ky. Rev. Stat. Ann. § 391.170 (Michie/Bobbs-Merrill 1984); Massachusetts, Mass. Ann. Laws ch. 214, § 1B (Law. Co-op. 1986); Nebraska, Neb. Rev. Stat. §§ 20-201 to 211 (1983); New York, N.Y. Civ. Rights Law L. §§ 50-51 (McKinney 1976); Okla. Stat. Ann. tit. 21, § 839.1 (West 1983); Rhode Island, R.I. Gen. Laws § 9-1-28 (1972); Tennessee, Tenn. Code Ann. §§ 47-25-1101 to 1108 (1984); Utah, Utah Code Ann. § 76-9-405 (1973); Virginia, Va. Code Ann. § 8.01-40 (1984).

10.
California, Cal. Civ. Code § 990 (West 1987); Florida, Fla. Stat. § 540.08 (1972); Kentucky, Ky. Rev. Stat. Ann. § 391.170 (Michie/Bobbs-Merrill 1984); Nebraska, Neb. Rev. Stat. § 20-208 (1983); Oklahoma, Okla. Stat. Ann., tit. 21, § 839.1 (West 1983); Tennessee, Tenn. Code Ann. § 47-25-1103 (1984); Tex. Prop. Code Ann. § 26.001 (Vernon 1988); Virginia, Va. Code Ann. § 8.01-40 (1977).

The court recognized that televising his act "goes to the heart of petitioner's right to earn a living as an entertainer."[5] It acknowledged that more people might be interested in seeing the "Human Cannonball" act by virtue of the television coverage, but said this went to the issue of damages rather than the issue of whether a right was violated.[6] The broadcaster's First Amendment defense that the event was news was rejected and the Ohio court's decision to protect the economic value of Zacchini's act was upheld.

The court's conclusion in *Zacchini*, while based on a publicity theory, is similar to the decision twenty years earlier in *Ettore* v. *Philco Television Broadcasting Corporation*.[7] There the court found that the rebroadcasting of the plaintiff's boxing match with Joe Louis, without his consent, was actionable as a property right. It said:

> *Where a professional performer is involved, there seems to be a recognition of a kind of property right in the performer to the product of his services. The theory may be summed up as follows: The performer, as a means of livelihood, contracts for his services with an entrepreneur. The finished product is, for example, a motion picture in which the performer's services are embodied. If the motion picture is employed for some use other than that for which it was intended by the performer and the entrepreneur, the motion picture is employed in such a way as to deprive the performer of his right to compensation for the new use of the product.*[8]

Today eleven states have statutes recognizing a person's right of privacy and/or cause of action for commercial use of one's name or likeness.[9] Moreover, eight states recognize a descendable right of publicity, one that can be asserted by a person's heirs for some period of time after his or her death.[10]

FILMING AND RECORDING PARTICIPANTS

To the extent that appearance in an event can be viewed as a performance, each participant should have rights similar to those in *Ettore* and *Zacchini*. The organizer should ask all participants to sign a release form in order to acquire all rights in their appearance and performance in an event. In other words, each participant should transfer his or her right of publicity to the organizer. (See Sample Participant's Release form in Chapter 5.)

It could be argued that, if one performs in a public place, one loses one's right of privacy or one's property right in that public performance. In *Man* v. *Warner Bros. Inc.*,[11] a professional musician objected to the filming of his performance at the Woodstock Festival. He claimed that "at someone's request" he climbed onstage and played "Mess Call" on his fluegelhorn and that the producers of the motion picture *Woodstock* included his performance in their film without his consent in violation of New York's privacy statute. The court held that the statute did not apply to a professional entertainer shown giving a performance before a public audience. The court said:

> *Plaintiff, by his own volition, placed himself in the spotlight of a sensational event which exposed him to the glare of publicity. That fact, without more, we think, makes him newsworthy and deprives him of any right to complain of a violation . . . .*[12]

The court held that in giving a performance before a vast audience, the privacy right was not at issue, although perhaps a property right was. As to that property right, the court found the incidental use of the entirety of his 45-second performance in the film to be *de minimus*. Participants in events like marathons may likewise be considered performers whose privacy rights are lost by the fact of their performance in a public place. Were their performances in a private place, perhaps the rationale of *Man* could be avoided, since *Man* predates *Zacchini*. In any event, organizers should avoid any question concerning their use of event footage that includes participants by using a broad form release.

11.
317 F. Supp. 50
(S.D.N.Y. 1970).

12.
Id. at 53.

FILMING AND RECORDING SPECTATORS

Spectators who are seen in a public place – such as at an outdoor concert or at a marathon – are deemed to have waived their privacy rights. Typically, releases for uses of their photographs or likenesses are not needed from mere spectators if they are filmed in their capacity as spectators.

13.
253 P.2d 441 (Cal. 1953).

For instance, in *Gill v. Hearst Pub. Co.*,[13] the court held that the unauthorized publication of a photograph of a husband and wife seated in an affectionate pose at their stall at a farmer's market was not an actionable invasion of their privacy. The court said that the photograph had no particular news value but did serve the function of entertainment as a matter of legitimate public interest. The court found that the same constitutional guarantees of freedom of expression apply to both news and entertainment features. Moreover, the court considered it important that the plaintiffs were photographed in a public place:

> In considering the nature of the picture in question, it is significant that it was not surreptitiously snapped on private grounds, but rather was taken of plaintiffs in a pose voluntarily assumed in a public place. . . . By their own voluntary action plaintiffs waived their right of privacy so far as this particular pose was assumed [citation omitted] for, "There can be no privacy in that which is already public." *Melvin v. Reid*, 112 Cal. App. 285, 290, 297 P. 91, 93. The photograph of plaintiffs merely permitted other members of the public, who were not at plaintiffs' place of business at the time it was taken, to see them as they had voluntarily exhibited themselves.[14]

14.
Id. at 444.

15.
318 N.Y.S.2d 474 (N.Y. 1971).

A similar result was reached in *Murray v. New York Magazine Company*.[15] There, the plaintiff's picture was used on the cover of *New York* magazine. Two years before, a freelance photographer had taken his picture in Irish garb at the St. Patrick's Day Parade in Manhattan. Later, it was used to illustrate an article entitled "The Last of the Irish Immigrants." The plaintiff allegations of violation of his rights under New York's privacy statute were denied on appeal. The court said:

> Dressed in striking attire to celebrate the occasion, he voluntarily became part of the spectacle and, since some newsworthy incident affecting him [was] taking place, [his] right of privacy is not absolute, but limited." *Gautier v. Pro-Football*, 304 N.Y. 354, 360, 107 N.E.2d 485, 489 [other citations omitted].

In other words, the plaintiff was singled out and photographed because his presence constituted a visual participation in a public event which invited special attention.[16]

16.
Id. at 476.

However, not all uses of spectators are permissible. In another case arising out of the Woodstock Festival, a man named Taggart who was filmed performing his job at the festival objected to the inclusion of footage featuring him.[17] Taggart had spoken freely to the filmmakers while they filmed him emptying portable latrines at the festival, but contended he did not know that they intended to publicly release a film. Moreover, he claimed that the sequence was edited into the documentary in such a way as to achieve, at his expense, a comic effect. He alleged that he suffered mental anguish, embarrassment, public ridicule and invasion of his right of privacy. The defendant asked the court to determine that it could not be held liable to Taggart under any circumstances, relying principally on *Man* v. *Warner Bros. Inc.*[18] The court denied defendant's motion, distinguishing *Man* on several grounds: (1) Taggart was not a professional musician performing for a public audience, (2) the footage of him in the movie was not *de minimus* and (3) the footage of him was not newsworthy. The court said:

17.
Taggart v. Wadleigh Maurice, Ltd., 489 F.2d 434 (3d Cir. 1973).

18.
317 F. Supp. 50 (S.D.N.Y 1970).

> [I]t would be one thing to photograph Taggart as he went about his duties at a newsworthy event and to include such a photograph in a factual description of the event, but quite another thing to deliberately draw him out in conversation for the purpose of making him an inadvertent performer in a sequence intended to be exploited for its artistic effect. The question of whether Taggart was an involuntary performer or a participant in a newsworthy event was left for the jury. (The outcome of the jury's determination is not reported.)[19]

19.
Taggart at 438.

Thus, those who appear on the public streets waive, perhaps involuntarily, part of their rights of privacy in favor of freedom of news and entertainment reporting. This rationale would allow *incidental* use of spectators' likenesses in film footage for home video and theatrical release, as well as incidental use in commercials for the event. Uses that focus on a single spectator may require his or her permission because such uses may constitute a commercial use of one's likeness.

FILMING AND RECORDING CELEBRITIES

Celebrities clearly have protectable rights in their performances. Those celebrities appearing in an event, particularly a musical event such as a concert, will carefully delineate by contract what can and cannot be done with respect to recording their performances. The Participant's Agreement provided in Chapter 5 would be modified accordingly.

It should be noted that some celebrities will require what is known as a "most favored nations" clause in their appearance contracts. This clause basically says that the celebrity is being compensated as well as any other celebrity who is being paid for his or her performance. Such a clause is often requested when several celebrities are donating their time in whole or in part and each wants to make sure that all the celebrities are being treated equally. However, saying "most favored nations" does not create any legal obligations; contracts must specifically address what the undertakings are with respect to equal treatment of participants. (*See* Sample Participant's Agreement in Chapter 5.)

NEWSWORTHINESS OF EVENTS

With respect to most special events, particularly those that take place on public streets, there must be some accommodation to the news value of what takes place. Fair comment, fair use or newsworthiness are but rubrics for the same principle: The press is free to report that the event took place. It may even be privileged to illustrate what the event looked like when it was happening.

In *Zacchini*, the court said:

> *If under this standard respondent [the TV station] had merely reported that petitioner [the Human Cannonball] was performing at the fair and described or commented on his act, with or without showing his picture on television, we would have a very different case.*[20]

The court further reasoned that there was a qualitative difference between taking a performance in its entirety and merely reporting on it:

> *It is evident . . . that petitioner's state-law right of publicity would not serve to prevent respondent from reporting the newsworthy facts about petitioner's act. [footnote omitted]. Wherever the line in particular situations is to be drawn between media reports that are protected and those that are not, we are quite sure that the First and Fourteenth Amendments do not immunize the media when they broadcast a performer's entire act without his consent.*[21]

The court in *Taggart* articulated a similar concern in allowing the jury to determine whether the latrine attendant's interview was newsworthy or a commercial exploitation of his privacy or publicity rights.

Numerous courts have limited the privacy right to accommodate the freedom of the press and the right of the public to know. As Prosser summarized in his seminal article:

> *The privilege of giving publicity to news, and other matters of public interest, arises out of the desire and the right of the public to know what is going on in the world, and the freedom of the press and other agencies of information to tell them.*[22]

Since the landmark cases of *New York Times Co.* v. *Sullivan*[23] and *Time* v. *Hill*,[24] the Supreme Court and lower federal courts have continued to define the limits of protection afforded to the media in reporting matters of legitimate public interest.

20.
Zacchini, supra note 2, at 569.

21.
Id. at 574-75.

22.
Privacy, *supra* note 1, at 412 (1960).

23.
376 U.S. 254 (1964).

24.
385 U.S. 374 (1976).

In *Time* v. *Hill*, the court considered a theater review that mistakenly reported that the play was based on an incident in which the Hill family was held hostage. The court said the report was privileged because it was not published with knowledge that it was false or with reckless disregard for the truth. Moreover, the court said the Hills were newsworthy:

> *Exposure of the self to others in varying degrees is a concomitant of life in a civilized community. The risk of this exposure is an essential incident of life in a society which places a primary value on freedom of speech and of press. "Freedom of discussion, if it would fulfill its historic function in this nation, must embrace all issues about which information is needed or appropriate to enable the members of society to cope with the exigencies of their period." Thornhill v. Alabama, 310 U.S. 88, 102 (60 S. Ct. 736, 84 L. Ed. 1093).*[25]

25.
Id. at 388.

26.
336 F. Supp. 133 (N.D. Cal. 1971).

The court in *Goldman* v. *Time, Inc.*[26] cited the above language from *Time* v. *Hill* in holding that a story about young Americans living abroad was newsworthy and did not invade their privacy. The plaintiffs had argued that the story was "manufactured" in the sense that there was no event about which to report. The Court said that California courts would look to three factors in determining whether a particular incident is newsworthy:

> *(1) the social value of the facts published; (2) the depth of the article's intrusion into ostensibly private affairs; and (3) the extent to which the party voluntarily acceded to a position of notoriety. [citation omitted].*[27]

27.
Id. at 138.

With respect to a parade, marathon or other public event, it is clear such factors make it newsworthy: (1) the social value does not turn on whether it is news or entertainment; (2) reporting the parade does not intrude on intrinsically private affairs; and (3) the participants and spectators, by appearing in public, have voluntarily waived some part of their privacy rights and have acceded to positions of notoriety, at least with respect to their involvement in the event.

RECORDING AND PERFORMING MUSIC

It is essential that event organizers understand how to use music legally in their events, even if the event itself is not a concert. Music is protected by copyright. Under the copyright law, the copyright owner (the composer or his or her transferee) controls the right to record the music, to arrange it and, perhaps most importantly for event organizers, to perform it publicly.

A public performance is one that occurs at a place open to the public (or at any place where a substantial number of people outside of a normal circle of a family and its social acquaintances is gathered) or that is transmitted to the public in different places (as via television) or at different times.[28] Playing a record on a jukebox is a public performance.[29] Broadcasting a song is a public performance.

Playing a radio station in a public place such as a store is a public performance if it is amplified by other than common home equipment. In *Twentieth Century Music Corp.* v. *Aiken*,[30] the court held that the playing of a radio over four ceiling speakers in a fast-food restaurant was not a public performance of copyrighted musical works. This exemption for the use in public establishments of "a single receiving apparatus of a kind commonly used in private homes" is now codified by the copyright law.[31]

Performances are either grand (dramatic) or small (nondramatic). Event organizers usually are concerned with small performance rights. Grand rights pertain to uses of music in furtherance of a story, as in an opera or a musical play. Small rights pertain to the simple performance in public of copyrighted music either as background or as the focus of attention. Most popular music is licensed for nondramatic public performance by the American Society of Composers, Authors and Publishers (ASCAP) or Broadcast Music, Inc. (BMI).

ASCAP and BMI are "performing rights societies." Their members are songwriters and music publishers. "Music publishing" in this sense means controlling the rights to the music. ASCAP and BMI pay both member publishers and member authors each time one of their songs is performed – on TV, on a radio, on a jukebox, in a concert, in a parade or otherwise. (The basic technique used by the societies to count public performances of songs in their respective repertoires is a sampling method that weights certain uses, like network TV's, heavier than others.)

ASCAP and BMI were formed because authors and publishers individually could not possibly administer or police all the public performances of their works. Popular songwriters thus grant to either ASCAP or BMI the right to license their music for nondramatic performances. ASCAP and BMI in turn grant public performances licenses to television and radio stations, concert halls and bars; they survey uses

28.
17 U.S.C. § 101.

29.
17 U.S.C. § 116(a)(2), (b)(1) (1976) provide for a compulsory license for the inclusion of recorded music in jukeboxes. The operator of the "coin operated phonorecord player" is entitled to the license. If a machine has been compulsorily licensed, the owner of an establishment in which the jukebox is located does not infringe the public performance rights of the copyright owner by allowing its use. This does not apply if one or more of the following circumstances applies: (1) the jukebox is not activated by the insertion of coins or currency; (2) a direct or indirect admission charge is made; (3) a list of the music is not affixed to the jukebox; or (4) the patrons don't get to choose the music.

30.
422 U.S. 151 (1975).

31.
17 U.S.C. § 110(5). *See also Broadcast Music, Inc. v. United States Shoe Corp.*, 211 U.S.P.Q. 43 (C.D. Cal. 1980), *aff'd*, 678 F.2d 816 (9th Cir. 1982) [Section 110(5) exemption did not apply because the "Bogen monaural receiver and the Bogen speaker used in the [defendant's] stores are not equipment of a kind commonly used in private homes" and the speakers were not "arranged within a narrow circumference from the receiver . . ."].

and pay authors and publishers their share of royalties after deducting an administrative fee. Again, ASCAP and BMI license only nondramatic performing rights. The rights to include a song in a stage show or pageant or to produce phonograph records are not within their control.

Essentially, ASCAP and BMI grant two kinds of licenses – blanket and single performance licenses. A *blanket license* is commonly granted to television and radio stations, to proprietors of public places and to festival promoters. It allows them to cause any song in the society's repertoire to be publicly performed an unlimited number of times during the period of the license. (The fact that a radio station has a blanket license does not allow a non-licensee to rebroadcast the radio's signal in a store, as previously discussed, except by the use of home amplifying equipment.)

Alternatively, a *single performance* license would allow an individual or a group to perform a musical number once at a given location on a given day.

The license fee for either a blanket or a single performance license varies with the capacity of the hall, whether it involves live or recorded music and whether or not there is dancing or an admission fee. ASCAP and BMI have many different standard contracts based on the kind of use being made. ASCAP's Concerts and Recitals License is reproduced in Appendix G. It is a blanket license for the period of the license.

It is the responsibility of the event organizer to obtain the requisite music licenses. Even if the musicians are independent contractors over whom the organizer has no control, the organizer is nonetheless liable for the unlicensed performance of copyrighted music. For instance, in *Famous Music Corp.* v. *Bay State Harness Horse Racing and Breeding Association*,[32] the court said it was well settled that the proprietor of a public establishment is responsible for all performance of music on his or her premises. Otherwise, the court said, the proprietor "could . . . reap the benefits of countless violations by orchestras, itinerant or otherwise, by merely claiming ignorance of any violation that would take place."[33] Arenas where music is frequently played – as background or at halftimes or during concerts – often have a blanket license; thus the organizer needs to insure only that all songs played are either ASCAP, BMI or public domain. The arena's rental agreement will often require the organizer to agree to pay only ASCAP, BMI or public domain music.

If an event organizer authorizes live broadcast of a parade or concert, for instance, it should require the broadcaster to have the necessary performance licenses, which

32.
554 F.2d 1213 (1st Cir. 1977).

33.
Id. at 1215.

often the broadcaster will have through the blanket license system discussed above. The organizer must then be certain that all music played is ASCAP, BMI or public domain.

If, on the other hand, the coverage of the event is delayed, or edited into a program or home video cassette, then the organizer needs to obtain a *synchronization license* to permit the recording of the music with the filmed action. (The broadcaster will still need to have a performance license.)

If an event is to be recorded, the organizer will need to obtain a *mechanical rights license* as well. Mechanical rights are rights to reproduce a copyrighted musical composition in copies of phonorecords. They are controlled by the owner of copyright in the song or by a licensing agency such as Harry Fox, Inc. "Phonorecords" includes all "material objects in which sounds, other than those accompanying a motion picture or other audiovisual work, are fixed by any method now know or later developed, and from which the sounds can be perceived, reproduced, or otherwise communicated, either directly or with the aid of a machine or device."[34] Simply put, phonorecords include phonograph records, tapes and CDs. If music is recorded for inclusion in motion pictures, television programs or video productions, the mechanical rights are called the *synchronization rights* (indicating the synchronization of music with visual images). Event organizers who desire to record music for use in a delayed broadcast of their event are most concerned with synchronization rights.

34.
17 U.S.C. § 101.

If a concert promoter has somehow garnered the right to produce a record album "Live at _____," the mechanical license known as the *compulsory license* would be available. Although it is typically cheaper to negotiate a royalty directly with the copyright proprietor, the copyright law does provide for a "compulsory license." A compulsory license allows anyone to record a composition once it has been recorded and publicly distributed. Of course, the event organizer must also negotiate with the musical talent to obtain rights in his or her particular performance of the underlying copyrighted material for purposes of the album. Compulsory licenses are not available for audiovisual works like television shows and videotapes.

The performer's record company may have contractual rights to prevent the celebrity from recording his or her performance in any manner. The sponsor should get a warranty that the talent is free to enter into videotaping and recording agreements.

ASCAP and BMI licensing requirements and applications can be obtained from the offices listed below:

ASCAP's Main Office:

American Society of Composers,
    Authors and Publishers
ASCAP Building
One Lincoln Plaza
New York, NY 10023
(212) 595-3050

Other Major ASCAP Offices:

6430 Sunset Boulevard
Hollywood, CA 90028
(213) 466-7681

2 Music Square East
Nashville, TN 37203
(615) 244-3936

BMI's Main Office:

Broadcast Music, Inc.
320 West 57th Street
New York, NY 10019
(212) 586-2000

Other Major BMI Offices:

10 Music Square East
Nashville, TN 37203
(615) 259-3625

8730 Sunset Boulevard
3rd Floor West
Hollywood, CA 90069
(213) 659-9109

TELEVISION

Program Sponsorship

Television rights to some events – such as holiday college football bowl games, the Olympics and other sporting events – can be quite valuable. In addition, the fee a sponsor is willing to pay usually depends on the amount of media coverage expected. Yet, sponsors cannot be assured that even their title sponsorship will be announced on TV. The networks may pay for the exclusive rights to cover the event, but they won't necessarily call it by the title sponsor's name. In a worst-case scenario, the lead broadcast sponsor could be the event sponsor's competitor!

Event organizers should attempt to have some broadcast commercial time "reserved" for the event sponsor to buy from the network. If a sponsor commits to enough commercial time – over and above the cost of the sponsorship of the event – the networks will probably pepper its broadcast with the title sponsor's name.

This is generally true even if the organizer has purchased the network's time and is producing the media coverage itself. The networks will impose their production and commercial standards on the organizer's coverage, and the same rules with respect to use of the title sponsor's name will apply. (In order to achieve uniformity, the networks usually also require organizers to use network announcers.)

Organizers can offer sponsors a greater array of options if they produce coverage of an event for sale to independent stations. An organizer might syndicate an event-based program for cash, commercial spots or for some combination of the two. Then the organizer sells the spots and can "give" some to the event sponsor.

In either case, the sponsor might require the organizer to guarantee that a certain percentage of the country will be covered or that a certain rating will be achieved. A rating point is a measure of audience. If a certain audience is not achieved, the sponsor might be entitled to a rebate, depending on its contract. The idea is to encourage the organizer to promote the event and generate enough interest that the television audience will be large. Perhaps the organizer should even be entitled to a bonus for achieving a greater rating. The organizer, however, cannot guarantee the success of any event and therefore should not bear the entire risk of a poor audience. The proportions of the carrot and the stick are negotiable.

If there is to be television coverage of an event, organizers should be aware of two pertinent legal issues: payola and blackouts.

Payola

"Payola" is a form of commercial bribery. The term refers generally to the payment of television producers, station managers or radio personnel for the inclusion of any commercial matter in a broadcast. For example, giving money or any other valuable consideration to a radio program director or disc jockey for playing a certain record is a form of payola. Paying a producer to show a television character drinking a certain brand of beverage is also payola. Plugging a hotel or airline that contributes to an event on the air is payola.

35.
47 U.S.C. § 508. (See Appendix H)

Payola in the television and radio industries has been a federal crime since 1960 and carries a fine of up to $10,000 or imprisonment for up to one year or both.[35] Payola is not an offense if the payment is disclosed to the station, to the producer of the program and to the public. This usually sounds something like: "Promotional consideration has been paid to (*name of station*) by (*sponsor*)."[36]

36.
See 47 C.F.R. § 73.4180 (1987) and Public Notice, FCC 70-593 (June 4, 1970), 23 F.C.C.2d 588.

Event organizers should be cognizant of their obligations under FCC rules if they intend to sell television or radio broadcast rights to their events.

Blackouts

When negotiating television coverage of an event, the organizer may need to negotiate for a blackout. In agreeing to black out an event, the network – free or cable – agrees not to broadcast the event to the area where it is taking place. This is important if the organizer is relying on live gate receipts as a significant source of revenues, as is the case with many athletic contests and concerts. It is less important, if at all, with large festival-type events or marathons.

A typical blackout covers a radius of 35 to 50 miles from the site of the event. During the blackout the local network affiliate has to substitute programming. For the blackout to be effective, network advertising for the event must prominently disclose the area of the blackout. (This also serves the interests of the affiliate by preventing a public relations disaster from dissatisfied viewers.)

In syndicating a broadcast, the organizer simply withholds the relevant market areas from the syndicator's territory. But the organizer should beware. The syndicator may sell the event coverage to a distant station whose signal is carried by a cable operator serving the supposedly blacked-out area. Some superstations, such as WGN in Chicago, present this problem because their signals are received in places as remote as Alaska. (See definition of "superstation" in the glossary.)

Sports events have some special protection from carriage of their events by cable operators. The FCC restricts a cable system's right to carry live sports events in certain narrowly defined situations.[37] The holder of broadcast rights to a sports event may prevent a cable system located within 35 miles of a television broadcast station licensed to a community in which a sports event is taking place from carrying the live broadcast of the sports event if the event is not broadcast by a television station that the cable system is required to carry pursuant to the FCC's former mandatory carriage rules.[38] Thus, for example, the holder of the broadcast rights to a boxing match in Las Vegas can prevent any cable system located within 35 miles of Las Vegas from carrying the fight live if no Las Vegas, Nevada or Henderson, Nevada television station is broadcasting the fight live.[39]

The request to prevent the broadcast of the live sports event must be made by the holder of the broadcast rights to the event, or by that holder's agent.[40] For regularly scheduled events, a party requesting deletion of sports broadcasts should ensure that such requests are received by the cable system no later than the Monday preceding the calendar week (Sunday through Saturday) during which the program deletion is to be made.[41] If events are not regularly scheduled, notice must be received by the cable system 24 hours after the time the telecast to be deleted becomes known, but never later than 24 hours before the event is to be broadcast.[42] Requests to delete a sports broadcast must include the name and address of the party requesting deletion, the date, time and expected duration of the sports event and the call letters of the station from which the deletion is to be made.[43] If the broadcast signal to be deleted is not regularly carried by the cable system, the station need not provide the call letters of the station from which the deletion is to be made.[44]

Local broadcast rights can also be protected from duplication by a cable system operation that carries a distant signal if the distant signal is duplicating the network programming of the local station.

The FCC provides non-duplication protection only for network programming. "Network" programming has been defined broadly by the FCC to include not merely programs carried by one of the three major national networks, but those carried by any group, on a regional basis, so long as the program is broadcast simultaneously in a discrete geographical area.[45] Thus, for example, the FCC has afforded non-duplication protection of the live and simultaneous broadcasts of Boston Bruins and Boston Red Sox games for only six New England-area television stations, based on the conclusion that such programming constitutes "network" programming broadcast by a regional television network.[46] Similarly, the simultaneous broadcast by two Minnesota television stations of high school tournament basketball games originated by a third Minnesota television station was found to constitute regional "network" programming for purposes of the non-

37.
47 C.F.R. § 76.67.

38.
47 C.F.R. § 76.67(a). The mandatory carriage rules were held unconstitutional in May 1988 in Century Communications Corporation v. F.C.C., No. 86-1683, slip op. at 4 (D.C. Cir. Dec. 11, 1984), cert. denied, 56 U.S.L.W. 3818 (May 31, 1988).

39.
If no television station is licensed to the community in which the sports event is taking place, the holder of the broadcast rights may prevent the live carriage of the sports event on any cable system located within 35 miles of a television station licensed to the community with which the sports event or local team is identified, provided the sports event is not carried by the cable system on a broadcast station that is a "must-carry" signal. 47 C.F.R. § 876.67(a). Finally, if no television station is licensed to the community in which the sports event is taking place and the event or team is not identified with any particular community, the holder of broadcast rights may prevent the carriage of the event on a television station licensed to the community nearest to the event if the event is not broadcast by any of the broadcast stations that are entitled to mandatory carriage on the cable system. 47 C.F.R. § 76.67(a).

40.
47 C.F.R. § 76.67(a).

41.
47 C.F.R. § 76.67(c).

42.
Id.

43.
47 C.F.R. § 76.67(b).

44.
Id.

45.
Maine Cable Television, Inc., 34 R.R.2d 1452 (1975).

46.
Id.

47.
Cable TV of Fairmount, 31 R.R.2d 671 (1974).

48.
WAPA-TV Broadcasting Corp., 37 R.R.2d 127 (1976); Cable Television of Puerto Rico, 34 R.R.2d 485 (1975).

49.
Cable systems having fewer than 1,000 subscribers are not subject to the network non-duplication protection requirements.
  There is one exception to the non-duplication protection afforded a local station; it provides that cable systems are not required to delete duplicated network programming of a "significantly viewed" station. 47 C.F.R. § 76.94(g).

50.
47 C.F.R. § 76.94.

51.
Id.

duplication rules.[47] Clearly, events distributed to television stations nationally and internationally by an event organizer constitute "network" programming for purposes of this rule.

A local broadcast station can claim non-duplication protection only for network programming that has not been altered. In this connection, network non-duplication protection is afforded only to programs duplicated in the same language.[48] A local television station that dubs the Spanish language into a program broadcast simultaneously in the English language cannot claim non-duplication protection against the English language program. Thus a Puerto Rican television station, for instance, that overrides WGN's English-language audio signal in the Spanish language cannot claim non-duplication protection from a local Puerto Rican cable system for a network program carried on WGN.

Generally, a local broadcast station is entitled to non-duplication protection for its network programs if the cable system importing the duplicative signal is located within 35 miles of the local television station and more than 35 miles from the station transmitting the duplicated programming.[49] Thus, for example, a Washington, D.C. television station carrying a boxing match live can require the Arlington, Virginia cable system to black out its live carriage on WGN. In addition, stations located in television markets outside the top 100 are entitled to protection from a cable system located within 55 miles of the local station if the cable system is not within 55 miles of the station transmitting the duplicated programming.

In order to receive protection, the television station seeking network non-duplication protection must give appropriate written notice to the cable system from which it requests protection. Stations must notify cable systems of non-duplication requests no later than the Monday preceding the calendar week (Sunday through Saturday) during which non-duplication protection is requested.[50] A station requesting such protection must provide the day, date and beginning and end times of the program to be protected and the day, date and beginning and end times of the program to be deleted.[51] The station seeking protection must also provide the call letters and channel number of the station from which the program is to be deleted.

SAMPLE TELEVISION AGREEMENT

THIS AGREEMENT is made as of (*date*) between (*Production Company or Organizer*) ("Licensor"), and (*Network*) ("Network").

Licensor hereby grants to Network exclusive television rights to broadcast of the Event described below (the "Program"), in accordance with the BASIC PROVISIONS set forth below and the attached GENERAL TERMS AND CONDITIONS.

This is the basic grant of rights in the Program. Here, the Licensor produces the Event and the television coverage (the "Program") and delivers it to the Network. This Paragraph should recite that the coverage is only to be live or delayed, depending on what rights are granted. There should be no significant differences between cable and free network agreements.

Basic Provisions

I. Event. The Event shall consist of (*describe*) scheduled to take place on (*date*) at (*location*) (the "Site"). The Event will be sanctioned by (*sanctioning body*). The Event shall consist of at least (*time*) hours of televisable activities and shall start at (*time*) ("Starting Time").

This paragraph will describe the event in some detail. For certain kinds of events, criteria may be specified, such as how many holes of golf will be covered, how many camera positions will be used, how many boxing matches, gymnastic events, hours of music, etc.

II. Consideration. A. In consideration of all rights granted to Network and the performance of all Licensor's obligations hereunder, Network hereby grants Licensor and the advertisers listed on Exhibit A attached hereto ("the Advertisers") national commercial time for the promotion during the Program of the products and services of the Advertisers as follows: (*specify*)

Here, the Licensor produces the Program and sells the commercial time to Advertisers (sponsors).

B. In the event of any extension of a Program (e.g., due to [a play-off, extra periods, curtain calls, etc.]) or reduction of a Program, each Advertiser shall receive a proportion of the available commercial time which equals such Advertiser's proportion of the commercial time during the planned Program length.

This allows the Licensor to get a proportion of the additional commercial time if the Program runs long and divides up the time if there is a shortfall.

C. In addition to the foregoing, 50% of the opening and closing billboards shall be provided to Advertisers. It is agreed that (*lead sponsor*) shall have exclusive presenter position on each Program, and that the first opening billboard shall be as follows: (*specify*). In producing the Program, Licensor agrees to adhere to the standard Network commercial format. Licensor further agrees to cooperate with appropriate Network personnel in the insertion of commercial positions in such Programs. In the event Licensor does not sell, or utilize for make-good purposes, all of the above-referenced commercial time, Licensor shall notify Network at least seven (7) days prior to the Event of the amount of any unsold time. After receipt of such notice, Network shall have the right, with respect to any unsold time, to insert other advertisers as Network may select in its discretion.

This paragraph requires the Licensor to follow Network standards regarding the Program and the use of commercial time in the Program. However, it requires the Licensor to return unsold time to the Network, which can sell it, here without commission or other compensation to the Licensor. This could be negotiated; the Licensor might be able to use the unsold time to hype other events. In the alternative, it could share in the Network's revenues from its sale.

D. In using such commercial time, Licensor shall, or, as the case may be, shall cause the Advertiser to:

1. consult regularly with the individual in Network's Advertising Sales Department designated by Network regarding plans for use of such time;

2. promptly advise Network of each committed use, specify the name of the Advertiser, the product or service to be advertised and such other relevant information as Network may reasonably request, and furnish Network, no later than seventy-two (72) hours before the telecast in question, with the videotapes and other requisite material for airing Advertisers' commercials;

3. observe Network's Advertising Regulations attached hereto as Exhibit B; and

4. refrain from "tags" or other promotional announcements on the part of Licensor's commentators except upon the prior approval of Network, which shall

not be unreasonably withheld. Licensor shall not withhold its approval of any such tag or promotional announcement for any category of product or service of an advertiser on the telecast or of other official suppliers to the Event.

The Licensor is required to adhere to the Network's commercial insertion standards and to refrain from "tags" or "plugs" without approval. This paragraph attempts to preapprove plugs for Advertisers and suppliers. Competitive protection for Licensor's Advertisers is provided elsewhere.

Any substitutions for, or changes to the Advertisers listed on Exhibit A shall be subject to the approval of Network, which shall not be unreasonably withheld. Any advertising in violation of Network's Advertising Regulations may be rejected by Network without liability or obligation to Licensor. [Network shall advise Licensor of any such rejection in time to permit broadcast of substitute materials already produced.]

The Network retains approval over the content of commercials and the identity of the advertisers. However, Licensor's Advertisers should be given prompt notice of rejection so alternative commercials can be used. This doesn't mean that the Advertisers must have time to produce new materials, just to substitute already produced commercials.

E. Network agrees not to sell commercial time on the Program for use in advertising any products or services in the following product categories: *(specify)*

This provides competitive protection to the Licensor's Advertisers. The Licensor may also wish to bar antithetical products even though not competitive to those of official sponsors.

F. Network hereby gives Licensor one (1) promotional position of sixty (60) seconds in length in the Program for the purpose of promoting the *(sanctioning body)*, provided that such promotional announcement shall not refer to third party commercial entities without the advance written approval of Network.

The sanctioning body often receives at least one minute of free time from the Network to promote itself.

G. In the case of a weather delay or force majeure (as hereinafter defined) which causes delay, postponement or cancellation of all or part of the Event, Licensor hereby authorizes Network to telecast, and Network hereby agrees to telecast, reruns of other Events previously distributed by Network or other programming provided by Licensor for this purpose (i.e., to fill time due to postponement or delay) ("Delay Programming"). Any Delay Programming shall include "on camera" introductory material containing an explanation of the weather delay or postponement necessitating the Delay Programming.

If the Event is postponed due to weather, the Network time must be filled. Here, the Licensor authorizes reruns of past events but also has the option to provide other programming to fill the delay.

III. Programs. Licensor shall produce and deliver to Network, at the site of the Event, the Program of the Event in accordance with the following:

Producer: . . . .   Licensor.

Director: . . . .   To be selected by Licensor in consultation with (*sanctioning body*) subject to Network's approval, not to be unreasonably withheld.

Commentators: . . . .   To be selected by Licensor in consultation with (*sanctioning body*) and subject to Network's approval, not to be unreasonably withheld.

Facilities/Equipment: . . . .   (*specify*)

Program Length: . . . .   (*number*) hours.

Delivery: . . . .   Live at the Site.

Other Terms: . . . .   Network will arrange and pay for transmission from the Site.

The Licensor agrees to provide the Program as specified here. The Network retains approval over announcers.

IN WITNESS WHEREOF, the parties hereto have executed this Agreement as of the day and year first written above.

Licensor

By: _____

Network

By: _____

General Terms and Conditions
I. The Event. A. As used herein, the term "Event" shall mean the event named in Paragraph I of the BASIC PROVISIONS and all events and activities taking place at the Site on the Date(s) of the Event. The Event shall be staged and conducted at the Site at the Starting Time(s) and on the Date(s) indicated in the BASIC PROVISIONS.

This refers back to the Basic Provisions, which may be tailor-made for this Event, while the General Terms are boilerplate.

B. As between Network and Licensor, Licensor shall be solely responsible for all arrangements (including any compensation) with the owner of the Site for the staging of the Event and all participants and any officials involved in the Event. If Network is furnishing announcers hereunder, Licensor shall supply Network suitable space for such persons.

The Licensor is required to make arrangements with the Site and to provide working space for the Network's announcers, if any.

C. At Network's request, Licensor shall furnish Network a reasonable number of choice complimentary tickets to the Event.

Complimentary tickets should be limited, particularly since the Network here is not paying for the Event.

II. The Program. A. As used herein, the term "Program" shall mean a television program based on or including the Event or any portion thereof. The Program shall be of at least the same quality and have at least the same production standards as other Network live programming currently being produced by Network.

Here the Network uses its own programming as the standard of quality.

B. Licensor shall consult with Network regularly throughout the development and production of the Program on the manner of production and other creative aspects of Program. The Program shall contain a closing credit which includes: "Produced in association with Network." [Other than a single credit which may be accorded to Licensor for its efforts in producing the Program, Licensor shall not, without first obtaining Network's written consent, include in the Program any credits to any other person, firm or corporation.]

This Paragraph requires the Licensor to consult with the Network on production and creative aspects of the Program. Licensor should attempt to retain final control, however, since it is the one at risk. Credits are always open to negotiation.

C. Licensor shall consult with Network on both the "above" and "below-the-line" personnel to be used by Licensor in the production of the Program. Network hereby approves of the personnel and elements, if any, specified in Paragraph II of the BASIC PROVISIONS. Network shall have the right to approve any material changes to such personnel and elements during the term of this Agreement.

Here the Network retains approval over production and creative personnel used by Licensor. Above-the-line items include the script, producer, director and on-camera talent. Below-the-line items are production, post production, sets, camera crews, make-up, transportation and the like.

D. Licensor shall cause one (1) or more Network and (*sanctioning body*) banners to be placed at the Site in such a manner and location that such banners will be reasonably and readily apparent to both the spectators at the Site and the viewers watching the Program as telecast by Network.

The Network wants visibility in the Program even though it is not buying it outright.

E. At Licensor's expense, Licensor shall deliver to Network at a point acceptable to Network at or immediately adjacent to the Site of the Event, or at such other point as may be specified in the BASIC PROVISIONS, an audio-video signal of the Program of acceptable technical quality meeting Federal Communications Commission requirements for television signals and suitable for retransmission by Network.

The point of delivery is important because of the expense of getting the signal to a remote site. The Licensor bears the cost of delivery.

F. If, prior to the Event Date, the Event is postponed due to any reason beyond the control of Licensor, Licensor and Network shall mutually agree on a Postponement Date.

If the Event is postponed, the parties agree on a new date so that television time can be made available.

III. Delayed Distribution and Exhibition. A. Network is hereby granted the exclusive right for one (1) year from the Event (the "License Period") in the geographic areas described in Exhibit C hereto (the "License Territory") and hereby agrees to distribute, transmit, exhibit, license, advertise, promote, publicize and perform (hereinafter "distribute") the Program and its constituent elements by means of Standard [and Nonstandard] Television, once live and not less than two (2) nor more than four (4) additional times on tape ("reruns"). Network shall have the right during the additional period ending one (1) year after the applicable License Period expires to (i) distribute an aggregate of ten percent (10%) of the Program, as part of a highlight show and (ii) re-exhibit the Program during any weather cancellation or delay occurring during a time period scheduled for telecast by Network of another Event organized by Licensor. Network also shall have the right for one (1) week after the Event, to permit others to tape and distribute up to three-minute excerpts of the Event as part of news and sports programs for exhibition over television. Network shall have the right in perpetuity to retain recordings of the Program for its files and reference, to use limited excerpts thereof (i.e., not to exceed three (3) minutes for any one use) for purposes of promoting itself in any medium, to use such excerpts as background material in reporting current news developments and, subject to Licensor's prior written approval, to distribute an aggregate of ten percent (10%) of the Program as part of a highlight show. As used herein the term "Nonstandard Television" shall include exhibition by direct satellite delivery, cable television, master antenna television, closed circuit television, and multipoint distribution service, all on a commercially supported or other basis of reception as Network may elect.

The Network must be required to broadcast the Event live – that's part of what the sponsors of the Event are paying for. Whether or not the Network gets any delayed rights is a matter of negotiation. The right to use 3 minutes of highlights for promotional purposes is standard. Use for a highlights film is negotiable; normally the Licensor, the producer of the Program, would retain those rights.

B. During the term of this Agreement, Licensor shall not license any other broadcast or cablecast or other exhibition whatsoever of the Event within the License Territory to any other party, without the advance written approval of Network. Notwithstanding the foregoing, Network hereby consents to Licensor's authorization of local, regularly scheduled news coverage, provided that Licensor requires each local broadcast to restrict its airing of such coverage to cumulative total of not more than three (3) minutes of the action of the Event.

Licensor here agrees that the Network's broadcast is exclusive. The Licensor should ask for a blackout of the Site if the Event is one to which tickets are sold. The blackout typically is lifted if the Event is 90% to 100% sold out.

C. At a minimum, Network shall distribute the Program over its network throughout the License Territory as set forth in Exhibit C.

The Network should be required to air the Program on the Network so that the Advertisers get their money's worth.

D. If Network distributes the Program outside the United States, it shall pay Licensor 50% of Network's revenues from sale or license of such rights. Such payment will be made by Network to Licensor within ten (10) days after the receipt of such revenues.

If the Network authorizes cable broadcast abroad, then the Licensor should share in revenues therefrom. A percentage of revenues is easier to calculate and audit than a percentage of profits.

IV. Expenses. A. Except to the extent provided otherwise in the BASIC PROVISIONS, Licensor shall, as between Licensor and Network, produce, film, and/or videotape the Program and pay all costs and expenses in connection therewith, including without limitation, all the above-the-line and below-the-line elements, post production, underlying rights, music synchronization, mechanical and performance rights and all material contained in the Program. Licensor shall be fully responsible for paying all persons providing services in connection with the Programs at least the amount required under any union or guild collective bargaining agreement applicable to the Program and the exercise of Network's rights hereunder. Licensor shall arrange and be responsible for all necessary licenses, clearances and permissions required to be obtained by Licensor pursuant to the terms of the Agreement.

All expenses of production are the Licensor's responsibility. The Licensor might want to except music performance rights from this paragraph if the Network has a blanket ASCAP or BMI License.

B. Except as otherwise specifically and explicitly set forth in the BASIC PROVISIONS hereof, Network shall have no obligation to make payments to Licensor or to anyone else with respect to the Event, the Program, the underlying material contained in the Paragraph and Network's distribution or exploitation of the Program pursuant to this Agreement.

This may be redundant, but it specifies explicitly that any reuse fees are the Licensor's responsibility.

V. Promotion and Publicity. Network, its sponsor(s) and their respective advertising agencies and each television or other distribution station, system or service scheduled to distribute the Program shall have the right and may grant to others the right to reproduce, print, publish or disseminate in any medium, the name and likeness and voice of each person appearing in or connected with the Program and biographical material concerning such persons as well as Licensor's name, the (*sanctioning body's*), the name of the Event and the Site, for purposes of trade or for advertising purposes, including, without limitation, "institutional" advertising, the distribution, exploitation, advertising and promotion of the Program and, in connection therewith, the products or services of any sponsors thereof, but not as an endorsement of any product or service.

It is standard to allow television outlets to use the Licensor's trademarks and the likenesses of key personnel to promote coverage of the Event.

VI. Force Majeure. If the staging or the coverage of any Event and the Delay Programming should be prevented or cancelled due to any act of God, inevitable accident, strike or other labor dispute, fire, riot or civil commotion, government action or decree, inclement weather, failure of technical, production or television equipment, or for any other reason beyond the control of any party hereto, then no party shall be obligated in any manner to the other with respect to the Program or the Event.

This paragraph lets both parties off the hook if the Event or its coverage (or the Delayed Coverage) is cancelled or prevented.

VII. Warranties. A. Licensor warrants and represents to Network that (1) it is free to enter into and perform this Agreement; (2) it has all rights necessary to its grant of rights to Network hereunder; (3) the commercials supplied by Advertisers hereunder are in compliance with Network's Advertising Regulations and will not infringe upon or violate the rights of any third party; (4) it will not do anything which might tend to interfere with or impair the rights which Network has acquired in this Agreement; [(5) the Event is sanctioned by such sports organizations and/or authorities as have jurisdiction over the Event and the Event will be conducted in accordance with all applicable rules and regulations of such organizations and/or authorities; and (6) a representative field of the top athletes in the applicable sport will participate in the Event.]

These are fairly standard warranties by the Licensor.

B. Network represents and warrants to Licensor that it has the right to enter into this Agreement and perform all of its obligations pursuant to this Agreement.

This is a fairly standard warranty but not terribly substantive.

VIII. Indemnification and Insurance. A. Each party will each indemnify, defend and hold the other harmless from any and all claims, costs, liabilities, judgments, expenses or damages (including reasonable attorneys' fees) arising out of any breach or alleged breach of this Agreement or any representation by it herein.

This is a standard indemnity.

B. In any case in which indemnification is sought hereunder:

1. The party seeking indemnification shall promptly notify the other of any claim or litigation to which the indemnification relates; and

2. The party seeking indemnification shall afford the other the opportunity to participate in and, at the other party's option, fully control any compromise, settlement, litigation or other resolution or disposition of such claim or litigation.

This requires notice and gives the indemnitor the right to control the litigation.

C. Each party shall maintain its own Comprehensive General & Automobile Liability Insurance Policy covering all of its activities under this Agreement in the minimum amount of $5,000,000 combined single limit bodily injury and property damage liability. Each party shall also maintain statutory workers' compensation insurance covering its employees with an Employers Liability limit of not less than $1,000,000 per occurrence.

Each party provides its own insurance. This paragraph could require that each party be named on the other's policy.

IX. Independent Contractors. Licensor and Network are independent contractors with respect to each other and nothing herein shall create any association, partnership, joint venture or agency relationship between them.

This paragraph disclaims any agency relationship between the parties.

X. Miscellaneous. A. All notices and other communication from any party to the other hereunder shall be in writing and shall be deemed received when delivered in person or five (5) days after deposit in the United States mails, postage prepaid, certified or registered mail, addressed to the other party at the address specified at the beginning of this Agreement, or at such other address as such other party may supply by written notice.

B. Each party hereto shall execute any and all further documents or amendments which either party hereto may deem necessary and proper to carry out the purposes of this Agreement.

C. This Agreement contains the full and complete understanding between the parties hereto, supersedes all prior agreements and understandings whether written or oral pertaining hereto, and cannot be modified except by a written instrument signed by each party hereto.

D. The descriptive headings of the several sections and paragraphs of this Agreement are inserted for convenience only and do not constitute a part of this Agreement.

E. This Agreement is to be governed by and construed in accordance with the laws of the State of (state) applicable to contracts entered into and to be fully performed therein.

F. Neither party hereto shall assign any of its rights or obligations hereunder without the prior written consent of the other party, and any purported assignment without such prior written consent shall be null and void and of no force and effect.

G. Any provisions hereof found by a court to be void or unenforceable shall not affect the validity or enforceability of any other provisions.

All of the above is boilerplate.

EXHIBIT A:
SPONSOR'S CURRENT AND PROSPECTIVE ADVERTISERS

EXHIBIT B:
ADVERTISING REGULATIONS

EXHIBIT C

The Territory is: (list states and/or countries)

SAMPLE SYNDICATION AGREEMENT

Syndicator's Letterhead

Owner of Event
Address

Ladies and Gentlemen:

This letter, when signed by us and countersigned by you, will constitute the agreement between us with respect to the distribution of the telecast of (*describe event*) (the "Event"). Our agreement is as follows:

1. Event.

1.01. The Event will take place in (*place*) on (*date*), beginning at approximately (*time*) and will consist of (*describe*).

This paragraph describes the Event, the site and the time.

1.02. (a) You shall undertake and cause the complete production of the Event and the telecast thereof, and shall be responsible for all costs relating thereto, including without limitation, all rights, all technical personnel, all facilities, the site, and all Event elements [including officiating and medical personnel.] The Event will be a production of (*name of Owner/Producer*) with announcers and color commentators subject to our prior written approval, which approval shall not be unreasonably withheld.

The Owner here arranges for the Event and the production of the coverage. The Syndicator retains approval rights over the announcers, since they affect the quality of the telecast.

[(b) No participant in the Event may be changed without our written consent, which consent shall not be unreasonably withheld.]

For some kinds of events, for instance, boxing events, the identity of participants is crucial to the attractiveness of the Event. If the participants were changed, the Event would be much less attractive to television stations and advertisers and the syndication effort would be less successful.

1.03. You shall be responsible for all arrangements for the terrestial facilities for the transmission of the telecast of the Event to a satellite and for the transmission of the telecast of the Event via satellite to receiving facilities for each television station licensed by us to telecast the Event. You agree to pay all costs in connection therewith, including the cost of integrating commercials into the telecast of the Event. You shall not be obligated to deliver the signal to more than one satellite.

The Organizer arranges to have the television coverage beamed to a satellite for delivery to the licensed television stations. The Organizer protects itself by specifying that it must deliver the signal to only one satellite. The Organizer here owns, and pays for, the production of the television coverage.

2. Syndicator's Rights

2.01. You hereby grant to us the exclusive right to license the live and delayed telecast of the Event throughout the geographic area (the "Territory") to [over-the-air] television stations as follows:

This Paragraph grants the Syndicator the right to distribute the event. Usually both over-the-air (traditional) and cable outlet rights are given.

(a) The Event will be telecast live from (*site*) on (*date*) from [approximately] (*time*) to (*time*) EST;

Obviously, the time of the broadcast, if it is to be live coverage, must be specified. Depending on the season, it is wise to specify daylight or standard time.

(b) The Event may be licensed for delayed telecast, only within 30 days of the Event.

Delayed telecast is especially important for foreign markets. A time frame for delayed broadcast protects the home video and theatrical markets, if those exist.

2.02. You hereby appoint us as the exclusive representative for the sale of advertising time, and we shall be solely and exclusively empowered to make arrangements and agreements with national advertisers for the sale, valuation and utilization of commercial time in connection with the Event. It is presently anticipated that the Event will be licensed to stations on a barter basis (*i.e.*, in exchange for commercial time) or on a cash or combination cash and barter basis.

Here, the Organizer recognizes that the Syndicator will set prices for commercial time and otherwise strike the deals with the stations without input from the Organizer.

3. Syndicator's Undertakings.

3.01. We shall secure for the Event a market coverage consisting of not less than (*number*) percent (_____%) of the households having television sets in the United States, as determined by the appropriate [Nielson NTI reports], and we agree to use our best efforts to provide maximum coverage for the live telecast of the Event.

This is a critical paragraph because it sets the standard of performance for the Syndicator. Seventy percent of Nielson NTI would be a common minimum performance criteria. Others may demand 90% coverage and/or utilize a different rating service. In any event, the Syndicator should use its best efforts to exceed the minimum criteria specified. For a discussion of best efforts clauses, see Chapter 1.

3.02. We shall be responsible for, and discharge all costs, charges and expenses incurred by us relating to the licensing of the telecast of the Event, including without limitation, all arrangements and agreements with advertisers; station clearances; sales expenses; accounting, legal and other internal costs, and all domestic taxes (other than income taxes) attributable to the licensing and distribution of the telecast of the Event.

Basically, the Syndicator pays its own costs with respect to the syndication effort.

3.03. We shall make arrangements for obtaining [Nielsen rating data] and supplying you with the applicable [Nielsen] reports.

The Syndicator has or arranges for access to rating reports and provides these to the Organizer (assuming, of course, that the Syndicator's contract with the rating service allows this sharing of data).

3.04. We agree not to license the live telecast, or delayed telecast on the same day as the Event, to any over-the-air television station [or cable system] licensed to broadcast within (*number*) miles of the arena in which the Event takes place. [We will notify you promptly of any sales or licenses to "superstations."]

The Organizer must protect the venue of the Event – that is, maximize the live gate.
The Syndicator therefore should not sell to stations that serve the venue area. How
to handle superstations (see the glossary for a definition) requires discussion between
the parties. The Organizer might wish to retain a veto over sales to superstations.

4. Fees and Financial Arrangements.

4.01. For the station clearance services to be provided by us pursuant to this
Agreement, we shall be paid either, (i) the sum of $_____ ("Syndication
Fee") [if Adjusted Gross Advertising Revenues (including revenues from advertising
sold by you), before the deduction of the Advertising Sales Commissions are at
least $_____, but if such Adjusted Gross Advertising Revenues for the
Event are less than $_____, the Syndication Fee shall be mutually agreed
upon;] or (ii) $_____ if the Event is not telecast, provided the failure to
telecast was not the result of a breach by us of any representation, warranty or
covenant contained herein.

A standard fee would be 20 to 40% of the advertising revenues. In the
parenthetical, the Syndicator here takes, in some way, less risk: if revenues fall below
a certain level, then it negotiates with the Organizer, but the higher number
psychologically frames the negotiation. There is, however, the risk that the
negotiation will not be successful. The Syndicator could assume a determinable
amount of risk by working solely on a percentage.

4.02. For purposes of this Agreement, the following terms shall have the following
meanings:

(a) "Adjusted Gross Advertising Revenues" shall mean the gross revenues actually
received by us (adjusted to reflect any cash rebates or the utilization of commercial
time in other programs ("make-goods") which Syndicator must provide to
advertisers pursuant to rating guarantees) from the sale of commercial time in
connection with the telecast of the Event, less standard advertising agency
commissions. Attached as Exhibit A is Syndicator's Program Audience Guarantee
Policy which sets forth Syndicator's policy and practice with respect to rating
guarantees. Advertising Revenues do not include sale of (*describe on-site*
advertising);

This is a very important paragraph. If the Syndicator guarantees an audience rating
to an advertiser and doesn't achieve that rating, it may have to make a cash or

other adjustment to the advertiser, thus reducing Gross Advertising Revenues. This paragraph also recognizes that advertising agencies typically earn a commission of 17.65% (15% of gross) on the cost of commercial time. On-site revenues (signs, etc.) are not included in the calculation of Adjusted Gross Advertising Revenues.

(b) "Advertising Sales Commission" shall mean (*number*) (____%) of Adjusted Gross Advertising Revenues.

A standard fee might be 10 or more percent. If the syndicator has a wholly owned or controlled sales arm, the amount of commission should be limited to avoid double-dipping.

(c) "Cable Royalties" shall mean any amounts received by any party from the Copyright Royalty Tribunal resulting from clearance of stations by us in connection with the Event. We shall have the sole right, responsibility and obligation for collection of Cable Royalties and you agree to remit to us immediately any Cable Royalties received by you from any person except us in connection with the Event.

The Copyright Royalty Tribunal collects fees from cable operators for over-the-air programming they pick up and remits royalties to copyright owners after adjudicating their claims. Here, the Syndicator takes on the responsibility for making the claim and, pursuant to the following paragraph, the Syndicator gets a fee for these efforts. This money is usually delayed pending Copyright Royalty Tribunal deliberations.

4.03. After the national [*service*] ratings of the Event are published, we shall pay to you an amount equal to the Adjusted Gross Advertising Revenues collected by us, less the sum of the Syndication Fee and the Advertising Sales Commission and any station compensation paid and any [*Nielsen rating*] adjustment, plus [*number*] percent (____%) of Cable Royalties received by us.

The Syndicator must wait until after the agreed-upon ratings service results are published in order to calculate advertising revenues, adjustments and commissions. Then it gets its fees and sales commission, if any, and its share of Cable Royalties (see Paragraph 4.02(c)), usually 10% or more.

4.04. We shall maintain accurate and complete books and records which shall reflect all transactions involving the Event. You shall have the right to have a representative of your choice examine said books and records during reasonable business hours upon reasonable advance notice to us.

This is a standard form audit clause.

4.05. We shall render or cause to be rendered to you on a quarterly basis, and within 30 days following the end of each quarter, reasonably detailed statements of all revenues and all authorized deductions relating to the Event. Such statements shall be accompanied by the payment to you of your share of the Adjusted Gross Advertising Revenues and Cable Royalties. All statements rendered hereunder shall be deemed final and incontestable unless objection is made by the objecting party within two (2) years after the date of submission.

The paragraph specifies the form of statement required by the Organizer. The Organizer may object to the two-year limitation on challenges to the accuracy of the statements.

5. Rights to Future Programming.

With respect to the future syndication of your events, you shall notify us of any such project and negotiate with us in good faith concerning the terms and conditions governing our involvement in such future productions. If we are unable to reach agreement concerning such terms and conditions, you shall be free to contract with any third party of your choosing concerning such third party's participation in such future production, on such terms and conditions, which may vary from those discussed with us, as may be acceptable to you.

An option to syndicate future events of the Organizer is negotiable. This paragraph only requires "good faith" negotiations – a requirement difficult to enforce. (See discussion of good faith negotiations in Chapter 1.)

6. Credits.

You shall be entitled to receive appropriate production credit; [however, any sponsor credit is subject to our prior written approval]. The telecast of the Event shall contain the following credit on a single frame for a minimum of four seconds duration as the last credit: Distributed by (Syndicator's Name).

Production credit, of course, goes to the Organizer. The Organizer should reject the parenthetical and retain approval over all sponsor credit in order to avoid having an advertiser sponsor the broadcast of an event title-sponsored or presented by a competitor. The Syndicator is entitled to distribution credit.

7. Insurance.

You shall procure the customary insurance carried by producers of television programs, including Errors and Omissions Insurance and Broadcasters Liability Insurance covering the Event and naming us as additional insured and insuring advertisers and the television stations broadcasting the Event, the limits of such insurance being $1,000,000 for a single claim and $3,000,000 for all claims in the aggregate [mutually agreeable].

The limits of insurance are negotiable, but it is customary for the producer (the Organizer) to indemnify all in the chain of distribution and broadcast.

8. Representations and Warranties.

8.01. You represent and warrant that:

(a) You are a corporation duly organized, validly existing and in good standing under the laws of the State of (*state*), and have the corporate power and authority to enter into and perform this agreement;

This is a standard corporate warranty.

(b) All corporate action necessary to authorize the execution, delivery and performance of this Agreement by you has been duly and properly taken, this Agreement has been duly and validly executed and delivered by you, and it constitutes a binding obligation enforceable against you in accordance with its terms;

This is a standard corporate warranty.

(c) You have [or will obtain] valid and binding agreements with all participants in the Event (the "Participants") pursuant to which each has agreed to participate in the Event (the "Event Agreements"). Each of the Event Agreements grants you the right to produce, sell and license the telecast of the Event as contemplated herein and make the representations, warranties and covenants contained in this Agreement;

The Organizer has the obligation to obtain all necessary releases from participants to allow broadcast of the Event.

(d) The execution, delivery and performance of this Agreement and the Event Agreements by you do not and will not require the consent of any third parties and will not conflict with, result in a breach of, or constitute a default under your Certificate of Incorporation or By-laws, any applicable law, judgment, order, injunction, decree, rule or regulation, or ruling of any court or governmental instrumentality; or conflict with, constitute grounds for termination of, result in a breach of or constitute a default under, any of the Event Agreements or any other agreement, instrument, license or permit to which you or the Event is subject;

This is a standard warranty that there will be no interference with the exercise of the Syndicator's rights.

[(e) The Event will be sanctioned by (name of body)];

This is an appropriate warranty for events that are sanctioned by official bodies such as the PGA, WBC or NASCAR.

(f) You are the sole owner of all right, title and interest in and to the Events, including all rights necessary for the live telecast of the Event;

This is a standard warranty.

(g) You have the sole authority to grant us the rights granted to us pursuant to this Agreement, and no consent or permit of any other person, entity, authority or commission is required to grant us such rights;

This is a standard warranty.

(h) The exercise by us of the rights granted to us under this Agreement will not infringe upon the rights of any third party; and upon exercise of such rights, no other person shall have any right or valid claim against us to any of the revenue to be derived by us from the exercise of such rights; and

This is a standard warranty, perhaps redundant to previous warranties.

(i) You have not entered and shall not enter into any arrangement or agreement which would or might diminish, derogate, encumber, interfere with or conflict with the rights granted to us by this Agreement.

Again, this is a standard warranty and perhaps redundant.

8.02. We represent and warrant that:

(a) We are a corporation duly organized, validly existing and in good standing under the laws of the State of (*state*) and have the corporate power and authority to enter into and perform this Agreement;

This is a standard corporate warranty.

(b) All corporate action necessary to authorize the execution, delivery and performance of this Agreement by us has been duly and properly taken; this Agreement has been duly and validly executed and delivered by us, and this Agreement constitutes a binding obligation of ours enforceable against us in accordance with its terms;

This is a standard corporate warranty.

(c) The execution, delivery and performance of this Agreement by us do not and will not require the consent of any third party and will not conflict with, result in a breach of, or constitute a default under, any applicable law, judgment, order, injunction, decree, rule or regulation, or ruling of any court or governmental instrumentality; or conflict with, constitute grounds for termination of, result in a breach of, or constitute a default under, any agreement, instrument, license or permit to which we are now subject; and

This is a standard corporate warranty.

(d) We shall comply with all laws and regulations applicable to the conduct of our business hereunder.

This is a standard corporate warranty.

9. Survival of Representations.

All representations, warranties and agreements made by you or us in this Agreement shall survive the telecast of the Event.

Boilerplate.

10. Indemnification.

10.01. Subject to the provisions of Paragraph 15 below, each party hereby agrees to indemnify and hold harmless the other, the television stations and advertisers, together with the officers, directors, agents, employees, successors and assigns of each of the foregoing, from and against all claims, liabilities, losses, damages, costs, or expenses incurred or suffered by it, including reasonable attorneys' fees and court costs incurred in defending or resisting any claim, action or proceeding or in enforcing this indemnity, arising out of, based upon, resulting from, in connection with or caused by, any inaccuracy, breach, failure to perform or violation by the other party of any representation, warranty, obligation or covenant set forth in this Agreement.

Indemnities are common; if the parties are not substantial, insurance to back them up would be an appropriate addition to this paragraph.

10.02. If any matter covered by the foregoing indemnities arises, the party seeking indemnification shall give written notice thereof to the other party promptly (in no event more than 30 days) after it learns of the existence of such matter.

Written notice of a claim giving rise to indemnification is common and may be a requirement under insurance policies.

10.03. Within 10 days after delivery of notice to the party from whom indemnification is sought, the party from whom indemnification is sought may make written objection, with explanation, to the party seeking indemnification. In such event, if the parties do not amicably dispose of the claim for indemnification within 30 days from the date of written objection, the party seeking indemnification may bring action on the claim. If no such written objection is delivered within such 10 day period, the party from whom indemnification is sought shall be conclusively presumed to have agreed to the claim for indemnification.

This paragraph is not particularly common, but may be useful in that it requires the parties to discuss an indemnification claim in situations where the parties might already be very antagonistic.

10.04. In the event that the party from whom indemnification is sought agrees to the claim for indemnification or is found by a court of competent jurisdiction to be liable for such indemnification, such indemnitor shall have full control of the defense of such litigation, and provided the indemnitor shall give the indemnitee at least five days' prior written notice thereof, the indemnitor may settle, compromise or adjust any such claim and/or litigation. If the indemnitee objects to any such settlement, compromise or adjustment proposed by the indemnitor, then the indemnitee shall be responsible for its own legal defense and costs after the date of such objection and the indemnitor's liability shall be limited to the amount which would have been involved in the settlement, compromise or adjustment proposed by the indemnitor.

If a party is required to indemnify another, it usually wants to control the defense and settlement of the litigation. If the party to be indemnified objects to a settlement, it assumes its further defense costs, and the indemnitor thereafter is liable only for the amount for which it would have settled the claims.

11. Station Compensation.
Station Compensation may be offered by us only with your consent; in the event that you give us such consent, you will be solely responsible for such compensation, and we will have no responsibility with respect thereto, except that, pursuant to Paragraph 4.03 above, we will deduct Station Compensation from amounts paid to you hereunder, and remit such amounts directly to such stations.

This presumes that the Station arrangement will be strictly barter; if the Syndicator agrees to pay cash to the station to carry the program, the cash comes out of the Organizer's pocket.

12. Confidentiality.

Due to the highly competitive nature of the industry in which we operate, it is agreed that any acquired operational and/or financial information or knowledge pertaining to the operation of either party hereto is privileged and confidential.

This provides that operational or financial information about each party will be treated as confidential by the other party. Absent disclosure of actual business information to other parties, it is difficult to enforce.

13. Compliance with Section 507 of the Communications Act of 1934, (As Amended).

13.01. Each party hereby certifies that it will comply with all provisions of Section 508 of the Communications Act of 1934, as amended (the "Act"), 47 U.S.C. § 508, and will make the appropriate disclosure required by such law.

See Appendix G for the text of 47 U.S.C. § 508. The FCC requires that if commercial matter is included in a program by a producer in exchange for consideration, such promotional consideration must be disclosed. This is a regulation enacted as a result of "payola" abuses in the early days of television.

13.02. The insertion into the telecast of the Event of any promotional announcements ("Plugs"), including but not limited to, wardrobe, airline and hotel and automobile rental announcements shall require our express approval, which approval shall not be unreasonably withheld. All Plugs shall be made in compliance with Section 508 of the Act. Any revenues derived from Plugs shall be included in Adjusted Gross Advertising Revenues.

See previous comment. The control over "plugs" is negotiable; the Organizer may want to control plugs since they are so integral to in-kind sponsorship donations. The Syndicator's interest seems more remote.

14. Default.

If either party shall default in the performance of any material obligation hereunder and such default shall not be cured within fourteen (14) days after written notice thereof is given by the other party, or if either party shall become insolvent, or if a petition under bankruptcy is filed by or against either party (which petition is not dismissed within thirty (30) days thereafter), or if either party executes an assignment for the benefit of its creditors, or if a receiver, trustee, liquidator, custodian or other officer is appointed for all or a substantial part of either party's assets, or if either party shall petition for or consent to any relief under any applicable insolvency or moratorium statute or other like statute, or if either party breaches the provisions of this Agreement (such party hereinafter called the "defaulting party" and any one of the above acts hereinafter called "event of default"), then in the event of any such event of default, in addition to any other rights or remedies the other party may have, such other party may terminate this Agreement by giving written notice thereof to the defaulting party at any time after the occurrence of such event of default.

These are very standard termination provisions. Note that termination in the event of bankruptcy or insolvency may not be effective under the Bankruptcy Code (see Chapter 1).

15. Force Majeure.

15.01. No party shall be liable to the other for any loss, damage or default occasioned by strike, civil disorder, Acts of God or any other Event of Force Majeure, as hereinafter defined. If any event of Force Majeure is of such nature that the continued performance hereunder is commercially impracticable, the parties agree that any and all guarantees made hereunder will be considered inoperative and without force and effect and the parties agree to negotiate in good faith the resolution of all other matters resulting from the Force Majeure including, but not limited to, the production and telecast of the Event at a future date.

This paragraph stipulates that each party bears its own risks if performance is interrupted for any reason beyond the control of the parties. If the syndication income is critical to the Organizer's bottom line, then the Organizer should provide for broadcast interruption insurance.

15.02 "Force Majeure" shall mean any act of God; inevitable accident; fire; lockout; strike or other labor dispute; riot or civil commotion; act of public enemy; law, enactment, regulation, rule, order or act of government or governmental instrumentality (whether Federal, state or local, foreign or other); failure of technical facilities, or other cause of similar or different nature beyond the control of any of the parties.

This is a standard contractual definition of Force Majeure.

16. Relationship of Parties.

Nothing contained in this Agreement shall create any partnership or joint venture between you and us. Neither party may pledge the credit of the other nor make any binding commitment on the part of the other, except as otherwise specifically provided herein. Without limiting the generality of the foregoing, we shall not be liable for any losses suffered by you in connection with the Event, and you shall have sole financial and other responsibility with respect to the production and delivery of and the telecast of the Event; our only responsibility in connection with the Event and the telecast of the Event is to clear stations and sell advertising time, as described herein.

This is a standard clause delineating the relationship of the parties.

17. Notices.

All notices to be sent to you shall be sent by registered or certified mail to: (*address*)

All notices to be sent to Syndicator shall be sent by registered or certified mail to: (*address*)

Boilerplate.

18. Publicity.

Syndicator shall have the right to use and license others to use the names and likenesses of the Participants for the purpose of advertising and publicizing of the Event, but not in connection with any endorsements of any product or services. Any expenses to be incurred in connection with the advertising and publicizing of the Event will be subject to your prior approval, and will be paid by you.

If an event has key participants who help to make the event sellable, then the Syndicator and its licensees have to be able to use their names and likenesses to promote broadcasts of the event.

19. Governing Law.

This Agreement and all matters collateral thereto shall be governed by the laws of (*state*) applicable to contracts executed and performed entirely therein.

Boilerplate.

20. Complete Agreement.

This Agreement constitutes the complete understanding between the parties and supersedes any other agreements and arrangements relating to the subject matter of this Agreement.

Boilerplate.

21. Severability.

Any provision of this Agreement found by a court of law to be void or unenforceable shall not affect the validity or enforceability of any other provision of this Agreement.

Boilerplate.

Syndicator

By: _____

Owner

By: _____

EXHIBIT A:
SYNDICATOR
PROGRAM AUDIENCE
GUARANTEE POLICY

With respect to advertising revenues, all agreements are based on a guaranteed audience delivery which is measured by the A.C. Nielsen Rating Service. In the event that these audience guarantees are not achieved, Syndicator is put in the position of having to "make good" the audience deficiency as follows:

(1) Syndicator will provide additional bonus spots, at no charge, within the program during specific weeks that are acceptable to the advertiser.

(2) An advertiser has the option to receive a cash rebate/credit equivalent to the amount of the deficiency.

(3) In the event of a cash rebate/credit, the advertiser has the option to reinvest the dollars in other Syndicator properties. This means that your program may also be the recipient of reinvested dollars.

In cases of over-delivery of audience guarantees, no additional revenues will be paid by clients since all agreements represent the maximum price.

SAMPLE HOME VIDEO DISTRIBUTION AGREEMENT

Principal Terms

THIS AGREEMENT, entered into as of this (*number*) day of (*month*), (*year*) by and between (*Name of Distributor*) ("Distributor") at (*address*) and (*Owner of Event*) ("*Owner*") at (*address*) for manufacture and distribution by Distributor of video recordings of an event commonly known as (*Name of Event*) (the "Property"), as more fully described below. The parties agree as follows:

1. Grant: Owner hereby grants to Distributor the exclusive right to manufacture, vend, rent, sell and otherwise distribute Copies of the Property in the Territory during the Term (and for the "sell-off period" described in the General Terms) on the terms and conditions set forth in these Principal Terms and the general terms attached hereto and incorporated herein by reference.[52]

This is the basic grant. This Agreement is used when the Owner of the Event controls the rights in existing footage.

2. Territory: Owner hereby grants Distributor the rights hereunder in the following geographical area(s): (*The World*) (*the "Territory"*).

It is fairly standard for a Distributor to take worldwide video rights and subdistribute in those territories where it does not have a distribution operation in place.

3. Programs: (a) The Property shall consist of not less than (*number*) minutes nor more than (*number*) minutes of video recording of the Event suitable for actual on-screen running time, to be selected, assembled, edited and otherwise produced from the Property by Distributor (the "Program").

(b) Owner and Distributor shall mutually agree upon the contents of the Program. Distributor shall designate a producer to review, assemble and edit material for the Program, and to create any new material that may be required in order to create the Program. Owner shall grant such producer full access to the Property. Distributor shall advance the actual direct costs of assembling and editing any existing or new material it deems desirable (not to exceed _____ Dollars ($_____)), and all such amounts shall be recoupable as part of the Advance as provided in Paragraph 10.

Here the Distributor advances the direct production costs for creating the Program and editing existing footage into a Program. Those costs are recoupable from revenues.

4. License Term: The term of the grant herein with respect to distribution of Copies of the Program (the "License Term") shall commence as of the date of execution hereof and continue until ten (10) years from the initial release of Copies of such Program by Distributor anywhere in the Territory.

A long term generally is appropriate to compensate the Distributor for its risk. However, some minimum performance or sales levels could be specified.

5. Advance: Distributor agrees promptly after full completion of the Event to pay to Owner the sum of _____ Dollars ($_____) (the "Advance"); provided that Distributor shall not release the Program hereunder prior to payment of the Advance. The Advance shall be non-returnable, but shall be an advance against and deducted from any and all amounts payable to Owner hereunder.

The Advance here is like a minimum guarantee.

6. Delivery: Owner agrees to make delivery of the Program, as described in the General Terms and Exhibit B, on or before the respective date set forth in Paragraph 2(a) of the General Terms; provided that Distributor shall cause the producer whose services are engaged by Distributor pursuant to Paragraph 3(b) hereof to render on a timely basis all services with respect to the Program in order to permit delivery in accordance with the terms hereof, it being understood that any delay in delivery caused by such producer shall not be considered a breach by Owner. Notwithstanding anything to the contrary contained herein, it is expressly agreed that delivery of the Program to Distributor will not be complete unless and until appropriate documents showing insurance and clear ownership of such Program by Owner have been delivered to Distributor in a form approved by Distributor, which approval shall not be unreasonably withheld; provided that such documents shall be reviewed and either approved or disapproved by Distributor not later than ten (10) business days after the delivery thereof. Distributor's failure to designate specific written objections with respect to any such documents within such 10-day period shall be deemed approval by Distributor and completion of delivery thereof by Owner.

The Owner has to deliver the Program with satisfactory evidence of ownership. However, the Owner will not be responsible if the producer fails to deliver on time. (The Distributor, after all, designated the producer under Paragraph 3(b).)

7. Rights and Exclusivity: It is expressly understood and agreed that, throughout the License Term hereof Distributor shall be the sole and exclusive licensee of all rights to manufacture, vend, sell, rent and otherwise deal with Copies throughout the Territory. Owner expressly represents, warrants and agrees that Owner has not prior to the date hereof and will not hereafter make any grant to any third party which will limit or infringe upon the exclusive rights granted to Distributor hereunder. Additionally, Owner agrees that it will not during the License Term authorize or allow any broadcast of any of the material contained in the Program except on a live basis or on a delayed basis within seven (7) days of the Event and except for clips not to exceed five minutes in length.

Since the home video market is affected by delayed broadcasts, this Agreement prohibits delayed coverage except during the time period very close to the Event. The warranties are standard.

8. Distribution Fees: Distributor shall be entitled to a distribution fee equal to _____% of Gross Receipts (as defined in the General Terms) (the "Distribution Fee") provided that to the extent Distributor sublicenses its rights in a particular territory to a subdistributor, Distributor shall be entitled, at its election, to either: (a) its Distribution Fee (inclusive of the subdistributor's fees), computed on Gross Receipts of the subdistributor; or (b) an Override (in addition to the subdistributors fees) equal to 15%, computed on the Gross Receipts of the subdistributor. Distributor represents and warrants that it currently distributes other home video properties directly in (*list countries*), and agrees that it will not subdistribute in such territories without Owner's consent, not to be unreasonably withheld.

A standard home video distribution fee is 30% of Gross Receipts. The Agreement alternatively could merely require the Distributor to pay the Owner a 20% royalty after recoupment of Distributor's Costs, including the Advance for production. Subdistribution can be expensive, and this paragraph seeks to cap subdistribution expenses. Here, the distributor is required to specify its international markets and not to use subdistributors there without the Owner's consent.

9. Distribution Expenses: The term "Distribution Expenses" shall mean (a) all actual direct costs incurred in connection with the exploitation or enforcement of any rights granted to Distributor herein, including without limitation all advertising costs; promotion costs; collection costs (including reasonable attorneys' fees, court costs and accounting fees and costs); all residuals and other rights payments (which Distributor shall have no obligation to pay); all costs associated with duplication and manufacture of Copies, and packaging, artwork and related materials, it being agreed that for the purposes hereof such costs shall be set at (*number*) dollars ($_____) per copy (subject to reasonable adjustment in the event such costs actually decrease or increase during the License Term); all costs resulting from or otherwise related to any default by Owner hereunder (including reasonable attorneys' fees and court costs) as determined pursuant to final judgment by a court of law; costs of insurance (Distributor being under no obligation to provide any insurance); costs of shipping, packing, storage, inspection, containers and cases, duties and imposts; taxes (other than net income taxes of Distributor); telephone tolls, costs of enforcement of any rights against third parties with respect to the Program (including reasonable attorneys' fees and court costs); plus (b) an advertising overhead charge of 10% on all third party advertising and promotion costs covered by (a) above. Distributor shall be entitled to establish reasonable reserves for anticipated Distribution Expenses.

This paragraph deserves intense scrutiny, since Distribution Expenses are paid before Net Profits are split. The overhead charge (here 10%) is negotiable – the Owner should try to reduce it to 0. Reserves for expenses could be capped.

10. Net Profits: (a) The term "Net Profits" shall mean the Gross Receipts remaining after deducting, in the following order:

(i) All Distribution Fees and Overrides; plus

(ii) All Distribution Expenses; plus

(iii) The unrecouped Advance, plus interest thereon at 1% over the prime lending rate in effect at (*bank*), from time to time, provided that such interest shall be calculated for a maximum of one year from payment of the Advance.

The Distributor here earns interest on the advance for one year and recoups its fees and its expenses before paying Net Profits to the Owner.

(b) Owner shall be entitled to a sum equal to 100% of the Net Profits.

Depending on the creativity of the accounting, if there are profits, they are to be paid to the Owner. Alternatively, one would expect the Distributor to bargain for part of the upside.

(c) In the event that Net Profits shall be less than the Distribution Fee in any accounting period (prior to deducting the amount of any unrecouped Advance then remaining), Owner and Distributor shall each be entitled to an amount equal to fifty percent (50%) of Gross Receipts, after deduction of Distribution Expenses.

If the Distribution Fee is greater than the Net Profits, then the Owner and the Distributor share the Gross Receipts after Distribution Expenses are paid (including recoupment of the Advance).

11. Packaging: Owner shall have right of approval with respect to the materials and design to be used in packaging the Property, which approval shall not be unreasonably withheld. All materials shall be deemed approved within ten (10) business days after Distributor's written request therefor, unless Owner shall provide specific [written] objection thereto.

The extent of Owner's approval is negotiable; the "deemed approved" language is useful to the Distributor to keep the project moving.

IN WITNESS WHEREOF, the parties hereto have executed this Agreement as of the date first noted above.

Owner

By: _____

Distributor

By: _____

VIDEO DISTRIBUTION AGREEMENT

General Terms

1. Grant: (a) *Basic Rights:* Owner grants to Distributor: (i) the exclusive and irrevocable right during the Term to assemble, edit and produce the Program identified in the Principal Terms hereof, and, in connection therewith, the exclusive right to use Owner's name in the home video market; (ii) the exclusive and irrevocable right during the License Term to manufacture Copies of the Property or any portion thereof and to sell, lease, license, rent, distribute, reproduce, exploit, advertise and otherwise market the same in the Territory, directly or through sublicensees as provided in the Principal Terms. Additionally, Distributor may during the six (6) month period following the License Term ("sell-off period") continue to sell and exploit all Copies made prior to the end of the License Term in all manners allowed during the License Term, but Distributor may not reproduce or manufacture new Copies during the sell-off period. As used herein, the term "Copies" shall include copies manufactured on video cassette, video disc or by any other analogous means (whether now known or hereafter invented) primarily intended for viewing of visual images by means of a device utilizing a television screen or comparable technology to exhibit such images located at the place of exhibition.

The Distributor has the right to cause a Program to be produced out of the Owner's coverage of the Event, and to distribute such programs in various video media, regardless of whether or not the media exists at the time the contract is written. There may be no real need for the sell-off period, especially if the agreement has a long term. This clause also grants rights in all video markets, including schools and other institutions.

(b) *Editing; Change of Title:* In manufacturing Copies, Distributor shall have the right to edit or modify the same in order to meet the requirements of censorship, foreign distribution, community standards in any portion of the Territory or physical limitations or economic constraints in the manufacturing of Copies, but Distributor may not change the title of the Event or Property except with Owner's prior written approval. Distributor will make no change in the titles or credits of the Property without Owner's prior written approval (which approval shall not be unreasonably withheld), except that Distributor's logos shall be included in such credits, subject to Owner's prior written approval, which approval shall not be unreasonably withheld.

The Distributor is allowed to cause the Event tape to be edited as it deems fit or, if the parenthetical is used, as needed to meet foreign and other requirements. The Owner should retain approval over the title because of the potential effect on its goodwill. The Distributor is entitled to credit.

(c) *Dubbing and Subtitling:* Distributor shall have the right to have the Property dubbed and/or subtitled in any language which Distributor may deem appropriate for distribution of Copies in the Territory. In the event that any dubbed or subtitled versions of the Property have been or are hereafter created, Owner shall include such dubbed or subtitled versions in Owner's delivery hereunder. The costs of creating any dubbed or subtitled versions of the Property required by Distributor and not heretofore created shall be advanced by Distributor and treated as a Distribution Expense hereunder.

If an event features celebrities, such as vocalists, they may well object to dubbing. Otherwise, this paragraph is fairly standard.

(d) *Advertising Rights:* In addition to the other rights granted to Distributor hereunder, Owner hereby grants to Distributor the right to use any portion of the Property, any stills therefrom, and all advertising materials delivered by Owner for the purpose of advertising and publicizing the sale, rental or other distribution of the Copies. Distributor shall similarly have the right to use the name, physical likeness, voice and biographical data of any party rendering services in connection with the Property for the purpose of advertising and publicizing the Copies. The advertising rights granted to Distributor hereunder are subject to any third party contractual requirements and/or limitations of which Distributor has been given prior written notification. In the event that in the exercise of any such rights, Distributor incurs any payment obligations pursuant to any collective bargaining agreements, Distributor shall be solely responsible therefor.

Typically, the Owner will have acquired all rights necessary to advertise and publicize the Event and recording thereof. (See Organizer contracts in Chapter 1). If there are restrictions, it is the Organizer's obligation to so inform the Distributor, but the Distributor pays any residuals.

2. Delivery: (a) *Initial Delivery:* Within thirty (30) days after the completion of production of the Program, Owner shall deliver to Distributor, at Distributor's office, or such other address(es) as Distributor shall designate, all the materials described in Exhibit B attached hereto with respect to the Program, with film elements in technically satisfactory condition so that Copies of first-class commercially acceptable quality may be manufactured therefrom, and with advertising and publicity material satisfactory for Distributor's use. Except as otherwise expressly provided herein, delivery and return of all materials shall be at Owner's cost and expense.

The Organizer should review the delivery schedule with its producer to be certain all elements will be available. Proof of ownership should be agreed upon before the Event takes place so that any objection by the Distributor to the forms of releases, etc., can be worked out. The Principal Terms, Paragraph 6, also deal with the Distributor's approval over delivered elements.

(b) *Cure:* In the event of defects or omissions in the delivered material for the Program or in the evidence of insurance or ownership thereof, Distributor shall either (i) request Owner to immediately cause such defects or omissions to be corrected and new or additional material to be made and delivered or new documentation of insurance or ownership to be delivered, such new or additional material or documentation to again be subject to Distributor's approval as described in the Principal Terms, or (ii) itself cause such defects or omissions to be corrected and deduct the cost thereof from any monies payable to Owner hereunder. In the event Distributor requests Owner to cause such defects or omissions to be corrected, and such cure is not made within thirty (30) days of Distributor's notice of its disapproval of the delivered materials or documentation, then Distributor may itself cause such defects or omissions to be corrected and deduct the cost thereof from any monies payable to Owner hereunder.

A Distributor might want the ability to satisfy itself that the necessary rights have been obtained. However, the Owner should resist a paragraph this broadly worded since the costs of the Distributor's cure are recouped from revenues. If the parties negotiate prior to the Event taking place, this paragraph should become unnecessary.

(c) *Return of Material:* As soon as practicable after the delivery of the material described herein, Distributor shall return to Owner the original print of the Program delivered hereunder. All other materials delivered hereunder, as well as the master videotape produced by Distributor from such original print shall be retained by Distributor for the use and distribution of Copies until the end of the License Term. Promptly after the end of the License Term, Distributor will return the master videotape of such Program to Owner or provide the Owner with a Certificate of Destruction. It is expressly understood and agreed that Distributor shall own all rights in the tangible materials manufactured by Distributor hereunder, including, without limitation, the master tape, the transfer tape, disc master, disc stampers and all Copies. Promptly following the end of the respective sell-off period, Distributor shall, at Owner's election, either:

(i) Destroy any remaining Copies in Distributor's possession; or

(ii) Sell to Owner the entire inventory of such Copies then in Distributor's possession at Distributor's average wholesale price for such Copies for the six months prior to the date of such sale.

At termination, it is common for the master to be destroyed or given to the Owner. The Owner has the right to purchase any remaining inventory at wholesale. Some time limits should be placed on the exercise of such rights.

3. Owner's Representations and Warranties: Owner represents, warrants and agrees that:

(a) *Ownership:* Owner solely owns and controls, without any limitations, restrictions or encumbrances whatsoever, all rights granted or purported to be granted to Distributor hereunder and all required rights in and to the literary, dramatic and musical material contained in the Property, and Owner has obtained all necessary licenses and permissions required for the manufacture, distribution, exhibition, advertising and exploitation of the Copies throughout the Territory as may be required for the full and unlimited exercise and enjoyment by Distributor of all the rights granted and purported to be granted to Distributor herein.

This is boilerplate. However, it should be noted that this paragraph makes music royalties the Owner's responsibility. All such charges could easily be deemed Distribution Expenses. A clause could be added disclaiming any responsibility of Distributor arising out of its review of documentation on delivery.

(c) *No Prior Sale:* No Copies have heretofore been manufactured, licensed or marketed in the Territory (other than Copies manufactured for Owner's use in the promotion of the Property.)

This warranty assures the Distributor that no copies have previously been authorized to be sold. However, it cannot protect the Distributor from pirates.

d. *Authority:* Owner has the full right, power, legal capacity and authority to enter into this agreement, to carry out the terms hereof and to grant the Distributor the rights, licenses and privileges granted or purported to be granted to it hereunder. If Owner is a corporation, Owner represents that it is duly incorporated, valid, existing and in good standing under the laws of the jurisdiction in which it was incorporated.

Boilerplate.

(e) *Non-Infringement:* Nothing in the Property shall infringe upon the copyright or violate any other personal or property rights of any kind or nature of any person, firm or corporation whatsoever, including without limitation, any rights to be free from defamation, any rights of privacy or publicity and any right to be free from unfair competition.

This is a standard warranty by the Owner.

(f) *Name and Likeness:* All persons, firms and corporations connected with the production of the Property and all other persons whose names, voices, photographs, likenesses, work, services and materials have been used in the Property or its exploitation have authorized the use of their names, voices, photographs, likenesses, performances and biographical data in connection with the advertising, promotion and exploitation of the Property, including such use and exploitation in connection with Copies manufactured hereunder.

This is a standard warranty.

(g) *Legal Requirements:* In the production of the Property, all laws, statutes, ordinances, rules and regulations of each country, state, city or other political entity having jurisdiction were complied with, as well as all of the rules, regulations and requirements of any union or guild having jurisdiction thereof.

Boilerplate.

(h) *Copyright:* The Property, as delivered, will contain all proper copyright notices required for protection of the Property, and Distributor agrees to include such copyright notices as so delivered on the Copies. The Property is not in the public domain and is or may be validly copyrighted throughout the Territory and Owner will not allow the Property to fall into the public domain anywhere in the Territory (where a protection system is in place) during the License Term.

This is a standard warranty.

(i) *Credits:* The credit lists and other materials delivered to Distributor under this Agreement will be complete and accurate and Distributor will incur no liabilities to any third parties arising out of its compliance with such lists and the use of such materials.

This is a standard warranty.

(j) *Insurance:* Owner will secure and maintain in full force and effect at its sole cost and expense during the initial (*number*) years after release of the Program, a standard producer's liability (errors and omissions) insurance policy issued by a company approved by Distributor (such approval not to be unreasonably withheld) with coverage of at least $_____ with respect to such Program. Such policy shall (i) name Distributor as an additional insured; (ii) cover all means and methods of exhibition of the Property licensed to Distributor hereunder and (iii) provide that it is not cancellable except upon thirty (30) days' prior written notice to Distributor.

While this is a standard warranty, the Distributor should also be required to have insurance on its activities.

4. Distributor's Representations and Warranties: Distributor warrants and represents that (a) it has the full right and power to enter into this Agreement, and to fully perform all of its obligations hereunder; (b) no promotion, advertising or materials created and utilized by Distributor in connection with the Property hereunder (other than materials provided by Owner) shall violate any rights whatsoever of any third parties; (c) Distributor shall not knowingly permit any unauthorized duplication, manufacture, sale or distribution of the Program, or permit or take any action which shall cause the Program or any portion thereof to fall into the public domain, and (d) Distributor shall accord and contractually require its sublicensees to accord all credits in connection with the Program as required pursuant to Owner's credit lists delivered to Distributor.

This is a fairly standard Distributor's warranty; it should be backed by insurance. The Distributor might want to specify that advertising approved by Owner is excepted from the warranty.

5. Indemnification: (a) *By Owner:* Owner hereby agrees to indemnify, save and hold harmless Distributor, and its respective successors, licensees, assigns, directors, shareholders, officers, employees, agents, attorneys and other representatives from and against any and all liability, loss, damage, cost and expense (including reasonable attorneys' fees) arising out of or relating to any breach or purported breach by Owner of any representation, warranty or covenant contained herein or from the use and exploitation by Distributor of any rights granted or purported to be granted hereunder.

(b) *By Distributor:* Distributor agrees to indemnify and hold harmless Owner and its successors, licensees, assigns, directors, shareholders, officers, employees, agents, attorneys and other representatives from and against any and all liability, loss, damage, cost and expense (including reasonable attorneys' fees) arising out of or relating to any breach of warranty, representation or covenant made or given by Distributor hereunder and/or relating to any use by Distributor of the Copies which exceeds the rights granted or purported to be granted to Distributor hereunder.

These are fairly standard warranties.

6. Accountings: "Gross Receipts" shall be defined and all monies due hereunder shall be paid in accordance with the following terms:

(a) *Definition of Gross Receipts:* "Gross Receipts" means all monies and other consideration (subject to the exclusions in subparagraph 6 (b) below) actually received by the Distributor or any affiliate of Distributor or credited to the account of Distributor or any such affiliate from the exploitation by Distributor of the rights granted to Distributor hereunder or due to recovery or settlement in connection with any claim by Distributor for any infringement relating to any such right.

This is a standard definition of Gross Receipts.

(b) *Exclusions from Gross Receipts:* Gross Receipts shall be determined after deduction of all refunds, credits, discounts, allowances and adjustments granted to sub-distributors, wholesalers, retailers and other purchasers and licensees, whether occasioned by condemnation by boards of censorship, settlement of disputes or otherwise. Neither advance payments nor security deposits shall be included in Gross Receipts until earned by the sale of Copies, forfeited or applied by Distributor to the Property; provided that nonrefundable and/or nonforfeitable advances shall be included in Gross Receipts no later than one year after receipt thereof by Distributor. Additionally, Gross Receipts shall not include and shall be reduced by:

Exclusions from Gross Receipts should be carefully reviewed.

(i) Any monies derived by any subdistributor, wholesaler, or retailer from the sale of Copies, or by any local sales or promotional organization for services rendered on their behalf, whether or not such subdistributor, wholesaler, retailer or sales or promotional organization is owned, operated, managed or controlled by Distributor; provided, however, that in the event Copies are sold or leased to any such owned, operated or managed subdistributor, wholesaler or retailer, Distributor agrees that the terms of such sale or lease shall be substantially the same as the terms of sale or lease of Copies to unrelated entities, in accordance with industry standards.

This mandates a third-party standard for the reasonableness of fees.

(ii) Any sums due, but not paid, to Distributor; provided, however, that Distributor agrees to use all reasonable efforts consistent with its prudent business judgment to collect any sums owed to it.

Uncollectable accounts do not become part of Gross Receipts.

(iii) The salvage value of any videotapes, cassettes or other materials purchased by or manufactured by Distributor and not sold as Copies.

The salvage value of the physical materials is not included in Gross Receipts.

(iv) Any sums received in a foreign currency and not readily convertible or not readily remittable; provided however, that Distributor shall, upon receipt of written request from Owner (but not more frequently than once in each accounting period) advise Owner in writing as to foreign revenues not included in Gross Receipts as aforesaid and Distributor shall, at the written request and expense of Owner (subject to any and all limitations, restrictions, laws, rules and regulations affecting such transactions), deposit into a bank designated by Owner in the country involved or pay to any other party designated by Owner in such country, such part thereof as would be payable to Owner hereunder as if all amounts received were Gross Receipts. Any such deposit or payment to or for Owner shall constitute due remittance to Owner, and Distributor shall have no further interest therein or responsibility therefor. Distributor makes no warranty or representation that any part of such foreign currencies may be converted or transferred to the account of Owner in any foreign country. All costs, discounts and expenses incurred in obtaining remittance of receipts and conversion of same, including costs of contesting imposition of restricted funds, shall be deducted in computing Gross Receipts hereunder.

Foreign receipts may not be readily convertible to dollars that can be sent to the United States. This paragraph allows for the possibility of segregation of foreign receipts in an account identified to the Owner.

(c) *Rendition of Statements:* Distributor shall account to Owner with regard to the monies due hereunder on a quarterly basis during the Term, and semiannually thereafter. The quarterly periods shall end March 31, June 30, September 30 and December 31 of each year, and semiannual accounting periods shall end on June 30 and December 31 of each year, or such other quarterly or semiannual period as Distributor and Owner may agree. Accountings shall be rendered by Distributor to Owner on or before the date sixty (60) days following the conclusion of each accounting period. Each statement shall show in summary form the appropriate calculations relating to the computation of Gross Receipts, if any, hereunder. Any portion of Gross Receipts payable to Owner hereunder shall be remitted to Owner with the particular statement indicating such amount to be due.

The parties should agree on a payment schedule.

(d) *Finality of Statements:* Each statement and all items contained therein shall be deemed correct and shall be conclusive and binding upon Owner, and shall constitute an account stated, upon the expiration of twenty-four (24) months from the date rendered unless, within such twenty-four (24) month period, Owner delivers a written notice to Distributor objecting to one or more items of such statement and such notice specifies in reasonable detail the items to which Owner objects and the nature and reason of Owner's objection thereto.

While the Distributor's desire for finality is understandable, the Owner usually should object to this paragraph.

(e) *Books of Account and Examinations:* Distributor shall keep books of account relating to the distribution of Copies. Such books shall be kept on the same basis and in the same manner and for the same periods as such records are customarily kept by Distributor for its other properties. Owner may, at its own expense and upon reasonable notice to Distributor, examine the applicable books and records with respect to any statements rendered by Distributor hereunder at the place where Distributor maintains same.

An audit clause is standard. Distributors may wish to place all sorts of restrictions on the right, such as requiring that it be conducted by CPAs, that only once per year, or that copies be given Distributor.

(f) *Allocations:* In any instance where revenues are earned or deductions allowed with regard to a group of motion pictures or programs which includes the Program, and such revenues or deductions are not specifically allocated among such group of motion pictures or programs, Distributor shall make such allocations as are determined by Distributor in good faith and Gross Receipts hereunder shall only include the amounts so allocated to the Property.

The Owner should here specify how the Distributor will make the allocation when it sells a package, e.g., by running time.

(g) *Returns:* Distributor shall establish an allowance of fifteen percent (15%) of Gross Receipts for returns of Copies, which fifteen percent (15%) shall be deducted from Gross Receipts hereunder. Distributor shall further be entitled, in the exercise of its reasonable business judgment, to establish reserves against additional returns or other items which Distributor reasonably anticipates may be deductible from Gross Receipts hereunder. Reserves established as aforesaid shall be liquidated within a reasonable time, not to exceed one (1) year after initially established.

The total reserve of the Distributor should be capped, to control what "other items" the Distributor may anticipate charging against Gross Receipts.

(h) *No Trust Imposed:* Gross Receipts are Distributor's sole and exclusive property and not trust funds nor otherwise held by Distributor for Owner's benefit. Distributor's obligation to make payments to Owner hereunder is that of a debtor only. Owner shall not own any interest whatsoever in the Copies or Gross Receipts or have any lien or other claim thereon. Distributor's obligation to pay Owner hereunder shall not bear interest nor entitle Owner to gains which may accrue to such funds prior to the payment thereof to Owner.

This paragraph reduces Owner to the position of any other general unsecured creditor in the event of Distributor's bankruptcy. While it is standard in Distributor's drafts, it should be negotiable.

(i) *Relationship of the Parties:* Nothing herein shall be construed to create a partnership or joint venture by or between Distributor and Owner or to make either the agent of the other. Each of Distributor and Owner agrees not to hold itself out as a partner or agent of the other or to otherwise state or imply by advertising or otherwise relationship between the parties in any manner contrary to the terms of this agreement and neither shall become liable or bound by any representation, act, omission or agreement. It is expressly agreed that Distributor shall have full and exclusive charge and control of the distribution, sale, exploitation, rental, leasing or other disposition of the Copies, and the Copies may be rented, leased, distributed, sold outright, exploited, marketed or otherwise disposed of by Distributor throughout the territory during the Term, and Distributor may in its sole discretion withhold or withdraw Copies from distribution, either entirely or with respect to any country or territory or portion thereof. Nothing herein contained shall be deemed to limit Distributor from entering into any agreement with any sub-distributor, wholesaler, retailer or otherwise with respect to Copies on whatever terms and conditions Distributor and such other party may agree. Distributor shall likewise have the right to cancel any such contracts in accordance with Distributor's good faith business judgment, to adjust and settle all disputes with any third parties regarding such agreements and to give standard industry allowances, rebates and credits to such persons. Notwithstanding the foregoing, in the event that that Distributor shall license, sell, lease or otherwise dispose of any rights in Copies to any party owning, owned by or under joint ownership with Distributor, such disposition shall be made on terms substantially equivalent to the terms which would apply had such disposition been made to an unrelated third party. It is the intent and purpose of this Agreement that absolute and sole control and discretion with reference to all matters involving the manufacture, production, distribution, lease, exhibition, sale, licensing and reissuing of Copies shall, as between Distributor and Owner, be vested solely and exclusively in Distributor and shall be exercised by Distributor in such manner as shall in Distributor's sole judgment and discretion be deemed proper, and Owner shall have no right of approval or control in connection therewith.

It is common for the parties to disclaim a partnership or agency relationship. The Owner here recognizes that most decisions regarding distribution are solely controlled by Distributor. However, third party dealings must be bona fide, as if all third party dealings were unrelated.

7. Force Majeure: In the event that Owner is unable to make delivery of part or all of the Property or Distributor is unable to accept delivery of the Property or, having accepted delivery of the Property, all or substantially all of Distributor's activities with regard to the Property are materially interfered with by reason of any cause of occurrence beyond the control of Distributor or Owner, including, without limitation, fire, flood, epidemic, earthquake, explosion, accident, war, blockade, embargo, act of a public enemy, civil disturbance, labor dispute (or threatened dispute), strike, lockout, new enactment of law or any act of God (all of the foregoing are referred to as events of "force majeure"), then the affected party shall immediately give notice of such event of force majeure to the other party hereto, and this agreement shall be suspended and the term extended for a period equal to the duration of such event of force majeure; provided, however, that in the event that such event of force majeure shall continue for a period in excess of six (6) months, then either party hereto shall have the right to terminate this Agreement by notice to the other.

This is a standard Force Majeure clause protecting the Distributor from unforeseen circumstances.

8. Assignability: Owner and Distributor, respectively, may assign this Agreement or any of their respective rights, licenses or privileges hereunder to any person, firm, corporation or other entity which assumes the obligations of the assignor hereunder, but no such assignment shall relieve the assignor of its obligations to the other party hereunder. Distributor's right to assign this Agreement to another unaffiliated distributor is subject to the prior written approval of Owner, not to be unreasonably withheld.

The terms on which the parties may assign the Agreement are negotiable.

9. Laws and Jurisdiction: It is the express intent of the parties that this agreement shall be governed by the laws of the State of (*state name*), United States of America, with the full force and effect as though this agreement had been executed in and fully performed in said state. In the event of any dispute hereunder, the parties hereto expressly agree that the courts of the State of New York shall have full jurisdiction over the parties hereto, and the parties hereby bind themselves over fully and completely to the jurisdiction of said courts. In the event that process must be served in connection with any such dispute, the parties agree that such process may be served by personal delivery within or without the State of New York or by registered mail, and the parties hereby appoint the Secretary of State of the State of New York as their agent for receipt of service of process in the event of any such dispute.

Unless both parties are located in the state, one will object to consenting to being sued (or suing) on the other's home turf. While specifying the law to govern is common, consent to jurisdiction is negotiable. It is most valuable when dealing with foreign parties.

10. Limitations on Remedies: It is expressly understood and agreed that, in the event of any breach or purported breach by Distributor hereunder, Owner's rights shall be limited to an action at law for money damages, if any, actually suffered by Owner as a result thereof, and in no event shall Owner be entitled to rescission, injunction or other equitable relief of any kind. All of Distributor's rights hereunder and Distributor's rights at law and equity shall be cumulative, and the exercise of one shall in no way limit any other right of Distributor in the event of any breach by Owner hereunder.

The Distributor obviously wants to avoid interruption of its business. However, if the breach affects the Owner's goodwill, then the Owner may want to negotiate a change in this paragraph.

11. Additional Documents/Enforcement of Rights: Owner agrees to execute such additional documents as may be necessary or desirable for Distributor to enforce its rights hereunder, including without limitation, a short form assignment in the form attached hereto as Exhibit A. In the event that Owner shall fail to deliver any such additional documents, Owner hereby irrevocably appoints Distributor to execute any such additional documents as Owner's attorney-in-fact. Owner also hereby irrevocably authorizes Distributor to proceed, whether in Distributor's name or Owner's name, with any appropriate action necessary to enforce Distributor's rights hereunder (including, without limitation, all rights of exclusivity and all holdback rights granted hereunder). Any such action shall be (subject to the indemnity provisions of Paragraph 5 of these General Terms) at Distributor's sole cost and expense.

This paragraph is fairly standard and ensures the Distributor that it can enforce its rights.

12. Notices: Any notice or statements which either party hereto may desire to give or which is required under the terms of this agreement shall be given in writing by registered or certified mail or by telex or telegraph or by personal service (in all cases, all charges prepaid) to the addresses first noted in the Principal Terms. In the event any such notice is given by mail, such notice shall be deemed given on the date five (5) business days following the date of such mailing. If notice is given by any other method, such notice shall be deemed given on the date deposited with the telegraph or telex company or on the date personal delivery is made. Copies of all notices to Distributor shall simultaneously be given by the same method to: (*Distributor's Lawyer*). Copies of all notices to Owner shall simultaneously be given by the same method to: (*Owner's Lawyer*).

Boilerplate.

13. Severability: Each and every provision of this Agreement shall be considered severable, and if for any reason any provision or provisions herein are determined to be invalid and contrary to any applicable existing or future laws, such invalidity shall not impair the operation or effect of any other portion of this agreement, and this agreement shall be deemed modified, but only to the extent necessary to conform with the requirement of such applicable law.

Boilerplate.

14. Waiver and Remedies: No waiver by either of the parties hereto of any failure by the other party to keep or perform any covenant or condition of this agreement shall be deemed a waiver of any preceding or succeeding breach of the same or any other covenant or condition. Except as expressly provided to the contrary, the remedies herein provided shall be deemed cumulative, and the exercise of one shall not preclude the exercise of any other remedy nor shall the specifications of remedies herein exclude any rights or remedies at law or in equity which may be available in the premises.

Boilerplate.

15. Headings: The title or headings of provisions herein are used for convenience only and shall in no way be used to construe the meaning of the provisions hereof.

Boilerplate.

16. Miscellaneous: This represents the entire agreement between the parties, superseding and replacing all prior oral or written understandings with regard to the subject matter hereof. No provision of this agreement may be waived or amended, except by a written instrument executed by the party to be charged. All terms used herein and not defined are used in accordance with their normal meaning in the entertainment industry in [New York, New York]. In the event of any inconsistency between these General Terms and those of the Principal Terms to which these General Terms are attached, the Principal Terms shall prevail.

Boilerplate.

EXHIBIT A:
SHORT FORM ASSIGNMENT

KNOW ALL MEN BY THESE PRESENTS: That the undersigned, for value received, hereby sells, grants, assigns and sets over unto (DISTRIBUTOR) and its successors and assigns (herein called "Assignee"), all home video rights and certain other allied rights in and to the motion picture or television program entitled _____ (which together with the title, themes, contents and characters and other versions thereof, is hereinafter called the "Property") with copyright in the name of (OWNER) and registered in the United States Copyright Office, No. _____ on _____, more particularly set forth and upon and subject to the terms and conditions in that certain Agreement between the undersigned (OWNER) and said Assignee dated _____.

The undersigned hereby assigns the rights set forth above under said copyrights to Assignee; and should the undersigned fail to do any of the foregoing, the undersigned hereby irrevocably appoints Assignee as attorney-in-fact, with full and irrevocable power and authority to do all such acts and things, and to execute, acknowledge, deliver, file, register and record all such documents, in the name and on behalf of the undersigned, as Assignee may deem necessary or proper in the premises to accomplish the same.

Assignee is also hereby empowered to bring, prosecute, defend and appear in suits, actions and proceedings of any nature under or concerning all said rights in and to said Property and all renewals thereof, or concerning any infringement thereof, or interference with any of the rights hereby granted under said copyrights or renewals thereof, in its own name or in the name of the (OWNER), but at the expense of Assignee, and, at its option, Assignee may join such (OWNER) and/or the undersigned as a party plaintiff or defendant in any such suit, action or proceeding.

Dated: _____

By: _____

State of _____ }
} ss.
County of _____ }

On this _____ day of _____, 198_____, before me _____ the undersigned Notary Public, personally appeared _____ personally known to me _____ proved to me on the basis of satisfactory evidence to be the person(s) who executed the within instrument _____ as _____ or on behalf of the corporation therein named, and acknowledged to me that the corporation executed it.

WITNESS my hand and official seal.

Notary's Signature _____

EXHIBIT B: DELIVERY REQUIREMENTS

DELIVERY ITEMS: Delivery of the Property shall consist of Owner making physical delivery of the items set forth herein, to such address as Distributor shall designate.

A. Picture Items

1. Print: One (1) first-class one-inch (1") NTSC master videotape of the Property, fully timed, fully titled, in aspect ratios of either 1:1.33, 1:1.85 or 1:1.66 with the soundtrack in perfect synchronization with photographic action, Dolby A encoded, and in all respects ready and suitable for the manufacture of first-class Copies.

2. Soundtracks: The separate dialogue tracks, sound effects tracks and music tracks, each recorded on 35mm magnetic tracks from which the original magnetic soundtrack was made. A separate dialogue track recorded on 35mm magnetic track in French, German, Spanish (Castillian and Latin American dialects) and Italian, and for each additional language, if any, into which the Property has been dubbed. All such soundtracks shall match the video element of the Property delivered hereunder.

3. Continuities: One (1) legible typewritten copy in the English language of a detailed, final dialogue and action continuity of the Property containing all dialogue, narration, song vocals, as well as a cut-by-cut description of the Property action, conforming exactly to the photographic action and Soundtrack of the completed Property as embodied in the Print in such form as to be suitable for transmittal to censorship authorities and for use in connection with dubbing and subtitling the Property. If the dialogue of the Property was recorded in a language other than English, the continuity shall contain a literal English translation.

4. Music Cue Sheets: One (1) copy of a music cue sheet showing the particulars of all music contained in the Property, in the English language, including the sound equipment used, the title of each composition, names of composers, publishers and copyright owners, the usages (whether instrumental, instrumental-visual, vocal, vocal-visual or otherwise), the place and number of such uses showing the film footage and running time for each cue, the performing rights society involved and any other information customarily set forth in music cue sheets.

5. Dubbed/Subtitled Versions: If the Property was recorded in a language other than English, Owner shall deliver a version of the Property dubbed in English or with English subtitles, as Distributor shall determine in its sole discretion. If a

Dubbed Version is required, Distributor shall have the right of approval of the voices and dubbing script. If a Subtitled Version is required, Distributor shall have the right of approval of the subtitling script. If versions of the Property have been or are hereafter created in more than one language, Owner shall deliver Copies of the print in each such language. Delivery of each of the dubbed, subtitled or foreign language versions of the Property previously created shall be concurrent with delivery of the Print referred to in Paragraph A.1 above.

B. Documentation

1. Employment List: One (1) copy of a complete list verified as true and correct by Owner of the names (and lending company, if services loaned to Owner) of all players, screenplay writers, directors (including assistant directors), individual producer, executive producer, unit production manager, composers, lyricists, vocalists, musicians (including orchestrators, copyists, conductors and leaders) and other personnel appearing in or rendering services in connection with the Property.

2. Dubbing Restrictions: A statement in the English language of any restrictions as to the dubbing of the voice of any player including dubbing dialogue in a language other than the language in which the Property was recorded, and any agreements in force with respect thereto between such player and Owner or any other party in connection with the Property.

3. Prior Distribution: An accurate statement in the English language of all prior distribution and exploitation of the Property in any and all media and a list of all agreements currently in force with regard to any such distribution, together with either copies of such agreements or an accurate summary of all rights granted and exclusivity and/or holdbacks agreed to.

4. Distribution Restrictions/Obligations: A statement in the English language of any restrictions and/or obligations set forth in agreements entered into by Owner with third parties (including artists, financial institutions and governmental agencies) regarding the exploitation of the Property.

5. Contracts: Duplicate originals or legible copies in the English language of all agreements, licenses, waivers or other documents relating to the production of the Property, including, but not limited to those covering the acquisition of literary, dramatic and other works and material of whatever nature upon which the Property may be based and/or used in the production of the Property.

6. Copyright Notice: A U.S. Copyright Registration Certificate (or application therefor if registration is not complete at the time of delivery) and a statement indicating the correct copyright notice for the Property to be included by Distributor on all Copies and the packaging thereof, including a U.S. copyright registration certificate.

7. Insurance: The insurance policy (or evidence thereof satisfactory to Distributor) referred to in the attached agreement.

8. Certificate of Origin: A fully completed, executed and notarized Certificate of Origin, in the form attached hereto as Exhibit C, for use in releasing the Property in each territory where such documentation is required. If Owner is not the copyright holder of the Property, then Owner shall obtain a completed Certificate of Origin for Distributor's use.

9. Subordinations, in form and substance satisfactory to Distributor, executed by all parties providing financing for the production of the Property or having any lien, charge or security interest in the Property or its revenues.

10. Assignment: One fully executed and notarized Short Form Assignment of Copyright with respect to the Property in the form annexed hereto.

C. Publicity and Advertising Materials

1. Stills: The original negative and one (1) positive print of fifty (50) different black and white still photographs, and color transparencies of fifty (50) different color still photographs photographed by an experienced still photographer. Said still photographs shall depict different scenes from the Property, production activities and information poses, all of which shall be accompanied by a notation identifying the Property, the persons and events depicted and shall be suitable for reproduction for advertising and publicity purposes. Where a player has still approval, Owner shall furnish Distributor with stills which have been approved for Distributor's use by the player depicted.

2. Biographies: One (1) biography (one to three typewritten pages in length) of each of the principal players, writers, individual producer and director of the Property.

3. Synopsis: One (1) copy of a brief synopsis in the English language (one typewritten page in length) of the story of the Property, which shall include the running time of the Property.

4. Advertising Materials: One (1) copy of all advertisements, paper accessories and other advertising materials prepared by Owner or by any other party in connection with the Property, and, without limiting the foregoing, samples of one-sheet posters, in color, and individual advertising art elements and transparencies necessary to make proofs thereof. The materials supplied to Distributor shall include all those created and used in connection with the theatrical release of the Property, if any.

5. Credits: The statements of credits applicable to the Property in the English language, photographic excerpts of all of Owner's obligations (taken from the actual contract) to accord credit on the screen, in advertising, in paperbacks and on recordings; and excerpts as to any restrictions as to use of name and likeness.

6. Cast: One (1) copy in the English language of a list indicating the name of the character portrayed by each player and a complete description of the character.

D. Completed Trailer Materials:
Owner shall deliver to Distributor the following items:

1. Trailer Print: One (1) first-class composite 35mm positive Print of the Trailer in the same language(s) as the language version(s) of the Property delivered hereunder, fully timed and color corrected, in aspect ratios of either 1:1.33, 1:1.85 or 1:1.66 with the Soundtrack printed thereon in perfect synchronization with photographic action in all respects ready and suitable for the manufacture of a first-class master videotape.

2. Trailer Soundtrack: The separate dialogue tracks, sound effects tracks, narration tracks and music tracks, each in 35mm magnetic tracks from which the original Trailer magnetic soundtrack was made.

3. Trailer Continuity: One (1) copy in the English language of a detailed, final dialogue and action continuity of the Trailer.

EXHIBIT C:
CERTIFICATE OF ORIGIN

Title:

Territory:

Term of Contract:

Original Producer:

Produced By (Company):

Filmed In (Country):

Nationality of Film:

Year of Production:

Sold To:

Distribution Rights in Territory:

Running Time:

Director:

Cast & Credit List:

Signature of Notary Public: _____

Signature of Notary Public: _____

Signature of Licensor: _____

(Stamp)

SAMPLE PAY-PER-VIEW SYSTEM
AGREEMENT WITH ORGANIZER

THIS AGREEMENT is made this _____ day of _____, between Organizer, (*address*) ("Organizer") and (*Licensee and address*) ("Licensee"), concerning certain rights for the live television broadcast of (*describe Event*) (the "Event") scheduled to take place at (*place*) (the "Site") on (date).

1. (a) Organizer warrants and represents that it possesses the exclusive rights to promote the Event and to grant television broadcast and distribution rights for the Event. Organizer hereby grants to Licensee the nonexclusive television exhibition rights for the Event, on a one time pay-per-view basis, for all the subscribers to Licensee's pay television system, (which system is described on Exhibit A attached hereto and incorporated herein by this reference). The right and license granted herein is only for a broadcast simultaneous with the Event. Licensee shall not broadcast the Event to any public places such as bars, restaurants and the like. Licensee shall use its best efforts to prevent unauthorized use or piracy of the broadcast signal of the Event.

This paragraph contains the basic grant of pay-per-view rights. The prohibitions on sales to bars is designed to protect the market. It is difficult to enforce. The Licensee is required to use its best efforts to protect its rights. In instance, if the Licensee learns that a bar is advertising that the Event can be seen there, it must try to stop it.

(b) The Event shall commence at approximately (*time*) Eastern Standard Time, and shall be of approximately (*number*) (_____) hours duration. The Event shall be broadcast from the Site or from the site at which it takes place.

Since the event is to be offered on a live basis, timing is important.

(c) Organizer agrees that it will not authorize any live television exhibition of the Event in the market area described on Exhibit A other than by Licensee. Organizer agrees and has agreed by contract that there will be no delayed broadcast of the Event until (*number*) days after the Event takes place and that no such delayed broadcast shall be announced until at least 24 hours after the Event takes place. If such an announcement is made prior to the Event, in its discretion, Organizer shall seek redress from the person(s) responsible for the damages suffered by Organizer, Licensee and Organizer's other licensees. Any recovery by Licensee against Organizer shall be limited to the proportionate amount of monetary damages recovered by Organizer because of its liability to Licensee for breach of this covenant compared to Organizer's other licensees and Organizer. This limitation on recovery by Licensee shall not apply if the announcement is made by Organizer.

This subparagraph is designed to protect the market by not announcing any delayed coverage until after the Event takes place. The Organizer here agrees to give a proportionate share of any recovery to the Licensee. However, that is the Licensee's maximum recovery. This subparagraph may not be particularly meaningful anymore. If any event is big enough to be offered on a pay-per-view basis, consumers may reasonably expect delayed (and perhaps even home video) coverage even if there is no prior announcement.

2. (a) The Event will be delivered by satellite or by land lines at Organizer's option. If the Event is delivered by satellite, Organizer shall be responsible, at its expense, for the delivery of the video and audio signal of the entire telecast to a satellite to be mutually agreed upon by the parties. Licensee agrees to be responsible at its expense for satellite downlink and for delivery of the video and audio signal from television receive-only earth stations to its subscribers.

The method of delivery here is at the Organizer's option. If delivery is by satellite, the Organizer pays the uplink and the Licensee the downlink. Many Licensees will require that the signal be scrambled to increase security.

(b) If the Event is to be delivered by land lines, Organizer shall be responsible for the delivery at Licensee's expense of the video and audio signal of the entire telecast to the local television operating center of the telephone company servicing each of Licensee's markets. Licensee agrees to pay its share of the expenses incurred relative to delivery of the Event to the local television operating center of each of Licensee's markets, that is, a sum equal to the total amount of such aggregate out-of-pocket expense divided by the number of parties or entities licensed by Organizer who actually receive or derive the telecast of the Event from the same or common land lines. Licensee agrees to be responsible, at its expense, for delivery of the video and audio signal from the television operating center to its subscribers.

If delivery is by land lines, many licensees will share the aggregate expense thereof. Delivery to individual subscribers is the Licensee's responsibility.

(c) Organizer will also use its best efforts to deliver at its expense a separate and complete back-up feed of the telecast to the local television operating center of the telephone company servicing each of Licensee's markets.

Many Licensees will demand a back-up. Here, delivery of the back-up is via the local phone company's operating center.

3. In consideration for the rights herein granted to Licensee, Licensee shall pay to Organizer a minimum guarantee of $_____ ("Minimum Guarantee") to be applied against (*number*) percent (____%) of the Gross Receipts received by Licensee from its authorized paying subscribers ("Licensee Subscribers") who subscribe to the Event, ("Gross Receipts") or a minimum of (*number*) ____% of the subscription price per each subscriber who subscribes to the Event (but not less than (number) dollars ($_____) per subscriber), whichever is greater. If Licensee's Gross Receipts yield a payment of the Minimum Guarantee to Organizer, then Licensee's next receipts totalling (*number*) percent (____%) of Licensee's Minimum Guarantee shall be retained by Licensee. After Licensee has retained said amount out of its Gross Receipts in excess of the Minimum Guarantee, Licensee shall pay to Organizer (*number*) percent (____%) of such Gross Receipts, or a minimum of (*number*) percent (____%) of the subscription price per each subscriber who subscribes to the Event (but not less than (*number*) dollars ($_____) per subscriber), whichever is greater. Uncollectible accounts, bad debts and unable-to-views shall be Licensee's sole responsibility.

Of course, payment terms are negotiable. This Paragraph puts much of the risk on the Licensee, at least to the level of the Minimum Guarantee. Thereafter, the Licensee gets a percentage of the revenues off the top; the balance is split with the Organizer, who most likely will take a 50% or greater share. The Licensee also takes the risk of uncollectible accounts, since it has the contact with, and ability to judge, their credit worthiness.

4. (a) The Minimum Guarantee shall be payable in full on (*date*), and shall be secured by an irrevocable letter of credit to be furnished within two (2) weeks after the execution of this Agreement, confirmed by and payable at (*bank*), which letter of credit shall be automatically payable on sight on and after (*date*) if presented with an article from a newspaper of daily circulation reporting that the Event took

place. Organizer agrees that it will not demand payment upon the letter of credit until noon Eastern Standard Time, on (*date*). Said letter of credit will expire at the close of business in (*place*) on (*date*).

This agreement secures the Minimum Guarantee with a letter of credit. The letter can be used by the Organizer to secure its own letters of credit or a loan. It also can protect the Licensee if the event doesn't take place as scheduled. It is risky to specify a particular newspaper for fear a strike or other Force Majeure.

(b) The balance of the Gross Receipts payable to Organizer hereunder shall be paid no later than thirty (30) working days after the date of the telecast of the Event, together with an accounting statement setting forth the basis upon which the Gross Receipts were calculated and verifying the number of subscribers to the event. Organizer shall have the right, at its own expense, upon reasonable notice to Licensee, to audit and inspect at Licensee's place of business, Licensee's books and records pertaining to the Event for the purpose of verifying Gross Receipts for a period of one year following the Event.

Since the Organizer participates in the Gross Receipts, an audit clause is appropriate. Licensees usually insist on notice of the audit.

5. The Event will be delivered to Licensee free of commercial announcements and/or commercial material, except for sponsorship signage and endorsements worn by participants, oral announcements for which will not be included on the telecast provided to Licensee.

The limitations, if any, on the Organizer's coverage are negotiable.

6. Organizer agrees to use its best efforts to make (*participants*) available at no charge to Licensee at a place or places and at a time or times reasonably convenient to (*participants*), for the production of television commercials and on-air promotional announcements. Said commercials and announcements shall be utilized solely for the purpose of advertising the broadcast of the Event in Licensee's markets. Said commercials and announcements shall not be used for the endorsements of any product or service, other than the Event. If (*participants*) make a personal appearance in Licensee's market area, Licensee shall reimburse Organizer for such (*participant's*) reasonable airfare, ground transportation and hotel expenses.

Depending on the kind of Event, the Organizer may be able to provide the Licensee with the services of key participants for publicity and advertising.

7. Licensee shall have the right to promote, publicize and advertise the Event. Organizer will provide film footage from previous Events, color transparencies or black and white glossy photographs and publicity materials for the use of Licensee in its promotional campaign and for its monthly program guide. Licensee may, in promoting, publicizing and advertising the telecast, use the name, photographs and biographical material of (Participants) but Licensee will not use or authorize the use of any of the foregoing for purposes of endorsement of any commercial product or service. Organizer agrees that Licensee shall have the right to use up to 60 seconds of film highlights of the Event only for future promotions of Licensee's services and only for a period not to exceed one year after the date of the Event.

This is a fairly standard grant of advertising rights, featuring key participants. The use of film clips for future promotion of Licensee's own services is fairly standard.

8. All rights of any kind in and ancillary to the Event and the telecast thereof, other than the rights specifically granted to Licensee herein, are reserved to Organizer. Licensee will not in any manner videotape, record, or otherwise use, authorize or permit the use of all or part of the broadcast of the Event for any purpose other than as provided herein.

The Organizer retains all rights not specifically granted.

9. If the Event or the telecast thereof is delayed or prevented from occurring on the scheduled date by reason of an Act of God, fire, flood, war, public disaster, other calamity, strike, or labor difficulties, or any governmental action, regulation or order, then Organizer shall immediately notify Licensee if the Event will not proceed as scheduled, and, within ten (l0) days of the occurrence of the Event causing the delay of the Event as described in this Paragraph, give Licensee written notice by registered or certified mail, of (i) the reason why the Event cannot be conducted as scheduled, and (ii) Organizer's decision, which decision shall be within Organizer's sole discretion, to (a) reschedule the Event ("Rescheduled Event") to another specified date and time ("Rescheduled Date") or (b) terminate this Agreement. Should Promoter determine to reschedule the Event, then all the terms and conditions of this Agreement shall apply to the Rescheduled Date, unless Licensee notifies Organizer within five (5) business days of receipt of notice from

Promoter of the Rescheduled Date that Licensee does not accept the Rescheduled Date, in which case this Agreement shall terminate and Organizer shall have no liability to Licensee except to return all monies previously paid to Organizer by Licensee [and to pay Licensee as compensation for its promotional expenses the amount described below]. Should Organizer determine to terminate this Agreement, then this Agreement shall be null and void and no payment shall be due to Organizer hereunder. [In the event the Event does not take place as contemplated herein on (*date*) then Organizer shall pay to Licensee as full compensation for its expenses, including without limitation, promotional expenses, Licensee's documented out-of-pocket costs up to a limit of (*number*) percent (_____%) of Licensee's Minimum Guarantee hereunder and no other payment will be due Licensee. Organizer shall obtain insurance adequate to cover these payments at its own expenses.]

This agreement allows the Organizer the option of rescheduling or terminating the Event without liability to Licensee. The parenthetical could be bargained for by the Licensee to reduce its risk with respect to out-of-pocket promotional expenses incurred by it. If such a clause is included, the Licensee should insist on insurance.

10. Organizer shall indemnify Licensee and hold Licensee and its respective officers, agents, directors, and employees harmless from any and all losses, claims, liabilities, damages, costs and expenses (including reasonable attorneys' fees) incurred by reason of violation by Organizer of any of the terms and conditions of this Agreement or breach of any warranty or representation made by it hereunder.

A standard warranty.

11. Licensee shall indemnify and hold Organizer, its respective officers, directors, agents, and employees harmless from and against all claims, liabilities, damages, costs and expenses (including reasonable attorneys' fees) arising out of or resulting from any action or activities by Licensee relative to Licensee's exhibition of the Event or incurred by reason of the violation by Licensee of any of the terms and conditions of this Agreement.

A standard warranty.

12. The obligations specified in Paragraphs 10 and 11 relative to indemnification of Organizer and Licensee shall be subject to the following provisions: (a) the party

seeking indemnification hereunder shall promptly notify the other of any claim or liability to which the indemnification relates; (b) the party seeking indemnification hereunder shall afford the other the opportunity to participate in any compromise, settlement, or other resolution or disposition of such claim or liability; and (c) the party seeking indemnification hereunder shall fully cooperate with the reasonable requests of the other in its participation in, and control, compromise, settlement, or resolution of, such claim or liability.

This is a fairly standard paragraph explaining the mechanism for enforcement of the indemnities.

13. If the Event is not transmitted by Organizer to the satellite or to the local television operating centers for any reason beyond Organizer's control, Organizer shall not be in breach of this Agreement, but will refund all sums paid by Licensee to Organizer. However, the provisions of this paragraph shall not apply to any failure of the live transmission resulting from inclement weather, failure of the satellite or land lines or failure of any services or equipment. Licensee shall insure against all such occurrences at its own expense and Organizer shall be named as a co-beneficiary of such insurance. Organizer represents and warrants that it will comply with the material conditions of Licensee's insurance policy of which Organizer is made aware by Licensee.

In the event of a broadcast failure (for a reason beyond the Organizer's control), the Organizer here has assumed no risk. The Minimum Guarantee is still due; the Licensee is required to buy insurance and name the Organizer as an insured. The Licensee has here at least required the Organizer to warrant compliance with insurance terms.

14. Each person executing this Agreement represents and warrants that he is fully authorized and has the power to execute this Agreement on behalf of such party. Licensee represents and warrants that there are no agent's or finder's fees due anyone regarding this Agreement and the grant of rights hereunder. Licensee further represents and warrants that it is presently and will continue to be duly authorized by law and by all governmental regulatory agencies claiming jurisdiction to regulate its business.

Boilerplate.

15. Nothing herein contained shall be deemed to constitute either of the parties a joint venturer or partner or agent of the other. Neither party shall hold itself out contrary to the terms of this Agreement and neither party shall become liable by any reason of any representation, act or omission of the other contrary to the provisions hereof.

Boilerplate.

16. Nothing herein contained shall require the commission of any act contrary to any express provision of law, or policy of law, or of any rule or regulation of any governmental authority, and if there shall exist any conflict between any provision of this Agreement and any such law, policy, rule, or regulation, the latter shall prevail; and the provision or provisions of this Agreement affected shall be curtailed, limited, or eliminated to the extent necessary to remove such conflict and as so modified this Agreement shall continue in full force and effect.

Boilerplate.

17. This Agreement shall be construed and interpreted under the laws of the State of (*state name*) with the same force and effect as if fully executed and to be fully performed therein.

Boilerplate.

18. Any notice, statement, demand, request, consent, approval, authorization, offer, Agreement or communication that either party hereto desires or is required to give to the other party shall be in writing and shall be sufficiently given and served upon the other party if delivered personally, or delivered by telegram or telex, or if sent by United States Postal Service, registered or certified mail, postage prepaid, to the appropriate party's address as first above mentioned, with a copy to (*lawyer's name*). Either party to this Agreement may change its address for the purpose of this Agreement by giving the other party appropriate notice.

Boilerplate.

19. This Agreement contains the full and complete understanding between the parties hereto and superseded any and all prior understandings, whether written or oral, pertaining to the subject matter hereof and cannot be modified except by a written instrument signed by both parties hereto.

Boilerplate.

20. This Agreement may not be assigned by Licensee or Organizer, either voluntarily or by operation of law, without the prior written consent of the other, and any such assignment shall not relieve the assignor of its obligations hereunder. Notwithstanding the foregoing, either Organizer or Licensee may assign this Agreement, or any of its rights hereunder, without the other's consent, to a parent company, subsidiary company or subsidiary of the parent company or any entity with which it may be merged or consolidated or which acquires all or substantially all of its assets, or any company owned or controlled by either party, provided that such entity with which it is merged or consolidated, or which acquires all or substantially all its assets agrees in writing to assume all of assignor's obligations under this Agreement.

Boilerplate.

IN WITNESS WHEREOF, the parties hereto have caused this Agreement to be signed by their respective duly authorized officers on the date written above.

Licensee

By: _____

Organizer

By: _____

EXHIBIT A

(List system members)

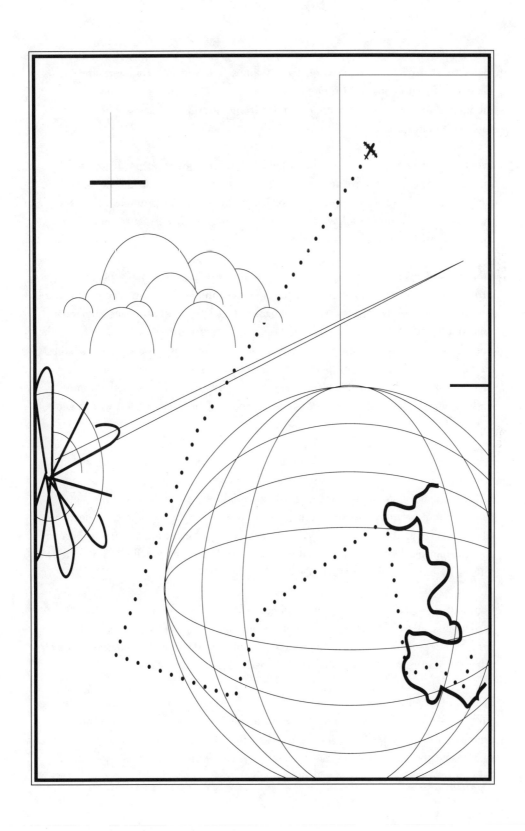

LIABILITY AND SPECIAL EVENTS

This chapter addresses the liability issues that can arise when presenting or sponsoring an event. It focuses on the liabilities imposed on promoters and, to some extent, on sponsors. Promoters are generally more active in actually conducting an event, so they appear more frequently in the cases. Where applicable, however, the liability of sponsors is discussed.

Event promoters generally have been held liable for injuries to participants and spectators. This has been true even where the injury was due to the negligence of the participant or of an independent contractor hired by the promoter. In a few cases, however, promoters have been relieved from liability because their actual connection with an event was minimal.

Promoters of events have an obligation to make sure they are not exposing participants to unreasonable risks of harm. For example, because race courses are inherently dangerous, promoters are obligated to inspect the premises and warn contestants of hidden dangers. In addition, promoters must rectify any dangers that come to their attention during an event. Promoters are not, however, responsible for injuries that arise due to the normal or ordinary risks inherent in an activity, such as a knee injury sustained as a result of being tackled in a football game. Under common law, participants assume the natural risks associated with a game or contest.

In addition, event promoters must ensure that a reasonably safe viewing area is provided for spectators. This includes an obligation to inspect the viewing premises before an event and to post warnings of potential hazards. Promoters are not, however, required to continuously inspect an area for dangers, and they need not take measures that would impair a spectator's enjoyment of an event. Furthermore, they are not guarantors of a spectator's safety and are thus not liable for injuries caused by unforeseeable occurrences.

Contractual releases have been used effectively as a method of limiting liability to participants. A waiver clause that clearly states the rights being waived and the persons released is upheld in most jurisdictions. However, waiver clauses cannot release a party from liability due to its grossly negligent conduct.

In unique circumstances, sponsors or promoters may contract to assume a third party's risks or liabilities. For instance, in arranging for a site for an event, the promoter usually agrees to hold the site harmless from any damages it may incur as a result of the event. This can include physical damage to the site as well as liability for personal injuries incurred by spectators.

THE CONCEPT OF DUTY AND THE STANDARD OF CARE

Generally, lawsuits brought against promoters allege that their conduct (1) created an unreasonable risk of harm to others and (2) resulted in an injury to a participant in or spectator of an event. The law calls this "negligent" conduct.

Promoters are not liable for their negligent conduct unless the injured party establishes four conditions. First, the promoter must have a duty or obligation to conform to a certain standard of conduct for the protection of others. Second, the organizer's conduct must have failed to meet the required standard. (Failure to do so is commonly known as a "breach of the duty of care.") Third, there must be a reasonably close causal connection between the promoter's conduct and the resulting injury. Finally, the complaining party must actually have suffered some injury or property damage that is compensable by law. Nominal damages, to vindicate a technical right, cannot be recovered in a negligence action where no *actual* loss has occurred.[1]

1.
See Prosser on Torts (5th ed. 1984), p. 165 [hereinafter, *Prosser*].

The threshold element for a finding of liability is the requirement of a duty. Thus, even if a promoter is found to be negligent, it will not be liable to a person unless it owed some duty of care to that person.

The determination of whether a duty exists is primarily a question of law.[2] A key factor in making this determination is whether an individual's conduct created a foreseeable risk of harm to others. All individuals are required to use ordinary care to prevent others from being injured as a result of their conduct.[3] Thus, when a promoter is able to anticipate a particular risk, it is generally under a duty to do so. Normally, a jury decides whether a risk was foreseeable, so each decision varies with the circumstances of the particular case.

2.
See Prosser, p. 358.

3.
Hilyar v. Union Ice Co., 45 Cal. 2d 30, 36, 286 P.2d 21, 24 (1955).

However, even if a promoter created a foreseeable risk, this does not automatically imply a duty to prevent injury. Nearly all human acts carry some recognizable degree of danger. Thus, a duty is generally imposed only upon an individual whose conduct creates an *unreasonable* foreseeable risk of harm.[4] A risk is unreasonable if the gravity and likelihood of the danger outweigh the utility of the conduct involved.[5]

4.
See Prosser, p. 170.

5.
Id. at 171.

Having a duty generally means having to do what an ideal individual would do in the same circumstances. The person's conduct must be a model of all the proper qualities of human behavior, with allowances for those shortcomings that society tolerates given the circumstances. This is referred to in law as the "reasonable person" standard.[6]

6.
Id. at 174.

Since the standard is a societal standard, the usual and customary conduct of others under similar circumstances has a bearing on whether the standard has been met. For example, safety precautions taken by a promoter of wrestling matches are compared with those considered customary among wrestling promoters in determining whether the promoter has violated its duty to protect spectators from harm.

The degree of care required of an individual depends on the nature and extent of the risks presented by his or her conduct. Normally, promoters are required to take measures that any ordinary person would in protecting others from potential hazards. On the other hand, promoters of inherently dangerous activities have sometimes been held liable for resulting damages regardless of their fault. (Liability without fault is called strict liability.)

7.
140 Cal. Rptr. 247 (1977).

For example, in *Ramsey* v. *Marutamaya Ogatsu Fireworks Co.*,[7] the organizer of a fireworks exhibition was held strictly liable for injuries suffered by an operator of the display. The operator was injured when a shell prematurely exploded. Despite a finding of negligence only on behalf of the fireworks manufacturer, the promoter was held liable to the operator for damages. The court explained that it is the event organizer's duty to protect the public from explosives. Furthermore, this duty cannot be delegated. Thus, the promoter's act of hiring an independent contractor was not sufficient to insulate it from liability.[8] Two corporate sponsors of the exhibit were also held liable because they had hired the organizer and the pyrotechnic operator and they were the ones primarily to be benefitted from the display. It should be noted, however, that both the promoter and sponsor were allowed to recover their losses from the fireworks manufacturer.[9]

8.
Id. at 253.

9.
Id. at 248. *See also Rill* v. *Chiarella*, 269 N.Y.S.2d 736 (Sup. 1966) [holding fireworks promoter liable for injuries to spectator notwithstanding negligence on the part of the independently contracted operator].

A promoter's ability to collect from the party ultimately responsible will depend in part on the financial strength of the liable party, the existence of insurance and perhaps on the contractual indemnity or release between the parties.

Promoters of activities involving an appreciable degree of risk should be aware that they may be held strictly liable for any damages. If a promoter subcontracts another party that exercises actual control over particular risks, the written contract should require the subcontractor to use due care and to indemnify the promoter from any loss or damages resulting from its failure to do so.

Duty to Protect from Unreasonable Foreseeable Risks
Promoters have been held liable for injuries resulting from unreasonable risks that were inherent in their promotions. The scope of this liability can be extensive. At least one court has found the promoter liable for an injury due to the negligence of

a third party, since the injury was related to the promotion and was foreseeable. A promoter's liability has been found to extend even to injuries that were unrelated to the promotion.

In *Weirum* v. *RKO General, Inc.*,[10] a radio station was held liable for the death of a man whose car was forced off a highway by teenagers participating in a promotion. The radio station, attempting to increase its audience, conducted a contest in which one of its disc jockeys drove around the city stopping at predetermined locations. The jockey drove a conspicuous automobile and periodically announced his intended destination over the radio. The first contestant to physically locate him at each site received a cash prize. Two teenagers in separate cars, racing to the announced destination, forced a man's car off the highway. The radio station was held liable because the risk that young listeners would speed while participating in the contest was foreseeable. The court found that the contest was directed at a teenage audience and was conducted during the summer when young people were "responsive to relief from vacation tedium."[11] Furthermore, the risk of a high-speed automobile chase far outweighed the promotional benefits to the station and was therefore unreasonable. The court stated that less dangerous alternatives were available and should have been adopted.[12] The court rejected the station's defense that it was not liable for the negligent conduct of its listeners. The radio station created the risk and was therefore in the best position to prevent the negligent conduct.

Reasonable Care in Protecting Invitees

Promoters of athletic events, rock concerts, and other entertainment activities often assume the position of occupiers of land. For example, the purchaser of a ticket to a wrestling match is considered an "invitee" of the promoter. Thus, the Court of Appeals of Georgia found that a promoter of a wrestling exhibition could be liable for an injury to a spectator who slipped and fell while attending the match.[13] The spectator slipped on a loose sheet of plastic that had been laid to protect the gymnasium floor where the event took place. Although the court did not make a final determination regarding liability, it did state that the issue turns on whether the promoter was negligent in not discovering the hazard and eliminating it or giving timely warning to the spectators.[14]

The law imposes a general duty upon an occupier of premises to keep them safe for those invited to enter ("invitees"). While the extent of this duty may vary by statute among states, the traditional rule is that an occupier of land must exercise the same care as an ordinarily careful and prudent person in the same position and circumstances, i.e., the reasonable person.[15] Included in this duty is an obligation to

10.
123 Cal. Rptr. 468, 539 P.2d 36 (1975).

11.
Id. at 472.

12.
Id.

13.
Begin v. *Georgia Championship Wrestling Inc.,* 172 Ga. App. 293, 322 S.E.2d 737 (1984).

14.
Id. at 297.

15.
Whitfield v. *Cox,* 189 Va. 219, 52 S.E.2d 72 (1949).

16.
See Prosser, pp. 425-26.

17.
See Restatement (Second) of Torts § 343.

18.
Winn-Dixie Stores, Inc. v. Hardy, 138 Ga. App. 342, 344, 226 S.E.2d 142, 144 (1976).

19.
Alterman Foods, Inc. v. Ligon, 246 Ga. 620, 622, 272 S.E.2d 327, 330 (1980).

inspect the premises to discover potential hazards and warn invitees of their existence.[16] Theoretically, an invitee enters the premises under an implied representation that the land has been prepared and made safe for him or her.[17]

The occupier of land is required only to use reasonable care and does not insure the safety of invitees.[18] Moreover, there is no duty to patrol the premises continuously to discover defects.[19]

Duty to Prevent Further Injury

Related to the previous duties is the duty to use reasonable care in rectifying subsequently arising dangers of which a person is, or should be, aware. The basis for this duty is the idea that, while the danger was not originally foreseeable, once it is known, the person becomes liable for failing to rectify the continued hazard.

Promoters should be aware of this ongoing duty. Any time a potential hazard comes to the promoters' attention, they should take steps to minimize the danger by correcting the problem or giving appropriate notice.

20.
J.C. Penney Co. v. Barrientz, 411 P.2d 841, 848 (Okla. 1966).

21.
Fleming v. Allied Supermarkets, Inc., 236 F. Supp. 306 (W.D. Okla. 1964).

22.
Id. at 308.

23.
Shircliff v. Kroger Co., 593 P.2d 1101 (Okl. Ct. App. 1979).

24.
Id. at 1106.

Whether reasonable care has been exercised in discovering and correcting a problem is a question of how long the actor knew about the dangerous condition. Usually the condition must exist for a "reasonable time" before liability arises.[20] What constitutes a reasonable time is determined by a jury and thus varies from case to case. However, the primary consideration is whether the actor had sufficient time and ability to prevent harm to others. Thus, a store owner has been held liable for injuries sustained by a customer who was knocked over by a child pushing a shopping cart.[21] The court found that the store owner had knowledge of the child's reckless behavior for at least eleven minutes and perhaps as much as thirty minutes.[22]

On the other hand, no liability was found where an individual was injured during a spontaneous assault while responding to an employment agency advertisement.[23] There, the plaintiff was assaulted and injured by another applicant for cutting in line. The court found that the store owner had no duty to protect the injured party from the assault. The fight itself was not a prolonged event, lasting only from one to ten minutes.[24] Furthermore, the only employee to witness the incident was a construction worker on stilts who was in no position to stop the fight.

SCOPE OF PROMOTER LIABILITY

Cases involving promoter liability for injuries fall into two groups: cases where the injured party was a participant in the advertised event, and cases where the injury involved a spectator. At least one court, however, has held a promoter liable for injuries sustained by an unrelated party.[25] The basic theories underlying liability are the same in all situations. In addition, promoters have escaped liability using the theories of assumption of risk and contributory negligence (negligence by the injured party).

25.
See Weirum v. RKO General, Inc., 123 Cal. Rptr. 468 (1975).

To Participants

Promoter liability to participants is qualified by the general rule that a participant in a lawful game or contest assumes the ordinary risks inherent in that game or contest.[26] Thus, in *McLeod Store* v. *Vinson*,[27] a promoter of a guinea hen chasing contest was found not liable for injuries sustained by a contestant. Contestants chased guinea hens on public streets, and a cash prize was awarded for each one caught. The plaintiff, while chasing a guinea hen, fell and broke his leg. The court ruled that, while the plaintiff was not yet 17 years of age, he still possessed ordinary intelligence and was able to assess the risks ordinarily inherent in such contests. Furthermore, the evidence revealed that the plaintiff had witnessed the actual event before participating. Thus, he had firsthand knowledge of the size of the crowd and the nature of the contest. Since he was a voluntary participant, he was held to have assumed the risk of falling, thereby releasing the promoter from liability.[28]

26.
7 A.L.R. 2d 707.

27.
213 Ky. 667, 281 S.W. 799 (1926).

28.
Id. at 668.

In a similar situation, the promoter of a hobbyhorse race on a restaurant's dance floor was found not liable for the injuries of a participant who fell during the race.[29] Although the plaintiff claimed she had not assumed the risk since she had never seen a hobbyhorse before, the court responded that adequate warning had been provided. Prior to the race, an announcement was made warning contestants of the dangers of falling off: "take your chances." Having received this warning, the plaintiff entered the race and, as she might have expected, was injured.[30]

29.
Knowles v. Roberts-at-the-Beach Co., 115 Cal. App. 2d 196,251 P.2d 389 (1953).

30.
See also Whipple v. Salvation Army, 261 Or. 453, 495 P.2d 739 (1972) [releasing promoter from liability because fifteen-year-old boy assumes the risk of injury in a tackle football game].

While participants are normally held to have assumed the ordinary risks of an activity, they do not automatically assume risks brought about by a promoter's negligence. Thus, in *Smith* v. *Hooper*,[31] the defendants, promoters of a balloon game for children, were found liable for an injury to a participant. The game required contestants, on horseback, to break with their hands balloons tied to other contestants' backs. The last contestant with his or her balloon intact received a prize. The plaintiff was injured when another contestant violated the contest's rules by using a whip to break balloons. The whip struck the plaintiff's horse, causing it

31.
89 N.H. 36, 192 A. 496 (1937).

to throw its rider to the ground. The court found the promoters negligent in failing to discover the use of the whip. The facts indicated that other riders had seen the whip and that no apparent attempt had been made to conceal its use.

32.
240 N.C. 470, 82 S.E.2d 417 (1954).

In *Midkiff* v. *National Assn. for Stock Car Auto Racing, Inc.*,[32] the court held that a race car driver's estate could pursue a legal claim against a corporate promoter/sponsor of a car race. Only a few seconds into the race, the car collided with a dead car on the track. The dead car had been left there after a series of test runs before the actual race. Race drivers were given no warning that such cars were on the course. Although the ultimate issue of the promoter/sponsor's negligence was not before the court, the court ruled that the promoter/sponsor was potentially liable for allowing the race to begin under such dangerous conditions.[33]

33.
Id. at 471.

34.
312 S.2d 300 (La. 1975).

The extent of promoter liability is further illustrated by the case of *Rosenberger* v. *Central Louisiana Dist. Livestock Show, Inc.*[34] There, the Supreme Court of Louisiana held a rodeo promoter liable for injuries sustained by a bareback bronco rider during competition. The rider was injured when his horse attempted to exit the arena through a gate that a rodeo employee had left partially open. The court found this to be clear negligence, relying upon testimony that it is common knowledge among rodeo professionals that a bucking horse will attempt to enter a partially open gate to dislodge a rider. The defendant was found to have breached his duties of inspection and prevention of further injury. Approximately forty-five minutes had elapsed between the last event in which the gate was used and the time of the plaintiff's injury.[35] Thus, the dangerous condition existed for an amount of time in which it would be reasonable to expect it to be discovered and remedied. The court rejected the promoter's argument that the rider assumed the risk of his injury and was contributorily negligent. Open gates in an arena are not commonplace during rodeo events. In addition, the court reasoned that it is unreasonable to expect a rider to be aware of surrounding hazards when his attention is focused on staying on the horse.[36]

35.
Id. at 304.

36.
Id.

The interesting aspect of *Rosenberger* is that the promoter was held liable even though organization and supervision of the event were the sole responsibility of an independent contractor. In fact, the gate was left open by a worker hired by the contractor. The court nevertheless found that the promoter retained complete control over the rodeo. In particular, all ticket proceeds and expenses were directed to the promoter. The promoter retained the right to determine whether or not the rodeo would take place and under what circumstances. Thus, it was held that the rodeo workers were all employees of the promoter for purposes of imputing their negligence to the promoter.[37]

37.
Id. at 305.

Promoters may also be responsible for injuries that are unnaturally incident to a game or contest. The law refers to such risks as "extraordinary."[38] Thus, a promoter of a cross-country horse race was held liable for the death of a participant whose horse stumbled into a hole on the course.[39] The hole, created during a Navy bombing demonstration, was approximately 3½ feet long, 2½ feet wide, and 18 inches deep. No prior warning about this condition was given to the riders. The court stated that, although an artificially created hole may not be more dangerous than a natural hazard, the law deems an invitee to have assumed only natural, ordinary dangers.[40] The court based the promoter's liability upon its duty as an occupier of land to provide a reasonably safe race course for its participants. At a minimum, the promoter should have had the course inspected and issued a timely warning of the potential hazard.[41]

Although the hazard may be an extraordinary one, a participant who knows about it and voluntarily assumes it will be precluded from recovering for injury or death. In *Paine* v. *Y.M.C.A.*,[42] the plaintiff, a basketball player, sued the organizer of a basketball game for injuries suffered from a fall during the game. While jumping for a ball, the plaintiff was knocked out of bounds and fell against some bleachers that were only 15 inches from the sidelines. The plaintiff asserted that the injury would not have occurred if the bleachers had been positioned farther back. The court disagreed. While the court acknowledged the existence of a hazard, the defendant was found not liable on the theory that the plaintiff knew the bleachers were there and was fully aware of the risk involved. The plaintiff was thus held to have assumed the extraordinary risk.[43]

Promoters have generally been held liable to participants only for those injuries sustained while engaged in the promoted activity. Thus, a car racing promoter was not held liable for injuries sustained by a racer while watching another race in the pit area.[44] In that case, the plaintiff was injured when a race car went out of control and catapulted into a spot in the pit area where the plaintiff was sitting. The court reasoned that the plaintiff, a race car driver, fully appreciated the danger of being in the pit area. Furthermore, the plaintiff was not required to watch the race from that vantage point and was free to observe from the safer confines of the grandstands.[45]

In a similar case, a promoter of horse and motorcycle races was found not liable when a motorcycle racer was injured while waiting for his event.[46] The promoter had scheduled several horse races, which were to be followed by motorcycle races on the same track. The racer watched the last horse race at an area alongside the track where there were no barricades. He was subsequently injured when a horse became excited and bolted through the opening where he was standing. The

38.
7 A.L.R. 2d 709.

39.
Hotels El Rancho, Inc. v. Pray, 64 Nev. 591, 187 P.2d 568 (1947).

40.
Id. at 611-12.

41,
Id. at 618.

42.
91 N.H. 78, 13 A.2d 820 (1940).

43.
Id. at 79.

44.
Hollamon v. Eagle Raceways, Inc., 187 Neb. 221, 188 N.W.2d 710 (1971).

45.
Id. at 225.

46.
Toole v. Erlanger Fair Assn., 269 S.W. 523 (Ky. 1925).

interesting aspect of *Toole* is that the promoter was held not liable even though one of the promoter's employees had directed the plaintiff to wait in that area. The plaintiff had been warming up on the racetrack prior to the last horse race and was ordered off the track. The court found that, notwithstanding the order, the plaintiff should have been aware of the potential danger and thus assumed the risk of his injury.[47]

47.
Id. at 524.

Race promoters should note, however, that if it is apparent that racers are using an unauthorized area for warming up, the promoters may be held liable for injuries unless they issue adequate warnings. In *Licato v. Eastgate*,[48] a race promoter, who was also a leaseholder of the racetrack, was held liable for an injury to a racer who was trespassing on adjacent property and struck an excavation. The facts indicated that racers often had been seen warming up on adjacent land and that there was no fence, sign or other demarcation to distinguish the racetrack from adjoining property. The court found that the risk of a participant's being injured on unauthorized property was foreseeable and that the promoter was therefore negligent in not providing course markers and warnings.[49]

48.
499 N.Y.S.2d 472 (App. Div. 1986).

49.
Id. at 474.

To Spectators

Promoter liability for spectator injuries has been based primarily on the promoter's duty, as an occupier of the premises, to provide a safe viewing area for the event. In a couple of instances, however, the extent of the promoter's control over an event has been a determining factor in establishing liability. Thus, a promoter may be released from liability if it can establish that it had the opportunity neither to foresee nor to control the hazard resulting in the injury. For example, in *Bowes* v. *Cincinnati Riverfront Coliseum, Inc.*,[50] an action for wrongful death against a national promoter for the rock group The Who was dismissed due to the promoter's tenuous connection with the concert. A fan was crushed to death while waiting for the gates to open at the stadium where the concert was held. Amidst charges of reckless conduct, the trial court found that the national promoter's involvement consisted only of a contractual agreement stating the time when the performance was to begin. The evidence indicated that no agents or employees of the promoter were present when the accident occurred. Thus, the court held that the promoter's conduct was not causally related to the tragedy.[51] Although the court did not make a final determination regarding liability, it did rule that a local promoter (in charge of the event's operation) was potentially liable for the tragedy.

50.
12 Ohio App. 3d 12, 465 N.E.2d 904 (1983).

51.
Id. at 22.

A promoter of a soapbox derby race avoided liability in a similar manner by establishing that the operation of the event was the sole responsibility of the city police department.[52] There, the plaintiff, a police officer, was injured when a

52.
Bango v. Carteret Lions Club, 12 N.J. Super. 52, 79 A.2d 57 (1951).

soapbox racer lost control and ran into him. The defendant promoter testified that operation of the event was turned over to the police department, which was responsible for positioning the plaintiff where he was.[53]

It should be noted, however, that the above instances are rare. In most cases, advertising an event and inviting the public to attend are sufficient to establish a promoter's duty of care to all spectators.

The more control a promoter has, the more certain his or her liability. In *McLaughlin* v. *Home Indemnity Insurance Co.*,[54] a rock concert promoter was held liable for injuries to a concertgoer who slipped on some wet stairs during an intermission. The promoter was found negligent in not allowing the concert hall lights to be turned on during the intermission period. Rather, to prevent destroying the "atmosphere," the promoter chose to rely only on the small exit lights located on each step. While the court stated that the promoter does not have a duty to continuously inspect the premises for hazards, it did find that leaving the lights off was unreasonable. The promoter was aware that beverages were being consumed and that spilling was inevitable. Under these circumstances, attendees' risk of falling was an unreasonable one because intermission is usually the time when people leave their seats. Above all, the risk involved was avoidable simply by turning the lights on.[55]

One specific obligation promoters must face is a duty to use reasonable care in inspecting the condition of seats prior to an event.[56] Thus, a promoter was held liable for injuries sustained by a spectator when bleachers broke, causing her to fall on a concrete floor.[57] The evidence indicated that the bleachers broke under the ordinary weight of the plaintiff and that there was no sign of tampering or negligence on the part of the spectator. The bleachers were built by an independent contractor hired by the promoter. The court found that the promoter had made no attempt to inspect the bleachers prior to the match and was therefore guilty of negligence.[58]

While promoters are expected to use reasonable care in protecting spectators, they are not insurers of their safety. In *Reynolds* v. *Deep South Sports, Inc.*,[59] a wrestling promoter was found not liable to a spectator who was hit by a bottle thrown by another spectator. The court found that the promoter had taken reasonable precautions to control the crowd and was under no duty to search all patrons for hazardous objects.[60]

Promoters have been successful in avoiding liability by showing that their conduct was consistent with the standard practice of the industry. In *Pierce* v. *Murnick*,[61] the

53.
Id. at 56.

54.
361 So. 2d 1227 (La. App. 1978).

55.
Id. at 1230.

56.
4 Am. Jur. 2d *Amusements and Exhibitions* § 57.

57.
Parker v. *Warren*, 503 S.W.2d 938 (Tenn. App. 1973).

58.
Id. at 943.

59.
211 So. 2d 37 (Fla. 1968).

60.
Id. at 39. *See also Whitfield* v. *Cox*, 189 Va. 219, 52 S.E.2d 72 (1949) [same facts]; *Stevenson* v. *Kansas City*, 187 Kan. 705, 360 P.2d 1 (1961) [holding no liability for an assault on a spectator en route to a wrestling exhibition].

61.
265 N.C. 707, 145 S.E.2d 11 (1965).

62.
Id. at 708.

63.
Id. at 709. *See also C & M Promotions v. Ryland,* 208 Va. 365, 158 S.E.2d 132 (1967) [rejecting claim that promoter was negligent in failing to provide additional protection for ringside spectators].

64.
McCarron v. Upper Peninsula Hauling Assoc., 13 Mich. App. 168, 163 N.W.2d 805 (1968).

65.
Id. at 173.

court found the defendant promoter not liable for personal injuries received by a spectator when a wrestler fell upon him. The spectator claimed that the promoter was negligent in not providing an additional barrier between the ring and the first row of seats. The ring was a standard wrestling ring consisting of a square platform with posts at each corner. The posts were connected by ropes that ran around the ring. It was noted that the usual practice is to leave ringside seats exposed. The court stated that the law does not require a promoter to take steps for the safety of spectators that will unreasonably impair their enjoyment of the exhibition.[62] Finding no departure from the standard practice and a voluntary act by plaintiff to sit at ringside, the court ruled that the defendant was not liable.[63]

Promoter liability has also been rejected where the spectator has assumed the risk of injury. For example, a spectator at a horse-team pulling contest was denied recovery for a broken leg caused by an uncontrolled horse.[64] The plaintiff chose to watch the contest from an entrance of the arena that was not barricaded. As a team was being prepared to be hitched, two horses escaped and bolted around the arena. The horses ran through the entrance, injuring the plaintiff. The promoter was not negligent in allowing the entrance to remain open because it was necessary for letting the horses through during the contest. Furthermore, the court ruled that there was no duty to warn spectators of the risk involved because the risk was obvious. Thus, the plaintiff was held to have assumed the risk of his injury.[65]

CONTRACTUAL RELEASES FROM
AND ASSUMPTIONS OF LIABILITY

Promoters have traditionally used release forms as a way of insulating themselves from liability to participants. Generally, these forms provide that a participant agrees not to hold the promoter liable for injuries resulting from an event. The use of such forms brings into conflict two tenets of law: first, that a party should be liable for the negligent breach of a duty he lawfully owes to another; and second, that a party should be free to contract about his or her affairs.

The following discussion offers four guidelines for promoters. First, waiver release forms should be identified clearly and presented in large, easily read type in a separate document, rather than being buried within an entry form. Second, the release form should specifically identify the parties that are being absolved from liability. Third, the risks being waived should be stated explicitly. For example, the language might read, "Participant hereby waives all claims arising out of . . . against promoter X and sponsor Y and their respective directors, officers, employees, designees and assigns." Fourth, promoters should instruct all agents administering such forms that they are responsible for informing participants of the existence of the release and its general nature. In addition, promoters should be aware that the existence of a signed waiver does not mean they are absolved from their legal duties to participants. Liability for grossly negligent or reckless conduct cannot be eliminated by contract.

In general, waiver clauses are disfavored under the law. They are strictly construed against the party relying on them, and clear and explicit language is required to relieve a person of liability.[66] In addition, such clauses have been ruled invalid when they conflict with a positive duty imposed by statute.[67] In *McCarthy*, a race car driver was severely burned when his car exploded upon completion of the race. The explosion could have been avoided had plaintiff's car been properly inspected before the race. Defendant promoter claimed no liability, relying upon a release form signed by plaintiff prior to the event. However, because a New Jersey state statute specifically required that race organizers inspect vehicles for the purpose of fire prevention, the court ruled the waiver form ineffective.[68]

In the context of sporting events, however, waiver release forms generally have been held enforceable under the theory that they are contracts regulating conduct between private parties.[69] Racers are always free to refuse participation in the race under the conditions imposed.[70] Thus, absent a conflict with a statute imposing a specific duty, promoters can usually rely on releases from participants.

Release forms are clearly effective where an injury results from a danger that is inherent in the activity. Thus, in *Okura* v. *U.S. Cycling Federation*,[71] a release form was held valid in barring recovery of a bike racer who fell when his bicycle hit

66.
17 C.J.S. Contracts
§ 262 (1963).

67.
See McCarthy v.
*National Assn. For Stock
Car Auto Racing, Inc.*,
87 N.J. Super. 442, 209
A.2d 668 (1965).

68.
Id. at 444.

69.
Gore v. *Tri-County Race-
way, Inc.*, 407 F. Supp.
489, 492 (M.D. Ala.
1974).

70.
Solodar v. *Watkins Glen
Grand Prix Corp.*, 317
N.Y.S.2d 228, 229
(1971).

71.
231 Cal. Rptr. 429
(1986).

72.
Prosser, pp. 483-84.

73.
Bennett v. *United States Cycling Federation*, 239 Cal. Rptr. 55 (1987).

74.
Id. at 59.

75.
See also Shelby Mutual Insurance Co. v. *Grand Rapids*, 6 Mich. App. 95, 148 N.W.2d 260 (1967); 6A *Corbin on Contracts*, pp. 596-97.

76.
See Young v. *City of Gadsden*, 482 S.2d 1158 (Ala. 1985) [a waiver form releasing promoter from "all liability" is effective against race car driver's injuries due to promoter's negligence].

77.
Ferrell v. *Southern Nevada Off-Road Enthusiasts, Ltd.*, 147 Cal. App. 3d 309, 314-15 (1983) [the language of a release was not clear; the form never used the words "release," "remise," "discharge," "waive" or the like].

78.
Celli v. *Sports Car Club of America, Inc.*, 29 Cal. App. 3d 511, 522 (1972) [pit pass release form, printed in 6-point type, did not specifically release defendants from their own negligence].

79.
45 Wash. App. 847, 728 P.2d 617 (1986).

80.
Id. at 849.

loose debris on the course. The court noted that the release form specifically insulated the promoter from all injuries incident to the sport of bicycle racing and any injuries due to the promoter's negligence or carelessness.

On the other hand, waivers are not enforceable where the terms expressed in the release do not apply to the particular misconduct of the defendant.[72] Thus, a promoter was held liable for injuries to a bicycle racer who collided with an automobile that was allowed to enter a closed course.[73] The rider had signed a release form identical to the one in *Okura*. Nevertheless, the court reasoned that the release form is valid as a waiver only of obvious or foreseeable hazards, such as collisions with other riders, negligently maintained equipment, bad road surfaces, bicycles unfit for racing, and so on. The form was not, however, effective in relieving the promoter from liability for an injury caused by an event that the rider could not reasonably have foreseen. The court thus held that, given plaintiff's knowledge that the course was in fact to be closed to automobiles, the waiver was unenforceable.[74] *Bennett* therefore illustrates that promoters cannot insulate themselves from their own grossly negligent conduct.[75]

In some cases, waiver forms have been effective in releasing a promoter from liability for negligence even though the term "negligence" was not stated in the form.[76] The general rule, however, is that the language in a release form must be clear, explicit and comprehensible in each of its essential details.[77] The agreement, read as a whole, must clearly notify the participant of the effect of signing it.[78]

Provided that a release form is clearly identified and its contents unambiguous, a participant who signs the release will be held to have understood its terms. Thus, in *Conradt* v. *Four Star Promotions, Inc.*,[79] a race car driver was charged with a duty to read the release form that barred his recovery. The driver testified that he was never told that he was signing any type of release agreement. The court found, however, that the form was entitled "Voluntary Waiver and Release from Liability and Indemnity Agreement" and was unambiguously addressed to the risks of automobile racing. Furthermore, above plaintiff's signature was the printed statement, "I have read this release." Thus, the release was held valid.[80]

Promoters, sponsors and subcontractors often use contracts to pass what liability they may have to the other. Such clauses may state that one or the other of the contracting parties is solely responsible for the fulfillment of certain obligations, for example, properly maintaining a marathon race course. But neither of the contracting parties can avoid a duty to a third party merely by agreeing among themselves who has "responsibility" for what. Instead, most commercial contracts have indemnity clauses stating that one party will pay all damages and expenses incurred by the other as a result of the first party's performance or non-performance of its obligations.

Site contracts – contracts with arenas, auditoriums, theaters and the like – typically require the organizers of an event to be solely responsible for everything that happens while they are in possession of the site. Thus, site contracts should be read carefully to determine whether insurance is required and whether the site has made any warranties regarding its physical condition. In the absence of any such representation or warranties, the promoter may need to inspect the physical site prior to the event. (Any liability the sponsor may have in that regard typically is passed on through contract.) The organizer is then contractually obligated, much like any lessee, to return the property as it was given, reasonable wear and tear excepted. If a riot breaks out and there is extensive damage, the lessee will be liable to the site for the damage.

SAMPLE PARTICIPANT'S AGREEMENT

Participant _____

Address _____

Social Security Number _____

Appearance Fee $_____

Agreed:

Participant's Signature: _____ Date: _____

Organizer's Signature: _____ Date: _____

Standard Terms and Conditions

1. Participant hereby agrees to participate as a (*runner, etc.*) in (*describe Event*) (the "Event") on (*date*) at (*site*) and hereby grants to (*Organizer*) ("Organizer") the right to record, broadcast and otherwise exploit his/her performance in such Event in any and all media throughout the world without territorial, time or other limitation. Participant will abide by all Event rules and Organizer's reasonable instructions with respect to Participant's performance.

This is a basic agreement with participants who are paid to participate. This paragraph gives Organizer all rights to exploit the Event in all media. In addition, the participant should sign a basic release and waiver of liability.

2. Participant hereby grants to Organizer the right to use Participant's name, likeness, voice and biographical information in advertising and exploiting the Event in any and all media without territorial, time or other limitation except that Organizer shall not use Participant's name or likeness as an endorsement of any product or service.

The Organizer should want merchandising rights from the Participant, but some participants will resist this paragraph and want to retain merchandising rights for themselves. The limitation here on endorsements is standard.

3. As full compensation for Participant's performance and for all rights granted Organizer therein, Organizer will pay Participant the Appearance Fee specified above, payable one-half on execution of this Agreement and one-half on the first

business day following the Event. [Organizer represents and warrants that it has not and will not pay or agree to pay any other participant in the Event an appearance or other fee greater than Participant's Appearance Fee.]

Appearance money is usually paid in installments agreed upon between the parties. Sometimes a participant may wish to defer the bulk of the payment to the next tax year. In an event with several key participants, such as a marathon, a participant may wish assurance that he or she is getting as much as his or her competitors.

4. Participant will cooperate with Organizer in publicizing the Event. Participant will attend the press conference on (*date*) at (*site*) and such other press conferences/publicity interviews/public appearances as Organizer reasonably requests [provided Participant shall not be required to give more than (*number*) such interviews or appearances].

The content of this paragraph is negotiable, and the reasonableness of the Organizer's requests is proportional to the amount of the Appearance Fee. The Participant should try to protect himself or herself by limiting the number of required appearances.

5. Organizer shall reimburse Participant for round trip [coach] transportation expenses from the commercial airport closest to Participant's address to the site of the Event and living expenses not to exceed $ _____ per day for (*number*) days prior to and (*number*) days after the Event, as well as during the duration of the Event itself, upon presentation of receipts therefor.

The Participant will usually want first-class airfare and accommodations to be provided and, unlike here, a fixed per diem so that he or she will not have to account to the Organizer.

6. If Participant does not participate due to physical or mental illness, incapacity or other default, Organizer may terminate this Agreement immediately upon notice to Participant and Participant shall immediately repay to Organizer all advances paid by Organizer for appearance fees and living and travel expenses. If the Event does not take place due to any labor dispute, fire, [rain], war, governmental action or other event beyond Organizer's reasonable control, then Organizer shall have the option either (i) to reschedule the Event to another date in which case Participant

will participate in the Event on such rescheduled date subject to Participant's prior professional commitments, of which it shall immediately inform Organizer, or (ii) to terminate this Agreement, in which case no further monies will be due Participant.

For a discussion of the consequences when an event is rained out or otherwise cannot take place due to some unforeseen occurrence, see discussion of insurance in Chapter 5. This paragraph presumes the Event feasibly can be rescheduled; if it cannot, the Participant keeps the advance but does not get the balance, the idea being here that the Participant is entitled to some compensation for being ready to perform and foregoing other opportunities. The Organizer can insure against these risks.

7. Organizer may secure life, health, accident, appearance or other insurance covering Participant and Participant shall have no right, title or interest in or to such insurance. Participant shall submit to usual and customary medical examinations and sign such applications and other documents relating to such insurance as Organizer shall reasonably request. Participant will not ride in any aircraft other than one flown by a United States or major international commercial carrier maintaining regularly published schedules or engage in any extra-hazardous activity without Organizer's prior written consent.

This paragraph is more important where there are only a few key participants. The prohibition on private air travel and other extra-hazardous activities should track with the insurance policy's exclusions. The Participant should attempt to have the latter clarified.

8. Organizer may assign this Agreement to any parent, subsidiary or affiliated corporation of Organizer or to any corporation with or into which Organizer may merge or consolidate or to any person, firm or corporation succeeding to all or a substantial portion of Organizer's assets.

This is boilerplate, but if the identity of the Organizer is important to the Participant, he or she should retain approval rights over assignment of this personal services contract.

9. Participant will not, without Organizer's prior written approval, issue or authorize the publication of any news stories or publicity relating primarily to the Event, Participant's participation in this Event or to this Agreement.

The Organizer may want to control the timing and content of publicity.

10. If Participant should, prior to or during the Event fail, refuse or neglect to govern his/her conduct with due regard to social conventions and public morals and decency or commit any act which brings Participant or Organizer into public disrepute, scandal, contempt or ridicule or which shocks, insults or offends a substantial portion or group of the community or reflects unfavorably on Organizer, then Organizer may terminate this Agreement upon written notice to Participant and Participant will thereupon return any advances paid by Organizer.

Participants will want to negotiate this paragraph to more objective limitations such as conviction of a felony (see discussion of morals clauses in Chapter 1). Depending on the kind of event, some specific language may be added here with respect to use of drugs (prescription as well as illegal). Sponsors might insist that the benefits of this paragraph extend to them.

11. Participant hereby grants to Organizer (*number*) consecutive options to require Participant's services in the next (*number*) events similar to the Event organized by Organizer. Participant agrees that between (*number*) days prior to and (*number*) days after the Event, he/she will not render his/her services to any person organizing an event substantially similar to the Event [within a (*number*) mile radius of the Event].

Getting commitments from key participants to participate in future events is a useful tool in avoiding competition (see Chapter 3). The limitation on the Participant's participation in similar events (in a given geographic area or during a particular time frame) also reduces the likelihood of a competitor's success. (See discussion on the enforceability of options at page 16.)

12. Participant agrees that his/her services are special, unique, unusual and extraordinary, giving them a peculiar value, the loss of which cannot be reasonably or adequately compensated in damages in an action at law and that in the event of any breach by Participant, Organizer shall be entitled to equitable relief by way of injunction or otherwise.

Injunctive relief is very difficult to obtain with respect to personal services, but this paragraph attempts to limit the Participant's defenses to Organizer's requests for equitable relief (see discussion of the enforceability of personal services contracts in Chapter 1.)

13. This Agreement is complete and contains the entire agreement of the parties. There are no representations or warranties other than those specifically set forth herein. This Agreement shall be governed by the laws of the State of (*name*). It may not be amended except in a writing signed by both parties.

Boilerplate.

SAMPLE PARTICIPANT'S RELEASE AND WAIVER OF LIABILITY

A form release should be reviewed by an attorney because each state may impose its own limits on its effectiveness or require specific wording.

I _____ [print name], ("Participant"), in consideration of my participation in a (*describe event*) known as (*name of Event*) (the "Event") hereby grant to (*name of Organizer*) ("Organizer") the right to record, broadcast and otherwise exploit in any and all media throughout the world my performance in the Event and to use my name, likeness, voice and biographical information concerning me in connection therewith.

I assume all risks associated with my participation in the Event and hereby release and hold harmless Organizer, the sponsors of and suppliers to the Event, and their respective directors, officers, employees, agents, successors and assigns, from and against any and all claims, damages, liabilities, costs and expenses, including reasonable attorneys' fees, arising out of my participation in the Event, including without limitation any personal injuries [or damage to my property] which I may incur as a result of [*describe known risks, e.g., conditions, other drivers, etc.*]. I warrant that I am of legal age and that I have read and fully understand the foregoing terms. (If not, parent or guardian must sign.)

Name: _____

Address: _____

Date: _____

Parent or Guardian's Guarantee

I represent and warrant that I am the parent or legal guardian of the Participant named above, that I am of legal age and that I have read and fully understand the foregoing Participant's release and agree for Participant and Participant's heirs, successors and assigns and for Participant's legal representatives to be bound by the terms thereof.

Parent or Legal Guardian: _____

Address: _____

Date: _____

LIABILITY FOR ACTS OF INTOXICATED PATRONS

Dramshop Acts and Common-Law Liability

One who serves alcohol at an event may be liable for damages caused to others by an intoxicated patron or guest. Thus, promoters need to consider carefully the implication of serving alcohol – free or through paid vendors – at events they organize. The extent of this liability varies widely among the states. Some states have "dramshop" acts; others have common-law liability; some have both. (See state-by-state Table of Liability on page 293 and the Illinois dramshop law in Appendix I.)

Traditionally, common law provided no cause of action against persons selling, giving or otherwise furnishing alcohol for injuries or damages resulting from the acts of intoxicated persons. The common-law rule derived from the theory that "the drinking of the liquor, not the furnishing of it, is the proximate cause of the injury."[81] More recently, however, many states have abolished this strict common-law rule. Fifteen states have passed "dramshop" statutes that give, generally, "a right of action to persons injured in person, property, or means of support, by an intoxicated person, or in consequence of the intoxication of any person, against the person selling or furnishing the liquor which caused the intoxication in whole or in part." Each state's dramshop law must be consulted to determine whether an event organizer – or even a sponsor – falls within its scope. (See, for example, the Illinois dramshop statute, Appendix I.)

In many states, the common-law tradition has been changed not by statute but by new court decisions. Courts in some of these jurisdictions have recently allowed a common-law cause of action on the premise that the serving of liquor to a minor or an inebriated person initiates a foreseeable chain of events for which the tavern owner may be held liable.[82] That is a traditional negligence theory based on the foreseeability of the probable injury. Other courts, assuming negligence *per se*, impose liability for injury upon a defendant who has violated a criminal statute proscribing sales of alcohol to certain classes of persons, such as minors or inebriated persons.[83]

Still other states, including California, continue to follow the strict common-law rule of no liability. Legislative bodies in these states have not passed dramshop acts, and the courts have not construed the common law to impose civil liability.

Finally, some states have both a legislatively enacted dramshop act *and* common-law liability. This means that in some states event organizers or sponsors could be liable for the acts of inebriated patrons regardless of whether they fall within the dramshop statute.

81.
45 Am. Jur. 2d *Intoxicating Liquors* § 553 (1969).

82.
See Campbell v. Carpenter, 279 Or. 237, 566 P.2d 893 (Or. 1977).

83.
See Ontiveros v. Borak, 136 Ariz. 500, 667 P.2d 200 (Ariz. 1983).

Liability of Property Owners

Often the owners of the premises where an event is to take place ask the event organizer to indemnify them against liability for acts of intoxicated participants or spectators. This is because the typical dramshop statute includes among those liable under the act:

> . . . any person owning, renting, leasing or permitting the occupation of any building or premises with knowledge that alcoholic liquors are to be sold therein, or who having leased the same for other purposes, shall knowingly permit therein the sale of any alcoholic liquors that have caused the intoxication of any person. . . .[84]

Some states construe their dramshop acts narrowly and do not hold the owner or lessor of the property liable. Others have held a lessor or owner liable under the act if he or she "knowingly rented or permitted his premises to be used for [selling intoxicating liquors]" even though the lessor did not personally sell the liquor.[85] It is thus probably appropriate for the owner or lessor of an event's premises to require indemnification from the organizer with respect to dramshop liability.

Liability of Sponsors

It is not clear whether a mere sponsor – or, for that matter, a title sponsor – will incur any liability at common law or under dramshop acts if it is not licensed to sell alcohol at the event.

Illinois has come closest to directly addressing this issue with respect to its dramshop act. In *Camille* v. *Berry Fertilizers, Inc.*,[86] a widow brought an action against the corporate sponsors of an event when her husband became inebriated at a party and died when his truck hit a utility pole on his way home. The corporate defendants had sponsored a "chicken fry" at which alcohol was sold. They in effect "hosted" the party by organizing and leasing the land where it took place. The plaintiffs argued that the corporation's "hope or expectation of future gains or profits from serving as hosts upon this occasion be[came] the equivalent of a sale of alcoholic liquor. . . ."[87] The court disagreed, holding that the corporation was not involved "in the business" of selling alcohol despite its expectation "that by selling or giving alcoholic liquors . . . defendants could reasonably expect to benefit their businesses by promoting good will, winning new customers, closing business deals, making new sales or contracts and, in general, enhance customer relations and the businesses' public image all to the result and effect of a pecuniary gain or profit."[88]

84.
Ill. Rev. Stat. ch. 43, para. 135 (1987).

85.
Annotation, *Liability of a Lessor or his Property for Damages Resulting from Lessee's Sale of Intoxicating Liquor*, 169 A.L.R. 1203 (1947).

86.
334 N.E.2d 205 (Ill. 1975).

87.
Id. at 206.

88.
Id.

The *Camille* case does not make clear whether the corporation itself sold the liquor or contracted with another to sell it. However, the court's ruling indicated that in a situation in which a corporation sponsors an event where alcohol is served, Illinois would not find a close enough tie between the actual sale of the alcohol and the sponsorship to find the corporation "in the business" of selling alcohol. Thus, in Illinois, sponsors are unlikely to be liable under that state's dramshop act.

Dramshop acts are "designed to suppress the evils of the liquor traffic and to alleviate as much as possible the injury to innocent persons by compensating them for the damages they may have suffered as a result of such traffic."[89] Conceivably, a court may someday decide to impose liability upon a corporate sponsor for any of several "public policy" reasons. First, in light of the state's concern for the injured party, the court might look to the "deepest pocket" to ensure compensation for the alcohol-related injury. Often, that would point to the corporate sponsor. Second, because the state may legally seek to control liquor consumption, a court may impose liability upon a corporate sponsor of a special event in order to discourage promotion of events where alcohol is served. To protect against such contingencies, both sponsors and organizers should be sure that their events are adequately insured. In addition, the establishment of a separate corporation to hold liquor licenses and to be responsible for "furnishing" alcoholic beverages may help to insulate the assets of both the organizer and the sponsor from dramshop liability, provided corporate formalities are observed.

89.
169 A.L.R., *supra*, note 85, at 1204.

TABLE OF LIABILITY FOR
FURNISHING ALCOHOLIC BEVERAGES

State	Dramshop Act	Common-Law Liability
ALABAMA	Ala. Code § 6-5-71 (1975)	No common-law vendor liability. *DeLoach* v. *Mayer Elec. Supply Co.*, 378 So. 2d 733 (Ala. 1979).
ALASKA	None	*Nazareno* v. *Urie*, 638 P.2d 671 (Alaska 1981); *Kavorkian* v. *Tommy's Elbow Room, Inc.*, 711 P.2d 521 (Alaska 1985).
ARIZONA	None	*Ontiveros* v. *Borak*, 136 Ariz. 500, 667 P.2d 200 (1983); *Brannigan* v. *Raybuck*, 136 Ariz. 513, 667 P.2d 213 (1983) [overruling earlier Arizona cases adhering to nonliability rule].
ARKANSAS	None	No common-law liability. *Carr* v. *Turner*, 238 Ark. 889, 385 S.W.2d 656 (1965).
CALIFORNIA	None	Prevailing common-law vendor liability for injury or damage resulting from intoxication abrogated in 1978 by Cal. Bus. & Prof. Code § 25602 (West 1985 Supp.) and Cal. Civ. Code § 1714 (West 1985).
COLORADO	None	*Kerby* v. *Flamingo Club*, 35 Colo. App. 127, 532 P.2d 975 (1974).
CONNECTICUT	Conn. Gen. Stat. § 30-102 (1985)	No common-law vendor liability. *Nelson* v. *Steffens*, 170 Conn. 356, 365 A.2d 1174 (1976); *Slicer* v. *Quigley*, 180 Conn. 252, 429 A.2d 855 (1980).
DELAWARE	None	No common-law liability. *Wright* v. *Moffitt*, 437 A.2d 554 (Del. 1981).
DISTRICT OF COLUMBIA	None	*Marusa* v. *District of Columbia*, 484 F.2d 828 (D.C. Cir. 1973).

State	Dramshop Act	Common-Law Liability
FLORIDA	None	Prevailing common-law vendor liability for injury or damage resulting from intoxication. *Davis* v. *Shiappacossee*, 155 So.2d 365 (Fla. 1963); *Prevatt* v. *McClennan*, 201 So. 2d 780 (Fla. Dist. Ct. App. 1967) limited in 1981 by Fla. Stat. § 768.125 (1983).
GEORGIA	Ga. Code § 3-3-22 (1982)	No common-law liability. *Keaton* v. *Kroger Co.*, 143 Ga. App. 23, 237 S.E.2d 443 (1977).
HAWAII	None	*Ono* v. *Applegate*, 62 Haw. 131, 612 P.2d 533 (1980).
IDAHO	None	*Alegria* v. *Payonk*, 101 Idaho 617, 619 P.2d 135 (1980) [overruling earlier Idaho case adhering to non-liability rule].
ILLINOIS	Ill. Ann. Stat. ch. 43, para. 135 (Smith-Hurd 1984 Supp.).	No common-law vendor liability. *Demchuk* v. *Duplancich*, 92 Ill. 2d 1, 440 N.E.2d 112 (1982); *Thompson* v. *Trickle*, 114 Ill. App. 3d 930, 449 N.E.2d 910 (1983).
INDIANA	None	*Elder* v. *Fisher*, 247 Ind. 598, 217 N.E.2d 847 (1966).
IOWA	Iowa Code Ann. § 123.92 (West 1984 Supp.)	*Haafke* v. *Mitchell*, 347 N.W.2d 381 (Iowa 1984) [vendor liability].
KANSAS	None	None
KENTUCKY	None	*Pike* v. *George*, 434 S.W.2d 626 (Ky. 1968).
LOUISIANA	None	*Thrahser* v. *Leggett*, 373 So. 2d 494 (La. 1979).

State	Dramshop Act	Common-Law Liability
MAINE	Me. Rev. Stat. Ann. tit. 28-A, § 2502 (1985)	Common-law liability possible. *Klingerman* v. *Sol Corporation of Maine*, 505 A.2d 474 (1986).
MARYLAND	None	No common-law liability. *Felder* v. *Butler*, 292 Md. 174, 438 A.2d 494 (1981); *Fisher* v. *O'Connor's Inc.*, 53 Md. App. 338, 452 A.2d 1313 (1982).
MASSACHUSETTS	None	*Adamian* v. *Three Sons, Inc.*, 353 Mass. 498, 233 N.E.2d 18 (1968); *Michnik-Zilberman* v. *Gordon's Liquor, Inc.*, 390 Mass. 6, 453 N.E.2d 430 (1983).
MICHIGAN	Mich. Stat. Ann. § 18.993 (Callaghan 1984 Supp.)	*Thaut* v. *Finley*, 50 Mich. App. 611, 213 N.W.2d 820 (1973) [vendor liability].
MINNESOTA	Minn. Stat. § 340.95 [1984]	*Trail* v. *Christian*, 298 Minn. 101, 213 N.W.2d 618 (1973). Recently, Minnesota Supreme Court refused to extend liability to a social host. *Holmquist* v. *Miller*, 367 N.W.2d 468 (1985).
MISSISSIPPI	None	*Munford, Inc.* v. *Peterson*, 368 So. 2d 213 (Miss. 1979).
MISSOURI	None	*Sampson* v. *W.F. Enterprise, Inc.*, 611 S.W.2d 333 (Mo. App. 1980); and *Carver* v. *Schaer*, 647 S.W.2d 570 (Mo. Ct. App. 1983).
MONTANA	None	*Nehring* v. *LaCounte*, 712 P.2d 1329 (Mont. 1986); *Swartzenberger* v. *Billings Labor Temple Assn.*, 179 Mont. 145, 586 P.2d 712 (1978).

State	Dramshop Act	Common-Law Liability
NEBRASKA	None	No common-law liability. *Holmes* v. *Circo*, 196 Neb. 496. 244 N.W.2d 65 (1976).
NEVADA	None	No common-law liability. *Hamm* v. *Carson City Nugget, Inc.*, 85 Nev. 99, 450 P.2d 358 (1969).
NEW HAMPSHIRE	None	*Ramsey* v. *Anctij*, 106 N.H. 375, 211 A.2d 900 (1965).
NEW JERSEY	None	Common-law liability established in *Rappaport* v. *Nichols*, 31 N.J. 188, 156 A.2d 1 (1959); recently extended to social hosts, *Kelly* v. *Gwinnell*, 96 N.J. 538, 476 A.2d 1219 (1984).
NEW MEXICO	None	*Lopez* v. *Maez*, 98 N.M. 625, 651 P.2d 1269 (1982); *MRQ Properties, Inc.* v. *Gries*, 98 N.M. 710, 652 P.2d 732 (1982); *Porter* v. *Ortiz*, 100 N.M. 58, 665 P.2d 1149 (Ct. App. 1983) [overruling earlier New Mexico cases adhering to nonliability rule].
NEW YORK	N.Y. Gen. Oblig. Law § 11-101 (McKinney 1984 Supp)	*Berkeley* v. *Park*, 47 Misc. 2d 381, 262 N.Y.S.2d 290 (1965).
NORTH CAROLINA	N.C. Gen. Stat. § 18B-121 *et seq.* (1983)	*Hitchens* v. *Hankins*, 63 N.C. App. 1, 303 S.E.2d 584, *reh'g. denied*, 309 N.C. 191, 305 S.E.2d 734 (1983).
NORTH DAKOTA	N.D. Cent. Code § 5-01-06 (1983 Supp.)	No common-law liability. *Thoring* v. *Bottonsek*, 350 N.W.2d 586 (N.D. 1984).

State	Dramshop Act	Common-Law Liability
OHIO	Ohio Rev. Code Ann. § 4399.01 (Page 1982).	*Mason* v. *Roberts*, 33 Ohio St. 2d 29, 294 N.E.2d 884 (1973) [vendor liability].
OKLAHOMA	None	Has not ruled on subject.
OREGON	None	Prevailing common-law vendor liability. *Campbell* v. *Carpenter*, 279 Or. 237, 566 P.2d 893 (1977), limited in 1979 by Or. Rev. Stat. § 30.950 *et seq.* (1983).
PENNSYLVANIA	None	*Jardine* v. *Upper Darby Lodge No. 1973*, 413 Pa. 626, 198 A.2d 550 (1964).
RHODE ISLAND	R.I. Gen. Laws § 3-11-1 (1976)	Status of common-law liability unclear.
SOUTH CAROLINA	None	Has not ruled on subject.
SOUTH DAKOTA	None	*Walz* v. *City of Hudson*, 327 N.W.2d 120 (S.D. 1982) [overruling earlier South Dakota case adhering to non-liability rule].
TENNESSEE	None	*Mitchell* v. *Ketner*, 54 Tenn. App. 656, 393 S.W.2d 755 (1964).
TEXAS	None	Has not ruled on subject.
UTAH	Utah Code Ann. § 32-11-1 (1983 Supp.)	Status of common-law liability unclear.
VERMONT	Vt. Stat. Ann. tit. 7, § 501, (1988)	Among others, *Langle* v. *Kurkul*, 146 Vt. 513, 510 A.2d 1301 (1986) [vendor liability].

State	Dramshop Act	Common-Law Liability
VIRGINIA	None	Has not ruled on subject.
WASHINGTON	None	Among others, *Callan* v. *O'Neil*, 20 Wash. App. 32, 578 P.2d 890 (1978); *Halligan* v. *Pupo*, 37 Wash. App. 84, 678 P.2d 1295 (1984).
WEST VIRGINIA	None	Has not ruled on subject.
WISCONSIN	None	*Sorensen* v. *Jarvis*, 119 Wis. 2d 627, 350 N.W.2d 108 (1984) [overruling earlier Wisconsin cases adhering to nonliability rule]; *Koback* v. *Crook*, 123 Wis. 2d 259, 366 N.W.2d 857 (1985) [Wisconsin Supreme Court imposes liability on social host who served liquor to a minor].
WYOMING	None	*McClellan* v. *Tottenhoff*, 666 P.2d 408 (Wyo. 1983) [overruling earlier Wyoming cases adhering to nonliability rule].

LIABILITY OF TRADEMARK LICENSORS

Sponsors may find themselves liable for injuries arising out of the sale of event souvenirs that bear the sponsor's trademark. However, responsibility for faulty merchandise purchased from the organizer or the organizer's licensees can be passed back to the organizer or licensee by contract. (See Paragraph 8 of the Sample Title or Lead Sponsorship Agreement in Chapter 1.)

As discussed in Chapter 2, trademark owners must control the quality of goods bearing their mark or else face potential loss of the trademark itself. It follows that trademark owners are responsible for their licensed products when they reach the ultimate consumer. Thus, the owners of trademarks may be held strictly liable for a defective product even when that product is manufactured by another entity.

An illustrative case is *Carter* v. *Joseph Bancroft & Sons Co.*[90] There, the plaintiff purchased a dress with a label reading "BAN-LON Fashion." The label stated that "BAN-LON" is a trademark identifying garment, fabrics, and articles made according to specifications and quality standards prescribed and controlled by Joseph Bancroft & Sons Co., a division of Indian Head, Inc." The reverse side of the tag said, "A Beautiful BAN-LON Fashion Anika New York." Anika was the manufacturer of the dress, while the defendants prescribed specifications for the fabric. The plaintiff wore the dress to a dinner party attended by seven other guests. As crepes suzette were being prepared by the host, a fire engulfed all of the guests. The plaintiff's clothes ignited, causing her to be severely burned. One man's coat sustained a small scorch mark; the clothing of the other six persons present did not burn. According to the court, Mrs. Carter's BAN-LON dress by Anika "flamed, burned, and vanished."

90.
360 F. Supp. 1103 (E.D. Pa. 1973).

Although the defendants maintained that they were merely licensors of the trademark BAN-LON and were not the manufacturers of the dress, the court still found that they could be held liable for the defective product. The court cited the *Restatement (Second) of Torts* § 400, which provides in part: "One puts out a chattel as his own product when he puts it out under his name or affixes to it his trade name or trademark." In essence, trademark owners are deemed to have induced use of a product by lending their credibility – their trademark – to it.

The Pennsylvania Supreme Court also justified the extension of liability beyond the manufacturer to the trademark licensor in *Forry* v. *Gulf Oil Corporation.*[91] The court held Gulf Oil liable as a manufacturer for injuries to the plaintiff that resulted when a tire exploded as it was being inflated. Gulf's name was imprinted on the tire, but B.F. Goodrich was the manufacturer. The court relied on the *Restatement (Second) of Torts* § 400 commented, which states in part that a trademark owner "frequently causes the chattel to be used in reliance upon a belief that he has

91.
428 Pa. 334, 237 A.2d 593 (1968).

required it to be made properly for him and that the actor's reputation is an assurance to the user of the quality of the product." In other words, the trade name gives the impression that the licensor is responsible for and stands behind the product, thus inducing the consumer's reliance on the licensor.

Because of the possible imposition of strict liability on trademark licensors for the acts of their licensees, matters of insurance and indemnity covering such actions should be addressed in sponsorship contracts, including contracts between sponsors and organizers and between organizers or sponsors and third-party suppliers.

INSURANCE

Because event promoters and sponsors face potential liability on a number of fronts, they should review their insurance needs with their insurance brokers. It is important to identify the risks involved in promoting or sponsoring an event, estimate the potential exposure and assess the extent of protection needed for one's assets. In addition, government and contractual requirements must be considered.

Generally, corporate sponsors are large companies with extensive insurance coverage. Well established promoters or events may have adequate insurance in place. New promoters may have no assets to protect; some may choose to go "bare," that is, to take the risk of a liability claim without the benefit of insurance since there are no assets that they fear losing. (The terms of government permits, however, might require some kinds of insurance, as may some site leases).

Sponsors may insist that promoters contractually indemnify and hold them harmless from liability. If a promoter has no assets, then such a contractual right to an indemnity is worthless unless backed by insurance. Even in the absence of an indemnity clause, the sponsor may nonetheless insist that the promoter carry insurance as a matter of responsible business practice.

Liability insurance covers the amounts an insured party may become legally obligated to pay as damages. In terms of insurance liability, there are three ways in which an insured can become legally obligated to pay damages to a third party: (1) through the insured's negligence, (2) by statute (such as workers' compensation or dramshop laws) and (3) by assuming the liability of others.

Acts of negligence are generally insured against under a *comprehensive general [or commercial] liability* ("CGL") policy. A standard CGL policy provides that the insurance company will defend any suit and pay any damages that the insured is liable to pay because of bodily injury or property damage caused by an "occurrence." "Occurrence" usually is defined in the CGL policy to mean "an accident, including continuous or repeated exposure to conditions, which results in bodily injury or property damage neither expected nor intended from the standpoint of the insured." Whether a CGL policy covers injuries to spectators at an auto race will depend largely on its exclusions and endorsements, which must be read carefully for what they subtract from or add to the policy's coverages. Some companies write insurance specifically for special events and spectator liability, but they may exclude coverage for participants, actions of security officers and mistakes of pyrotechnicians on fireworks displays, all of which would require separate coverage.

It should be noted that the standard CGL policy does not usually cover *professional liability*. As an organizer of an event rendering professional services, an organizer might become liable for the failure to use due care and the degree of skill expected of a person in that particular profession. Insurance for this exposure is called *professional liability insurance* or *malpractice insurance* (generally pertaining to doctors and lawyers) or *errors and omissions* ("E&O") insurance (generally pertaining to other professionals). E&O insurance is not limited to injury caused by an "occurrence." In fact, in many cases, the professional exercises as much care and skill as can be reasonably expected; however, his or her judgment might be faulty and injury might result. For instance, a promoter who fails to provide emergency medical services at a marathon might have need to call on its E&O insurance for injuries arising out of that error in judgment.

The CGL policy typically does not cover purely personal, as opposed to bodily, injury. A personal injury could be invasion of privacy, slander or the like. Professional liability covers both kinds of injuries, but those in the business of producing or disseminating words and images – advertisers, broadcasters, program producers, advertising agencies – should insure these risks separately. A few companies write policies specifically for those groups, covering libel, slander, copyright, plagiarism and privacy. Those not in the advertising/broadcasting/ publication/telecasting business may elect *personal and advertising injury liability* coverage as part of their CGL coverage.

Liability imposed by statute may also be insured against. A *Workers' Compensation and Employers' Liability* policy covers both liability imposed on the insured under state law and liability imposed by law but not compensable under workers' compensation.

A standard CGL policy excludes liability for organizations involved in the alcoholic beverages industry if they incur that liability by violating any statute or regulation pertaining to alcohol. In addition, liability arising out of serving minors or intoxicated persons is also excluded. This exclusion is quite broad. Therefore, *liquor liability* insurance is needed to cover both liability imposed by dramshop acts and common-law liability.

The third type of liability commonly insured against is assumed liability, often called *contractual liability*. "Hold harmless" clauses or "contracts of indemnity" are subject to contractual liability insurance coverage. It should be emphasized that contractual liability coverage has nothing to do with liability for breach of contract.

In some cases, the parties to a contract will not agree to hold each other harmless, but one party will instead require the other to maintain certain kinds of insurance with certain limits. If that party fails to obtain such insurance, then there is a cause of action for breach of contract, but not a viable claim under the contractual liability policy. To enforce such provisions, the parties should require that evidence of the coverage be provided to them. An even better approach is to require that the insurance be in the indemnitee's name or that the indemnitee be named on the other's insurance as an additional insured.

Standard CGL insurance includes property damage insurance but may have exclusions that should be carefully reviewed. For instance, an organizer who takes possession of a sponsor's signs or automobiles or equipment, such as an expensive timing device, might want coverage for property in his care, custody and control, which might otherwise be excluded.

Event promoters might consider other specialty insurance coverages appropriate to their particular events. For instance, rain insurance might be appropriate for a golf or other outdoor tournament. Broadcast interruption insurance might be necessary for pay-per-view events or other broadcasts where revenue will not be generated if the television signal is not delivered. It may also be possible to obtain some form of *business interruption* insurance to protect loss of business income in case there is physical damage to the site of a planned event that cannot easily be moved.

Three other aspects of insurance policies deserve mention. First, one should be certain that the policy requires the insurer to defend, not merely to indemnify. This means that the insurer will provide the defense costs as incurred rather than the insured having to pay out-of-pocket costs and then seek reimbursement from the insurer. Moreover, the insurer typically is bound to defend as long as there is a possibility that at least one of the claimant's allegations is within the policy's coverage. Even if there are allegations clearly outside the coverage, a single allegation within the coverage requires the insurer to defend. The insurer cannot escape this duty by characterizing the allegations as "groundless, false or fraudulent."[92]

Next, the triggering event under an insurance policy must be considered. Insurance policies are written on an "occurrence" basis or a "claims-made" basis. If "occurrence" is the trigger, then the insurance policy applies to losses arising out of occurrences during the term of the policy, even if the claim is made after the policy period. In contrast, if "claims-made" is the trigger, then if the claim is first made during the policy period, there is coverage. (A "claims-made" policy contains a retroactive date. If a claim is made for injury or damage that occurred *before* the retroactive date, coverage will be denied even though the claim was properly made during the policy period.)

Many insureds have typically preferred occurrence-type coverage. However, there are several pitfalls here. One is that, after a business ceases, it may continue to have liability exposure if its products are still on the market. If coverage is wanted for any such later occurrences, a policy must be purchased separately. In addition,

92.
A comprehensive discussion of an insurer's duty to defend can be found in 14 *Couch on Insurance (2nd)* (Rev. ed 1912) § 51:35.

the limits of occurrence coverage may have become inadequate due to inflation in the years prior to the claim being made, or the limits may have been reduced by prior claims. Promoters of one-time or short-lived events may find none of these pitfalls troublesome. It is clearly easier to avoid coverage gaps using occurrence rather than claims-made insurance.

If claims-made coverage is used, an extended reporting period or "tail" may be necessary. The tail covers claims made *after* the policy period arising out of occurrences *during* the period.

Lastly, it should be noted that not all liability damages may be insurable. Punitive damages are damages awarded to a person not to compensate for injury but to punish the wrongdoer. Punitive damages are usually awarded when the complained of conduct was intentional, malicious or grossly negligent or in reckless disregard for the safety of others. Only four states – Louisiana, Massachusetts, Nebraska and Washington – do not recognize punitive damages. In the remaining states, there is considerable confusion over whether punitive damages should be insurable. Some states believe that insurance against intentional wrongdoing is against public policy; others allow recovery against the insurer.

In some instances, local governments or sponsors may require event promoters to post surety bonds to guarantee performance of some kind. For instance, a city might require a promoter to post a bond guaranteeing cleanup after the event. In addition, a rock concert promoter might want a performance bond from particularly tempermental talent.

In general, a *contract bond* guarantees the fulfillment of contract specifications. A *performance bond* guarantees that work will be performed according to specifications and on time. If either is not satisfied, the surety is obligated to the person requiring the work. A *bid bond* guarantees the bid price on a contract. A *payment bond* usually is covered by a performance bond but covers payment of labor and materials.

License and permit bonds usually guarantee that the bonded person will comply with all laws and regulations applicable to their activities.

Court bonds are posted in injunction and other equity proceedings to protect the enjoined party in case it later prevails on the merits. Court bonds may also be used to obtain the release of persons charged in civil or criminal suits, such as bail bonds.

Such bonds often are arranged through the organizer's insurer or insurance broker.

NOT-FOR-PROFIT ORGANIZATIONS

"We're not doing this because we're greedy –
We're doing this to feed the needy."

– The Super Bowl Shuffle

Some events are organized around a non profit organization, the organization acting
as either organizer/producer or as the mere recipient of all or a portion of the
proceeds of the event. LIVE-AID and FARM-AID are examples of cause-oriented,
charitable events. The Los Angeles Marathon has also been organized as a not-for-
profit event. There are, of course, some essential tensions between for-profit and
not-for-profit event producers. There are also some specific restrictions on the
not-for-profit mode of organization and on charitable solicitation that require
attention. Those restrictions are discussed in this chapter.

ORGANIZATION AND EXEMPTION
FROM TAXATION

Most states have laws that provide for the organization of a corporation as a
not-for-profit entity. A sample state not-for-profit incorporation law appears in
Appendix J. The federal government recognizes several categories of tax-exempt,
not-for-profit organizations under Section 501 of the federal Internal Revenue
Code. Section 501(c)(3) describes corporations organized *exclusively* for educational, religious, charitable, scientific, public safety, literary or educational
purposes, including organizations operated for the purpose of fostering national or
international amateur sports competitions or for the prevention of cruelty to animals
or children; Section 501(c)(4) describes civic leagues and social welfare
organizations; 501(c)(5), labor, agricultural and horticultural associations;
501(c)(6), trade and professional organizations; and 501(c)(7), social clubs.

A 501(c)(3) tax-exempt not-for-profit organization escapes corporate income tax,
and donors to such an organization may deduct their charitable donations thereto.
Other 501(c) organizations escape corporate tax, but contributions are not
deductible.

A corporation may qualify under a state's not-for-profit law but still not be tax
exempt, if it has not demonstrated to the IRS that it qualifies under the IRS code.
The primary characteristics of a not-for-profit are that it is *not* organized for private
gain and that it is possessed of a donative intent – that is, an interest in benefitting
the public.

For-profit corporations distribute their profits to their owners – the shareholders.
Not-for-profits, on the other hand, are constrained. They cannot take their earnings
or profits in a way which would pay their employees more than a commercially
reasonable amount, either as salary or as bonus. There are also limits on what
non-profits can pay to outside consultants as fees. For instance, if a not-for-profit
hires a third-party event producer, it cannot pay fees greater than the "going rate."
The relationship between the not-for-profit and the third party is particularly
suspect if there is an identity of ownership between the for-profit and the not-for-
profit. The IRS may well scrutinize such relationships very carefully in an audit.

Event promoters, as individuals, most often seek to profit from the risks they have
taken in producing an event. Under not-for-profit laws, the profits of a corporation
must be devoted to the charitable or educational or scientific purposes of the
corporation. Unlike a normal corporation, a not-for-profit does not have shareholders who participate in the profits through dividends earned on shares. Nor can
a not-for-profit pay unreasonably high salaries or bonuses to its employees or
founders. Moreover, on dissolution, the profits of a non profit must be transferred

to other qualified non profit organizations. Thus, it is difficult for an individual to personally profit significantly from employment by or organization of a non profit corporation.

UNRELATED BUSINESS INCOME

Not all of a not-for-profit's income is tax exempt. Unrelated trade or business income is taxable at corporate rates; too much unrelated trade or business income can cause an organization to lose its tax-exempt status.

An "unrelated trade or business" is one that does *not* "contribute importantly" to accomplishing a Section 501(c)(3)'s exempt purposes. It is (i) a trade or business, (ii) regularly carried on and (iii) substantially unrelated to the organization's exempt purposes. The third factor usually is the most important. (Even though an event like the Rose Bowl is annual, the IRS has not considered that to be "regular.")

Exceptions to the unrelated business income rule are royalties and rent from real property. In addition, income from volunteer work, from sales for the convenience of members and from the sale of donated merchandise has also not taxable.

Four sorts of income are of particular interest to event producers: programs, advertising, concessions and souvenirs.

The sale of advertising space in a souvenir event program is not unrelated business income. On the other hand, an annual directory of suppliers or services is deemed to be more like the Yellow Pages, and thus income from its sale is taxable. Program income should also be distinguished from income from the sale of a journal or other periodical. In the latter case, the subscription income is exempt but the advertising revenue is not.

Advertising revenue generated by an event by way of corporate sponsorships presumably is related to the exempt purpose of the not-for-profit, which usually is to raise money for some cause. Similarly, money raised from the sale of food and beverage concessions is also exempt, since it is for the convenience of attendees. (It may also be exempt because a sponsor donated the food or beverage.) Souvenir sales (unless the merchandise is donated) may run a risk of being deemed unrelated.

The scope of the unrelated business tax is a subject recently of much debate, as the for-profit sector seeks to reduce competition from the not-for-profit sector. Non-profit organizations should seek special tax counsel in this tricky and changing area of law.

RELATIONSHIP TO FOR-PROFITS

Some events are organized to benefit not-for-profits but are run by for-profit producers. There are many ways to structure such arrangements: the for-profit producer may guarantee the not-for-profit a minimum contribution or a portion of the ticket price; the for-profit producer can be hired by the not-for-profit for a set fee or for a percentage of the sponsorships raised, or the for-profit and not-for-profit may be partners. Since often the for-profit producer has also been instrumental in the organization of the not-for-profit, it is important that the relationship be structured in a manner that does not jeopardize the not-for-profit's tax-exempt status. In other words, the relationship must be of the sort that unrelated parties, bargaining at arm's length, would create. For instance, a not-for-profit could not in most circumstances agree that a for-profit producer would be entitled to substantially all of the non-profit's revenues from an event.

1.
74 T.C. 1324 (1980),
aff'd per curiam, 675
F.2d 244 (9th Cir. 1982).

Partnerships with a for-profit do not necessarily jeopardize a not-for-profit's tax exemption. In *Plumstead Theatre Society, Inc. v. C.I.R.*,[1] the court concluded that a non profit theater was operated exclusively for charitable purposes and thus was tax exempt. The fact that the theater had entered into a limited partnership agreement with investors (and another non-profit entity) did not undermine its charitable purpose (promotion of public appreciation of American theater). No personal profit or self-dealing was involved in the structure of the Plumstead relationship. The partnership was fairly organized in terms of risk and return. Thus, its tax-exempt status was affirmed.

CHARITABLE SOLICITATION LAWS

At least 34 states (see Appendix K) have a statute governing charitable solicitations. These generally require anyone who solicits or collects funds from the public for a charitable cause to register with the Secretary of State. The purpose of the charitable solicitation statutes is to prevent fraud in raising funds for charity. The statutes seek to ensure that a significant portion of the money raised in a charitable solicitation actually goes toward charitable purposes. They also seek to inform persons from whom money is solicited of the portion that will go toward charitable purposes.[2] (See Sample Charitable Solicitation Laws in Appendix L.)

For the purposes of the charitable solicitation statutes, the term "charitable" is interpreted quite broadly. This means that organizations that are not traditionally considered charities may fall within the purview of the charitable solicitation laws. In California, for instance, any "governmental employee organization" that solicits funds is considered a charity. A police officers' union or a highway patrol union, in which the union members themselves stand to benefit from solicitations, is defined as a charity. As such, they are required to register.[3] Illinois law provides another example of how broadly the term "charitable" can be defined. The Illinois charitable solicitation law was held to apply to an organization that claimed to be "strictly political" in *People ex rel Hartigan* v. *National Anti-Drug Coalition*.[4] There, the court said that the definition of charity includes:

> *anything that tends to promote the improvement, well doing and well being of social man. Moreover, charitable organizations may include organizations whose primary purpose is not to provide money or services for the poor, the needy or other worthy objects of charity, but to gather and disseminate information about and to advocate positions on matters of public concern. These organizations characteristically use paid solicitors who "necessarily combine" the solicitation of financial support with the functions of information dissemination. They may also pay other employees to obtain and process the necessary information and to announce in suitable form the organization's preferred positions on the issue of interest to them.[5]*

Such organizations are often referred to in the statutes as "professional fund raisers."

A "professional fund raiser" is usually defined as one who, for compensation or other consideration, plans, conducts or manages any drive or campaign for the purpose of soliciting contributions for or on behalf of a charitable organization. If, for example, an event organizer advertised that it will donate to a charity a portion

2.
See, e.g., Cal. Bus. & Prof. Code 17510(a)(b) (West 1987).

3.
See 66 Op. Att'y Gen. Cal. 40 (1983); see also 1980 Op. Att'y Gen. N.Y. 74 (1980).

4.
124 Ill. App. 3d 269, 464 N.E.2d 690, 694 (1984).

5.
Id. at 274.

of the ticket price or the entry fee, the organizer may be considered a professional fund raiser because the required ticket purchase or entry would be deemed "other consideration." This is so even though the organizer is not directly compensated for raising those funds. Another common example of a professional fund raiser is a person who distributes the charity's solicitations and collects the donations on behalf of the charity. In other words, any organization "that provides all the services necessary to conduct a fund raising drive is a professional fund raiser."[6]

6.
983 Op. Att'y Gen. N.Y. 24 (1983).

Before engaging in a promotion with a charity, an organizer should ascertain whether the charity involved is registered with the state within which the event will be held. An organizer should also determine whether it will itself have to be registered.

Beyond the registration requirement, professional fund raisers often must post bond before they may make any charitable solicitations. In some states, they must file annual reports and keep detailed financial records. Also, a professional fund raiser is often required by statute to enter into written contracts with the organization for whom it will raise funds. In New York and Illinois, for instance, the contract must be filed with the Secretary of State before any charitable solicitations may be made by the professional fund raiser.[7] Likewise, a charity is prohibited in those states from hiring a professional fund raiser who has not filed the written contract.

7.
N.Y. Exec. Law § 173(a) (McKinney 1988); Ill. Rev. Stat. ch. 23, para. 5107 (1987).

Potential questions as to whether the registration, bond and record-keeping requirements apply to certain organizers have been anticipated by New York's charitable solicitation statute. There, the legislature has defined in more detail the role of those who help raise funds for charity. In addition to defining a "professional fund raiser," the statute defines a "professional solicitor" as any person who is paid by a professional fund raiser to solicit funds from the public.[8] A "fund raising counsel" is defined as a person who is paid to give advice to a charity with regard to its solicitation of contributions, but who "does not have access to contributions . . . or authority to pay expenses . . . and who does not solicit."[9] This definition does not include an attorney, volunteer or employee of the charity. A "commercial co-venturer" is defined as a person who is "regularly and primarily" engaged in commercial trade, but who "advertises that the purchase or use of goods, services, entertainment . . . will benefit a charitable organization."[10] In New York, professional fund raisers, commercial co-venturers and fund raising counsel are required to register with the Secretary of State, to post bond and to file a written contract before they may act on behalf of a charity. Professional solicitors are required only to register.

8.
N.Y. Exec. Law § 171(a)(5) (McKinney 1988).

9.
N.Y. Exec. Law § 171(a)(9).

10.
N.Y. Exec. Law § 171(1)(6).

If a national event organizer fell within the purview of this statute, or other states' more general statutes, it would be burdened with detailed registration, record-keeping and in some states, disclosure requirements. In New York, it seems clear that an event organizer would need to register as a commercial co-venturer; in other states, it may be sufficient that the charity is registered.

Strict attention usually should be paid to these regulations. It added to the embarrassment of the Chicago Bears that the producers of "The Super Bowl Shuffle" failed to comply with the Illinois Charitable Solicitation Act. The producers advertised that the proceeds from the sale of the "The Super Bowl Shuffle" record and video would go to charity, but they failed to register with the Attorney General's office as required. Since the registration requirement is the means by which Illinois monitors charitable solicitations, the failure to register prompted an inquiry by the Attorney General's office. The producers thereupon registered, and two years later, the charities received the promised proceeds.

The failure to register could cause more than embarrassment. An organization can be enjoined from making charitable solicitations if it is not registered as a professional fund raiser or if it fails to file a written contract. A New York organization that claimed it was making donations to charity but at the same time claimed it was not a professional fund raiser was enjoined from soliciting funds until it registered as a professional fund raiser or as a commercial co-venturer in *State* v. *Richard A. Viguerie Co. Inc.*[11] Since the organization was paid to provide the charity with donor lists as well as its expertise and aid in preparing a direct mail solicitation, it was required to register under New York's law.

11.
86 Misc. 2d 506, 382
N.Y.S.2d 622 (1976).

In states with a registration requirement, the attorney general usually is empowered to sue to enjoin violations. Willful violation usually constitutes a misdemeanor for which damages may be recovered.

Some states also require certain disclosures to be made in advertising that solicits funds. California, for instance, requires that all charitable solicitations disclose to the prospective donor the name and address of the charity, the amount of the purchase price being donated, the cost of fund raising expenses, whether the charitable organization is tax exempt and, among other requirements, how much, if any, of the purchase price is tax deductible as a charitable contribution.[12] These disclosures may be made on a separate card or in brochures. Television commercials of 60 seconds or less are exempted from the disclosure requirements. These disclosure requirements apply to the sale of items such as coupons and merchandise, and to the sale of admission tickets and entry fees of which a part or all of the purchase price is donated to charity.

12.
Cal. Bus. & Prof.
Code § 17510.3 (McKin-
ney 1988).

California's disclosure requirement is perhaps the most detailed and burdensome of the charitable solicitation statutes. Most other states' laws are less demanding. Illinois, for example, has no specific disclosure requirements in its charitable solicitation law.

13.
N.Y. Exec. Law § 174(c)
(McKinney 1988).

New York requires disclosures similar to those in California, but only in advertising for the sale of an item, including entertainment, that will benefit charity.[13] New York's requirement is further limited in that it does not apply unless a professional fund raiser or a commercial co-venturer is involved in the fund raising effort.

14.
106 A.D.2d, 484
N.Y.S.2d 245 (1984).

A producer of shows for charities' fund raising events was enjoined from making further charitable solicitations because he failed to comply with New York's disclosure requirements and failed to file his contracts with the charities in *People v. United Funding Co., Inc.*[14] As a registered commercial co-venturer, the producer would enter into contracts with charities for which he was to raise funds. In violation of the law, he failed to file these contracts with the Secretary of State. He then solicited contributions by selling tickets to a show and encouraged contributors to buy extra tickets to give to handicapped children. The charity received only between 10 percent and 15 percent of the ticket sales. For its repeated failure to comply with the disclosure requirements, the producer was enjoined from producing shows and making charitable solicitations in New York.

The requirements pertaining to the charitable solicitation of funds are different in every state. Organizers of events that will benefit charity should be aware that these requirements may apply to their fund raising efforts.

FALSE ADVERTISING AND CHARITIES

If the proceeds of an event are going to charity, how can/should the organizer of the event advertise that fact?

Obviously, if the organizer says $1.00 per ticket goes to charity, $1.00 per ticket must in fact be donated to charity. More frequently, however, the phrase "Proceeds to benefit _____" is used. That is probably understood as a statement that the profits will go to charity. But everyone knows that "profits" is a funny term. Can the organizer charge overhead against the event, recovering direct and indirect costs? Whenever such terms are used, care should be taken to clarify what is meant in order to avoid challenge by the Internal Revenue Service, state attorneys general and consumer advocates.

Recently, the Internal Revenue Service has become concerned with how charities advertise the deductibility of donations to fund-raising events. The IRS is concerned that taxpayers are being misled by questionable solicitation practices which make it appear that the taxpayer's payment for a ticket to an event or for a "free" gift or premium is a contribution to the charity in instances where the payment is really the purchase price of admission or of an item offered for sale.

To be deductible as a charitable contribution for federal income tax purposes, a payment to a charitable organization must in fact be a gift. To be a gift, there must be a payment of money or a transfer of property without adequate consideration. When a corporation sponsors a fund-raising event, it is not so concerned with deductibility of the sponsorship fee, which can be expensed as an advertising cost. The fee paid is probably not a charitable gift because the sponsor is getting valuable advertising exposure in return.

Individuals, however, have the burden of proving to the IRS that the amount paid to the charity is in excess of the fair market value of the benefits or premiums received. It is the policy of the IRS that charitable organizations should make clear what portion of a ticket price, for instance, is a gift and what portion is the fair market value of the benefits to be received by the purchaser. Where an event such as a concert or an athletic event has an established ticket price, it is relatively easy to establish what portion of a higher-priced charity event ticket is the fair market value for the admission and what portion may be a gift. When the event has no standarized admission fee or no comparable counterpart, a reasonable estimate must be made of the fair market value of the admission and of the gift. For instance, if a concert seat is usually $10, and a charity sponsors a concert and sells tickets at the usual concert prices, the ticket price is not deductible by the individual patron, even though the ticket says the concert is for the benefit of the charity. However, if the charity charges $30 per ticket, $20 would be a gift and $10 would be the fair market value of the admission.

The IRS has published a number of examples to provide guidelines on the proper disclosure of deductibility (see Appendix M). One example concerns a women's club whose monthly membership luncheon meetings include both entertainment and business. The example shows a sample ticket that says, "Suburban Women's Club of X County Luncheon-Benefit of The Handicapped Children's Fund of X Charity/Readings by GASTON Noted Lecturer and Author/The Z Country Club, Tuesday, October 31, 1967/12:00 Noon/$5.50 Donation." The IRS says the use of the word "donation" is misleading because it suggests that the price of the ticket is a charitable contribution and, therefore, tax deductible. However, since there is no showing in the example that any part of the ticket price is in fact a gift of an amount in excess of the value of the luncheon and the entertainment, no part of the payment is deductible.

In another example, the IRS supposes that all the costs of a charity ball are underwritten by individuals in the community (which individuals could be corporate sponsors). Even if the entire gross receipts of the sale of tickets to the ball go to a charity, no part of the ticket price is deductible unless the price of the ticket is in excess of the fair market value of the event. It would be misleading to lead individuals to believe that they could deduct the price of the ticket. The charity should disclose that the ticket price is not deductible. The sponsors of the event may be able to deduct all or part of their underwriting of the event.

Other than through charitable solicitation laws, most states regulate advertising practices through consumer protection statutes and laws against false or deceptive trade practices. It is probably not a violation of such laws to say that a certain level of profits is hoped for, as long as the stated amount is reasonable and is reasonably calculated in accordance with generally accepted accounting principles. However, charitable solicitation laws should be reviewed for specific limitations they may impose.

The charitable solicitation statute in New York is illustrative of the treatment such statutes give to advertising charitable solicitations. The statute makes it illegal to:

> engage in any fraudulent or illegal act, device, scheme, artifice to
> defraud or for obtaining money . . . by means of a pretense . . . in

connection with any solicitation for charitable purposes . . . or . . .
use or intend to use false or materially misleading advertising or
promotional material.[15]

15.
N.Y. Exec. Law
§ 172(d)(2)(3) (McKinney 1988).

Thus, organizers must avoid advertising that has the potential to mislead the public.

An organizer who advertises that the proceeds of an event are going to charity might find that the determination of whether the advertising is misleading can be tricky. For instance, a peace officers' union is required to register as a charity under California's charitable solicitation law. However, the union may not advertise that the proceeds of an event will go to charity if the proceeds are used for the lobbying and promotional activities of the union's members, because the public would not traditionally consider the lobbying and promotional activities of the union charitable activities. Thus, advertising that contributions "go directly to charity" might mislead the public and is likely to violate the charitable solicitation or false advertising laws of California.[16]

16.
66 Op. Att'y Gen. Cal. 40 (1983).

The question of whether an advertisement is misleading often arises when an organizer uses phrases like "proceeds to benefit charity" or "XYZ Event to raise $100,000 for charity." Such a solicitation might lead the public to believe that most, if not all, of its contributions will go directly to the charitable cause. A portion of the contributions, however, will inevitably be used for administrative expenses in connection with raising funds. Organizers should be aware that there have been various efforts by the states to regulate the uses to which proceeds may be put. Such regulations aim to prevent fraudulent solicitation of funds through misleading advertisements and to address the concern that too much money is spent on "administrative" costs, while too little money goes to the charitable cause.

Generally, the statutes are designed to ensure that contributions actually go to the charity by imposing a strict limit on the amount that can be spent on administration. These statutes have been successfully challenged on constitutional grounds.

Since the charitable solicitation of funds involves the "communication of information, the dissemination of ideas, and the advocacy of causes," it is a form of protected speech under the First Amendment.[17] While charitable solicitations are protected by the First Amendment, they are "undoubtedly subject to reasonable regulation but the latter must be undertaken with due regard for the reality that solicitation is characteristically intertwined with informative and perhaps persuasive speech seeking support for particular causes or for particular views on economic, political or social issues."[18]

17.
Schaumburg v. *Citizens for a Better Environment,* 444 U.S. 620, 632 (1980).

18.
Id.

Since charitable solicitations are protected under the First Amendment, a charitable solicitation law will be scrutinized to determine whether it unnecessarily infringes on First Amendment interests.[19] For instance, a regulation that prohibited door-to-door solicitation by charitable organizations that spend less than 75 percent of the funds raised on charitable purposes, excluding solicitation expenses, salaries, overhead and administrative expenses, was held to be an unconstitutional infringement on First Amendment rights in *Schaumburg* v. *Citizens for a Better Environment*.[20] The court said that the regulation restricted the use to which donations could be put. This effectively limited the charity in its exercise of First Amendment rights. The state argued that the regulation was reasonable in order to prevent fraud in the solicitation of funds. It reasoned that a charity that spends more than 25 percent of its proceeds on administrative, fund raising and overhead expenses is "not a charitable, but a commercial, for-profit enterprise and that to permit it to represent itself as a charity is fraudulent."[21] The U.S Supreme Court disagreed and emphatically stated that high costs do not necessarily mean that a charity is fraudulent.[22] A charity's high costs might be due to expensive fund raising techniques that are particularly effective for the charity, such as direct mailings. Moreover, the court said there were better and more accurate ways to prevent fraudulent charities, methods that would be "less destructive of First Amendment interests."[23]

A similar statute was struck down by the Supreme Court as an unconstitutional infringement of First Amendment rights in *Secretary of State* v. *Joseph H. Munson Co.*[24] In that case, a Maryland statute that prohibited a charity from spending more than 25 percent of its donations from charitable solicitations on fund raising expenses was held unconstitutional.[25] This statute was actually more flexible than the one struck down by the Supreme Court in *Schaumburg* v. *Citizens for a Better Environment*. Although not more than 25 percent of the total contributions could be spent on fund raising expenses, the cost of "goods, food, entertainment, or drink sold or provided to the public" in addition to postage and printing costs were exempted from the 25 percent limit.[26] The statute also provided for an administrative waiver of the 25 percent limit if the charity could "demonstrate financial necessity."[27] Despite the added provisions that allowed for greater protection of First Amendment rights, the Supreme Court struck down this statute as an unconstitutional infringement on the charity's First Amendment rights.

Recently, the Supreme Court reaffirmed these two decisions in *National Federation of the Blind of N.C., Inc.* v. *Riley*.[28] In this case, the court struck down North Carolina's charitable solicitation statute as an unconstitutional infringement on First Amendment rights. The statute prohibited a professional fund raiser from charging an "excessive" or "unreasonable fee."[29] Under the statute, it was reasonable for

19.
Id.

20.
Id. at 636.

21.
Id.

22.
Id. at 637.

23.
Id. at 636.

24.
467 U.S. 947 (1984).

25.
Id. at 968.

26.
Id. at 951.

27.
Id.

28.
101 L. Ed. 2d 669 (1988)

29.
Id. at 681.

the professional fund raiser to charge 20 percent of the contributions, while it was unreasonable to charge between 20 percent and 35 percent of the contributions if there was to be no dissemination of information.[30] Finally, it was clearly excessive to charge 35 percent of the contributions unless it was shown that the fee was necessary "either 1) because the solicitation involved the dissemination of information or advocacy of public issues directed by the charity, or 2) because otherwise the charity's ability to raise money or communicate would be significantly diminished."[31] The statute was held unconstitutional by the court because:

> *prior cases teach that the solicitation of charitable contributions is protected speech, and that using percentages to decide the legality of the fund raiser's fee is not narrowly tailored to the state's interest in preventing fraud. That much established, unless the state can meaningfully distinguish its statute from those discussed in our precedents, its statute must fall.*[32]

The state distinguished its statute from the *Citizens for a Better Environment* and *Joseph H. Munson Co.* precedents on two grounds. First, it argued that the statute ensured that contributions actually go to charity. Second, it argued that the statute prevented fund raisers from charging an unreasonable fee. Neither argument sufficiently distinguished the statute from the precedents. Thus, the statute was held to be unconstitutional.

In the wake of this recent decision, it seems clear that a statute that limits the fund raising costs of a charity by use of a percentage limit is likely to be held unconstitutional.

In Illinois, for example, it is fraudulent under the charitable solicitation statute to solicit funds where less than 75 percent of the gross receipts of the charity are used for charitable purposes. Gross receipts are defined as "receipts after the legitimate and reasonable cost of any merchandise for resale or . . . of services required with the fund raising event or program are deducted. . . ."[33] Even though this percentage limit may be generous, unless Illinois can meaningfully distinguish this statute from those struck down by the Supreme Court, it will likely be held unconstitutional and will not therefore be vigorously enforced.

Disclosure requirements and antifraud laws are the primary means by which a state may address its concerns regarding fraudulent charities. In fact, in *Citizens for a Better Environment*, the court explained that concerns about unscrupulous

30.
Id.

31.
Id. at 8.

32.
Id. at 684.

33.
Ill. Rev. Stat. ch. 23, para. 5109(c) (1987).

34.
444 U.S. at 636-37.

professional fund raisers and charities are addressed directly by disclosure and registration requirements and penalties for fraudulent conduct.[34] The court explained further that:

> *Efforts to promote disclosure of the finances of charitable organizations also may assist in preventing fraud by informing the public of the ways in which their contributions will be employed. Such measures may help make contribution decisions more informed, while leaving to individual choice the decision whether to contribute to organizations that spend large amounts on salaries and administrative expenses.*[35]

35.
Id. at 637-38.

36.
95 Misc. 2d 381, 407
N.Y.S.2d 611 (1978).

37.
407 N.Y.S.2d at 613.

38.
Id. at 614.

Under New York's charitable solicitation law, it is not illegal for the professional fund raiser to retain a "lion's share" of the money donated to the charity, but he or she must inform the public of that fact. The court in *State* v. *Francis*[36] held it would be "unconscionable, deceptive and a fraud on the public" to fail to inform the public that 75 percent of the funds solicited for charity was actually to be paid to the professional fund raiser.[37] The court reasoned that "contracts with the not-for-profit corporation are not merely bilateral, but rather establish triangular relationships with the public as the third party whose interest should be protected."[38] So, although a professional fund raiser may freely contract with a charitable organization, he or she must comply with disclosure laws and deceptive advertising and fraud laws.

Useful guidelines on charitable solicitations are published by the Council of Better Business Bureaus, Inc. in *Do's and Don'ts in Advertising Copy* (1984). Their standards address public accountability, use of funds, solicitation materials and fund raising practices. They provide in part that "total fund raising and administrative costs shall be reasonable," and they define "reasonable" as follows:

> *Reasonable use of funds requires that a) at least 50% of total income from all sources be spent on programs and activities directly related to the organization's purpose; b) at least 50% of public contributions be spent on the programs and activities described in solicitations, in accordance with donor expectations; c) fund raising costs not exceed 35% of related contributions; and d) total fund raising and administrative costs not exceed 50% of total income. An organization which does not meet one or more of these percentage limitations may provide evidence to demonstrate that its use of funds is reasonable. The higher fund raising and administrative costs of a newly created organization, donor restrictions on the use of funds, exceptional bequests, a stigma*

associated with a cause, and environmental or political events beyond an organization's control are among the factors which may result in costs that are reasonable although they do not meet these percentage limitations.

SAMPLE AGREEMENT FOR CHARITY TIE-IN

Charity
Address
City/State/Zip

Dear *Charity:*

This will confirm our Agreement concerning the (*describe event*) ("Event") to be promoted by us ("we") in part for the benefit of (*charitable organization*) ("Charity" or "you") on the terms and conditions contained herein.

A letter agreement sometimes appears more informal, but it is nonetheless binding on both parties when signed.

1. Event. We will use our best efforts to organize and promote the Event at (*site*) on (*date(s)*). We shall be solely responsible for all costs incurred in connection with the advertising, promotion and production of the Event. We shall solely own all rights of any kind in the Event and any film, videotape, sound recording, book or other subsequent exploitation of the Event and in the trademarks and logos identifying the Event (the "Event Trademarks").

This paragraph describes the basic event and recites the Organizer's ownership of the Event. If the Charity is a more active participant than the passive role assumed here, then the Charity might be in the position of Organizer or at the least would assert some ownership rights in the Event.

2. Sponsors. Charity understands that we will seek corporate sponsors and suppliers for the Event (the "Sponsors"). Understanding that the identity of such Sponsors may reflect on Charity's reputation, Charity will have the right to approve the identity of the Sponsors, which approval shall not be unreasonably withheld.

The Charity probably will insist on approval of sponsors and suppliers, particularly if the Charity is cause oriented, such as an environmental group.

3. Tie-In. Charity hereby agrees to cooperate with us as reasonably requested to promote the Event. Charity hereby grants us the right to use the name and logos of Charity ("Charity's Trademarks") in advertising and promoting the Event, including Event souvenirs and related merchandise. Charity shall use its reasonable efforts to cause its mailings and press releases, if any, prior to the Event to refer to the Event and to the Sponsors thereof. Charity shall recognize us and Sponsors as major contributors for calendar year (*year*) in any printed literature of any kind recognizing donors and/or contributors generally.

The nature of the Charity's obligations may be passive, as here, or fairly active. For instance, a charity may be required to contract with musical talent for a concert or music festival to benefit a specific cause. The talent would be more likely to donate his or her services in such a case. Recognition of the Organizer and its Event Sponsors as major benefactors of the Charity is a nice perk for both Organizers and Sponsors.

4. Donation. In consideration of all of Charity's services and all rights granted us hereunder, we will donate the following to Charity (*state when*): (*describe donation*) (the "Donation").

The "donation" could be a percentage of the total revenues or net profits, which would then require a definition of how revenues or profits will be calculated. If a per-ticket or entry-fee donation is made, the Organizer should provide a ticket manifest or some certification of the number of entries. Such donations should probably be made within 30 to 60 days after the Event takes place. Alternatively, the Organizer may guarantee a flat amount that could be paid up front or in installments.

5. Indemnification. We hereby indemnify and hold Charity and its directors, officers, employees, agents and assigns, harmless from any damages, liabilities, claims, losses and expenses, including reasonable attorneys' fees and court costs, arising in any way out of the Event, except for Charity's own acts. We shall cause Charity to be named as an additional insured on our comprehensive general liability and other insurance policies.

If the Charity is truly passive, the total indemnity is appropriate. If Charity undertakes to perform any affirmative obligations, then it should indemnify Organizer for its failure to perform its obligations properly.

6. Charity's Warranty. Charity represents and warrants that it is and shall remain until the completion of the Event duly organized as a not-for-profit corporation under the laws of (*state*) and that it is and will so remain in good standing [and is

currently duly registered under the laws of (*list*) to solicit charitable donations].
Charity further represents and warrants that it has been recognized by the Internal
Revenue Service as an exempt organization under Section 501(c)(3) of the Internal
Revenue Code and that it will immediately notify us of any change in such status.

*This paragraph assures the Organizer that it is dealing with a bona fide charity. It
may or may not be necessary for the Charity to be registered to solicit donations.*

7. Our Additional Obligations. We shall provide Charity, upon request, with the
following: (*list*).

*The Charity might want to have a courtesy tent for big donors, a page of program
advertising, or a free copy of any film or videotape made of the Event and the right
to use it in private or internal presentations, or in public service announcements, etc.
Such additional rights or perks should be described.*

8. Organizer's Warranty. We represent and warrant that we will abide by all laws
and regulations applicable to the Event and that the Event and its exploitation will
not infringe the personal or proprietary rights of any person.

*This is basically a warranty that the Event will be conducted in a lawful manner.
Other kinds of warranties, such as that the Event will be sanctioned by an official
athletic body, might be in order, but a warranty that the Event will be first-class or
will reflect well upon the Charity might well be considered by the Organizer to be
too vague.*

9. Termination. Either party shall have the right to terminate this Agreement upon
30 days' written notice to the other of the other's material breach of this
Agreement, provided such breach is not cured within such period. In addition, we
may terminate this Agreement upon written notice to Charity if on or before (*date*)
we have not obtained contractual commitments from Sponsor of at least
[$_____] [an amount of funding we deem reasonably necessary to conduct
the Event in a professional manner]. In any event this Agreement will terminate
three months after the Event takes place.

*The right to terminate for breach is standard. However, the Organizer also needs to
retain the right to terminate if adequate Sponsorship monies are not raised.*

10. Effect of Termination. Upon termination, all rights granted either party shall cease, except that the provisions of Paragraph 5 shall continue in full force and effect. Charity understands that if termination is due to a lack of funding or Charity's breach, the Donation described in Paragraph 4 hereof will not be made and we shall have no liability to Charity therefor. In addition, we may liquidate and/or utilize any materials, merchandise or souvenirs bearing Charity's Trademarks produced or in process prior to termination, provided termination has not been caused by our breach of this Agreement.

Here the indemnification obligation survives termination but all other rights cease, except that Organizer may liquidate or utilize any materials, merchandise or souvenirs produced prior to termination if termination is not caused by Organizer's breach. In the alternative, the Charity may require some reduced Donation for its lost time and effort.

11. Non-Compete. Charity represents and warrants that for a period of (*number*) years following termination of this Agreement, Charity will not, directly or indirectly, participate or allow its name to be used in connection with any event substantially similar to the Event hereunder.

Some of the Organizer's goodwill in connection with the Event derives from the Charitable tie-in. This paragraph is designed to prevent the Charity from stealing the substance of the Event and calling it something else.

12. Force Majeure. In the event the Event does not take place due to any cause beyond the reasonable control of the parties, then we shall have the right to terminate this Agreement upon our written notice to Charity of the occurrence of such event or to postpone the Event to a mutually agreeable date within six months of the scheduled date. If we terminate this Agreement, we shall have no liability to Charity for the Donation described in Paragraph 4, but shall otherwise have the rights specified in Paragraph 10 and shall continue to indemnify the Charity as provided therein. If we postpone the Event, all the terms and conditions of this Agreement shall apply.

If the Event cannot take place as scheduled, the Organizer can postpone or terminate. If it chooses termination, there may be no money for the Donation.

13. Miscellaneous. This Agreement sets forth our entire Agreement and supersedes all prior understandings, oral or written. No representations have been relied upon by either party except as specifically set forth herein. This Agreement shall be governed by the laws of the State of (*state*). Neither party may assign this Agreement without the consent of the other except that we may assign it to any entity wholly owned or controlled by us. Any amendments or modifications must be in a writing signed by both parties.

This is boilerplate. Other boilerplate that might be added would include a right to injunctive relief in the event of breach, a "notice" paragraph and/or an arbitration clause.

If this accurately sets forth our Agreement, please so indicate by signing below and returning a copy to us.

Sincerely,

Organizer

Agreed and Accepted this _____ day of _____, 19____

Charity: _____

CHAPTER 7:
SPECIAL INDUSTRIES

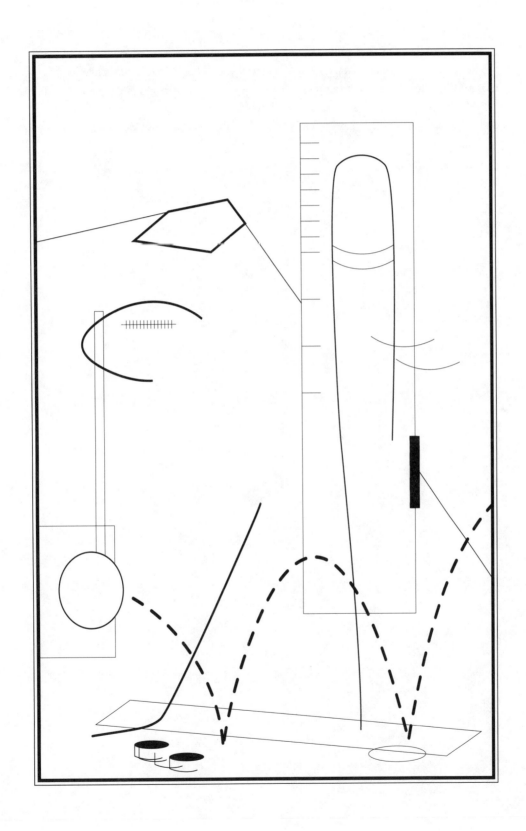

SPECIAL INDUSTRIES

If an industry is regulated under either federal or state law, its advertising and promotional activities are likely to be regulated too. The alcoholic beverage and tobacco industries are two examples. While members of both industries have been actively involved in sponsorship, particularly of sports events, the legal constraints under which they operate cause some special problems for event organizers.

ALCOHOLIC BEVERAGES

The alcoholic beverage industry – the only industry to have two U.S. constitutional amendments devoted to it – is plagued by a panoply of state and federal laws, as well as local ordinances. While the sale and advertising of alcohol is legal in most areas of the United States, many sales promotion techniques common in other industries – such as cooperative advertising – are simply illegal in the alcoholic beverage business. This creates some unique problems – though not insurmountable ones – for event promoters.

Each state has its own laws regulating the sale and distribution of alcoholic beverages. This discussion will illustrate some of the constraints on event sponsors in the alcoholic beverage industry.

The Treasury Department's Bureau of Alcohol, Tobacco and Firearms (BATF) administers the Federal Alcohol Administration (FAA) Act.[1] In this capacity, the BATF regulates the advertising of wine,[2] malt beverages (beer)[3] and distilled spirits.[4] BATF regulations also enforce the "tied house" provisions of the FAA Act.[5] The term "tied house" refers to distribution arrangements between various industry members, such as brewers, wholesalers and retailers. The object of tied house regulations is to prevent inducements to retailers to purchase one industry member's product to the exclusion of another's.[6] (Another word for "inducement" might be "bribe.") It is thus illegal for an industry member to have an interest, direct or indirect, in a retail licensee.[7] (The BATF's tied house regulations are reprinted in Appendix N.)

With certain exceptions, it is also illegal for an industry member to furnish a retailer with anything of value.[8] This includes giving, renting, lending or selling the retailer any equipment, fixtures, signs, supplies, money or services. The rule applies whether or not the transaction appears to be an inducement.[9]

Many event promoters consider becoming licensees of the local and state liquor authorities in order to sell alcoholic beverages – usually beer and wine – at an event. However, as retail licensees, they are subject to tied house regulations when dealing with sponsors from the alcoholic beverage industry. If the sponsor pays a fee to the promoter-retailer, that fee could be deemed "furnishing something of value." Moreover, the sponsor clearly could not require that its brand be the only brand sold at the event. That would fly in the face of the prohibition on activities

1.
27 U.S.C. § 201 (Cum. Supp. 1988).

2.
27 C.F.R. § 4.6 et seq. (1984).

3.
27 C.F.R. § 7.50 et seq. (1984).

4.
27 C.F.R. § 5.61 et seq. (1984).

5.
27 U.S.C. § 205(b).

6.
27 C.F.R. § 6.11 defines industry member as "Any person engaged in business as a distiller, brewer, rectifier, blender, or other producer, or as an importer or wholesaler, of distilled spirits, wine or malt beverages, or as a bottler, or warehouseman and bottler, of distilled spirits; industry member does not include an agency of a state or political subdivision thereof, or an officer or employee of such agency."

7.
27 C.F.R. § 6.21.

8.
27 C.F.R. § 6.41.

9.
Id.

10.
27 C.F.R. § 6.2.

that "prevent, deter, hinder or restrict other persons from selling or offering for sale any such products to such retailer. . . ."[10] Some sponsors use specific disclaimers in their contracts, such as:

Brewer represents, warrants and covenants to Organizer as follows:

(i) This Agreement is entered into solely for the purchase of advertising as described herein and for no other purposes.

(ii) Brewer's purchase of advertising under this Agreement is in no way conditioned on any agreement or understanding that Organizer will require any alcoholic beverage retail licensee to purchase any alcoholic beverage produced, sold or offered for sale by Brewer.

(iii) By the purchase of advertising under this Agreement, Brewer does not agree, expect or intend to induce the purchase by or through Organizer or any alcoholic beverage retail licensee of any alcoholic beverage produced, sold or offered for sale by Brewer.

Organizer represents, warrants and covenants to Brewer as follows:

(i) Organizer is not a retailer of alcoholic beverages at any Event site or elsewhere and has no ownership interest in any alcoholic beverage retail license at any Event site or elsewhere.

(ii) No monies paid by Brewer for the advertising purchased under this Agreement are intended to be or will be passed on by Organizer to any alcoholic beverage retail licensee as an inducement to any such retailer to purchase any alcoholic beverage produced, sold or offered for sale by Brewer.

(iii) There is no agreement or understanding between Brewer and Organizer that, as consideration for Brewer's purchase of advertising under this Agreement, Organizer will require any alcoholic beverage retail licensee to purchase any alcoholic beverage produced, sold or offered for sale by Brewer.

The purpose of the clause is to give the brewer/sponsor a defense if in fact only one brand of beer is sold. The clause also assures the sponsor that it is not dealing with a retail licensee.

Some promoters set up a separate corporation to hold the necessary liquor licenses. Sponsorship fees are then paid to the event organizer, who is not a retail alcoholic beverage licensee. Because it is so transparent an attempt to evade the law, this practice might not work on a long-term basis. However, on a one-time basis it seems to work satisfactorily, as enforcement authorities tend to believe special events are in the public interest.

There may be additional advantages to using a separate corporation for the sale of alcoholic beverages. The sale of alcoholic beverages can give rise to liability for injuries caused to or by persons who become intoxicated at a licensee's establishment (see Chapter 5). A *bona fide* separate corporation with its own capitalization and insurance may serve to insulate the bulk of the organizer's assets in the event of liability.

Setting up a separate corporation can also insulate a sponsor from illegally "furnishing something of value" to the promoter. For instance, BATF regulations prohibit cooperative advertising between industry members and retailers.[11] In addition, industry members are prohibited from giving ballpark, racetrack and stadium retail concessionaires signs, scoreboards, scorecards, programs and the like.[12]

11.
27 C.F.R. § 6.52

12.
27 C.F.R. §§ 6.53, 6.54.

Finally, it must be emphasized that even if an activity is legal under federal law, it may be prohibited by state law.[13]

13.
27 C.F.R. § 6.1.

Some states specifically regulate the kinds of events that a member of the alcoholic beverage industry can sponsor. For instance, California regulations permit manufacturers to sponsor contests, races, tournaments and other similar activities, both on and off licensed premises. However, sponsorships can only be in the form of monetary payments to "bona fide amateur or professional organizations established for the encouragement and promotion of the activities involved."[14] This does not mean, however, that alcoholic beverage manufacturers must involve non-profits in these events. But, as discussed above, it may be impossible for a manufacturer to work directly with a for-profit promoter or if the latter holds a liquor license. In such a situation, payments to the promoter or venue would violate California's "tied house" laws. This problem is solved practically if a third party holds the liquor license.

14.
California Alcholic Beverage Control Department, Rule 106.

California regulations also specify that the sponsor cannot require that its products be the only ones sold at the event. No money or other thing of value other than approved advertising specialties can be given to anyone other than the organizations sponsoring the event. Participants may be charged an entry fee, but entry cannot be conditioned on the purchase of the sponsor's products.[15]

15.
Id.

In a case involving Miller Brewing Company in 1988, a California court held that the Department of Alcoholic Beverage Control could validly enforce its rules against giving away promotional merchandise in connection with its sponsorship of a concert.[16] Miller was sponsoring a comedy concert tour featuring comedian Joe Piscopo. Some of the concerts were held in California, and the proceeds were given to the Olympic Training Center, a non-profit corporation providing free training facilities to amateur athletes training for the Olympics. Miller planned to co-promote the tour with radio stations and to give the stations concert tickets and jackets to be given to listeners who won on-air promotional contests. The tickets would identify Miller as a sponsor of the concert and the jackets would bear logos of a Miller product and the concert. Recipients of the promotional merchandise were not required to buy any Miller product. The Department refused to approve the giveaways. It said it would consider the furnishing of free tickets and jackets a violation of its rules, which prohibit a licensee from giving any premium, gift or free goods in connection with the sale or distribution of any alcoholic beverage, except for advertising specialties of only nominal value. The court upheld the Department's very broad reading of "sale" and "distribution" as including merchandising and advertising. Despite this ruling, sponsors are free to give free premiums of nominal value directly to consumers at events, and to conduct sweepstakes and other promotions in California under other rules of the Department. (See Appendix O (1) for California Alcoholic Beverage Control Department Regulations.)

16.
Miller Brewing Company v. Department of Alcoholic Beverage Control,
204 Cal. App. 3d 5, 250 Cal. Rptr. 845 (Cal. App. 1988).

Utah regulations provide another example of how a state may regulate sponsorship of events.[17] Distillers may not sponsor athletic events in Utah without the prior approval of the Liquor Control Commission. The sponsor must submit a written description of the event and the type and scope of the distiller's participation. The event may not take place at a licensed premises or at an educational institution. Free products may not be given to the general public. (It would seem, however, that a sponsor could invite V.I.P.s to a promotional party where free beverages are served.) Drinking scenes may not be displayed in connection with the event and the event cannot "unduly increase the consumption of alcoholic products."[18] (See Appendix O (2) for Utah Liquor Control Commission regulations.)

17.
Utah Reg. 96-1-7(1).

18.
Id.

TOBACCO

Somewhat less regulated than the alcohol industry, but possibly even more controversial, is the tobacco industry. Although some organizers are reluctant to accept sponsorship dollars from tobacco companies, some tobacco interests have remained fairly active in sponsorship. Organizers of events sponsored by tobacco companies face several unique problems.

The first problem is fairly straightforward: the requirement to provide warnings. The Federal Cigarette Labelling and Advertising Act,[19] provides that each cigarette package and advertisement bear one of four warnings:

19.
15 U.S.C. § 1331 et seq.
(Cum. Supp. 1987).

> *Surgeon General's Warning: Smoking Causes Lung Cancer, Heart Disease, Emphysema, and may complicate pregnancy.*
>
> *Surgeon General's Warning: Quitting Smoking Now Greatly Reduces Serious Risks to Your Health.*
>
> *Surgeon General's Warning: Smoking by Pregnant Women May Result in Fetal Injury, Premature Birth and Low Birth Weight.*
>
> *Surgeon General's Warning: Cigarette Smoke Contains Carbon Monoxide.*[20]

20.
15 U.S.C. § 1333.

Abbreviated warnings are specified and required on outdoor billboards. Arguably, sponsorship signs at an event are advertising or billboards requiring these warnings. The organizer should defer to the cigarette company's judgment on this issue, since the statute's requirements are imposed only on manufacturers and importers of cigarettes. On the other hand, as the publisher of a souvenir program, the organizer will want to make sure the tobacco company has included the warning in its advertising pages. (See Appendix P for federal cigarette labelling regulations.)

21.
15 U.S.C. § 1334 (1982).

The federal law preempts any state-required packaging or advertising warning or other statement relating to health.[21] However, cities may impose non-health-related labelling requirements, such as clear disclosure of price lists and prices in advertising.[22] In addition, cities may require nonsmoking seating or eating areas at an event.

22.
See Long Island Tobacco Co., Inc. v. Lindsay, 343 N.Y.S.2d 122, 42 A.D. 2d 1056, aff'd, 357 N.Y.S.2d 504, 34 N.Y.2d 748, 313 N.E.2d 794 (1973).

Federal law poses another, perhaps more serious problem: it is unlawful to "advertise cigarettes and little cigars on any medium of electronic communication subject to the jurisdiction of the Federal Communications Commission."[23] This prohibition was upheld as a rational regulation of interstate commerce by the FCC.[24] If a cigarette company is a title sponsor of an event, will a broadcaster be able to

23.
15 U.S.C. § 1335.

24.
Capital Broadcasting Company v. Mitchell, 333 F. Supp. 582 (D.D.C. 1971), aff'd, 405 U.S. 1000 (1972).

use the name of the manufacturer in broadcasting the event? Can cigarette signage be shown on television? The FCC and the U.S. Department of Justice have taken the position that the name can be used, for example, Virginia Slims Tennis Tournament, but that logos and signs cannot be shown. Broadcasters must avoid all but the most fleeting or incidental coverage of signage. The same prohibitions apply to cable operators and other nonstandard television and radio stations subject to the jurisdiction of the FCC. Moreover, under the Comprehensive Smokeless Tobacco Health Education Act of 1986,[25] it is also illegal to advertise smokeless tobacco on any medium of electronic communications subject to the jurisdiction of the FCC.

State and local laws must also be consulted with respect to two other common event activities – promotional tie-ins and sampling. Some states, such as Virginia, do not allow sweepstakes in connection with tobacco products. Federal law prohibits sweepstakes and chance promotions that are delivered to consumers on the cigarette package,[26] but allows skill contests. Local ordinances govern whether passing out samples of cigarettes is allowed. If it is, measures should be taken to ensure that free samples are not given to minors.

25.
15 U.S.C. § 4401.

26.
26 U.S.C. § 5723
(reprinted in Appendix Q).

CHAPTER 8:
MUNICIPAL ORDINANCES AND THE
FIRST AMENDMENT

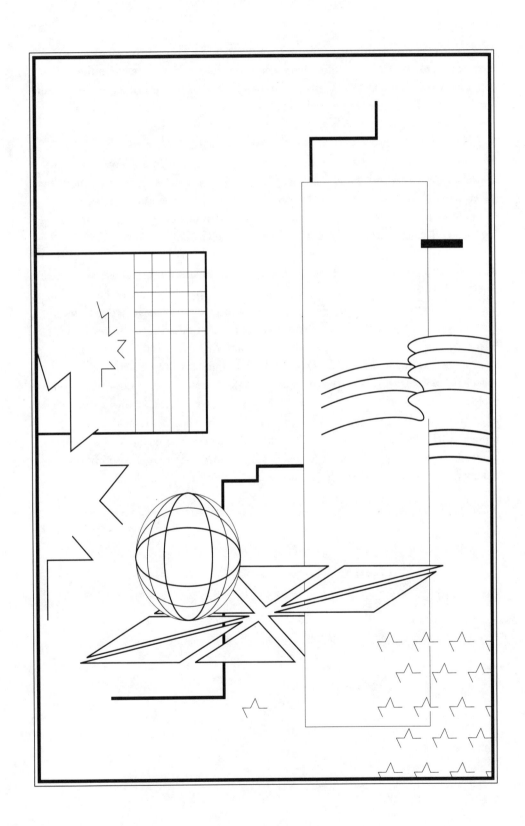

MUNICIPAL ORDINANCES AND THE FIRST AMENDMENT

1.

In relevant part, the First Amendment reads: "Congress shall make no law . . . abridging freedom of speech." The Supreme Court has ruled that the limitations of the First Amendment apply to all government action. *See, e.g., Heffron v. International Society for Krishna Consciousness*, 452 U.S. 640, 69 L. Ed. 2d 298, 101 S. Ct. 2559 (1981). As will be discussed later, qualifying for First Amendment protection does not exempt speech from all regulations.

2.
452 U.S. 61 (1981).

3.
Id. at 65.

4.
427 U.S. 297 (1976).

5.
See City of Lakewood v. *Plain Dealer Publishing Co.*, 108 S. Ct. 2138, 100 L. Ed.2d 771 (1988).

The success of an event often relies on cooperation between event sponsors and municipal authorities. Many cities have enacted ordinances that regulate the conduct of festivals on publicly owned property. Typically, the ordinances empower a municipal commissioner to evaluate requests for permits to hold events and specify conditions upon which such requests may be granted.

Because many events involve First Amendment[1] interests in free speech and free association, a city government's authority to regulate events is limited. In short, the government's regulation of events protected by the First Amendment must be content-neutral; that is, the government cannot discriminate against an event merely because it disagrees with the event's purpose or philosophy.

An event is protected by the First Amendment if it involves a protected form of speech. The definition of constitutionally protected "speech" is somewhat elusive, but it is clear that events must involve some form of expression in order to merit First Amendment protection. That expression need not be political; in *Schad* v. *Mount Ephraim*,[2] the court specifically found that "[l]ive entertainment such as musical and dramatic works fall within the First Amendment guarantee of free speech."[3] In contrast, the purely commercial sale of merchandise does not enjoy such protection. For instance, in *City of New Orleans* v. *Dukes*,[4] the court upheld a city ban on pushcart vending. However, if the merchandise being sold is itself protected by the First Amendment, its sale is protected. For example, the municipal licensing of newspaper racks is subject to constitutional scrutiny because newspapers are products clearly protected under the First Amendment.[5]

ACCESS AND PERMITS

Even if speech is protected by the First Amendment, it may be regulated by the government depending on the nature of the forum in which the speaker seeks to speak. The Supreme Court has divided publicly owned property into three categories for the purposes of First Amendment analysis: (1) nonpublic forums, (2) limited public forums and (3) public forums.

A nonpublic forum is a place that the government has not opened for public speech at all. There is no First Amendment right of access to a nonpublic forum. For instance, a post office is a government building, but it is not one to which the government routinely grants access for rallies or concerts.

A limited public forum is property that the government has opened "for use by certain speakers or for the discussion of certain topics."[6] For instance, the government could exclude legal defense and political organizations from a combined charity drive aimed at federal employees in a nonpublic context because the drive was organized pursuant to an Executive Order which specifically excluded political organizations.[7] In addition, the court in *Calash* v. *City of Bridgeport*[8] denied a rock concert promoter access to a municipal stadium dedicated to noncommercial use by civic, charitable and nonprofit organizations. The court reasoned that "[w]hen the government creates a limited public forum for use of certain individuals or for the discussion of certain subjects, the First Amendment protections . . . only apply to entities of a character similar to those the government admits to the forum."[9] Since a for-profit promoter did not fall into the category of not-for-profit entities to whom the city had opened the stadium, the city could constitutionally exclude the promoter.

If, however, a municipal authority does not limit access to a facility, the authority has created a public forum. Public plazas in front of government buildings are often such public forums. As a general rule, a city may not deny access to a public forum. However, it may impose reasonable time, place and manner restrictions in a public forum if (1) the restrictions advance a substantial state interest and (2) there are alternative channels for expression.[10] If, however, a regulation is content-based, then it must (1) promote a compelling state interest and (2) be narrowly tailored to serve that interest.[11] Thus, a city can not deny access to a public forum because it disapproves of a speaker's message.

For example, in *Southeastern Promotions, Inc.* v. *Conrad*,[12] the Supreme Court ruled that municipally owned theaters in Chattanooga, Tennessee, could not prohibit the performance of the musical *Hair*. The court reasoned that the theaters were public forums and that exclusion of the production was content-based. More recently, in *Cinevision* v. *City of Burbank*,[13] a concert promoter filed a suit against

6.
Cornelius v. *NAACP*, 473 U.S. 788, 802, 105 S. Ct. 3439, 3449 (1985).

7.
Id.

8.
788 F.2d 80 (2d Cir. 1985).

9.
Id. at 82.

10.
See, e.g., Heffron v. *International Society for Krishna Consciousness*, 452 U.S. 640 (1981).

11.
See Renton v. *Playtime Theatres*, 475 U.S. 41 (1986).

12.
420 U.S. 546 (1975).

13.
745 F.2d 560 (9th Cir. 1984).

Burbank, California, claiming that the city unconstitutionally denied its request for permission to sponsor a number of concerts in the city-owned Starlight Bowl. The city objected to the concerts because it considered them "hard rock." The court regarded the city's refusal to grant a permit as a content-based discrimination and, as a result, required the city to demonstrate a compelling state interest that was advanced by disallowing "hard rock." The court suggested that noise, crowd control and traffic were legitimate matters of concern but that a generalized fear that narcotics or other laws would be broken was not sufficient to justify the exclusion. The former are content-neutral; the latter is not.[14] The court held that the city had failed to demonstrate a compelling state interest and therefore violated the promoter's First Amendment rights. It said:

> Excluding a performer because of his political views, or those of the crowd that he might attract, or because the performer might say unorthodox things, as well as considering such arbitrary factors as the lifestyle or race of the crowd that a performer would attract, is not constitutionally permissible.[15]

The opinions in these cases raise troubling questions. The Court in *Cornelius*, for example, noted that the government has the power to create a limited public forum "for use by certain speakers or for the discussion of certain subjects."[16] Yet, if the forum were public, limiting its use to "certain speakers" would undoubtedly violate the First Amendment. Thus, determining whether a forum is a limited public forum or whether instead there has been an impermissible exclusion from a public forum is difficult. Justice Rehnquist dissented in the *Hair* case, in part because of his difficulty in drawing that distinction. He said: "[m]ay an opera house limit its productions to opera, or must it show rock musicals? May a municipal theater devote its entire season to Shakespeare or is it required to book any potential producer on a first come, first served basis?"[17]

The court in the Cinevision "hard rock" case attempted to answer those questions:

> A court must scrutinize closely a government's dedication of a forum to a particular type of expression and fully consider a number of factors before deciding the constitutionality of such an action. As a threshold matter, the court is required to review with particular care any claim that the governmental body is actually attempting to suppress controversial, political, or other forms of expression, rather than attempting to promote certain limited forms of entertainment.

14.
Id. at 572.

15.
Id. at 577.

16.
105 S. Ct. at 3449.

17.
Southeastern Promotions, 420 U.S. at 572-73.

Once it is clearly established that the purpose of the conduct is not to suppress protected expression, the reviewing court should consider the category of expression that a municipality has dedicated the use of a public forum to, how that category is defined, and what standards will be used to determine whether particular performances or works fall within that category. The exclusive use of an auditorium or theater for a form of expression that is well defined, historically recognized, readily identifiable, and susceptible to objective classification is likely to be found permissible. The more subjective the standard used, the more likely that the category will not meet the requirements of the first amendment; for, when guided only by subjective, amorphous standards, government officials retain the unbridled discretion over expression that is condemned by the first amendment.[18]

18.
745 F.2d at 575.

As this passage suggests, courts are most likely to uphold a government's exclusion of an event from a forum if the criteria for the exclusion conform to generally accepted standards. In approaching a particular case, a court is likely to assess the motive of officials who exclude an event and examine the historic use of the facility. It is clear, in any case, that cities do not have unfettered discretion.

To avoid suppressing free speech, legislative bodies must limit the discretion of those authorities who grant or deny licenses for conducting activities protected by the First Amendment. In *Shuttlesworth* v. *Birmingham*,[19] the Supreme Court struck down a local ordinance that required individuals to obtain a permit in order to organize protest marches. The court reasoned that the ordinance afforded too much discretion to the official who was empowered to grant the permit. The court said that, because First Amendment rights were at stake, the ordinance must articulate "narrow, objective and definite standards to guide the licensing authority."[20] Otherwise, the statute would be unconstitutional.

19.
394 U.S. 147 (1969).

20.
Id. at 151.

Courts have applied the *Shuttlesworth* standard to municipal regulation of entertainment. In *Grandco Corp.* v. *Rochford*,[21] the court invalidated a Chicago ordinance empowering the mayor to grant movie theater licenses "upon a satisfactory showing that the applicant is a fit and proper person."[22] The court held that this ordinance failed the test articulated in *Shuttlesworth* because it vested too much discretion in the mayor to determine what was "fit and proper."

21.
536 F.2d 197 (7th Cir. 1976).

22.
Id. at 201.

In order to conform to this constitutional requirement, many municipal event codes limit the permit-granting discretion of administrators. Atlanta, for example, requires its commissioner to consider the following factors in evaluating an application for a permit to hold an event:

> *(1) [T]he effects the proposed festival will have upon the environment and the public health and safety; (2) Whether any inconvenience which may be suffered by the general public is outweighed by the potential benefit to the community as a whole; (3) Whether budgetary considerations at the time of the application create such a heavy burden upon the city's financial resources that it would not be practical to hold the proposed festival at the time requested; (4) Whether the holding of the festival as planned would create an undue burden upon the manpower resources of the city; and (5) Whether the public safety would be compromised substantially.*[23]

The San Francisco ordinance vests its park officials with the discretion to determine "which park facility . . . is the most suitable facility to accommodate the interests of the permittee."[24] The officials are required to consider:

> *the nature of the event, anticipated impact on the neighborhood, anticipated attendance, the policies and guidelines set forth in this resolution, the expertise and experience of the committee in organizing the type of event proposed, and any other facts and circumstances that relate to any potential adverse impact on the park property, the neighborhood or the public so long as such impacts are unrelated to the content of the event.*[25]

It is difficult to assess whether these criteria would pass the *Shuttlesworth* test. To be sure, if a court determines that a local official is considering the content of the event or otherwise abusing discretion in order to suppress particular protected expression, the court will grant relief and require the permit to be granted.

Administrative discretion is not the only means by which municipalities determine who receives a permit. San Francisco's ordinance limits to four the number of events with an anticipated audience of over 25,000 that may occur in Golden Gate Park in a year.[26] This limitation is designed to protect the park's eroding soil base. If there are more than four applications for such events, the city holds a lottery to determine who will receive the permits. Municipal code provisions that establish such methods for deciding who may receive a permit have not yet faced constitutional challenge. Presumably, if the mechanism used to determine who receives a permit is content-neutral, it will pass constitutional scrutiny.

23.
See Appendix R(1).

24.
See Appendix R(2).

25.
Id.

26.
Id.

FEES, BONDS AND INSURANCE

Municipal codes often require event organizers to pay permit fees, post bonds and obtain liability insurance in order to receive a permit. For instance, Atlanta requires applicants to pay a permit fee that is linked to the number of overtime hours that city employees will work in connection with an event.[27] Atlanta also requires an event organizer that wishes to handle clean-up responsibilities itself to post a "Sanitation Bond" to guarantee that it will adequately perform the sanitation duties.[28]

Courts will scrutinize these types of requirements under the First Amendment. For example, in *Rock Against Racism* v. *Ward*,[29] a concert promoter sued to invalidate a number of New York City regulations pertaining to the use of the Naumberg Bandshell in Central Park. Generally, the city guidelines required applicants to pay a "nonrefundable processing fee" of between $50 and $100 and to obtain liability insurance. The promoter challenged both of these requirements.

The court, in upholding the processing fee, said that permit fees that affect First Amendment rights must meet constitutional standards: "A fee must be 'closely scrutinized' to see whether it is reasonably necessary to a legitimate goal . . . [A] fee which does not exceed the cost to the city is reasonable and enforceable."[30] The court also noted that if the applicant could demonstrate indigence, the city is constitutionally obligated to waive the fee.

The city's insurance requirement did not fare as well; the court struck it down on two grounds. First, the court held that the regulation establishing the insurance requirement vested too much authority in administrative officials.[31] Second, the court reasoned that the city failed to demonstrate that requiring liability insurance was the "least restrictive means" to protect itself from damages. The court noted that the city neglected to provide evidence of any instances in which a city had incurred liability as a result of a concert by this promoter.

If a city were able to demonstrate a likelihood of facing liability, a court would probably uphold an insurance requirement. However, if the sponsor were to show that the insurance requirement would result in cancellation of the event, the First Amendment might require waiver of insurance requirements. Many local ordinances do require insurance. In order to conform to the constitutional principles articulated in *Rock Against Racism*, San Francisco's ordinance exempts First Amendment activities from bond and insurance requirements when there is evidence that compliance would be so financially burdensome as to preclude the applicant from using city property for the activity.[32] It is likely that courts would compel cities that

27.
See Appendix R(1).

28.
Id.

29.
658 F. Supp. 1346 (S.D.N.Y. 1987), *rev'd in part on other grounds,* 848 F.2d 367 (2d Cir. 1988).

30.
Id. at 1354.

31.
See Shuttlesworth, 394 U.S. 147.

32.
See Appendix Q(2).

do not have such an exception to grant one, the threshold question always being whether the First Amendment applies. Still, insurance is usually desirable from the organizer's point of view, regardless of local ordinances (see Chapter 5).

In another case involving Naumberg Bandshell and Rock Against Racism, the U.S. Supreme Court in 1989 clarified the legal standard applicable to government regulation of the time, place or manner of protected speech.[33] The Court upheld a city regulation requiring Bandshell performers to use sound-amplification equipment and a sound technician provided by the city. The Court found that the city's purpose in passing the regulation was noise control, not disagreement with the message of rock music. The Court said the relevant test of the constitutionality of the regulation was not whether there were less intrusive means of accomplishing the city's objective, but rather whether it was "narrowly tailored to serve a significant governmental interest." Under this standard, many time, place and manner restrictions on special events are likely to be upheld.

33.
Ward v. Rock Against Racism, ___ U.S. ___ (1989).

APPENDIX A
AMATEUR ELIGIBILITY SAMPLE PARAGRAPH

Sponsor covenants that it will fully cooperate with _____ to take all appropriate measures reasonably requested and deemed necessary by _____ to protect the amateur status of team members and ensure their eligibility to compete in competitions, including the (*competition*), and Sponsor covenants that it will not knowingly and willfully take or omit to take any action placing a team member's amateur status in jeopardy. Sponsor agrees that no remuneration has been or will be paid to any team member or to anyone on a team member's behalf without the prior consent and approval of _____. Appearance fees and any travel and incidental meal and lodging expenses payable by Sponsor under the terms of this Agreement will be paid or reimbursed by Sponsor in accordance with _____'s instructions.

APPENDIX B
TRADEMARK APPLICATION

In the United States Patent and Trademark Office

Mark: _____

Int'l Class No.: _____

The Commissioner of Patents and Trademarks
Trademark Operations
Washington, D.C. 20231

TRADEMARK APPLICATION

_____ is a(n)
_____ corporation with its
principal place of business at _____
_____.

1. The above identified applicant has adopted and is using the mark shown in the accompanying drawing for the following goods: (LIST ITEMS IN CAPITAL LETTERS) _____

_____

in International Class _____, and requests that said mark be registered in the United States Patent and Trademark Office on the Principal Register established by the Act of July 5, 1946.

2. The trademark was first used on the goods on _____;
was first used in interstate commerce on _____; and is
now in use in such commerce.

3. The mark is used by applying it to (the goods/the containers for the goods/displays associated with the goods/tags or labels affixed to the goods) and
five specimens showing the mark as actually used are presented herewith.

4. Applicant hereby appoints _____ and
_____, and each of them of the law firm
of _____(name of law firm)_____,
each of whom is a member of the Bar of the State of (name), to prosecute this
application for registration, to transact all business in the Patent and Trademark
Office in connection therewith, and to receive the Certificate of Registration.

(name of officer of corporation) being hereby warned that willful false statements and the like so made are punishable by fine or imprisonment, or both, under Section 1001 of Title 18 of the United States Code and that such willful false statements may jeopardize the validity of the application or any registration resulting therefrom, declares that he/she is _____(official title)_____ of applicant corporation and is authorized to execute this instrument on behalf of said corporation; he/she believes said corporation to be the owner of the trademark sought to be registered; to the best of his/her knowledge and belief, no other person, firm, corporation or association has the right to use said mark in commerce, either in the identical form or in such near resemblance thereto as may be likely, when applied to the goods of such other person, to cause confusion, or to cause mistake or to deceive; the facts set forth in this application are true, and all statements made of his/her own knowledge are true and all statements made on information and belief are believed to be true.

(name of corporation) _____

By: (signature of officer of corporation and official title of officer.) _____

(date) _____

APPENDIX C
COPYRIGHT OFFICE NOTICE REGULATIONS

37 C.F.R. § 201.20(c) Manner of affixation and position generally. (1) In all cases dealt with in this section, the acceptability of a notice depends upon its being permanently legible to an ordinary user of the work under normal conditions of use, and affixed to the copies in such manner and position that, when affixed, it is not concealed from view upon reasonable examination.

(2) Where, in a particular case notice does not appear in one of the precise locations prescribed in this section but a person looking in one of those locations would be reasonably certain to find a notice in another somewhat different location, that notice will be acceptable under this section.

(d) *Works published in book form.* In the case of works published in book form, a notice reproduced on the copies in any of the following positions is acceptable:

(1) The title page, if any;

(2) The page immediately following the title page, if any;

(3) Either side of the front cover, if any; or, if there is no front cover, either side of the front leaf of the copies;

(4) Either side of the back cover, if any; or, if there is no back cover, either side of the back leaf of the copies;

(5) The first page of the main body of the work;

(6) The last page of the main body of the work;

(7) Any page between the front page and the first page of the main body of the work, if: (i) There are no more than ten pages between the front page and the first page of the main body of the work; and (ii) the notice is reproduced prominently and is set apart from other matter on the page where it appears;

(8) Any page between the last page of the main body of the work and back page, if: (i) There are no more than ten pages between the last page of the main body of the work and the back page; and (ii) the notice is reproduced prominently and is set apart from the other matter on the page where it appears.

(9) In the case of a work published as an issue of a periodical or serial, in addition to any of the locations listed in paragraphs (d)(1) through (8) of this section, a notice is acceptable if it is located: (i) As a part of, or adjacent to, the masthead;

(ii) on the page containing the masthead if the notice is reproduced prominently and is set apart from the other matter appearing on the page; or (iii) adjacent to a prominent heading, appearing at or near the front of the issue, containing the title of the periodical or serial and any combination of the volume and issue number and date of the issue.

(10) In the case of a musical work, in addition to any of the locations listed in paragraphs (d)(1) through (9) of this section, a notice is acceptable if it is located on the first page of music.

(e) *Single-leaf works.* In the case of single-leaf works, a notice reproduced on the copies anywhere on the front or back of the leaf is acceptable.

(f) *Contribution to collective works.* For a separate contribution to a collective work to be considered to "bear its own notice of copyright,: as provided by 17 U.S.C. 404, a notice reproduced on the copies in any of the following positions is acceptable:

(1) Where the separate contribution is reproduced on a single page, a notice is acceptable if it appears: (i) Under the title of the contribution on that page; (ii) adjacent to the contribution; or (iii) on the same page if, through format, wording, or both, the application of the notice to the particular contribution is made clear;

(2) Where the separate contribution is reproduced on more than one page of the collective work, a notice is acceptable if it appears: (i) Under a title appearing at or near the beginning of the contribution; (ii) on the first page of the main body of the contribution; (iii) immediately following the end of the contribution; or (iv) on any of the pages where the contribution appears, if: (A) The contribution is reproduced on no more than twenty pages of the collective work; (B) the notice is reproduced prominently and is set apart from other matter on the page where it appears; and (C) through format, wording, or both, the application of the notice to the particular contribution is made clear.

(3) Where the separate contribution is a musical work, in addition to any of the locations listed in paragraphs (f)(1) and (2) of this section, a notice is acceptable if it is located on the first page of music of the contribution;

(4) As an alternative to placing the notice on one of the pages where a separate contribution itself appears, the contribution is considered to "bear its own notice" if the notice appears clearly in juxtaposition with a separate listing of the

contribution by title, or if the contribution is untitled, by a description reasonably identifying the contribution: (i) on the page bearing the copyright notice for the collective work as a whole, if any; or (ii) in a clearly identified and readily-accessible table of contents or listing of acknowledgments appearing near the front or back of the collective work as a whole.

(g) *Works reproduced in machine-readable copies.* For works reproduced in machine-readable copies (such as magnetic tapes of disks, punched cards, or the like, from which the work cannot ordinarily be visually perceived except with the aid of a machine or device,[1] each of the following constitute examples of acceptable methods of affixation and position of notice:

(1) A notice embodied in the copies in machine-readable form in such a manner that on visually perceptible printouts it appears either with or near the title, or at the end of the work;

(2) A notice that is displayed at the user's terminal at sign on;

(3) A notice that is continuously on terminal display; or

(4) A legible notice reproduced durably, so as to withstand normal use, on a gummed or other label securely affixed to the copies or to a box, reel, cartridge, cassette, or other container used as a permanent receptacle for the copies.

(h) *Motion pictures and other audiovisual works.* (1) The following constitute examples of acceptable methods of affixation and positions of the copyright notice on motion pictures and other audiovisual works: A notice that is embodied in the copies by a photomechanical or electronic process, in such a position that it ordinarily would appear whenever the work is performed in its entirety, and that is located; (i) With or near the title; (ii) with the cast, credits, and similar information; (iii) at or immediately following the beginning of the work; or (iv) at or immediately preceding the end of the work.

(2) In the case of an untitled motion picture or other audiovisual work whose duration is sixty seconds or less, in addition to any of the locations listed in paragraph (h)(1) of this section, a notice that is embodied in the copies by a photomechanical or electronic process, in such a position that it ordinarily would appear to the projectionist or broadcaster when preparing the work for performance, is acceptable if it is located on the leader of the film or tape immediately preceding the beginning of the work.

1.
Works published in a form requiring the use of a machine or device for purposes of optical enlargement (such as film, filmstrips, slide films, and works published in any variety of microform) and works published in visually perceptible form but used in connection with optical scanning devices, are not within this category.

(3) In the case of a motion picture or other audiovisual work that is distributed to the public for private use, the notice may be affixed, in addition to the locations specified in paragraph (h)(1) of this section, on the housing or container, if it is a permanent receptacle for the work.

(i) *Pictorial, graphic, and sculptural works.* The following constitute examples of acceptable methods of affixation and positions of the copyright notice on various forms of pictorial, graphic, and sculptural works:

(1) Where a work is reproduced in two-dimensional copies, a notice affixed directly or by means of a label cemented, sewn, or otherwise attached durably, so as to withstand normal use, of the front or back of the copies, or to any backing, mounting, matting, framing, or other material to which the copies are durably attached, so as to withstand normal use, or in which they are permanently housed, is acceptable.

(2) Where a work is reproduced in three-dimensional copies, a notice affixed directly or by means of a label cemented, sewn, or otherwise attached durably, so as to withstand normal use, to any visible portion of the work, or to any base, mounting, framing, or other material on which the copies are durably attached, so as to withstand normal use, or in which they are permanently housed, is acceptable.

(3) Where, because of the size or physical characteristics of the material in which the work is reproduced in copies. It is impossible or extremely impracticable to affix a notice to the copies directly or by means of a durable label, a notice is acceptable if it appears on a tag that is of durable material, so as to withstand normal use, and that is attached to the copy with sufficient durability that it will remain with the copy while it is passing through its normal channels of commerce.

(4) Where a work is reproduced in copies consisting of sheet-like or strip material bearing multiple or continuous reproductions of the work, the notice may be applied: (i) To the reproduction itself; (ii) to the margin, selvage, or reverse side of the material at frequent and regular intervals; or (iii) if the material contains neither a selvage nor a reverse side, to tags or labels, attached to the copies and to any spools, reels, or containers housing them in such a way that a notice is visible while the copies are passing through their normal channels of commerce.

(5) If the work is permanently housed in a container, such as a game or puzzle box, a notice reproduced on the permanent container is acceptable.

FORM TX
UNITED STATES COPYRIGHT OFFICE

REGISTRATION NUMBER

_____

TX _____ TXU _____

EFFECTIVE DATE OF REGISTRATION

_____

Month   Day   Year

DO NOT WRITE ABOVE THIS LINE. IF YOU NEED MORE SPACE, USE A SEPARATE CONTINUATION SHEET.

1

TITLE OF THIS WORK ▼

_____

PREVIOUS OR ALTERNATIVE TITLES ▼

_____

PUBLICATION AS A CONTRIBUTION If this work was published as a contribution to a periodical, serial, or collection, give information about collective work in which the contribution appeared. **Title of Collective Work ▼**

If published in a periodical or serial give: **Volume ▼**   **Number ▼**   **Issue Date ▼**   **On Pages ▼**

2

a

NAME OF AUTHOR ▼

DATES OF BIRTH AND DEATH
Year Born ▼   Year Died ▼

Was this contribution to the work a "work made for hire"?
☐ Yes
☐ No

AUTHOR'S NATIONALITY OR DOMICILE
Name of Country
OR { Citizen of ▶_____
     { Domiciled in ▶_____

WAS THIS AUTHOR'S CONTRIBUTION TO THE WORK
Anonymous? ☐ Yes ☐ No
Pseudonymous? ☐ Yes ☐ No

If the answer to either of these questions "Yes," see detailed instructions.

NATURE OF AUTHORSHIP Briefly describe nature of the material created by this author in which copyright is claimed. ▼

NOTE

Under the law, the "author" of a "work made for hire" is generally the employer, not the employee (see instructions). For any part of this work that was "made for hire" check "Yes" in the space provided, give the employer (or other person for whom the work was prepared) as "Author" of that part, and leave the space for dates of birth and death blank.

b

NAME OF AUTHOR ▼

DATES OF BIRTH AND DEATH
Year Born ▼   Year Died ▼

Was this contribution to the work a "work made for hire"?
☐ Yes
☐ No

AUTHOR'S NATIONALITY OR DOMICILE
Name of Country
OR { Citizen of ▶_____
     { Domiciled in ▶_____

WAS THIS AUTHOR'S CONTRIBUTION TO THE WORK
Anonymous? ☐ Yes ☐ No
Pseudonymous? ☐ Yes ☐ No

If the answer to either of these questions "Yes," see detailed instructions.

NATURE OF AUTHORSHIP Briefly describe nature of the material created by this author in which copyright is claimed. ▼

c

NAME OF AUTHOR ▼

DATES OF BIRTH AND DEATH
Year Born ▼   Year Died ▼

Was this contribution to the work a "work made for hire"?
☐ Yes
☐ No

AUTHOR'S NATIONALITY OR DOMICILE
Name of Country
OR { Citizen of ▶_____
     { Domiciled in ▶_____

WAS THIS AUTHOR'S CONTRIBUTION TO THE WORK
Anonymous? ☐ Yes ☐ No
Pseudonymous? ☐ Yes ☐ No

If the answer to either of these questions "Yes," see detailed instructions.

NATURE OF AUTHORSHIP Briefly describe nature of the material created by this author in which copyright is claimed. ▼

3

YEAR IN WHICH CREATION OF THIS WORK WAS COMPLETED This information must be given in all cases.
_____ ◀ Year

DATE AND NATION OF FIRST PUBLICATION OF THIS PARTICULAR WORK
Complete this information ONLY if this work has been published.
Month ▶_____ Day ▶_____ Year ▶_____
_____ ◀ Nation

4

See instructions before completing this space.

COPYRIGHT CLAIMANT(S) Name and address must be given even if the claimant is the same as the author given in space 2. ▼

TRANSFER If the claimant(s) named here in space 4 are different from the author(s) named in space 2, give a brief statement of how the claimant(s) obtained ownership of the copyright. ▼

APPLICATION RECEIVED
_____

ONE DEPOSIT RECEIVED
_____

TWO DEPOSITS RECEIVED
_____

REMITTANCE NUMBER AND DATE
_____

MORE ON BACK ▶
• Complete all applicable spaces (numbers 5-11) on the reverse side of this page.
• See detailed instructions.
• Sign the form at line 10.

DO NOT WRITE HERE

Page 1 of _____ pag

DO NOT WRITE ABOVE THIS LINE. IF YOU NEED MORE SPACE, USE A SEPARATE CONTINUATION SHEET.

PREVIOUS REGISTRATION Has registration for this work, or for an earlier version of this work, already been made in the Copyright Office?

Yes ☐ No If your answer is "Yes," why is another registration being sought? (Check appropriate box) ▼

This is the first published edition of a work previously registered in unpublished form.

This is the first application submitted by this author as copyright claimant.

This is a changed version of the work, as shown by space 6 on this application.

If your answer if "Yes," give: **Previous Registration Number ▼**   **Year of Registration ▼**

5

DERIVATIVE WORK OR COMPILATION Complete both space 6a & 6b for a derivative work; complete only 6b for a compilation.

Preexisting Material Identify any preexisting work or works that this work is based on or incorporates. ▼

Material Added to This Work Give a brief, general statement of the material that has been added to this work and in which copyright is claimed. ▼

6

See instructions before completing this space.

—space deleted—

7

REPRODUCTION FOR USE OF BLIND OR PHYSICALLY HANDICAPPED INDIVIDUALS A signature on this form at space 10, and a check in one of the boxes here in space 8, constitutes a non-exclusive grant of permission to the Library of Congress to reproduce and distribute solely for the blind and physically handicapped and under the conditions and limitations prescribed by the regulations of the Copyright Office: (1) copies of the work identified in space 1 of this application in Braille (or similar tactile symbols); or (2) phonorecords embodying a fixation of a reading of that work; or (3) both.

a ☐ Copies and Phonorecords   **b** ☐ Copies Only   **c** ☐ Phonorecords Only

8

See instructions.

DEPOSIT ACCOUNT If the registration fee is to be charged to a Deposit Account established in the Copyright Office, give name and number of Account.

Name ▼   **Account Number ▼**

9

CORRESPONDENCE Give name and address to which correspondence about this application should be sent.   Name/Address/Apt/City/State/Zip ▼

Area Code & Telephone Number ▶

Be sure to give your daytime phone number. ◀

CERTIFICATION* I, the undersigned, hereby certify that I am the

Check one ▶ ☐ author
☐ other copyright claimant
☐ owner of exclusive right(s)
☐ authorized agent of _____

of the work identified in this application and that the statements made by me in this application are correct to the best of my knowledge.

Name of author or other copyright claimant, or owner of exclusive right(s). ▲

10

Typed or printed name and date ▼ If this is a published work, this date must be the same as or later than the date of publication given in space 3.

_____ date ▶ _____

Handwritten signature (X) ▼

MAIL CERTIFICATE TO

Name ▼

Number/Street/Apartment Number ▼

City/State/ZIP ▼

Certificate will be mailed in window envelope

YOU MUST:
• Complete all necessary spaces
• Sign your application in space 10

SEND ALL 3 ELEMENTS IN THE SAME PACKAGE:
1. Application form
2. Non-refundable $10 filing fee in check or money order payable to *Register of Copyrights*
3. Deposit material

MAIL TO:
Register of Copyrights
Library of Congress
Washington, D.C. 20559

11

APPENDIX D (2)
COPYRIGHT FORM VA

FORM VA
UNITED STATES COPYRIGHT OFFICE

REGISTRATION NUMBER

VA   VAU

EFFECTIVE DATE OF REGISTRATION

Month   Day   Year

DO NOT WRITE ABOVE THIS LINE. IF YOU NEED MORE SPACE, USE A SEPARATE CONTINUATION SHEET.

1

TITLE OF THIS WORK ▼   NATURE OF THIS WORK ▼ See instructions

PREVIOUS OR ALTERNATIVE TITLES ▼

PUBLICATION AS A CONTRIBUTION If this work was published as a contribution to a periodical, serial, or collection, give information about collective work in which the contribution appeared. **Title of Collective Work ▼**

If published in a periodical or serial give: **Volume ▼**   **Number ▼**   **Issue Date ▼**   **On Pages ▼**

2

a

NAME OF AUTHOR ▼   DATES OF BIRTH AND DEATH
Year Born ▼   Year Died ▼

Was this contribution to the work a "work made for hire"?
☐ Yes
☐ No

AUTHOR'S NATIONALITY OR DOMICILE
Name of Country
OR { Citizen of ▶_____
{ Domiciled in ▶_____

WAS THIS AUTHOR'S CONTRIBUTION TO THE WORK
Anonymous?   ☐ Yes ☐ No
Pseudonymous?   ☐ Yes ☐ No

If the answer to ei of these questions "Yes," see detaile instructions.

NATURE OF AUTHORSHIP Briefly describe nature of the material created by this author in which copyright is claimed. ▼

NOTE

Under the law, the "author" of a "work made for hire" is generally the employer, not the employee (see instructions). For any part of this work that was "made for hire" check "Yes" in the space provided, give the employer (or other person for whom the work was prepared) as "Author" of that part, and leave the space for dates of birth and death blank.

b

NAME OF AUTHOR ▼   DATES OF BIRTH AND DEATH
Year Born ▼   Year Died ▼

Was this contribution to the work a "work made for hire"?
☐ Yes
☐ No

AUTHOR'S NATIONALITY OR DOMICILE
Name of Country
OR { Citizen of ▶_____
{ Domiciled in ▶_____

WAS THIS AUTHOR'S CONTRIBUTION TO THE WORK
Anonymous?   ☐ Yes ☐ No
Pseudonymous?   ☐ Yes ☐ No

If the answer to eit of these questions "Yes," see detailed instructions.

NATURE OF AUTHORSHIP Briefly describe nature of the material created by this author in which copyright is claimed. ▼

c

NAME OF AUTHOR ▼   DATES OF BIRTH AND DEATH
Year Born ▼   Year Died ▼

Was this contribution to the work a "work made for hire"?
☐ Yes
☐ No

AUTHOR'S NATIONALITY OR DOMICILE
Name of Country
OR { Citizen of ▶_____
{ Domiciled in ▶_____

WAS THIS AUTHOR'S CONTRIBUTION TO THE WORK
Anonymous?   ☐ Yes ☐ No
Pseudonymous?   ☐ Yes ☐ No

If the answer to eit of these questions "Yes," see detailed instructions.

NATURE OF AUTHORSHIP Briefly describe nature of the material created by this author in which copyright is claimed. ▼

3

YEAR IN WHICH CREATION OF THIS WORK WAS COMPLETED This information must be given in all cases.
_____ ◀ Year

DATE AND NATION OF FIRST PUBLICATION OF THIS PARTICULAR WORK
Complete this information ONLY if this work has been published.
Month ▶_____ Day ▶_____ Year ▶_____
◀ Natic

4

See instructions before completing this space.

COPYRIGHT CLAIMANT(S) Name and address must be given even if the claimant is the same as the author given in space 2. ▼

TRANSFER If the claimant(s) named here in space 4 are different from the author(s) named in space 2, give a brief statement of how the claimant(s) obtained ownership of the copyright. ▼

APPLICATION RECEIVED

ONE DEPOSIT RECEIVED

TWO DEPOSITS RECEIVED

REMITTANCE NUMBER AND DATE

MORE ON BACK ▶ • Complete all applicable spaces (numbers 5-9) on the reverse side of this page.
• See detailed instructions.   • Sign the form at line 8.

DO NOT WRITE HERE

Page 1 of _____ pag

EXAMINED BY		FORM VA
CHECKED BY		

☐ CORRESPONDENCE
Yes

☐ DEPOSIT ACCOUNT
FUNDS USED

FOR
COPYRIGHT
OFFICE
USE
ONLY

DO NOT WRITE ABOVE THIS LINE. IF YOU NEED MORE SPACE, USE A SEPARATE CONTINUATION SHEET.

PREVIOUS REGISTRATION Has registration for this work, or for an earlier version of this work, already been made in the Copyright Office?

Yes ☐ No If your answer is "Yes," why is another registration being sought? (Check appropriate box) ▼

☐ This is the first published edition of a work previously registered in unpublished form.

☐ This is the first application submitted by this author as copyright claimant.

☐ This is a changed version of the work, as shown by space 6 on this application.

If your answer if "Yes," give: **Previous Registration Number** ▼   **Year of Registration** ▼

5

DERIVATIVE WORK OR COMPILATION Complete both space 6a & 6b for a derivative work; complete only 6b for a compilation.

Preexisting Material Identify any preexisting work or works that this work is based on or incorporates. ▼

Material Added to This Work Give a brief, general statement of the material that has been added to this work and in which copyright is claimed. ▼

6

See instructions
before completing
this space.

DEPOSIT ACCOUNT If the registration fee is to be charged to a Deposit Account established in the Copyright Office, give name and number of Account.

Name ▼   **Account Number** ▼

7

CORRESPONDENCE Give name and address to which correspondence about this application should be sent.   Name/Address/Apt/City/State/Zip ▼

Area Code & Telephone Number ▶

Be sure to
give your
daytime phone
◀ number.

CERTIFICATION* I, the undersigned, hereby certify that I am the

check only one ▼

☐ author

☐ other copyright claimant

☐ owner of exclusive right(s)

☐ authorized agent of _____
Name of author or other copyright claimant, or owner of exclusive right(s) ▲

of the work identified in this application and that the statements made
by me in this application are correct to the best of my knowledge.

Typed or printed name and date ▼ If this is a published work, this date must be the same as or later than the date of publication given in space 3.

_____ date ▶ _____

Handwritten signature (X) ▼

8

**MAIL
CERTIFI-
CATE TO**

Certificate
will be
mailed in
window
envelope

| Name ▼ |
| Number/Street/Apartment Number ▼ |
| City/State/ZIP ▼ |

Have you:
• Completed all necessary
  spaces?
• Signed your application in space
  8?
• Enclosed check or money order
  for $10 payable to *Register of
  Copyrights?*
• Enclosed your deposit material
  with the application and fee?

MAIL TO: Register of Copyrights,
Library of Congress, Washington,
D.C. 20559.

9

☆ U.S. GOVERNMENT PRINTING OFFICE: 1985: 461-584/20,002

June 1985—100,000

APPENDIX E
COPYRIGHT REVISION ACT OF 1976
SELECTED PROVISIONS

Sec. 101. Definitions

A work is "fixed" in a tangible medium of expression when its embodiment in a copy or phonorecord, by or under the authority of the author, is sufficiently permanent or stable to permit it to be perceived, reproduced or otherwise communicated for a period of more than transitory duration. A work, consisting of sounds, images or both that are being transmitted, is "fixed" for purposes of this title if a fixation of the work is being made simultaneously with its transmission.

To "perform" a work means to recite, render, play, dance or act it, either directly or by means of any device or process or, in the case of a motion picture or other audiovisual work, to show its images in any sequence or to make the sounds accompanying it audible.

"Phonorecords" are material objects in which sounds, other than those accompanying a motion picture or other audiovisual work, are fixed by any method now known or later developed, and from which the sounds can be perceived, reproduced or otherwise communicated, either directly or with the aid of a machine or device. The term "phonorecord" includes the material object in which the sounds are first fixed.

To perform or display a work "publicly" means –

(1) to perform or display it at a place open to the public or at any place where a substantial number of persons outside of a normal circle of a family and its social acquaintances are gathered; or

(2) to transmit or otherwise communicate a performance or display of the work to a place specified by clause (1) or to the public by means of any device or process, whether the members of the public capable of receiving the performance or display receive it in the same place or in separate places and at the same time or at different times.

"Sound recordings" are works that result from the fixation of a series of musical, spoken or other sounds, but not including the sounds accompanying a motion picture or other audiovisual work, regardless of the nature of the material objects, such as disks, tapes or other phonorecords, in which they are embodied.

A "work made for hire" is –

(1) a work prepared by an employee within the scope of his or her employment; or

(2) a work specially ordered or commissioned for use as a contribution to a collective work, as a part of a motion picture or other audiovisual work, as a translation, as supplementary work, as a compilation, as an instructional text, as a test, as answer material for a test, or as an atlas, if the parties expressly agree in a written instrument signed by them that the work shall be considered a work made for hire. For the purpose of the foregoing sentence, a "supplementary work" is a work prepared for publication as a secondary adjunct to a work by another author for the purpose of introducing, concluding, illustrating, explaining, revising, commenting upon or assisting in the use of the other work, such as forewords, afterwards, pictorial answer material for tests, bibliographies, appendixes and indexes, and an "instructional text" is a literary, pictorial or graphic work prepared for publication with the purpose of use in systematic instructional activities.

Sec. 102. Subject Matter of Copyright: In General

(a) Copyright protection subsists, in accordance with this title, in original works of authorship fixed in any tangible medium of expression, now known or later developed from which they can be perceived, reproduced or otherwise communicated, either directly or with the aid of a machine or device. Works of authorship include the following categories:

(1) literary works;

(2) musical works, including any accompanying words;

(3) dramatic works, including any accompanying music;

(4) pantomimes and choreographic works;

(5) pictorial, graphic and sculptural works;

(6) motion pictures and other audiovisual works; and

(7) sound recordings.

(b) In no case does copyright protection for an original work of authorship extend to any idea, procedure, process, system, method of operation, concept, principle or discovery, regardless of the form in which it is described, explained, illustrated or embodied in such work.

Sec. 106. Exclusive Rights in Copyrighted Works

Subject to sections 107 through 118, the owner of copyright under this title has the exclusive rights to do and to authorize any of the following:

(1) to reproduce the copyright work in copies or phonorecords;

(2) to prepare derivative works based upon the copyrighted work;

(3) to distribute copies or phonor cords of the copyrighted work to the public by sale or other transfer of ownership, or by rental, lease or lending;

(4) in the case of literary, musical, dramatic and choreographic works, pantomimes and motion pictures and other audiovisual works, to perform the copyrighted work publicly; and

(5) in the case of literary, musical, dramatic and choreographic works, pantomimes and pictorial, graphic or sculptural works, including the individual images of a motion picture or other audiovisual work, to display the copyrighted work publicly.

Sec. 107. Limitations on Exclusive Rights: Fair Use

Notwithstanding the provisions of section 106, the fair use of a copyrighted work, including such use by reproduction in copies or phonorecords or by any other means specified by that section, for purposes such as criticism, comment, news reporting, teaching (including multiple copies for classroom use), scholarship or research, is not an infringement of copyright. In determining whether the use made of a work in any particular case is a fair use, the factors to be considered shall include:

(1) the purpose and character of the use, including whether such use is of a commercial nature or is for nonprofit educational purposes;

(2) the nature of the copyrighted work;

(3) the amount and substantiality of the portion used in relation to the copyrighted work as a whole; and

(4) the effect of the use upon the potential market for or value of the copyrighted work.

Sec. 115. Scope of Exclusive Rights in Nondramatic Musical Works: Compulsory License for Making and Distributing Phonorecords

In the case of nondramatic musical works, the exclusive rights provided by clauses (1) and (3) of section 106, to make and to distribute phonorecords of such works, and subject to compulsory licensing under the conditions specified by this section.

(a) Availability and scope of compulsory license:

(1) When phonorecords of a nondramatic musical have been distributed to the public in the United States under the authority of the copyright owner, any other person may, by complying with the provision of this section, obtain a compulsory license to make and shirtwaist phonorecords of the work. A person may obtain a compulsory license only if his or her primary purpose in making phonorecords is to distribute them to the public for private use. A person may not obtain a compulsory license for use of the work in the making of phonorecords duplicating a sound recording fixed by another unless:

(i) such sound recording was fixed lawfully; and

(ii) the making of the phonorecords was authorized by the owner of copyright in the sound recording or, if the sound recording was fixed before February 15, 1972, by any person who fixed the sound recording pursuant to an express license from the owner of the copyright in the musical work or pursuant to a valid compulsory license for use of such work in sound recording.

(2) A compulsory license includes the privilege of making a musical arrangement of the work to the extent necessary to conform it to the style or manner of interpretation of the performance involved, but the arrangement shall not change the basic melody or fundamental character of the work and shall not be subject to protection as a derivative work under this title, except with the express consent of the copyright owner. In any case, however, where the deposit, application and fee required for registration have been delivered to the Copyright Office in proper form and registration has been refused, the applicant is entitled to institute an action for infringement if notice thereof, with a copy of the complaint, is served on the Register of Copyrights. The Register may, at his or her option, become a party to the action with respect to the issue of registerability of the copyright claim by entering an appearance within sixty days after such service, but the Register's failure to become a party shall not deprive the court of jurisdiction to determine that issue.

(b) In the case of work consisting of sounds, images or both, the first fixation of which is made simultaneously with its transmission, the copyright owner may, either before or after such fixation takes place, institute an action for infringement under section 501, fully subject to the remedies provided by sections 502 through 506 and sections 509 and 510 if, in accordance with requirements that the Register of Copyrights shall prescribe by regulation, the copyright owner:

(1) serves notice upon the infringer, not less than ten or more than thirty days before such fixation, identifying the work and the specific time and source of its first transmission, and declaring an intention to source copyright in the work; and

(2) makes registration for the work within three months after its first transmission.

APPENDIX F
36 U.S.C. § 380. USE OF OLYMPIC SYMBOLS, EMBLEMS, TRADEMARKS AND NAMES

(a) Unauthorized use; civil action; lawful use prior to September 21, 1950

Without the consent of the Corporation, any person who uses for the purpose of trade, to induce the sale of any goods or services, or to promote any theatrical exhibition, athletic performance, or competition –

(1) the symbol of the International Olympic Committee, consisting of 5 interlocking rings;

(2) the emblem of the Corporation, consisting of an escutcheon having a blue chief and vertically extending red and white bars on the base with 5 interlocking rings displayed on the chief;

(3) any trademark, trade name, sign, symbol, or insignia falsely representing association with, or authorization by, the International Olympic Committee or the Corporation; or

(4) the words "Olympic," "Olympiad," "Citius Altius Fortius," or any combination or simulation thereof tending to cause confusion, to cause mistake, to deceive, or to falsely suggest a connection with the Corporation or any Olympic activity;

shall be subject to suit in a civil action by the Corporation for the remedies provided in the Act of July 5, 1946 (60 Stat. 427; popularly known as the Trademark Act of 1946) [15 U.S.C.A. 1051 et seq.]. However, any person who actually used the emblem in subsection (a)(2) of this section, or the words, or any combination thereof, in subsection (a)(4) of this section for any lawful purpose prior to September 21, 1950, shall not be prohibited by this section from continuing such lawful use for the same purpose and for the same goods or services. In addition, any person who actually used, or whose assignor actually used, any other trademark, trade name, sign, symbol, or insignia described in subsections (a)(3) and (4) of this section for any lawful purpose prior to September 21, 1950, shall not be prohibited by this section from continuing such lawful use for the same purpose and for the same goods or services.

(b) Contributors and suppliers

The Corporation may authorize contributors and suppliers of goods or services to use the trade name of the Corporation as well as any trademark, symbol, insignia, or emblem of the International Olympic Committee or of the Corporation in advertising that the contributions, goods, or services were donated, supplied, or furnished to or for the use of, approved, selected, or used by the Corporation or United States Olympic or Pan-American team or team members.

(c) Exclusive right of Corporation

The Corporation shall have exclusive right to use the name "United States Olympic Committee"; the symbol described in subsection (a)(1) of this section; the emblem described in subsection (a)(2) of this section; and the words "Olympic," "Olympiad," "Citius Altius Fortius" or any combination thereof subject to the preexisting rights described in subsection (a) of this section.

APPENDIX G
ASCAP CONCERT AND FESTIVALS LICENSE

AGREEMENT between AMERICAN SOCIETY OF COMPOSERS, AUTHORS, AND PUBLISHERS ("SOCIETY"), located at _____ and _____ ("LICENSEE"), located at _____ as follows:

1. Grant and Term of License

(a) SOCIETY grants and LICENSEE accepts for a term of one year, commencing _____, and continuing thereafter for additional terms of one year each unless terminated by either party as hereinafter provided, a license to perform publicly at each of the locations specified in Schedule "A," annexed hereto and made a part hereof, as said schedule may be amended as hereinafter provided ("the premises"), and not elsewhere, nondramatic renditions of the separate musical compositions now or hereafter during the term hereof in the repertory of SOCIETY, and of which SOCIETY shall have the right to license such performing rights.

(b) LICENSEE agrees to give SOCIETY notice in advance of any additional premises owned or operated by LICENSEE where music is to be performed during the term hereof, and Schedule "A" shall thereafter be deemed amended to include such additional premises. Such notice shall include all information as to "LICENSEE's Operating Policy" (as hereinafter defined) required for each of the premises by this agreement.

(c) Either party may, on or before thirty days prior to the end of the initial term or any renewal term, give notice of termination to the other. If such notice is given the agreement shall terminate on the last day of such initial or renewal term.

2. Limitations on License

(a) This license is not assignable or transferable by operation of law or otherwise, and is limited to the LICENSEE and to the premises.

(b) This license does not authorize the broadcasting, telecasting, or transmission by wire or otherwise, of renditions of musical compositions in SOCIETY's repertory to persons outside of the premises.

(c) This license is limited to nondramatic performances, and does not authorize any dramatic performances. For purposes of this agreement, a dramatic performance shall include, but not be limited to, the following:

(i) performance of a "dramatico-musical work" (as hereinafter defined) in its entirety;

(ii) performance of one or more musical compositions from a "dramatico-musical work" (as hereinafter defined) accompanied by dialogue, pantomime, dance, stage action, or visual representation of the work from which the music is taken;

(iii) performance of one or more musical compositions as part of a story or plot, whether accompanied or unaccompanied by dialogue, pantomime, dance, stage action, or visual representation;

(iv) performance of a concert version of a "dramatico-musical work" (as hereinafter defined). The term "dramatico-musical work" as used in this agreement, shall include, but not be limited to, a musical comedy, oratorio, choral work, opera, play with music, revue, or ballet.

3. License Fee

(a) In consideration of the license granted herein, LICENSEE agrees to pay SOCIETY the applicable license fee set forth in the rate schedule annexed hereto and made part hereof, based on "LICENSEE's Operating Policy" (as hereinafter defined) for each of the premises, payable quarterly in advance on January 1, April 1, July 1 and October 1 of each year. The term "Licensee's Operating Policies," as used in this agreement, shall be deemed to mean all of the factors which determine the license fee applicable to each of the premises under said rate schedule.

(b) LICENSEE warrants that the Statement of LICENSEE's Operating Policy annexed hereto for each of the premises is true and correct.

(c) Said license fee totals _____ Dollars ($_____) annually, based on the facts set forth in said Statement(s) of LICENSEE's Operating Policy.

4. Changes in Licensee's Operating Policy

(a) LICENSEE agrees to give SOCIETY thirty days' prior notice of any change in LICENSEE's Operating Policy for any of the premises. For purposes of this agreement, a change in LICENSEE's Operating Policy shall be one in effect for no less than thirty days.

(b) Upon any such change in LICENSEE's Operating Policy resulting in an increase in the license fee, based on the annex rate schedule, LICENSEE shall pay said increased license fee, effective as of the initial date of such change, whether or not notice of such change has been given pursuant to paragraph 4(a) of this agreement.

(c) Upon any such change in LICENSEE's Operating Policy resulting in a reduction of the license fee, based on the annexed rate schedule, LICENSEE shall be entitled to such reduction, effective as of the initial date of such change, and to a pro rata credit for any unearned license fees paid, in advance, provided LICENSEE has given SOCIETY thirty days notice of such change. If LICENSEE fails to give such prior notice, any such reduction and credit shall be effective thirty days after LICENSEE gives notice of such change.

(d) In the event of any such change in LICENSEE's Operating Policy, LICENSEE shall furnish a current Statement of LICENSEE's Operating Policy and shall certify that it is true and correct.

(e) If LICENSEE discontinues the performance of music at all of the premises, LICENSEE or SOCIETY may terminate this agreement upon thirty days' prior notice, the termination to be effective at the end of such thirty-day period. In the event of such termination, SOCIETY shall refund to LICENSEE a pro rata share of any unearned license fees paid in advance. For purposes of this agreement, a discontinuance of music shall be one in effect for no less than thirty days.

5. Breach or Default

Upon any breach or default by LICENSEE of any term or condition herein contained, SOCIETY may terminate this license by giving LICENSEE thirty days' notice to cure such breach or default, and in the event that such breach or default has not been cured within said thirty days, this license shall terminate on the expiration of such thirty-day period without further notice from SOCIETY. In the event of such termination, SOCIETY shall refund to LICENSEE any unearned license fees paid in advance.

6. Notices

All notices required or permitted hereunder shall be given in writing by certified United States mail sent to either party at the address stated above. Each party agrees to inform the other of any change of address.

IN WITNESS WHEREOF, this agreement has been duly executed by SOCIETY and LICENSEE this _____ day of _____, 19_____.

AMERICAN SOCIETY OF COMPOSERS, AUTHORS AND PUBLISHERS

By: (District Manager) _____

(Licensee) _____

By: (Title) _____

_____

(Fill in capacity in which signed: (a) if corporation, state corporate office held; (b) if partnership, write word "partner" under signature of signing partner; (c) if individual owner, write "individual owner" under signature.)

SCHEDULE "A"

List of the Premises

Name   **Address**

RATE SCHEDULE –
FESTIVALS AND SIMILAR EVENTS

Capacity (As Specified by Local Fire Code)	Rate Per Day
Up to 6,000 persons	$ 50.00
6,001 to 12,000 persons	$ 75.00
12,001 to 25,000 persons	$100.00
Over 25,001 persons	$150.00

The above rate schedule covers the use of live and mechanical music in conjunction with each festival. However, it is not applicable to musical events (such as live concerts or dances) presented before or after the show. In such circumstances, SOCIETY's concert rate schedule shall apply.

DISCOUNTS: Twenty-five or more shows. A discount of 20% may be deducted from the above fees for payment for each show in excess of twenty-five performed by LICENSEE during the contract year or any renewal term thereof. _____

STATEMENT OF LICENSEE'S OPERATING POLICY

1) Name of Event _____

2) Days Presented: From _____ To _____

3) Number of days event will be presented: _____

4) Capacity:
   Day (1) _____
   Day (2) _____
   Day (3) _____
   Day (4) _____

(If festival exceeds four days, please indicate daily capacity for remaining days on the back of this form.)

Rate based on above policy: $_____

CERTIFICATE

I hereby certify that the foregoing Statement of Operating Policy is true and correct as of this _____ day of _____, 19_____.

LICENSEE

By: _____

Capacity:
Day (5) _____
Day (6) _____
Day (7) _____
Day (8) _____
Day (9) _____
Day (10) _____
Day (11) _____
Day (12) _____

CONCERTS AND RECITALS
PER CONCERT LICENSE AGREEMENT

AGREEMENT between AMERICAN SOCIETY OF COMPOSERS, AUTHORS, AND PUBLISHERS ("SOCIETY"), located at _____
and _____ ("Licensee"),
located at _____ as follows:

1. Grant and Term of License

(a) SOCIETY grants and LICENSEE accepts for a term of one year commencing _____, and continuing thereafter for additional terms of one year each unless terminated by either party as hereinafter provided, a license to perform publicly at concerts or recitals in the United States presented by or under the auspices of LICENSEE, and not elsewhere, nondramatic renditions of the separate musical compositions now or hereafter during the term hereof in the repertory of SOCIETY, and of which society shall have the right to license such performing rights.

(b) This agreement shall inure to the benefit of and shall be binding upon the parties hereto and their respective successors and assigns, but no assignment shall relieve the parties hereto of their respective obligations hereunder as to performances rendered, acts done and obligations incurred prior to the effective date of the assignment.

(c) Either party may, on or before thirty days prior to the end of the initial term or any renewal term, give notice of termination to the other. If such notice is given the agreement shall terminate on the last day of such initial or renewal term.

2. Limitations on License

(a) This license is not assignable or transferable by operation of law, devolution or otherwise, except as provided in Paragraph "1(b)" hereof, and is strictly limited to the LICENSEE and to the premises where each concert or recital is presented.

(b) This license does not authorize the broadcasting or telecasting or transmission by wire or otherwise, of renditions of musical compositions in SOCIETY's repertory to persons outside of the premises.

(c) This license is limited to nondramatic performances, and does not authorize any dramatic performances. For purposes of this agreement, a dramatic performance shall include, but not be limited to, the following:

(i) performance of a "dramatico-musical work" (as hereinafter defined) in its entirety;

(ii) performance of one or more musical compositions from a "dramatico-musical work" (as hereinafter defined) accompanied by dialogue, pantomime, dance, stage action, or visual representation of the work from which the music is taken;

(iii) performance of one or more musical compositions as part of a story or plot, whether accompanied or unaccompanied by dialogue, pantomime, dance, stage action, or visual representation;

(iv) performance of a concert version of a "dramatico-musical work" (as hereinafter defined). The term "dramatico-musical work" as used in this agreement, shall include, but not be limited to, a musical comedy, oratorio, choral work, opera, play with music, revue, or ballet.

(d) This license does not authorize the performance of any special orchestral arrangements or transcriptions of any musical composition in the repertory of SOCIETY, unless such arrangements or transcriptions have been copyrighted by members of SOCIETY or foreign societies which have granted SOCIETY the right to license such performances.

(e) SOCIETY reserves the right at any time to restrict the first American performance of any composition in its repertory and further reserves the right at any time to withdraw from its repertory and from operation of this license, any musical work as to which any suit has been brought or threatened on a claim that such composition infringes a composition not contained in SOCIETY's repertory, or on a claim that SOCIETY does not have the right to license the performing rights in such composition.

3. License Fees

In consideration of the license granted herein, LICENSEE agrees to pay SOCIETY the applicable license fee set forth in the rate schedule annexed hereto and made a part hereof, for each concert or recital at which a nondramatic performance of any copyrighted musical composition in the SOCIETY's repertory occurs.

4. Reports of Concerts and Payment of License Fees

(a) At least one week prior to the presentation of any concert or recital by LICENSEE, LICENSEE shall submit to SOCIETY:

(i) Written notice of such concert or recital, on forms supplied free of charge by SOCIETY, including the date and place of such concert or recital, name of the artists or performers appearing, seating capacity, and highest price of admission exclusive of tax; and

(ii) Payment of any license fee required by and set forth in Paragraph "3" hereof.

(b) Within one week after the presentation of any concert or recital licensed hereunder, LICENSEE shall submit to SOCIETY a program containing a list of all musical works, including encores, performed at such concert or recital.

5. Breach or Default

Upon any breach or default by LICENSEE of any term or condition herein contained, SOCIETY may terminate this license by giving LICENSEE thirty days' notice to cure such breach or default, and in the event that such breach or default has not been cured within said thirty days, this license shall terminate on the expiration of such thirty-day period without further notice from SOCIETY.

6. Failure to Report Concerts or Recitals and Pay License Fees

In the event LICENSEE presents any concert or recital during the course of which any copyrighted musical composition in SOCIETY's repertory is performed, and LICENSEE fails to report such concert or recital and pay license fees to SOCIETY as required by Paragraph "4" hereof, this license shall not extend to such concert or recital and such performances shall be deemed to be infringements of the respective copyrights unless such performances have been licensed by SOCIETY's member(s) in interest. Such failure to report and pay license fees shall be a breach and default under this agreement pursuant to Paragraph "5" hereof.

7. Interference in Society's Operations
In the event of:

(a) any major interference with the operations of SOCIETY in the state, territory, dependency, possession or political subdivision in which LICENSEE is located, by reason of any law of such state, territory, dependency, possession or political subdivision; or

(b) any substantial increase in the cost to SOCIETY of operating in such state, territory, dependency, possession or political subdivision, by reason of any law of such state, territory, dependency, possession or political subdivision, which is applicable to the licensing of performing rights, SOCIETY shall have the right to terminate this agreement forthwith by written notice.

8. Notices
All notices required or permitted hereunder shall be given in writing by certified United States mail sent to either party at the address stated above. Each party agrees to inform the other of any change of address.

IN WITNESS WHEREOF, this agreement has been duly executed by SOCIETY and LICENSEE this day of _____, 19_____.

AMERICAN SOCIETY OF COMPOSERS, AUTHORS AND PUBLISHERS

By: _____

(Licensee)

By: _____

(Title)_____

(Fill in capacity in which signed: (a) if corporation, state corporate office held; (b) if partnership, write word "partner" under signature of signing partner; (c) if individual owner, write "individual owner" under signature.)

PER CONCERT LICENSE RATE SCHEDULE

Seating Capacity*	Ticket Price									
	$0.00 to $3.00	$3.01 to $6.00	$6.01 to $9.00	$9.01 to $12.00	$12.01 to $15.00	$15.01 to $18.00	$18.01 to $21.00	$21.01 to $25.00	$25.01 to $30.00	OVER $30.00
0 - 250	11	21	35	53	71	90	113	135	158	188
251 - 500	17	27	41	59	78	98	120	143	165	195
501 - 750	23	33	47	66	86	105	128	150	173	203
751 - 1,000	29	39	54	77	99	120	146	173	195	233
1,001 - 1,500	36	50	66	90	113	135	165	195	225	263
1,501 - 2,000	44	62	80	105	128	150	188	225	263	308
2,001 - 3,000	53	71	89	116	138	168	206	248	285	338
3,001 - 4,000	62	80	98	128	150	188	225	270	315	375
4,001 - 5,500	80	98	120	150	188	225	270	315	360	420
5,501 - 7,500	98	120	150	188	225	270	315	360	405	465
7,501 - 10,000	120	150	188	225	270	315	360	405	450	510
10,001 - 15,000	150	188	225	270	315	360	405	450	495	555
15,001 - 20,000	188	225	270	315	360	405	450	495	540	600
20,001 - 25,000	225	270	315	360	405	450	495	540	585	660
25,001 - 30,000	270	315	360	405	450	495	550	600	660	735
30,001 - 40,000	315	360	405	450	495	540	615	675	735	810
40,001 - 50,000	375	420	465	510	555	615	675	750	810	885
50,001 - 60,000	435	480	525	570	615	675	750	825	885	975
over 60,000	525	570	615	660	705	765	825	900	975	1088

* Where concert or recital occurs at a location whose total seating capacity has been altered to accommodate a particular performance, the term "seating capacity" shall mean the total number of seats made available for that particular performance.

APPENDIX H
47 U.S.C. § 508. "PAYOLA"

(a) Subject to subsection (d) of this section, any employee of a radio station who accepts or agrees to accept from any person (other than such station), or any person (other than such station) who pays or agrees to pay such employee, any money, service or other valuable consideration for the broadcast of any matter over such station shall, in advance of such broadcast, disclose the fact of such acceptance or agreements to such station.

(b) Subject to subsection (d) of this section, any person who, in connection with the production or preparation of any program or program matter which is intended for broadcasting over any radio station, accepts or agrees to accept, or pays or agrees to pay, any money, service or other valuable consideration for the inclusion of any matter as a part of such program or program matter shall, in advance of such broadcast, disclose the fact of such acceptance or payment or agreement to the payee's employer, or to the person for whom such program or program matter is being produced, or to the licensee of such station over which such program is broadcast.

(c) Subject to subsection (d) of this section, any person who supplies to any other person any program or program matter which is intended for broadcasting over any radio station shall, in advance of such broadcast, disclose to such other person any information of which he has knowledge, or which has been disclosed to him, as to any money, service or other valuable consideration which any person has paid or accepted, or has agreed to pay or accept, for the inclusion of any matter as a part of such program or program matter.

(d) The provisions of this section requiring the disclosure of information shall not apply in any case where, because of a waiver made by the Commission under section 317(d) of this title, an announcement is not required to be made under section 317 of this title.

(e) The inclusion in the program of the announcement required by section 317 of this title shall constitute the disclosure required by this section.

(f) The term "service or other valuable consideration" as used in this section shall not include any service or property furnished without charge or at a nominal charge for use on, or in connection with, a broadcast, or for use on a program which is intended for broadcasting over any radio station unless it is so furnished in consideration for an identification in such broadcast or in such program of any person, product, service, trademark or brand name beyond an identification which is reasonably related to the use of such service or property in such broadcast or such program.

(g) Any person who violates any provision of this section shall, for each such violation, be fined not more than $10,000 or imprisoned not more than one year, or both.

APPENDIX I
ILLINOIS DRAMSHOP ACT

Ill. Rev. Stat. Chp. 43 ¶ 135. Actions for damages caused by intoxication – Lessor's liability – Forfeiture of lease – Maximum recovery – Limitations – Jurisdiction – Service

§ 6.21. **(a)** Every person who is injured within this State, in person or property, by any intoxicated person has a right of action in his or her own name, severally or jointly, against any person, licensed under the laws of this State or of any other state to sell alcoholic liquor, who, by selling or giving alcoholic liquor, within or without the territorial limits of this State, causes the intoxication of such person.*** Any person owning, renting, leasing or permitting the occupation of any building or premises with knowledge that alcoholic liquors are to be sold therein, or who having leased the same for other purposes, shall knowingly permit therein the sale of any alcoholic liquors that have caused the intoxication of any person, shall be liable, severally or jointly, with the person selling or giving the liquors.*** All damages recovered by a minor under this Act shall be paid either to the minor, or to his or her parent, guardian or next friend as the court shall direct. The unlawful sale or gift of alcoholic liquor works a forfeiture of all rights of the lessee or tenant under any lease or contract of rent upon the premises where the unlawful sale or gift takes place. All actions for damages under this Act may be by any appropriate action in the circuit court. An action shall lie for injuries to means of support caused by an intoxicated person or in consequence of the intoxication of any person resulting as hereinabove set out. The action, if the person from whom support was furnished is living, shall be brought by any person injured in means of support in his or her name for his or her benefit and the benefit of all other persons injured in means of support. However, any person claiming to be injured in means of support and not included in any action brought hereunder may join by motion made within the times herein provided for bringing such action or the personal representative of the deceased person from whom such support was furnished may so join. In every such action the jury shall determine the amount of damages to be recovered imposed by this Section. The amount recovered in every such action is for the exclusive benefit of the person injured in loss of support and shall be distributed to such persons in the proportions determined by the verdict rendered or judgment entered in the action. If the right of action is settled by agreement with the personal representative of a deceased person from whom support was furnished, the court having jurisdiction of the estate of the deceased person shall distribute the amount of the settlement to the person injured in loss of support in the proportion, as determined by the court, that the percentage of dependency of each such person upon the deceased person bears to the sum of the percentage of dependency of all such persons upon the deceased person.*** For all causes of action involving persons injured, killed, or incurring property damage after September 12, 1985, in no event shall the judgment or recovery for injury to the person or property of any person exceed $30,000 for each person incurring damages, and recovery under this Act for loss of means of support resulting from the death or injury of any person shall not exceed $40,000. Nothing in this Section bars any person from making separate claims which, in the aggregate, exceed any one limit where such person incurs more than one type of compensable damage, including personal injury, property damage, and loss to means of support. However, all persons claiming loss to means of support shall be limited to an aggregate recovery not to exceed the single limitation set forth herein for the death or injury of each person from whom support is claimed.

Nothing in this Act shall be construed to confer a cause of action for injuries to the person or property of the intoxicated person himself, nor shall anything in this Act be construed to confer a cause of action for loss of means of support on the intoxicated person himself or on any person claiming to be supported by such intoxicated person. In conformance with the rule of statutory construction enunciated in the general Illinois saving provision in Section 4 of "An Act to revise the law in relation to the construction of the statutes," approved March 5, 1874, as amended, no amendment of this Section purporting to abolish or having the effect of abolishing a cause of action shall be applied to invalidate a cause of action accruing before its effective date, irrespective of whether the amendment was passed before or after the effective date of this amendatory Act of 1986.

Each action hereunder shall be barred unless commenced within one year next after the cause of action accrued.

However, a licensed distributor or brewer whose only connection with the furnishing of alcoholic liquor which is alleged to have caused intoxication was the furnishing or maintaining of any apparatus for the dispensing or cooling of beer is not liable under this Section, and if such licensee is named as a defendant, a proper motion to dismiss shall be granted.

(b) Any person licensed under any state or local law to sell alcoholic liquor, whether or not a citizen or resident of this State, who in person or through an agent causes the intoxication, by the sale or gift of alcoholic liquor, of any person who, while intoxicated, causes injury to any person or property in the State of Illinois thereby submits such licensed person, and, if an individual, his or her personal representative, to the jurisdiction of the courts of this State for a cause of action arising under subsection (a) above.

Service of process upon any person who is subject to the jurisdiction of the courts of this State, as provided in this subsection, may be made by personally serving the summons upon the defendant outside this State, as provided in the Code of Civil Procedure, as now or hereafter amended, with the same force and effect as though summons had been personally served within this State.

Only causes of action arising under subsection (a) above may be asserted against a defendant in an action in which jurisdiction over him or her is based upon this subsection.

Nothing herein contained limits or affects the right to serve any process in any other manner now or hereafter provided by law.

APPENDIX J
ILLINOIS NOT-FOR-PROFIT
INCORPORATION LAW

Article 3. Purposes and Powers

Ill. Rev. Stats. Chp. 32 § 103.05. Purposes and authority of corporations – particular purposes – exemptions.

§ 103.05. Purposes and authority of corporations – particular purposes – exemptions. (a) Not-for-profit corporations may be organized under this Act of any one or more of the following or similar purposes:

(1) Charitable;

(2) Benevolent;

(3) Eleemosynary;

(4) Educational;

(5) Civic;

(6) Patriotic;

(7) Political;

(8) Religious;

(9) Social;

(10) Literary;

(11) Athletic;

(12) Scientific;

(13) Research;

(14) Agricultural;

(15) Horticultural;

(16) Soil improvement;

(17) Crop improvement;

(18) Livestock or poultry improvement;

(19) Professional, commercial, industrial or trade association;

(20) Promoting the development, establishment or expansion of industries; * * *

§ 103.10. General powers. Each corporation shall have power:

(a) To have perpetual succession by its corporate name unless a limited period of duration is stated in its articles of incorporation;

(b) To sue and be sued, complain and defend, in its corporate name;

(c) To have a corporate seal which may be altered at pleasure, and to use the same by causing it, or a facsimile thereof, to be impressed or affixed or in any other manner reproduced, provided that the affixing of a corporate seal to an instrument shall not give the instrument additional force or effect, or change the construction thereof, and the use of a corporate seal is not mandatory;

(d) To purchase, take, receive, lease as lessee, take by gift, devise, or bequest, or otherwise acquire, and to own, hold, hold as trustee, use, and otherwise deal in and with any real or personal property, or any interest therein situated in or out of this State;

(e) To sell and convey, mortgage, pledge, lease as lessor, and otherwise dispose of all or any part of its property and assets;

(f) To lend money to its officers, employees and agents except as limited by Section 108.80 of this Act;

(g) To purchase, take, receive, subscribe for, or otherwise acquire, own, hold, vote, use, employ, sell, mortgage, loan, pledge, or otherwise dispose of, and otherwise use and deal in and with, shares or other interests in, or obligations of, other domestic or foreign corporations, whether for profit or not for profit, associations, partnerships or individuals;

(h) To incur liabilities, to borrow money for its corporate purposes at such rates of interest as the corporation may determine without regard to the restrictions of any usury law of this State, to issue its notes, bonds and other obligations; to secure any of its obligations by mortgage, pledge, or deed of trust of all or any of its property, franchises, and income; and to make contracts, including contracts of guaranty and suretyship;

(i) To invest its funds from time to time and to lend money for its corporate purposes, and to take and hold real and personal property as security for the payment of funds so invested or loaned;

(j) To conduct its affairs, carry on its operations, and have offices within and without this State and to exercise in any other state, territory, district, or possession of the United States, or in any foreign county, the powers granted by this Act;

(k) To elect or appoint officers and agents of the corporation, and define their duties and fix their compensations;

(l) To make and alter bylaws, not inconsistent with its articles of incorporation or with the laws of this State, except as provided in Section 102.30 of this Act, for the administration and regulation of the affairs of the corporation;

(m) To make donations in furtherance of any of its purposes, to lend money to the State or Federal government; and to conduct any lawful affairs in aid of the United States;

(n) To cease its corporate activities and surrender its corporate franchise;

(o) To establish deferred compensation plans, pension plans, and other incentive plans for its directors, officers and employees and to make the payments provided for therein;

(p) To indemnify its directors, officers, employees or agents in accordance with and to the extent permitted by Section 108.75 of this Act and other applicable provisions of law;

(q) To be a promoter, partner, member, associate or manager of any partnership, joint venture or other enterprise; and

(r) To have and exercise all powers necessary or convenient to effect any or all of the purposes for which the corporation is formed.

Article 6. Shares; Dividends; Contributions

§ 106.05. Shares and dividends prohibited. A corporation shall not have or issue shares. No dividend shall be paid and no part of the money, property or other assets of a corporation shall be distributed to its members, directors, officers; provided, however, that a corporation may pay compensation in a reasonable amount to members, officers or directors for services rendered, including for service as a director only, and may make distributions pursuant to Section 109.10 of this Act or upon dissolution or final liquidation as permitted by Article 12 of this Act.[1]

1.
Paragraph 112.05 *et seq.* of this chapter.

§ 106.10. Evidence of contribution. A contribution of a member may be evidenced by a written instrument delivered to the member, but such instrument shall not be denominated a "share of stock" or by any word or term implying that the instrument is a share as such term is used in the Business Corporation Act of 1983 as now in effect or as hereafter amended.[2]

2.
Paragraph 1.01 *et seq.* of this chapter.

Article 7. Members

§ 107.03. Members. (a) A corporation may have one or more classes of members or may have no members.

(b) If the corporation has one or more classes of members, the designation of such class or classes and the qualifications and rights of the members of each class shall be set forth in the articles of incorporation or the bylaws.

(c) If the corporation is to have no members, that fact shall be set forth in the articles of incorporation or the bylaws.

(d) A corporation may issue certificates evidencing membership therein.

(e) The transfer of a certificate of membership in a not-for-profit corporation in which assets are held for a charitable, religious, eleemosynary, benevolent or educational purpose, shall be without payment of any consideration of money or property of any kind or value to the transferor in respect to such transfer. Any transfer in violation of this Section shall be void.

(f) Where the articles of incorporation or bylaws provide that a corporation shall have no members, or where a corporation has under its articles of incorporation, bylaws or in fact no members entitled to vote on a matter, any provision of this act requiring notice to, the presence of, or the vote, consent or other action by members of the corporation in connection with such matter shall be satisfied by notice to, the presence of, or the vote, consent or other action of the directors of the corporation.

* * *

Article 8. Directors and Officers
§ 108.05. Board of directors. (a) Each corporation shall have a board of directors and the affairs of the corporation shall be managed by or under the direction of the board of directors.

(b) The articles of incorporation or bylaws may prescribe qualifications for directors. A director need not be a resident of this State or a member of the corporation unless the articles of incorporation or bylaws so prescribe. The articles of incorporation or the bylaws may prescribe other qualifications for directors.

(c) Unless otherwise provided in the articles of incorporation or bylaws, the board of directors, by the affirmative vote of a majority of the directors then in office, shall have authority to establish reasonable compensation of all directors for services to the corporation as directors, officers or otherwise, notwithstanding the provisions of Section 108.60 of this Act.

(d) No director may act by proxy on any matter.

* * *

§ 108.40. Committees. (a) If the articles of incorporation or bylaws so provide, a majority of the directors may create one or more committees and appoint directors or such other persons as the board designates, to serve on the committee or committees. Each committee shall have two or more directors, a majority of its membership shall be directors, and all committee members shall serve at the pleasure of the board.

(b) Unless the appointment by the board of directors requires a greater number, a majority of any committee shall constitute a quorum, and a majority of committee members present and voting at a meeting at which a quorum is present is necessary for committee action. A committee may act by unanimous consent in writing without a meeting and, subject to the provisions of the bylaws or action by the board of directors, the committee by majority vote of its members shall determine the time and place of meetings and the notice required therefor.

(c) To the extent specified by the board of directors or in the articles of incorporation or bylaws, each committee may exercise the authority of the board of directors under Section 108.05 of this Act; provided, however, a committee may not:

(1) Adopt a plan for the distribution of the assets of the corporation, or for dissolution;

(2) Approve or recommend to members any act this Act requires to be approved by members;

(3) Fill vacancies on the board or on any of its committees;

(4) Elect, appoint or remove any officer or director or member of any committee, or fix the compensation of any member of a committee;

(5) Adopt, amend, or repeal the bylaws or the articles of incorporation;

(6) Adopt a plan of merger or adopt a plan of consolidation with another corporation, or authorize the sale, lease, exchange or mortgage of all or substantially all of the property or assets of the corporation; or

(7) Amend, alter, repeal or take action inconsistent with any resolution or action of the board of directors when the resolution or action of the board of directors provides by its terms that it shall not be amended, altered or repealed by action of a committee.

(d) The board of directors may create and appoint persons to a commission, advisory body or other such body which may or may not have directors as members, which body may not act on behalf of the corporation or bind it to any action but may make recommendations to the board of directors or to the officers.

* * *

§ 108.50. Officers. (a) A corporation shall have such officers as shall be provided in the bylaws. Officers and assistant officers and agents as may be deemed necessary may be elected or appointed by the board of directors or chosen in such other manner as may be prescribed by the bylaws. If the bylaws so provide, any two or more offices may be held by the same person. One officer, in this Act generally referred to as the secretary, shall have the authority to certify the bylaws, resolutions of the members and board of directors and committees thereof, and other documents of the corporation as true and correct copies thereof.

(b) All officers and agents of the corporation, as between themselves and the corporation, shall have such express authority and perform such duties in the management of the property and affairs of the corporation as may be provided in the bylaws, or as may be determined by resolution of the board of directors not inconsistent with the bylaws and such implied authority as recognized by the common law from time to time.

(c) The articles of incorporation or the bylaws may provide that any one or more officers of the corporation or any other person holding a particular office outside the corporation shall be a director or directors while he or she holds that office. Unless the articles of incorporation or the bylaws provide otherwise, such director or directors shall have the same rights, duties and responsibilities as other directors.

* * *

§ 108.65. Liability of directors in certain cases. (a) In addition to any other liabilities imposed by law upon directors of a corporation, they are liable as follows:

(1) The directors of a corporation who vote for or assent to any distribution not authorized by Section 109.10 or Article 12 of this Act[3] shall be jointly and severally liable to the corporation for the amount of such distribution.

(2) If a dissolved corporation shall proceed to bar any known claims against it under Section 112.75 of this Act, the directors of such corporation who fail to take reasonable steps to cause the notice required by Section 112.75 of this Act to be given to any known creditor of such corporation shall be jointly and severally liable to such creditor for all loss and damage occasioned thereby.

(3) The directors of a corporation that conducts its affairs after the filing by the Secretary of State of articles of dissolution, otherwise than so far as may be necessary for the winding up thereof, shall be jointly and severally liable to the creditors of such corporation for all debts and liabilities of the corporation incurred in so conducting its affairs.

3.
Paragraph 11.205 *et seq.* of this chapter.

(b) A director of a corporation who is present at a meeting of its board of directors at which action on any corporate matter is taken is conclusively presumed to have assented to the action taken unless his or her dissent or abstention is entered in the minutes of the meeting or unless he or she files his or her written dissent or abstention to such meeting with the person acting as the secretary of the meeting before the adjournment thereof or forwards such dissent or abstention by registered or certified mail to the secretary of the corporation immediately after the adjournment of the meeting. Such right to dissent or abstain does not apply to a director who voted in favor of such action.

(c) A director shall not be liable for a distribution of assets to any person in excess of the amount authorized by Section 109.10 or Article 12 of this Act if he or she relied and acted in good faith upon a balance sheet and profit and loss statement of the corporation represented to him or her to be correct by the president or the officer of such corporation having charge of its books of account, or certified by an independent public or certified public accountant or firm of such accountants to fairly reflect the financial condition of such corporation, nor shall he or she be so liable if in good faith in determining the amount available for any such distribution he or she considered the assets to be of their book value.

(d) Any director against whom a claim is asserted under this Section and who is held liable thereon is entitled to contribution from the other directors who are likewise liable thereon. Any director against whom a claim is asserted for the improper distribution of assets of a corporation, and who is held liable thereon, is entitled to contribution from the persons who knowingly accepted or received any such distribution in proportion to the amounts received by them respectively.

§ 108.70. Limited liability of directors, officers and persons who serve without compensation. (a) No director or officer serving without compensation, other than reimbursement for actual expenses, of a corporation organized under this Act and exempt, or qualified for exemption, from taxation pursuant to Section 501(c) of the Internal Revenue Code of 1986, as amended, shall be liable, and no cause of action may be brought for damages resulting from the exercise of judgment or discretion in connection with the duties or responsibilities of such director or officer unless the act or omission involved willful or wanton conduct.

(b) No director of a corporation organized under this Act for the purposes identified in items (14), (19), (21) and (22) of subsection (a) of Section 103.05 of this Act, and exempt or qualified for exemption from taxation pursuant to Section 501(c) of the Internal Revenue Code of 1986, as amended, shall be liable, and no cause of action may be brought for damages resulting from the exercise of judgment or discretion in connection with the duties or responsibilities of such director unless: (1) such director earns in excess of $5,000 per year from his duties as director, other than reimbursement for actual expenses; or (2) the act or omission involved willful or wanton conduct.

(c) No person, who, without compensation, other than reimbursement for actual expenses, renders service to or for a corporation organized under this Act and exempt, or qualified for exemption from taxation pursuant to Section 501(c)(3) of the Internal Revenue Code of 1986, as amended, shall be liable, and no cause of action may be brought for damages resulting from an act or omission in rendering such services unless the act or omission involved willful or wanton conduct.

(d) As used in this Section "willful or wanton conduct" means a course of action which shows an actual or deliberate intention to cause harm or which, if not intentional, shows an utter indifference to or conscious disregard for the safety of others or their property.

(e) Nothing in this Section is intended to bar any cause of action against the corporation or change the liability of the corporation arising out of an act or omission of any director, officer or person exempt from liability for negligence under this Section.

§ 108.75. Indemnification of officers, directors, employees and agents; insurance.
(a) A corporation may indemnify any person who was or is a party, or is threatened to be made a party to any threatened, pending or completed action, suit or proceeding, whether civil, criminal, administrative or investigative (other than an action by or in the right of the corporation) by reason of the fact that he or she is or was a director, officer, employee or agent of the corporation, or who is or was serving at the request of the corporation as a director, officer, employee or agent of another corporation, partnership, joint venture, trust or other enterprise, against expenses (including attorneys' fees), judgments, fines and amounts paid in settlement actually and reasonably incurred by such person in connection with such action, suit or proceeding, if such person acted in good faith and in a manner he or she reasonably believed to be in, or not opposed to, the best interests of the corporation, and, with respect to any criminal action or proceeding, had no reasonable cause to believe his or her conduct was unlawful. The termination of any action, suit or proceeding by judgment, order, settlement, conviction, or upon a plea of *nolo contendere* or its equivalent, shall not, of itself, create a presumption that the person did not act in good faith and in a manner which he or she

reasonably believed to be in or not opposed to the best interests of the corporation or, with respect to any criminal action or proceeding, that the person had reasonable cause to believe that his or her conduct was unlawful.

(b) A corporation may indemnify any person who was or is a party, or is threatened to be made a party to any threatened, pending or completed action or suit by or in the right of the corporation to procure a judgment in its favor by reason of the fact that such person is or was a director, officer, employee or agent of the corporation, or is or was serving at the request of the corporation as a partnership, joint venture, trust or other enterprise, against expenses (including attorneys' fees) actually and reasonably incurred by such person in connection with the defense or settlement of such action or suit, if such person acted in good faith and in a manner he or she reasonably believed to be in, or not opposed to, the best interests of the corporation, provided that no indemnification shall be made in respect of any claim, issue or matter as to which such person shall have been adjudged to be liable for negligence or misconduct in the performance of his or her duty to the corporation, unless, and only to the extent that the court in which such action or suit was brought shall determine upon application that, despite the adjudication of liability, but in view of all the circumstances of the case, such person is fairly and reasonably entitled to indemnity for such expenses as the court shall deem proper.

(c) To the extent that a director, officer, employee or agent of a corporation has been successful, on the merits or otherwise, in the defense of any action, suit or proceeding referred to in subsections (a) and (b), or in the defense of any claim, issue or matter therein, such person shall be indemnified against expenses (including attorneys' fees) actually and reasonably incurred by such person in connection therewith.

(d) Any indemnification under subsections (a) and (b) (unless ordered by a court) shall be made by the corporation only as authorized in the specific case, upon a determination that indemnification of the director, officer, employee or agent is proper in the circumstances because he or she has met the applicable standard of conduct set forth in subsections (a) or (b). Such determination shall be made (1) by the board of directors by a majority vote of a quorum consisting of directors who were not parties to such action, suit or proceeding, or (2) if such a quorum is not obtainable, or even if obtainable, if a quorum of disinterested directors so directs, by independent legal counsel in a written opinion, or (3) by the members entitled to vote, if any.

(e) Expenses incurred in defending a civil or criminal action, suit or proceeding may be paid by the corporation in advance of the final disposition of such action, suit or proceeding, as authorized by the board of directors in the specific case, upon receipt of an undertaking by or on behalf of the director, officer, employee or agent to repay such amount, unless it shall ultimately be determined that he or she is entitled to be indemnified by the corporation as authorized in this Section.

(f) The indemnification provided by this Section shall not be deemed exclusive of any other rights to which those seeking indemnification may be entitled under any bylaw, agreement, vote of members or disinterested directors, or otherwise, both as to action in his or her official capacity and as to action in another capacity while holding such office, and shall continue as to a person who has ceased to be a director, officer, employee or agent, and shall inure to the benefit of the heirs, executors and administrators of such a person.

(g) A corporation may purchase and maintain insurance on behalf of any person who is or was a director, officer, employee or agent of the corporation, or who is or was serving at the request of the corporation as a director, officer, employee or agent of another corporation, partnership, joint venture, trust or other enterprise, against any liability asserted against such person and incurred by such person in any such capacity, or arising out of his or her status as such, whether or not the corporation would have the power to indemnify such person against such liability under the provisions of this Section.

(h) In the case of a corporation with members entitled to vote, if a corporation has paid indemnity or has advanced expenses under this Section to a director, officer, employee or agent, the corporation shall report the indemnification or advance in writing to the members entitled to vote with or before the notice of the next meeting of the members entitled to vote.

(i) For purposes of this Section, references to "the corporation" shall include, in addition to the surviving corporation, any merging corporation (including any corporation having merged with a merging corporation) absorbed in a merger which, if its separate existence had continued, would have had the power and authority to indemnify its directors, officers, employees or agents, so that any person who was a director, officer, employee or agent of such merging corporation, or was serving at the request of such merging corporation as a director, officer, employee or agent of another corporation, partnership, joint venture, trust or other enterprise, shall stand in the same position under the provisions of this Section with respect to the surviving corporation as such person would have with respect to such merging corporation if its separate existence had continued.

(j) For purposes of this Section, references to "other enterprises" shall include employee benefit plans; references to "fines" shall include any excise taxes assessed on a person with respect to an employee benefit plan; and references to "serving at the request of the corporation" shall include any service as a director, officer, employee or agent of the corporation which imposes duties on, or involves services by such director, officer, employee, or agent with respect to an employee benefit plan, its participants, or beneficiaries. A person who acted in good faith and in a manner he or she reasonably believed to be in the best interests of the participants and beneficiaries of an employee benefit plan shall be deemed to have acted in a manner "not opposed to the best interests of the corporation" as referred to in this Section.

§ 108.80. Prohibited loans to directors and officers. Except as permitted by subsection (e) of Section 108.75, no loan shall be made by a corporation to a director or officer except that a loan may be made to a director or officer who is employed by the corporation, is authorized by a majority of the non-employed directors and either (a) in the case of a corporation organized for and holding property for any charitable, religious, eleemosynary, benevolent, educational or similar purpose, the purpose of such loan is to provide financing for the principal residence of the employed director or officer upon receipt of adequate collateral consisting of marketable real estate or securities readily capable of valuation or (b) the loan is otherwise in furtherance of the purposes of the corporation and in the ordinary course of its affairs. The directors of a corporation who vote for or assent to the making of a loan to any non-employed director or non-employed officer of the corporation, or otherwise prohibited by this Section, and any other person knowingly participating in the making of such loan, shall be jointly and severally liable to the corporation for the amount of such loan until the repayment thereof.

* * *

Article 9. Distributions

§ 109.10. Distributions prior to dissolution. (a) The board of directors of a corporation may authorize, and the corporation may make, distributions of its money, property, or other assets, other than upon dissolution and final liquidation, subject to the limitations of subsection (d) of this Section, only:

(1) To any person or organization who or which has made payments to the corporation for goods or services, as a fractional repayment of such payments, provided all such persons or organizations in any category are repaid on an equal pro rata basis; or

(2) To any person or organization as a repayment of his, her or its contribution of an amount not to exceed the amount of the contribution, provided that any assets held for any charitable, religious, eleemosynary, benevolent, educational or similar purpose or held upon a condition requiring return, shall continue to be so restricted. The articles of incorporation or the bylaws may provide that the membership rights of a member cease upon the repayment, in whole, of the contribution of such member.

(b) Any payment or transfer of money, property or other assets in furtherance of any of the purposes of the corporation shall not be deemed a distribution for the purposes of this Article and this Section shall not be construed as limiting the purposes and powers of a corporation as set forth in Article 3 of this Act.[4]

(c) All distributions by a corporation permitted by this Section shall be at the option of the corporation only and at such amount or amounts, within the period or periods, and on such terms and conditions, not inconsistent with the purpose of the corporation and this Act, as are stated in, or fixed by the board of directors pursuant to authority granted by, the articles of incorporation or the bylaws.

(d) No distribution under subsection (a) may be made if, after giving it effect:

(1) The corporation would be insolvent; or

(2) The net assets of the corporation would be less than zero; or

(3) The corporation would be rendered unable to carry on its corporate purposes.

(e) The board of directors may base a determination that a distribution may be made under subsection (d) either on financial statements prepared on the basis of accounting practices and principles that are reasonable in the circumstances or on a fair valuation or other method that is reasonable in the circumstances.

(f) The effect of a distribution under subsection (d) is measured as of the earlier of:

(1) The date of its authorization if payment occurs within 120 days after the date of authorization or the date of payment if payment occurs more than 120 days after the date of authorization; or

(2) In the case of a repayment of a contribution in which the membership rights of a member cease, the earlier of (i) the date money or other property is transferred or debt incurred by the corporation or (ii) the date the membership rights of the member cease.

* * *

Article 12. Dissolution

§ 112.16. Distribution of assets. The assets of a corporation in the process of dissolution shall be applied and distributed as follows:

(a) All liabilities and obligations of the corporation shall be paid, satisfied and discharged, or adequate provision shall be made therefor;

(b) Assets held by the corporation upon condition requiring return, transfer or conveyance, which condition occurs by reason of the dissolution, shall be returned, transferred or conveyed in accordance with such requirements;

(c) Assets held for a charitable, religious, eleemosynary, benevolent, educational or similar use, but not held upon a condition requiring return, transfer or conveyance by reason of the dissolution, shall be transferred or conveyed to one or more domestic or foreign corporations, societies or organizations engaged in activities substantially similar to those of the dissolving corporation, pursuant to a plan of distribution adopted as provided in this Act;

(d) To the extent that the articles of incorporation or bylaws determine the distributive rights of members, or any class or classes of members, or provide for distribution to others, other assets, if any, shall be distributed in accordance with such provisions;

(e) Any remaining assets may be distributed to such societies, organizations or domestic or foreign corporations, whether for profit or not for profit, as may be specified in a plan of distribution adopted as provided in Section 112.17 of this Act.

* * *

§ 112.30. Effect of dissolution. (a) Dissolution of a corporation terminates its corporate existence and a dissolved corporation shall not thereafter conduct any affairs except those necessary to wind up and liquidate its affairs, including:

(1) Collecting its assets;

(2) Disposing of its assets that will not be distributed in kind;

(3) Giving notice in accordance with Section 112.75 of this Act and discharging or making provisions for discharging its liabilities;

(4) Distributing its remaining assets in accordance with this Act; and

(5) Doing such other acts as are necessary to wind up and liquidate its affairs.

(b) After dissolution, a corporation may transfer good and merchantable title to its assets as authorized by its board of directors or in accordance with its bylaws.

(c) Dissolution of a corporation does not:

(1) Transfer title to the corporation's assets;

(2) Effect any change in the bylaws of the corporation or otherwise affect the regulation of the affairs of the corporation except that all action shall be directed to winding up the affairs of the corporation;

(3) Prevent suit by or against the corporation in its corporate name;

(4) Abate or suspend a proceeding pending by or against the corporation on the effective date of dissolution.

§ 112.35. Grounds for administrative dissolution. The Secretary of State may dissolve any corporation administratively if:

(a) It has failed to file its annual report as required by this Act before the first day of the anniversary month of the corporation of the year in which such annual report becomes due;

(b) It has failed to file in the office of the Secretary of State any report after the expiration of the period prescribed in this Act for filing such report;

(c) It has failed to appoint and maintain a registered agent in this State; or

(d) The Secretary of State receives notification from a local liquor commissioner, pursuant to Section 4-4(3) of "The Liquor Control Act of 1934," as now or hereafter amended,[5] that an organization incorporated under this Act and functioning as a club has violated that Act by selling or offering for sale at retail alcoholic liquors without a retailer's license.

* * *

5.
Chapter 43, ¶ 112.

APPENDIX K
STATE LAWS REGULATING CHARITABLE SOLICITATIONS

As of December 31, 1987

State/Regulatory Agency	Charitable Organizations Registration or Licensing Requirements	Fund Raisers Counsel Registration and Bonding Requirements
Alabama Attorney General Consumer Protection Div. Montgomery, AL 36130 205-261-3550	–	–
Alaska Attorney General Dept. of Law 1301 W. 4th Avenue Anchorage, AK 99501 907-276-3550	–	–
Arizona Attorney General 1275 West Washington Phoenix, AZ 85007 602-255-1719	–	–
Arkansas Secretary of State Trademarks Department Little Rock, AR 72201 501-371-5167	Registration	Registration. $5,000 Bond.
California Registry of Charitable Trusts 1718 3rd Street Sacramento, CA 94203-4470 916-445-2021	Registration	–
Colorado Attorney General Dept. of Law 1525 Sherman Street Denver, CO 80203 303-866-3611	–	–
Connecticut Attorney General Public Charities Unit 30 Trinity Street Hartford, CT 06106 203-566-5836	Registration	Registration. $20,000 bond if fund raiser has custody or control of contributions. Must file contracts with Department.

State/Regulatory Agency	Charitable Organizations Registration or Licensing Requirements	Fund Raisers Counsel Registration and Bonding Requirements
Delaware Attorney General Civil Division The Wilmington Tower Wilmington, DE 19899 302-571-2528	–	–
District of Columbia Dept. of Consumer & Regulatory Affairs 614 H Street NW Washington, DC 20001 202-727-7086	Licensing	–
Florida Department of State Division of Licensing The Capital-#4 Tallahassee, FL 32399 904-488-5381	Registration	Licensing. $10,000 bond for professional solicitors. No bond requirement for Consultant.
Georgia Secretary of State Office of Special Services 2 Martin Luther King Dr. Suite 802-West Tower Atlanta, GA 30334 404-656-4910	Registration	Registration. $10,000 or 50% of fund raiser's income for preceding year, whichever is greater.
Hawaii Dept. of Commerce & Consumer Affairs P.O. Box 40 Honolulu, HI 96810 808-548-5319	Registration	Licensing. $5,000 bond.
Idaho Attorney General Statehouse Boise, ID 83720 208-334-2400	–	–

State/Regulatory Agency	Charitable Organizations Registration or Licensing Requirements	Fund Raisers Counsel Registration and Bonding Requirements
Illinois Attorney General Charitable Trust Div. 100 West Randolph 12th Floor Chicago, IL 60601-3175 312-917-2595	Registration, Religious organization also required to register, but may apply for exemption.	Registration. $5,000 bond.
Indiana Attorney General Consumer Protection Div. 219 State House Indianapolis, IN 46204 317-232-4522	–	Registration
Iowa Attorney General Consumer Protection Div. 1300 East Walnut Hoover State Off. Bldg. Des Moines, IA 50319	Registration with Secretary of State. [Requirement has been declared unconstitutional, but is still on the books.]	–
Kansas Secretary of State Capitol Bldg.- 1st Floor Topeka, KS 66612 913-296-3751	Registration	Registration. $5,000 bond.
Kentucky Attorney General Division of Consumer Protection Frankfort, KY 40601 502-564-2200	Registration if required to file 990.	Registration
Louisiana Attorney General Dept. of Justice Consumer Protection Div. Baton Rouge, LA 70806 504-342-7013	Registration	Registration

State/Regulatory Agency	Charitable Organizations Registration or Licensing Requirements	Fund Raisers Counsel Registration and Bonding Requirements
Maine Dept. of Business, Occupation & Professional Regulation Station #35 August, ME 04333 207-289-3671	Registration	Registration. $10,000 bond.
Maryland Secretary of State State House Annapolis, MD 21401 301-974-3425	Registration	Registration
Massachusetts Attorney General Division of Public Charities One Ashburton Place Boston, MA 02108 617-727-2235	Registration	Licensing. $10,000 bond. Bond only for solicitors.
Michigan Attorney General Charitable Trust Section 690 Law Building 525 West Ottawa Street Lansing, MI 48913 517-335-0855	Licensing	Licensing. $10,000 Bond.
Minnesota Attorney General Charities Division 340 Bremer Tower 7th Pl. & Minnesota St. St. Paul, MN 55101 612-296-6172	Registration	Registration. $20,000 bond if fund-raiser has custody of funds.
Mississippi Attorney General Carroll Gartin Justice Bldg. P.O. Box 220 Jackson, MS 39205-0220 601-359-3680	–	Registration

State/Regulatory Agency	Charitable Organizations Registration or Licensing Requirements	Fund Raisers Counsel Registration and Bonding Requirements
Missouri Attorney General P.O. Box 899 Jefferson City, MO 65102 314-751-2616	Registration	Registration
Montana Secretary of State Room 225 Capitol Station Helena, MT 59520 406-444-3665	–	–
Nebraska Secretary of State Lincoln, NE 68509 402-471-2554	Certificate granted on basis of letter of approval obtained from county attorney of home office county.	–
Nevada Attorney General Carson City, NV 89710 702-687-4170	–	–
New Hampshire Attorney General Charitable Trust Concord, NH 03301 603-271-3591	Registration	Registration if fund-raiser has custody of funds: $10,000 bond.
New Jersey Charities Registration Section 1100 Raymond Blvd. Newark, NJ 07102 201-648-4002	Registration	Registration. $10,000 bond.
New Mexico Attorney General Charitable Organization Registry P.O. Drawer 1508 Santa Fe, NM 87504-1508 505-827-6910	Registration	Registration

State/Regulatory Agency	Charitable Organizations Registration or Licensing Requirements	Fund Raisers Counsel Registration and Bonding Requirements
New York Office of Charities Registration Department of State Albany, NY 12231 518-474-3720	Registration	Registration. $10,000 bond.
North Carolina Department of Human Resources Solicitation Licensing Branch 701 Balbour Drive Raleigh, NC 27603 919-733-4510	Registration [Some provisions of statute ruled unconstitutional by U.S. District Court. Case on appeal before U.S. Supreme Court.]	Licensing. $20,000 bond if fund raiser has custody of funds.
North Dakota Secretary of State Bismark, ND 58505 701-466-3180	Licensing	Registration
Ohio Attorney General Charitable Foundation Section State Office Tower 30 East Broad Street Columbus, OH 43266-0410 614-466-3180	Registration	Registration. $5,000 bond.
Oklahoma Income Tax Division Oklahoma Tax Commission 2501 Lincoln Boulevard Oklahoma City, OK 73194 405-521-4293	Registration	Registration. $2,500 bond.
Oregon Attorney General Portland, OR 97204 503-229-5725	Registration	Registration
Pennsylvania Dept. of State Bureau of Charitable Organizations Room 308, North Office Bldg. Harrisburg, PA 17120 717-783-1720	Registration	Registration. $10,000 bond.

State/Regulatory Agency	Charitable Organizations Registration or Licensing Requirements	Fund Raisers Counsel Registration and Bonding Requirements
Rhode Island Dept. of Business Regulations Providence, RI 02903 401-277-3048	Registration	Registration. $10,000 bond.
South Carolina Secretary of State Columbia, SC 29211 803-734-2169	Registration	Registration. $5,000 bond.
South Dakota Attorney General State Capitol Pierre, SD 57501 605-773-3215	Registration	–
Tennessee Secretary of State James K. Polk Bldg. Suite 500 Nashville, TN 37219-5040	Registration	Registration. $10,000 bond.
Texas Attorney General Charitable Trust Section P.O. Box 12548 Austin, TX 78711 512-463-2002	–	–
Utah Dept. of Business Reg. Div. of Consumer Prot. P.O. Box 45802 Salt Lake City, UT 84145-0801 801-530-6601	Registration/Permit. (Application for permit must include estimate of % of proceeds allocated to charity.)	Registration. $10,000 bond.
Vermont Attorney General 109 State Street Montpelier, VT 05602 802-828-3171	–	–

State/Regulatory Agency	Charitable Organizations Registration or Licensing Requirements	Fund Raisers Counsel Registration and Bonding Requirements
Virginia Office of Consumer Affairs P.O. Box 1163 Richmond, VA 23209 804-786-1343	Registration	Registration. $20,000 bond.
Washington Charities Division Office of the Secretary of State Legislative Building (MS-AS-22) Olympia, WA 98504 206-753-7121	Registration	Registration. $15,000 bond for paid if paid counsel has custody of funds.
West Virginia Secretary of State Capitol Building Charleston, WV 25305 304-345-4000	Registration	Registration. $10,000 bond.
Wisconsin Dept. of Regulation & Licensing P.O. Box 8935 Madison, WI 53708 608-266-0829	Registration	Registration. $5,000 bond.
Wyoming Secretary of State Capitol Building 200 W. 24th Cheyenne, WY 82002 307-777-7378	–	–

APPENDIX L (1)
CALIFORNIA BUSINESS AND PROFESSIONS CODE § 17510. CHARITABLE SOLICITATIONS

§ 17510. Legislative findings and declaration

(a) The Legislature finds that there exists in the area of solicitations and sales solicitations for charitable purposes a condition which has worked fraud, deceit and imposition upon the people of the state which existing legal remedies are inadequate to correct. Many solicitations or sales solicitations for charitable purposes have involved situations where funds are solicited from the citizens of this state for charitable purposes, but an insignificant amount, if any, of the money solicited and collected actually is received by any charity. The charitable solicitation industry has a significant impact upon the well-being of the people of this state. The provisions of this article relating to solicitations and sale solicitations for charitable purposes are, therefore, necessary for the public welfare.

(b) The Legislature declares that the purpose of this article is to safeguard the public against fraud, deceit and imposition, and to foster and encourage fair solicitations and sales solicitations for charitable purposes, wherein the person from whom the money is being solicited will know what portion of the money will actually be utilized for charitable purposes. This article will promote legitimate solicitations and sales solicitation for charitable purposes and restrict harmful solicitation methods, thus the people of this state will not be misled into giving solicitors a substantial amount of money which may not in fact be used for charitable purposes.

§ 17510.2. Definitions

(a) As used in this article, "solicitation for charitable purposes" means any request, plea, entreaty, demand or invitation, or attempt thereof, to give money or property in connection with which:

(1) any appeal is made for charitable purposes; or

(2) the name of any charity, philanthropic or charitable organization is used or referred to in any such appeal as an inducement for making any such gift; or

(3) any statement is made to the effect that such gift or any part thereof will go to or be used for any charitable purpose or organization.

(b) As used in this article, "sales solicitation for charitable purposes" means the sale of, offer to sell, or attempt to sell any advertisement, advertising space, book, card, chance, coupon device, magazine subscription, membership, merchandise, ticket of admission or any other thing or service in connection with which:

(1) any appeal is made for charitable purposes; or

(2) the name of any charity, philanthropic or charitable organization is used or referred to in any such appeal as an inducement for making any such sale; or

(3) any statement is made to the effect that the whole or any part of the proceeds from such sale will go to or be used for any charitable purpose or organization.

(c) A solicitation for charitable purposes, or a sale, offer or attempt to sell for charitable purposes, shall include the making or disseminating or causing to be made or disseminated before the public in this state, in any newspaper or other publication, or any advertising device, or by public outcry or proclamation, or in any other manner or means whatsoever any such solicitation.

(d) For purposes of this article, "charity" shall include any person who, or any nonprofit community organization, fraternal, benevolent, educational, philanthropic or service organization, or governmental employee organization which, solicits or obtains contributions solicited from the public for charitable purposes or holds any assets for charitable purposes.

§ 17510.3. Solicitation or sales solicitation for charitable purposes; disclosure requirements; noncompliance by volunteer solicitor

(a) Prior to any solicitation or sales solicitation for charitable purposes, the solicitor or seller shall exhibit to the prospective donor or purchaser a card entitled "Solicitation or Sale for Charitable Purposes Card." The card shall be signed and dated under penalty of perjury by an individual who is a principal, staff member or officer of the soliciting organization. The card shall give the name and address of the soliciting organization or the person who signed the card and the name and business address of the paid individual who is doing the actual soliciting.

In lieu of exhibiting a card, the solicitor or seller may distribute during the course of the solicitation any printed material, such as a solicitation brochure, provided such material complies with the standards set forth below, and provided that the solicitor or seller informs the prospective donor or purchaser that such information as required below is contained in the printed material.

Information on the card or printed material shall be presented in at least 10-point type and shall include the following:

(1) the name and address of the combined campaign, each organization or fund on behalf of which all or any part of the money collected will be utilized for charitable purposes.

(2) if there is no organization or fund, the manner in which the money collected will be utilized for charitable purposes.

(3) the amount, stated as a percentage of the total gift or purchase price, that will be used for charitable purposes.

(4) if paid fund raisers are paid a set fee rather than a percentage of the total amount raised, the card shall show the total cost that is estimated will be used for direct fundraising expenses.

(5) if the solicitation is not a sale solicitation, the card may state, in place of the amount of fundraising expenses, that an audited financial statement of such expenses may be obtained by contacting the organization at the address disclosed.

(6) the nontax-exempt status of the organization or fund, if the organization or fund for which the money or funds are being solicited does not have a charitable tax exemption under both federal and state law.

(7) the percentage of the total gift or purchase price which may be deducted as a charitable contribution under federal and state law. If no portion is so deductible, the card shall state that "this contribution is not tax deductible."

(8) if the organization making the solicitation represents any nongovernmental organization by any name which includes, but is not limited to, the terms "officer," "peace officer," "police," "law enforcement," "reserve officer," "deputy," "California Highway Patrol," "Highway Patrol," or "deputy sheriff," which would reasonably be understood to imply that the organization is composed of law enforcement personnel, the solicitor shall give the total number of members in the organization and the number of members working or living within the country where the solicitation is being made, and if the solicitation is for advertising, the statewide circulation of the publication in which the solicited ad will appear.

(b) Knowing and willful noncompliance by any individual volunteer who receives no compensation of any type from or in connection with a solicitation by any charitable organization shall subject the solicitor or seller to the penalties of the law.

(c) When the solicitation is not a sale solicitation, any individual volunteer who receives no compensation of any type from, or in connection with, a solicitation by any charitable organization may comply with the disclosure provisions by providing the name and address of the charitable organization on behalf of which all or any part of the money collected will be utilized for charitable purposes, by stating the charitable purposes for which the solicitation is made, and by stating to the person solicited that information about revenues and expenses of such organization, including its administration and fundraising costs, may be obtained by contacting the organization's office at the address disclosed. Such organization shall provide such information to the person solicited within seven days after receipt of the request.

(d) A volunteer who receives no compensation of any type from, or in connection with, a solicitation or sale solicitation by a charitable organization which has qualified for a tax exemption under Section 501(c)(3) of the Internal Revenue Code of 1954, and who is 18 years of age or younger, is not required to make any disclosures pursuant to this section.

§ 17510.4. Initial solicitation without direct personal contact; disclosure of information; delivery of card

If the initial solicitation or sales solicitation is made by radio, television, letter, telephone or any other means not involving direct personal contact with the person solicited, this solicitation shall clearly disclose the information required by Section 17510.3. This disclosure requirement shall not apply to any radio or television solicitation of 60 seconds or less. If the gift is subsequently made or the sale is subsequently consummated, the solicitation or sale for charitable purposes card shall be mailed to or otherwise delivered to the donor, or to the buyer with the item or items purchased.

§ 17510.7. In lieu compliance with city or county ordinances; preemption

Compliance with any city or county ordinance which provides for disclosure of information relating to solicitations or sales solicitations for charitable purposes substantially similar to and no less than the disclosure requirements of this article shall be deemed to satisfy the requirements of this article. The provisions of this article are not intended to preempt any city or county ordinance.

APPENDIX L (2)
ILLINOIS REV. STATS. CH. 23.
SOLICITATION OF FUNDS FOR CHARITABLE PURPOSES

5101. Definitions

§ 1. The following words and phrases as used in this Act shall have the following meanings unless a different meaning is required by the context.

(a) "Charitable organization." Any benevolent, philanthropic, patriotic or eleemosynary person or one purporting to be such which solicits and collects funds for charitable purposes and includes each local, county or area division within this State of such charitable organization, provided such local, county or area division has authority and discretion to disburse funds or property otherwise than by transfer to any parent organization.

(b) "Contribution." The promise or grant of any money or property of any kind or value, including the promise to pay, except payments by members or an organization for membership fees, dues, fines or assessments, or for services rendered to individual members, if membership in such organizations confers a bona fide right, privilege, professional standing, honor or other direct benefit, other than the right to vote, elect officers or hold offices, and except money or property received from any governmental authority. Reference to the dollar amount of "contributions" in this Act means, in the case of promises to pay or payments for merchandise or rights of any other description, the value of the total amount promised to be paid or paid for such merchandise or rights and not merely that portion of the purchase price to be applied to a charitable purpose.

(c) "Person." Any individual, organization, group, association, partnership, corporation, trust or any combination of them.

(d) "Professional fund raiser." Any person who, for compensation or other consideration, plans, conducts, manages or carries on any drive or campaign in this State for the purpose of soliciting contributions for or on behalf of any charitable organization or any other person, or who engages in the business of, or holds himself out to persons in the State as independently engaged in the business of, soliciting contributions for such purposes. A bona fide officer or employee of a charitable organization shall not be deemed a professional fund raiser unless his salary or other compensation is computed on the basis of funds to be raised or actually raised.

(e) "Professional solicitor." Any person who is employed or retained for compensation by a professional fund raiser to solicit contributions for charitable purposes from persons in this State.

(f) "Charitable purpose." Any charitable, benevolent, philanthropic, patriotic or eleemosynary purpose.

5102. Registration statement – Filing – Contents – Duration – Notice of changes – Reports – Books and records – Administration of Act.

§ 2. (a) Every charitable organization, except as otherwise provided in Section 3 of this Act, which solicits or intends to solicit contributions from persons in this State by any means whatsoever shall, prior to any solicitation, file with the Attorney General upon forms prescribed by him a registration statement which shall include the following information:

1. The name of the organization and the name or names under which it intends to solicit contributions.

2. The names and addresses of the officers, directors, trustees and chief executive officer of the organization.

3. The addresses of the organization and the addresses of any offices in this State. If the organization does not maintain a principal office, the name and address of the person having custody of its financial records.

4. Where and when the organization was legally established, the form of its organization and its tax exempt status.

5. The purpose for which the organization is organized and the purpose or purposes for which the contributions to be solicited will be used.

6. The date on which the fiscal year of the organization ends.

7. Whether the organization is authorized by any other governmental authority to solicit contributions and whether it is or has ever been enjoined by any court from soliciting contributions.

8. The names and addresses of any professional fund raisers who are acting or have agreed to act on behalf of the organization.

9. Methods by which solicitation will be made.

10. Copies of contracts between charitable organizations and professional fund raisers relating to financial compensation or profit to be derived by the professional fund raisers. Where any such contract is executed after filing of registration statement, a copy thereof shall be filed within 10 days of the date of execution.

11. Board, group or individual having final discretion as to the distribution and use of contributions received.

(b) The registration statement shall be signed by the president or other authorized officer and the chief fiscal officer of the organization.

(c) Such registration shall remain in effect unless it is either cancelled as provided in this Act or withdrawn by the organization.

(d) Every registered organization shall notify the Attorney General within 10 days of any change in the information required to be furnished by such organization under paragraphs 1 through 11 of subdivision (a) of this Section.

(e) In no event shall a registration of a charitable organization continue, or be continued, in effect after the date such organization should have filed, but failed to file, an annual report in accordance with the requirements of Section 4 of this Act, and such organization shall not be eligible to file a new registration until it shall have filed the required annual report with the Attorney General. If such report is subsequently filed, such organization may file a new registration.

(f) Subject to reasonable rules and regulations adopted by the Attorney General, the register, registration statements, annual reports, financial statements, professional fund raisers' contracts, bonds, applications for registration and re-registration, and other documents required to be filed with the Attorney General shall be open to public inspection.

Every person subject to this Act shall maintain accurate and detailed books and records at the principal office of the organization to provide the information required herein. All such books and records shall be open to inspection at all reasonable times by the Attorney General or his duly authorized representative.

(g) Where any local, county or area division of a charitable organization is supervised and controlled by a superior or parent organization, incorporated, qualified to do business, or doing business within this State, such local, county or area division shall not be required to register under this Section if the superior or parent organization files a registration statement on behalf of the local, county or area division in addition to or as part of its own registration statement. Where a registration statement has been filed by a superior or parent organization as provided in Section 2(g) of this Act, it shall file the annual report required under Section 4 of this Act on behalf of the local, county or area division in addition to or as part of its own report, but the accounting information required under Section 4 of this Act shall be set forth separately and not in consolidated form with respect to every local, county or area division which raises or expends more than $4,000.

(h) The Attorney General may make rules of procedure and regulations necessary for the administration of this Act. Copies of all such rules of procedure and regulations and of all changes therein, duly certified by the Attorney General, shall be filed in the office of the Secretary of State.

5103. Exemptions from registration

§ 3. (a) Upon initial filing of a registration statement pursuant to Section 2 of this Act and notification by the Attorney General of his determination that the organizational purposes specified in this paragraph for exemption are actual and genuine, this Act shall not apply to a corporation sole or other religious corporation, trust or organization incorporated or established for religious purposes, nor to any agency or organization incorporated or established for charitable, hospital or educational purposes and engaged in effectuating one or more of such purposes that is affiliated with, operated by, or supervised or controlled by a corporation sole or other religious corporation, trust or organization incorporated or established for religious purposes, nor to other religious agencies or organizations which serve religion by the preservation of religious rights and freedom from persecution or prejudice or by fostering religion, including the moral and ethical aspects of a particular religious faith.

(b) The following persons shall not be required to register with the Attorney General:

1. The University of Illinois, Southern Illinois University, Eastern Illinois University, Illinois State Normal University, Northern Illinois University, Western Illinois University, all educational institutions that are recognized by the State Board of Education or that are accredited by a regional accrediting association or by an organization affiliated with the National Commission on Accrediting, any foundation having an established identity with any of the aforementioned educational institutions, any other educational institution confining its solicitation of contributions to its student body, alumni, faculty and trustees, and their families, or a library established under the laws of this State, provided that the annual financial

report of such institution or library shall be filed with the State Board of Education, Governor, Illinois State Library, County Library Board or County Board, as provided by law.

2. Fraternal, patriotic, social, educational, alumni organizations and historical societies when solicitation of contributions is confined to their membership. This exemption shall be extended to any subsidiary of a parent or superior organization exempted by Subparagraph 2 of Paragraph (b) of Section 3 of this Act where such solicitation is confined to the membership of the subsidiary, parent or superior organization.

3. Persons requesting any contributions for the relief or benefit of any individual, specified by name at the time of the solicitation, if the contributions collected are turned over to the named beneficiary, first deducting reasonable expenses for costs of banquets or social gatherings, if any, provided all fund raising functions are carried on by persons who are unpaid, directly or indirectly, for such services.

4. Any charitable organization which does not intend to solicit and receive and does not actually receive contributions in excess of $4,000 during any 12 month period ending June 30th of any year, provided all of its fund raising functions are carried on by persons who are unpaid for such services. However, if the gross contributions received by such charitable organization during any 12 month period ending June 30th of any year shall be in excess of $4,000, it shall, within 30 days after the date it shall have received total contributions in excess of $4,000, register with the Attorney General as provided in Section 2.

5. Any charitable organization receiving an allocation from an incorporated community chest or united fund, provided such chest or fund is complying with the provisions of this Act relating to registration and filing of annual reports with the Attorney General, and provided such organization does not actually receive, in addition to such allocation, contributions in excess of $4,000 during any 12 month period ending June 30th of any year, and provided further that all the fund raising functions of such organization are carried on by persons who are unpaid for such services. However, if the gross contributions other than such allocation received by such charitable organization during any 12 month period ending June 30th of any year shall be in excess of $4,000, it shall, within 30 days after the date it shall have received such contributions in excess of $4,000, register with the Attorney General as required by Section 2.

6. A bona fide organization of volunteer firemen, or a bona fide auxiliary or affiliate of such organization, provided all its fund raising activities are carried on by members of such an organization or an affiliate thereof and such members receive no compensation, directly or indirectly, therefor.

7. Any charitable organization operating a nursery for infants awaiting adoption providing that all its fund raising activities are carried on by members of such an organization or an affiliate thereof and such members receive no compensation, directly or indirectly, therefor.

8. Any corporation established by the Federal Congress that is required by federal law to submit annual reports of its activities to Congress containing itemized accounts of all receipts and expenditures after being duly audited by the Department of Defense or other federal departments.

9. Any boys' club which is affiliated with the Boys' Club of America, a corporation chartered by Congress; provided, however, that such an affiliate properly files the reports required by the Boys' Club of America and that the Boys' Club of America files with the Government of the United States the reports required by its federal charter.

5104. Annual reports to attorney general – Cancellation for non-compliance

§ 4. (a) Every charitable organization registered pursuant to Section 2 of this Act which shall receive in any 12 month period ending June 30th of any year contributions in excess of $50,000 and every charitable organization whose fund raising functions are not carried on solely by persons who are unpaid for such services shall file a written report with the Attorney General upon forms prescribed by him on or before June 30 of each year, if its books are kept on a calendar basis, or within 6 months after the close of its fiscal year, if its books are kept on a fiscal year basis, which shall include a financial statement covering the immediately preceding 12 month period of operation. Such financial statement shall include a balance sheet and statement of income and expense, and shall be consistent with forms furnished by the Attorney General clearly setting forth the following: gross receipts and gross income from all sources, broken down into total receipts and income from each separate solicitation project or source; cost of administration; cost of solicitation; cost of programs designed to inform or educate the public; funds or properties transferred out of this State, with explanation as to recipient and purpose; and total net amount disbursed or dedicated for each major purpose, charitable or otherwise. Such report shall also include a statement of any changes in the information required to be contained in the registration form filed on behalf of such organization. The report shall be signed by the president or other authorized officer and the chief fiscal officer of the organization, and shall be accompanied by an opinion signed by an independent certified public accountant that the financial statement therein fairly represents the financial operations of the organization in sufficient detail to permit public evaluation of its operations.

(b) Every organization registered pursuant to Section 2 of this Act which shall receive in any 12 month period ending June 30th of any year contributions not in excess of $50,000 and all of whose fund raising functions are carried on by persons who are unpaid for such services shall file a written report with the Attorney General upon forms prescribed by him on or before June 30 of each year, if its books are kept on a calendar basis, or within 6 months after the close of its fiscal year, if its books are kept on a fiscal year basis, which shall include a financial statement covering the immediately preceding 12-month period of operation limited to a statement of such organization's gross receipts from contributions, fund raising expenses including a separate statement of the cost of any goods, services or admissions supplied as part of its solicitations, and the disposition of the net proceeds from contributions. Such report shall also include a statement of any changes in the information required to be contained in the registration form filed on behalf of such organization. The report shall be signed by the president or other authorized officer and the chief fiscal officer of the organization who shall certify that the statements therein are true and correct to the best of their knowledge.

(c) For any fiscal or calendar year of any organization registered pursuant to Section 2 of this Act in which such organization would have been exempt from registration pursuant to Section 3 of this Act if it had not been so registered, or in which it did not solicit or receive contributions, such organization shall file, on or before June 30 of each year if its books are kept on a calendar basis, or within 6 months after the close of its fiscal year if its books are kept on a fiscal year basis, instead of the reports required by subdivisions (a) or (b) of this Section, a report in the form of an affidavit of its president and chief fiscal officer stating the exemption and the facts upon which it is based or that such organization did not solicit or receive contributions in such fiscal year. The affidavit shall also include a statement of any changes in the information required to be contained in the registration form filed on behalf of such organization.

(d) The Attorney General may, in his discretion, cancel the registration of any organization which fails to comply with subdivision (a), (b) or (c) of this Section within the time therein prescribed, or fails to furnish such additional information as is requested by the Attorney General within the required time; except that the time may be extended by the Attorney General for a period not to exceed 3 months.

The Attorney General shall, by rule, set forth the standards used to determine whether a registration shall be cancelled as authorized by this subsection. Such standards shall be stated as precisely and clearly as practicable, to inform fully those persons affected. Notice of such cancellation shall be mailed to the registrant at least 15 days before the effective date thereof.

5105. Organizations or persons having no office within state – Service of process.
§ 5. Any charitable organization, person, professional fund raiser or professional solicitor which or who solicits contributions in this State, but does not maintain an office within the State, shall be subject to service of process as follows:

(a) By service thereof on its registered agent within the State, or if there be no such registered agent, then upon the person who has been designated in the registration statement as having custody of books and records within the State; where service is effected upon the person so designated in the registration statement, a copy of the process shall, in addition, be mailed to the charitable organization at its last known address.

(b) When a charitable organization has solicited contributions in this State, but maintains no office within the State, has no registered agent within the State, and no designated person having custody of its books and records within the State, or when a registered agent or person having custody of its books and records within the State cannot be found as shown by the return of the sheriff of the county in which such registered agent or person having custody of books and records has been represented by the charitable organization as maintaining an office, service may be made by delivering to and leaving with the Secretary of State, or with any deputy or clerk in the corporation department of his office, three copies thereof and a fee of $6.

(c) Following service upon the Secretary of State, the provisions of law relating to service of process on foreign corporations contained in the "Business Corporation Act of 1983," as amended, shall thereafter govern.

(d) The solicitation of any contribution within this State shall be deemed to be the agreement of the charitable organization that any process against it which is so served in accordance with the provisions of this Section shall be of the same legal force and effect as if served personally within the State.

5106. Registration and re-registration of professional fund raisers – Application – Bond – Duration – Annual report – Violations

§ 6. (a) No person shall act as a professional fund raiser for a charitable organization required to register pursuant to Section 2 of this Act, or for any religious organization as described in Section 3(a) of this Act, before he has registered with the Attorney General or after the expiration or cancellation of such registration or any renewal thereof. Applications for registration and re-registration shall be in writing, under oath, in the form prescribed by the Attorney General. The applicant shall, at the time of making application, file with and have approved by, the Attorney General a bond in which the applicant shall be the principal obligor, in the sum of $5,000, with one or more corporate sureties licensed to do business in this State whose liability in the aggregate will at least equal such sum. The bond shall run to the Attorney General for the use of the State and to any person who may have a cause of action against the obligor of the bond for any malfeasance or misfeasance in the conduct of such solicitation; provided that the aggregate limit of liability of the surety to the State and to all such persons shall, in no event, exceed the sum of such bond. Registration or re-registration when effected shall be for a period of one year, or a part thereof, expiring on the 30th day of June, and may be renewed upon written application, under oath, in the form prescribed by the Attorney General and the filing of the bond for additional one year periods. Every professional fund raiser required to register pursuant to this Act shall file an annual written report with the Attorney General containing such information as he may require by rule.

(b) Any person who violates the provisions of this Section is guilty of a Class A misdemeanor.

5107. Contracts between charitable organizations and professional fund raisers

§ 7. All contracts entered into between professional fund raisers and charitable organizations shall be in writing and a true and correct copy of each such contract shall be filed by the professional fund raiser who is party thereto with the Attorney General within 10 days after it is made. True and correct copies of such contracts shall be kept on file in the offices of the charitable organization and the professional fund raiser during the term thereof and until the expiration of a period of 3 years subsequent to the date the solicitation of contributions provided for therein actually terminates. Any person who violates the provisions of this Section is guilty of a Class A misdemeanor.

5108. Registration and re-registration of professional solicitors – Application – Duration – Renewal – Penalty

§ 8. (a) No person shall act as a professional solicitor in the employ of a professional fund raiser required to register pursuant to Section 6 of this Act before he has registered with the Attorney General or after the expiration or cancellation of such registration or any renewal thereof. Application for registration or re-registration shall be in writing, under oath, in the form prescribed by the Attorney General. Such registration or re-registration when effected shall be for a period of one year, or a part thereof, expiring on the 30th day of June, and may be renewed upon written application, under oath, in the form prescribed by the Attorney General for additional one year periods.

(b) Any person who violates the provisions of this Section is guilty of a Class A misdemeanor.

5109. Actions for violation of Act – Injunctions – Recovery of costs

§ 9. (a) An action for violation of this Act may be prosecuted by the Attorney General in the name of the people of the State, and in any such action, the Attorney General shall exercise all the powers and perform all duties which the State's Attorney would otherwise be authorized to exercise or to perform therein.

(b) This Act shall not be construed to limit or restrict the exercise of the powers or the performance of the duties of the Attorney General which he otherwise is authorized to exercise or perform under any other provision of law by statute or otherwise.

(c) Whenever the Attorney General shall have reason to believe that any charitable organization, professional fund raiser or professional solicitor is operating in violation of the provisions of this Act, or if any of the principal officers of any charitable organization has refused or failed, after notice, to produce any records of such organization or there is employed or is about to be employed in any solicitation or collection of contributions for a charitable organization any device, scheme or artifice to defraud or for obtaining money or property by means of any false pretense, representation or promise, or any false statement has been made in any application, registration or statement required to be filed pursuant to this Act, or the solicitation of funds includes the sending of goods, wares and merchandise not ordered or requested by the recipient and where more than 25% of the total funds so raised are paid over to the manufacturer, supplier or agent thereof of the goods, wares and merchandise, or where less than 75% of the gross receipts, excluding any bequests or gifts by will or other testamentary device, of such charitable organization as defined in Section 1 are used for charitable purposes.

Gross receipts shall mean receipts after the legitimate and reasonable cost of any merchandise for resale or the legitimate and reasonable cost of services required with the fund raising event or program are deducted; in addition to any other action authorized by law, he may bring in the circuit court an action in the name, and on behalf of the people, of the State of Illinois against such charitable organization and any other person who has participated or is about to participate in such solicitation or collection by employing such device, scheme, artifice, false representation or promise, to enjoin such charitable organization or other person from continuing such solicitation or collection or engaging therein or doing any acts in furtherance thereof, or to cancel any registration statement previously filed with the Attorney General.

In connection with such proposed action, the Attorney General is authorized to take proof in the manner provided in Section 2-1003 of the Code of Civil Procedure.

(d) Upon a showing by the Attorney General in an application for an injunction that any person engaged in the solicitation or collection of funds for charitable purposes, either as an individual or as a member of a copartnership, or as an officer of a corporation or as an agent for some other person, or co-partnership or corporation has been convicted in this State or elsewhere of a felony or of a misdemeanor where such felony or misdemeanor involved the misappropriation, misapplication or misuse of the money or property of another, he may enjoin such persons from engaging in any solicitation or collection of funds for charitable purposes.

(e) The Attorney General may exercise the authority granted in this Section against any charitable organization or person which or who operates under the guise of pretense of being an organization exempted by the provisions of Section 3 and is not in fact an organization entitled to such an exemption.

(f) In any action brought under the provisions of this Act, the Attorney General is entitled to recover costs for the use of this State.

5110. Attendance of witnesses and hearings

§ 10. When the Attorney General requires the attendance of any persons, as provided in Section 9, he shall issue an order setting forth the time when and the place where attendance is required and shall cause the same to be served upon the person in the manner provided for service of process in civil cases at least 14 days before the date fixed for attendance. Such order shall have the same force and effect as a subpoena and, upon application of the Attorney General, obedience to the order may be enforced by any court having jurisdiction in the county where the person receiving it resides or is found in the same manner as though the notice were a subpoena. Such court may, in case of contumacy or refusal to obey the order issued by the Attorney General, issue an order requiring such person to appear before the Attorney General or to produce documentary evidence, if so ordered, or to give evidence touching the matter in question, and any failure to obey such order of the court may be punished by that court as a contempt upon itself. The investigation or hearing may be made by or before any Assistant Attorney General designated in writing by the Attorney General to conduct such investigation or hearing on his behalf. Witnesses ordered to appear shall be paid the same fees and mileage as are paid witnesses in the circuit courts of this State, and witnesses whose depositions are taken and the persons taking the same shall severally be entitled to the same fees as are paid for like services in the circuit courts of this State. The Attorney General or the Assistant Attorney General acting in his behalf is empowered to administer the necessary oath or affirmation to such witnesses.

5111. Use of name of other person – Exception – Acts constituting – Publication of names of contributors – Violations

§ 11. (a) No person shall, for the purpose of soliciting contributions from persons in this State, use the name of any other person, except that of an officer, director or trustee of the charitable organization by or for which contributions are solicited, without the written consent of such other persons.

(b) A person shall be deemed to have used the name of another person for the purpose of soliciting contributions if such latter person's name is listed on any stationery, advertisement, brochure or correspondence in or by which a contribution is solicited by or on behalf of a charitable organization or his name is listed or referred to in connection with a request for a contribution as one who has contributed to, sponsored or endorsed the charitable organization or its activities.

(c) Nothing contained in this Section shall prevent the publication of names of contributors, without their written consents, in an annual or other periodic report issued by a charitable organization for the purpose of reporting on its operations and affairs to its membership or for the purpose of reporting contributions to contributors.

(d) No charitable organization or professional fund raiser soliciting contributions shall use a name, symbol or statement so closely related or similar to that used by another charitable organization or governmental agency that the use thereof would tend to confuse or mislead the public.

(e) Any person who willfully violates the provisions of this Section is guilty of a Class A misdemeanor.

5112. Effect of registration – Representation of registration or compliance with Act – Cancellation of registration

§ 12. Registration under this Act shall not be deemed to constitute an endorsement by the State of Illinois of the charitable organization, professional fund raiser or professional solicitor so registered. It shall be unlawful for any charitable organization, professional fund raiser or professional solicitor so registered. It shall be unlawful for any charitable organization, professional fund raiser or professional solicitor to represent, directly or indirectly, for the purpose of solicitation and collection of funds for charitable purposes, in any form or manner whatsoever by advertising or otherwise, that it has registered or otherwise complied with the provisions of this Act. The Attorney General may, in his discretion, cancel the registration of any organization, professional fund raiser or professional solicitor which or who violates the provisions of this Section. The Attorney General shall, by rule, set forth the standards by which he shall make this determination. Such standards shall be stated as precisely and clearly as practicable, to inform fully those persons affected.

5113. Exchange of information – Agreements with other States

§ 13. The Attorney General may enter into reciprocal agreements with a like authority of any other State or States for the purpose of exchanging information made available to the Attorney General or to such other like authority.

5114. Severability clause

§ 14. If any provision of this Act, or the application of such provision to any persons, body or circumstances, shall be held invalid, the remainder of this Act, or the application of such provision to persons, bodies or circumstances other than those as to which it shall have been held invalid, shall not be affected thereby.

APPENDIX L (3)
NEW YORK'S CHARITABLE SOLICITATION LAW
EXECUTIVE LAW, ARTICLE 7-A

§ 171-a. Definitions

The following words and phrases as used in this article shall have the following meanings unless a different meaning is required by the context.

1. "Charitable organizations." Any benevolent, philanthropic, patriotic, or eleemosynary person or one purporting to be such.

2. "Contribution." The promise or grant of any money or property of any kind or value, whether or not in combination with the sale of goods, services, entertainment or any other thing of value, including a grant or other financial assistance from any agency of government, but except payments by members of any organization for membership fees, dues, fines, or assessments, or for services rendered to individual members, if membership in such organization confers a bona fide right, privilege, professional standing, honor or other direct benefit, other than the right to vote, elect officers, or hold offices.

3. "Person." Any individual, organization, group, association, partnership, corporation, or any combination of them.

4. "Professional fund raiser." Any person who directly or indirectly: (a) for compensation or other consideration plans, manages, conducts, carries on, or assists in connection with a charitable solicitation or individually solicits or who employs or otherwise engages on any basis another person to solicit in this state for or on behalf of any charitable organization or any other person, or who engages in the business of, or holds himself out to persons in this state as independently engaged in the business of soliciting for such purpose; (b) solicits by telephone or door-to-door and advertises a sale, performance, or event will benefit a charitable organization; or (c) who advertises a sale, performance, or event will benefit a charitable organization but is not a commercial co-venturer. A bona fide officer, volunteer or employee of a charitable organization or fund raising counsel shall not be deemed a professional fund raiser.

5. "Professional solicitor." Any person who is employed or retained for compensation by a professional fund raiser to solicit contributions for charitable purposes from persons in this state.

6. "Commercial co-venturer." Any person who for profit is regularly and primarily engaged in trade or commerce other than in connection with the raising of funds or any other thing of value for a charitable organization and who advertises that the purchase or use of goods, services, entertainment, or any other thing of value will benefit a charitable organization.

7. "Secretary." The secretary of state.

8. "Membership." The collective body of any charitable organization comprised of persons having voting rights and other powers of governance and who derive a direct benefit or privilege as a member thereof.

9. "Fund-raising counsel." Any person who for compensation consults with a charitable organization or who plans, manages, advises, or assists with respect to the solicitation in this state of contributions for or on behalf of a charitable organization, but who does not have access to contributions or other receipts from a solicitation or authority to pay expenses associated with a solicitation and who does not solicit. A bona fide officer, volunteer, or employee of a charitable organization or an attorney at law retained by a charitable organization, shall not be deemed a fund-raising counsel.

10. "Solicit." To directly or indirectly make a request, whether express or implied, through any medium. A "solicitation" shall be deemed to have taken place whether or not the solicitor receives a contribution. For purposes of this article, a "solicitation" or a "solicitation of contributions" includes any advertising which represents that the purchase or use of goods, services, entertainment or any other thing of value will benefit a charitable organization. Provided, however, that the preparation and the mailing of a written solicitation for funds or any other thing of value to benefit a charitable organization shall not alone constitute soliciting on the part of persons who prepared and mailed such solicitation if such person does not receive or have access to such contributions.

§ 172. Registration of Charitable Organizations
1. Every charitable organization, except as otherwise provided in Section 172-a of this article, which intends to solicit contributions from persons in this state or from any governmental agency by any means whatsoever shall, prior to any solicitation, file with the secretary upon forms prescribed by it, the following information:

(a) The name of the organization and the name or names under which it intends to solicit contributions.

(b) The names and business, residence, or other addresses where each can regularly be found of the officers, directors, trustees, and executive personnel of the organization.

(c) The addresses of the organization and the addresses of any offices in this state. If the organization does not maintain an office, the name and address of the person having custody of its financial records.

(d) Where and when the organization was established, the form of its organization, its tax exempt status together with a copy of the letter of exemption, if any, issued by the internal revenue service and a copy of any certificate of incorporation, by-laws, amendments and other operative organizational documents.

(e) A clear description of the specific programs stating whether in existence or planned for which the contributions to be solicited will be used.

(f) The date on which the fiscal year of the organization ends.

(g) Whether the organization is authorized by any other governmental authority to solicit contributions and whether it or any of its present officers, directors, executive personnel or trustees are or have ever been enjoined by any court from soliciting contributions or have been found to have engaged in unlawful practices regarding solicitation of contributions or administration of charitable assets and where its registration or license has been suspended or cancelled by any governmental agency together with the reasons for such suspension or cancellation.

(h) The names and addresses of any professional fund raisers, fund-raising counsels and commercial co-venturers who are acting or have agreed to act on behalf of the organization.

(i) A copy of its annual report, if any, for the immediately preceding fiscal year in accordance with the requirements of Section 172-b of this article.

(j) The names and addresses of any chapters, branches, affiliates or organizations that share in the contributions or other revenue raised in this state.

2. The registration form shall be signed by the president or other authorized officer and the chief fiscal officer of the organization and shall be verified under oath.

3. For filing such registration, the secretary shall receive a fee of twenty-five dollars, to be paid at the time of registration.

4. Such registration shall remain in effect unless it is either cancelled as provided in this article or withdrawn by the organization.

5. Every registered organization shall notify the secretary within thirty days of any material change in the information required to be furnished by such organization under subdivision 1 of this section.

6. In no event shall a registration of a charitable organization continue, or be continued, in effect after the date such organization should have filed, but failed to file, an annual report in accordance with the requirements of Section 172-b of this article, and such organization shall not be eligible to file a new registration until it shall have filed the required annual report with the secretary. If such report is subsequently filed, such organization may file a new registration upon the payment of a fee of one hundred fifty dollars to the secretary.

7. Registration statements, financial reports, professional fund raisers' contracts, and other documents required to be filed pursuant to this article become public records in the office of the secretary.

8. No charitable organization, professional fund raiser, fund-raising counsel or commercial co-venturer shall use or exploit the fact of registration so as to lead the public to believe that registration in any manner constitutes an endorsement or approval by the state.

9. To the extent practicable, the secretary of state and the attorney general shall jointly develop a single registration and uniform set of reporting forms to be filed in accordance with the requirements of this subdivision and those of Section 8-1.4 of the estates, powers and trusts law. These forms shall avoid duplication with and make maximum use of information required in federal reporting forms, which are also filed with the secretary and the attorney general.

§ 172-a. Certain Persons Exempted

1. This article shall not apply to corporations organized under the religious corporations law, and other religious agencies and organizations, and charities, agencies, and organizations operated, supervised, or controlled by or in connection with a religious organization.

2. The following persons shall not be required to register with the secretary:

(a) An educational institution confining its solicitation of contributions to its student body, alumni, faculty and trustees, and their families.

(b) Fraternal, patriotic, social, alumni organizations and historical societies chartered by the New York State board of regents when solicitation of contributions is confined to their membership.

(c) Persons requesting any contributions for the relief of any individual, specified by name at the time of the solicitation, if all of the contributions collected, without any deductions whatsoever, are turned over to the named beneficiary.

(d) Any charitable organization which does not intend to solicit and receive and does not actually receive contributions in excess of twenty-five thousand dollars during a fiscal year of such organization, provided none of its fund-raising functions are carried on by professional fund raisers or commercial co-venturers. However, if the gross contributions received by such charitable organization during any fiscal year of such organization shall be in excess of twenty-five thousand dollars, it shall within thirty days after the date it shall have received total contributions in excess of twenty-five thousand dollars register with the secretary as required by Section 172 of this article.

(e) Any charitable organization receiving an allocation from a federated fund, incorporated community appeal or a united way, provided such fund, appeal or united way is complying with the provisions of this article relating to registration and filing of annual reports with the secretary, and provided such organization does not actually receive, in addition to such allocation, contributions in excess of twenty-five thousand dollars during the fiscal year, and provided further that all the fund-raising functions of such organizations are carried on by persons who are unpaid for such services. However, if the gross contributions other than such allocation received by such charitable organization during any fiscal year of such organization shall be in excess of twenty-five thousand dollars, it shall within thirty days after the date it shall have received such contributions in excess of twenty-five thousand dollars register with the secretary as required by Section 172 of this article.

(f) A local post, camp, chapter or similarly designated element, or a county unit of such elements, of a bona fide veterans' organization which issues charters to such local elements throughout this state, a bona fide organization of volunteer firemen, an organization providing volunteer ambulance service (as defined in Section 3001 of the public health law) or a bona fide auxiliary or affiliate of such organizations, provided all its fund-raising activities are carried on by members of such an organization or an affiliate thereof and such members receive no compensation, directly or indirectly, therefor.

(g) An educational institution which files annual financial reports with the regents of the university of the state of New York as required by the education law or with an agency having similar jurisdiction in another state or a library which files annual financial reports as required by the state education department.

(h) A charitable organization which receives all or substantially all of its funds from a single governmental agency and reports annually to that agency provided such reports contain financial information substantially similar in content to that required by subdivision 1 of Section 172-b of this article; provided, however, that such organization may receive no more than twenty-five thousand dollars from sources other than the government agency to which it reports.

§ 172-b. Reports of Registered Charitable Organizations; Registration to Be Cancelled for Failure to File

1. Every charitable organization registered pursuant to Section 172 of this article which shall receive in any fiscal year of such organization total revenue and support in excess of one hundred fifty thousand dollars and every charitable organization whose fund-raising functions are not carried on solely by persons who are unpaid for such services shall file an annual written report with the secretary upon forms prescribed by the secretary, on or before the fifteenth day of the fifth calendar month after the close of such fiscal year, which shall include a financial statement covering such fiscal year, clearly setting forth the gross income, expenses, and net income inuring to the benefit of the charitable organization, a balance sheet as of the close of such fiscal year and a schedule of activities carried on by the organization in the performance of its purposes, and the amounts expended thereon, during such fiscal year. Each such organization shall file its annual financial statement in accordance with standards and classifications of accounts prescribed by the secretary to effect uniform reporting by organizations having similar activities and programs. Such standards shall be in accordance with the generally accepted accounting principles set forth in the "Industry Audit Guides" for colleges and universities, hospitals and voluntary health and welfare organizations published by the American Institute of Certified Public Accountants or in its Statement of Position 78-10 or in accordance with any modification thereof adopted by the Financial Accounting Standards Board. Such report shall also include a statement of any changes in the information required to be contained in the registration form filed on behalf of such organization. The report shall be signed by the president or other authorized officer and the chief fiscal officer of the organization who shall certify that the statements therein are true and correct to the best of their knowledge, and shall be accompanied by an opinion signed by an independent public accountant that the financial statement and balance sheet

therein present fairly the financial operations and position of the organization. A fee of twenty-five dollars payable to the secretary shall accompany such report at the time of filing.

2. Every organization registered pursuant to Section 172 of this article which shall receive in total revenue and support in any fiscal year at least seventy-five thousand dollars but not more than one hundred fifty thousand dollars shall file an annual financial statement accompanied by an independent certified public accountant's review report as defined by the American Institute of Certified Public Accountants in their publication of "Statement on Standards for Accounting and Review Service." Such financial statement shall be in accordance with the generally accepted accounting principles set forth in the "Industry Audit Guides" for colleges and universities, hospitals and voluntary health and welfare organizations published by the American Institute of Certified Public Accountants or in its Statement of Position 78-10 or in accordance with any modification thereof adopted by the Financial Accounting Standards Board. Such financial statement shall be filed with the secretary, upon forms prescribed by the secretary on an annual basis on or before the fifteenth day of the fifth calendar month after the close of such fiscal year, which shall include a financial statement covering such fiscal year in accordance with such requirements as the secretary may prescribe. Such report shall also include a statement of any changes in the information required to be contained in the registration form filed on behalf of such organization. The report shall be signed by the president or other authorized officer and the chief fiscal officer of the organization who shall certify that the statements therein are true and correct to the best of their knowledge. A fee of ten dollars payable to the secretary shall accompany such report at the time of filing.

2-a. Every organization registered pursuant to Section 172 of this article which shall receive in any fiscal year of such organization total revenue and support not in excess of seventy-five thousand dollars shall file an unaudited financial report with the secretary upon forms prescribed by the secretary, on or before the fifteenth day of the fifth calendar month after the close of such fiscal year, which shall include a financial statement covering such fiscal year in accordance with such requirements as the secretary may prescribe. Such report shall also include a statement of any changes in the information required to be contained in the registration form filed on behalf of such organization. The report shall be signed by the president or other authorized officer and the chief fiscal officer of the organization who shall certify that the statements therein are true and correct to the best of their knowledge. A fee of ten dollars payable to the secretary shall accompany such report at the time of filing.

3. For any fiscal year of any organization registered pursuant to Section 172 of this article in which such organization would have been exempt from registration pursuant to Section 172 of this article if it had not been so registered, or in which it did not solicit or receive contributions, such organization shall file, instead of the reports required by subdivisions one or two of this section, a report in the form prescribed by the secretary stating the exemption and the facts upon which it is based or that such organization did not solicit or receive contributions in such fiscal year. The report shall also include a statement of any changes in the information required to be contained in the registration form on behalf of such organization.

4. (a) Any charitable organization registered pursuant to Section 172 of this article, which is the parent organization of one or more affiliates thereof within the state, and such affiliates, may comply with the reporting requirements of subdivision 1, 2, 2-a or 3 of this section, by filing a combined written report upon forms prescribed by the secretary.

(b) As used in this subdivision the term "affiliate" shall include any chapter, branch, auxiliary, or other subordinate unit of any registered charitable organization, howsoever designated, whose policies, fund-raising activities, and expenditures are supervised or controlled by such parent organization.

(c) There shall be appended to each combined report a schedule, containing such information as may be prescribed by the secretary, reflecting the activities of each affiliate, which shall contain a certification, under penalty of perjury, by an official of the organization, certifying that the information contained therein is true.

(d) The failure of a parent organization to file an appropriate combined written report shall not excuse either the parent organization or its affiliates from complying with the provisions of subdivision 1, 2, 2-a or 3 of this section.

(e) A combined report filed pursuant to this subdivision shall be accompanied by a fee of twenty-five dollars plus ten dollars for each organization included in such report, but the aggregate fee shall not exceed five hundred dollars.

5. The secretary shall cancel the registration of any organization which fails to comply with subdivision 1, 2, 2-a or 3 of this section within the time therein prescribed, or fails to furnish such additional information as is requested by the secretary within the required time; except that the time may be extended by the secretary for a period not to exceed one hundred eighty days. Notice of such cancellation shall be mailed to the registrant at least twenty days before the effective date thereof.

6. Every charitable organization registered or required to register pursuant to Section 172 of this article shall keep and maintain records, books and reports for at least three years after the end of the period of registration to which they relate which shall at all times be available for inspection at the principal office of such organization, by the secretary or the attorney general, or their duly authorized representatives.

7. The secretary may accept a copy of a current annual report previously filed by a charitable organization with any other governmental agency in compliance with the provisions of this article provided that the report filed with such other governmental agency shall be substantially similar in content to the report required by this section.

§ 172-c. Non-Resident Charitable Organizations; Designation of Secretary of State as Agent for Service of Process; Service of Process
(Omitted)

§ 172-d. Prohibited Activity
Except as exempted pursuant to subdivision 1 of Section 172-a of this article, in addition to other violations of this article no person shall:

1. Make any material statement which is untrue in an application for registration, registration statement, a claim of exemption, or written annual report; or fail to disclose a material fact in an application for registration, registration statement, claim of exemption, or written annual report; or

2. Engage in any fraudulent or illegal act, device, scheme, artifice to defraud or for obtaining money or property by means of a false pretense, representation or promise, transaction or enterprise in connection with any solicitation for charitable purposes, any solicitation or collection of funds or other property for a charitable organization, any commercial co-venture, or with the registration, reporting and disclosure provisions of this article. The term "fraud" or "fraudulent" as used herein shall include those acts which may be characterized as misleading or deceptive including but not limited to those acts covered by the term "fraud" or "fraudulent" under subdivision 12 of Section 63 of this chapter. To establish fraud neither intent to defraud nor injury need to be shown; or

3. Use or intend to use false or materially misleading advertising or promotional material in connection with any solicitation for charitable purposes or with any commercial co-venture; or

4. Fail to apply contributions in a manner substantially consistent with the solicitation for charitable purposes or the registration statement of the charitable organization or the purposes expressed therein; or

5. Enter into any contract or agreement with or employ any unregistered professional fund raiser, fund-raising counsel or professional solicitor; or

6. Enter into any contract or agreement with or raise any funds for any charitable organization, required to be registered pursuant to this article unless such charitable organization is duly registered; or

7. Repeatedly and willfully fail to file as required by this article any fund-raising contract, closing statement or written report or any documents; or

8. Fail to respond or comply within sixty days with any cease and desist order of the Secretary of State; or

9. Represent in any manner that registration constitutes an endorsement or approval by the state; or

10. Solicit contributions for a charitable purpose without either being a registered charitable organization, if required to be registered, or having a written contract or agreement with a charitable organization or registered charitable organization if required to be registered, authorizing solicitation on its behalf; or

11. Continue soliciting on behalf of a charitable organization more than fifteen days after the cancellation in accordance with subdivision 6 of Section 174-a of this article of a contract between the person soliciting and the charitable organization; or

12. Act as or enter any contract as a professional fund raiser, fund-raising counsel, or professional solicitor without having registered; or

13. Fail to maintain books and records or refuse or fail within fifteen days after receiving written notice by certified mail, to produce any books and records, as required by this article; or

14. Fail to discontinue solicitation immediately or to register in accordance with the provisions of this article within fifteen days after the attorney general or the secretary has given notice pursuant to subdivision 2 of Section 175 of this article of violation of subdivision 1, 2, or 3 of Section 174 of this article; or

15. Fail to provide a charitable organization with an accurate accounting of a sale advertised for its benefit as prescribed by subdivision 3 of Section 173-a of this article; or

16. Knowingly use in the course of soliciting contributions for or on behalf of a charitable organization a name, symbol, or service mark so closely related or similar to that used by another established charitable organization that the use thereof would tend to confuse or mislead the public; or

17. Solicit contributions in a manner or with words which are coercive as such term is defined pursuant to Section 135.65 of the penal law; or

18. Vote or use personal influence as an officer or member of the board of directors of a charitable organization, a majority of whose members are professional fund raisers or their designees on matters on which such officer or member has a financial or material conflicting interest.

§ 173. Professional Fund Raisers, Commercial Co-venturers and Fund-Raising Counsel

1. Registration and bond required. No person shall act as a professional fund raiser or fund-raising counsel before he has registered with the secretary or after the expiration or cancellation of such registration or any renewal thereof. Applications for registration and re-registration shall be in writing, under oath, in the form prescribed by the secretary and shall be accompanied by an annual fee in the sum of two hundred dollars. A professional fund raiser shall at the time of making application, file with, and have approved by, the secretary a bond. In said bond, the filer shall be the principal obligor, in the sum of ten thousand dollars, with one or more sureties whose liability in the aggregate as such sureties will at least equal the said sum. The said bond which may be in the form of a rider to a larger blanket liability bond shall run to the secretary for the use of the state and to any person who may have a cause of action against the obligor of said bond for any malfeasance or misfeasance in the conduct of such solicitation. Registration or re-registration when effected shall be for a period of one year, or a part thereof, expiring on the thirty-first day of August, and may be renewed upon written application, under oath, in the form prescribed by the secretary and the filing of the bond and the fee prescribed herein for additional one-year periods. Applications for registration and re-registration and bonds, when filed with the secretary, shall become public records in the office of the secretary. If there is any material change in the information provided in any such application for registration and re-registration, the applicant or registrant shall notify the secretary in writing within twenty days of such change.

2. Books and records. A professional fund raiser, commercial co-venturer and fund-raising counsel shall maintain accurate and current books and records of all activities as such while required to be registered under subdivision 1 of this section; and, until at least three years shall have elapsed after the end of the effective period of the registration to which they relate, he shall keep such books and records in his office available for inspection and examination by the secretary or the attorney general or their duly authorized representatives; provided, however, that any such books and records obtained by the secretary or the attorney general shall not be available to the public for inspection.

3. Violations. Any person who willfully violates the provisions of this section is guilty of a misdemeanor.

§ 173-a. Contracts of Professional Fund Raisers, Fund-Raising Counsel and Commercial Co-venturers; Closing Statements; Final Accountings

1. No person shall act as a professional fund raiser, fund-raising counsel or commercial co-venturer before he has a written contract with the charitable organization or other person benefitting from his services. A true and correct copy of each contract entered into between a professional fund raiser or fund-raising counsel and a charitable organization shall be filed by the professional fund raiser or fund-raising counsel who is a party thereto with the secretary within ten days after it is made. When the services to be performed under such contracts include the oral solicitation of funds from the public, such oral presentations shall be deemed to be part of the contract and shall be reduced to a writing which in the case of a professional fund raiser shall be filed with the secretary by the registrant at the time such contracts are filed. If there is any change in the presentation filed with the secretary, the registrant shall notify the secretary in writing within five days of such change. No services shall be performed under such a contract until the professional fund raiser shall have received an acknowledgement from the secretary of the receipt of a copy of such contract and such contract shall have been on file with the secretary for at least fifteen days. True and correct copies of such contracts shall be kept on file in the offices of the charitable organization and the professional fund raiser or fund-raising counsel during the term thereof and until the expiration of a period of three years subsequent to the date the solicitation of contributions provided for therein actually terminates. Within ninety days after the termination of any such contract, the professional fund raiser shall file a closing statement with the secretary disclosing gross receipts, and all expenditures incurred in the performance of the contract. In the event that a contract term is longer than a one-year period, the professional fund raiser shall file an interim statement, at least annually. Willful violation of this section shall be a misdemeanor.

2. Every contract between a professional fund raiser and a charitable organization shall contain or shall be deemed to contain a provision that within five days of receipt all funds received from solicitation shall be deposited in a bank account under the exclusive control of the charity.

3. A commercial co-venturer, within ninety days after the termination of a sales promotion which it has advertised will benefit a charitable organization shall provide such organization with an interim report showing the number of items sold and the dollar amount of each sale and a final accounting at least once a year for all sales promotions during the year. In the event that such sales promotion is longer than a one-year period, the commercial co-venturer shall provide an interim statement, at least annually.

4. A charitable organization which enters into a contract with a commercial co-venturer shall file with the secretary on the date that the next annual report is due to be filed the following information signed by an officer: (a) a list of all commercial co-ventures authorized by the charitable organization to use its name during the preceding year covered by that annual report and, if known, during the year following the year covered by the annual report, (b) a statement of the financial terms and any conditions of each co-venture contract, and (c) a statement whether each commercial co-venturer has provided the charitable organization with an accounting as prescribed by subdivision 3 of this section.

§ 173-b. Professional Solicitor

1. Registration required. No person shall act as a professional solicitor in the employ of a professional fund raiser required to register pursuant to Section 173 of this article before he has registered with the secretary or after the expiration or cancellation of such registration or any renewal thereof. Application for registration or re-registration shall be in writing, under oath, in the form prescribed by the secretary and shall be accompanied by a fee in the sum of twenty dollars. Such registration or re-registration when effected shall be for a period of one year, or a part thereof, expiring on the thirty-first day of August, and may be renewed upon written application, under oath, in the form prescribed by the secretary and the payment of the fee prescribed herein, for additional one-year periods. Applications for registration and re-registration, when filed with the secretary, shall become public records in the office of the secretary.

2. Violations. Any person who willfully violates the provisions of this section is guilty of a misdemeanor.

§ 173-c. Non-Resident Professional Fund Raisers, Fund-Raising Counsel, Professional Solicitors and Commercial Co-venturers; Designation of Secretary of State as Agent for Service of Process; Service of Process.

Any professional fund raiser, fund-raising counsel, professional solicitor or commercial co-venturer resident or having his or its principal place of business without the state or organized under and by virtue of the laws of a foreign state, who or which shall solicit contributions or act as a fund-raising counsel in this state, shall be deemed to have irrevocably appointed the secretary of state as his or its agent upon whom may be served any summons, subpoena, subpoena duces tecum, or other process directed to such professional fund raiser, fund-raising counsel, professional solicitor, commercial co-venturer or any partner, principal, officer, or director thereof, in any action or proceeding brought by the attorney general under the provisions of this act. Any such professional fund raiser, fund-raising counsel, professional solicitor or commercial co-venturer may file with the secretary of state a designation, in terms complying herewith, duly acknowledged, irremovably appointing the secretary of state as his or its agent upon whom may be served any such process; provided, however, that a designation filed with the secretary of state pursuant to Section 352-a of the general business law, Section 1304 of the not-for-profit corporation law, or Section 1304 of the business corporation law shall serve also as such designation. Service of such process upon the secretary of state shall be made by personally delivering to and leaving with him or a deputy secretary of state a copy thereof at the office of the department of state in the city of Albany, and such service shall be sufficient service provided that notice of such service and a copy of such process are forthwith sent by the attorney general to such professional fund raiser, fund-raising counsel, professional solicitor or commercial co-venturer by registered mail with return receipt requested, at his or its office as set forth in the registration form required to be filed with the secretary pursuant to Sections 173 and 173-b of this article, or in default of the filing of such form, at the last address known to the attorney general. Service of such process shall be complete ten days after the receipt by the attorney general of a return receipt purporting to be signed by the addressee or a person qualified to receive his or its registered mail, in accordance with the rules and customs of the post office department, or, if acceptance was refused by the addressee or his or its agent, ten days after the return to the attorney general of the original envelope bearing a notation by the postal authorities that receipt thereof was refused.

§ 174. Solicitation by Unregistered Charitable Organizations, Professional Fund Raisers or Commercial Co-venturers a Fraud upon the People of the State.

1. No charitable organization shall employ any professional fund raiser or commercial co-venturer unless and until such fund raiser or commercial co-venturer is registered pursuant to this article. Any such contract of employment shall be voidable at the option of the charitable organization.

2. No professional fund raiser or commercial co-venturer shall enter into any contract or raise any funds for any organization required to be registered pursuant to this article unless such charitable organization actually so registered.

3. No professional fund raiser required to be registered under this article shall employ any professional solicitor who is not registered in accordance with this article.

4. In addition to all other remedies provided by law the attorney general may bring an action to enjoin the violation of the provisions of this section. The attorney general may give notice of at least fifteen days in writing by registered or certified mail to the organization, person or persons violating the provisions hereof, requiring that registration be accomplished or that the solicitation funds be immediately terminated. The failure to immediately discontinue solicitation or to register in accordance with the provisions of this article within fifteen days of service of such notice shall be deemed to be a continuing fraud upon the people of the state of New York.

§ 174-a. Contracts with Charitable Organizations

1. Whenever a charitable organization contracts with a professional fund raiser or fund-raising counsel, the charitable organization shall have the right to cancel the contract without cost, penalty, or liability for a period of fifteen days following the date on which said contract is filed with the secretary pursuant to the provision of this article. Any provision in the contract that is intended to waive this right of cancellation shall be void and unenforceable.

2. A charitable organization may cancel a contract signed pursuant to subdivision one of this section by a written notice of cancellation. If given by mail, cancellation shall be deemed effective when deposited in a mailbox, properly addressed and postage prepaid. The notice shall be sufficient if it indicates that the charitable organization does not intend to be bound by the contract.

3. Whenever a charitable organization cancels a contract pursuant to the provisions of this section, it shall mail a duplicate copy of the notice of cancellation to the secretary of state.

4. Every contract entered into pursuant to subdivision one of this section shall contain, in a conspicuous typeface:

(a) a concise, accurate statement of the charitable organization's right to cancel;

(b) a concise, accurate statement of the period during which the contract may be cancelled;

(c) the address to which the notice of cancellation is to be sent;

(d) the address of the secretary of state to which a duplicate of the notice of cancellation is to be sent; and

(e) a clear statement of the financial arrangement including, if applicable, a statement of the percentage of the total funds collected on behalf of the charitable organization which shall be retained by the professional fund raiser for purposes other than the exclusive benefit of the charitable organization.

5. Any funds collected in violation of this section shall be deemed to be held in trust for the benefit of the charitable organization without deduction for costs or expenses of any nature. A charitable organization shall be entitled to recover all funds collected in violation of this section together with costs, disbursements and allowances.

6. The failure of a professional fund raiser or co-venturer to immediately discontinue solicitation in accordance with the provisions of this article within fifteen days of the cancellation of the contract shall be deemed to be a continuing fraud upon the people of the state of New York. In addition to all other remedies provided by law the attorney general may bring an action to enjoin the violation of the provisions of this section.

§ 174-b. Solicitation
1. Any solicitation used by a charitable organization which is required to have previously filed an annual report pursuant to this article, shall include therein a statement that upon request, a person may obtain from the organization or from the secretary, a copy of the last annual report filed by the organization with the secretary. Such statement shall specify the address of the organization and the

address of the secretary in Albany, to which such request should be addressed and in the case of a written solicitation, must be placed conspicuously in the material with print no smaller than ten-point boldface type or, alternatively, no smaller than the size print used for the most number of words in the statements. Provided, however, such statement need not be made where the space for a printed advertisement or promotional time in the broadcast media has been donated or made available to the charitable organization at no cost and such space or times does not reasonably permit inclusion of such statement.

2. Any solicitation used by or on behalf of any charitable organization shall provide a clear description of the programs and activities for which it has requested and has expended or will expend contributions or shall include therein a statement that, upon request, a person may obtain from the organization such a description.

3. If any charitable organization makes contributions to another organization which is not its affiliate as defined by paragraph (b) of subdivision 4 of Section 172-b of this article, such solicitation shall include a statement that such contributions have been made and that a list of all organizations which have received contributions during the past twelve months from the soliciting organization may be obtained from that organization; provided, however, a united way, federated fund or incorporated community appeal, by or through which a donation is merely transferred to a charity selected by the donor, need not include such donor selected organization in the list.

4. A charitable organization shall comply with all requests made pursuant to subdivisions 1, 2, and 3 of this section within fifteen days of their receipt. In the event that a charitable organization required to register pursuant to this article has not previously been required to file an annual report with the secretary, the solicitation shall state the date when such report will be filed; provided, however, that no additional solicitation shall be permitted by charitable organizations until an annual report is filed, if the report is delayed beyond one year.

§ 174-c. Sales Advertised to Benefit a Charitable Organization.
All advertising, of every kind and nature, that a sale of goods, services, entertainment or any other thing of value will benefit a charitable organization shall set forth the anticipated portion of the sales price, anticipated percentage of the gross proceeds, anticipated dollar amount per purchase, or other consideration or benefit the charitable organization is to receive; provided, however, that advertising for sales by a charitable organization that has not used the services of a professional fund raiser or commercial co-venturer in any way for the sale shall not be subject to the requirement of this section.

§ 174-d. Unauthorized Use of Names When Soliciting or Collecting Contributions

1. No person shall, for the purpose of soliciting contributions from persons in this state, use the name of any other person, except that of an officer, director or trustee of the charitable organization by or for which contributions are solicited, without the written consent of such other person.

2. A person shall be deemed to have used the name of another person for the purpose of soliciting contributions if such latter person's name is listed on any stationery, advertisement, brochure or correspondence in or by which a contribution is solicited by or on behalf of a charitable organization or his name is listed or referred to in connection with a request for a contribution as one who has contributed to, sponsored or endorsed the charitable organization or its activities.

3. Nothing contained in this section shall prevent the publication of names of contributors without their written consents, in an annual or other periodic report issued by a charitable organization, for the purpose of reporting on its operations and affairs to its membership or for the purpose of reporting contributions to contributors.

§ 175. Enforcement by Attorney General

1. An action for violation of this article may be prosecuted by the attorney general, or his deputy, in the name of the people of the state, and in any such action, the attorney general or his deputy, shall exercise all the powers and perform all duties which the district attorney would otherwise be authorized to exercise or to perform therein.

2. In addition to any other action authorized by law and any action or proceeding by the secretary, the attorney general may bring an action or special proceeding in the Supreme Court, in the name and in its behalf of the people of the state of New York, against a charitable organization and any other persons acting for it or in its behalf to enjoin such organization and persons from continuing the solicitation or collection of funds or property or engaging therein or doing any acts in furtherance thereof, and to cancel any registration statement previously filed with the secretary and for an order awarding restitution and damages and costs; and removing any director or other person responsible for the violation of this article; dissolving a corporation and other relief which the court may deem proper, whenever the attorney general shall have reason to believe that the charitable organization or other person:

(a) is operating in violation of the provisions of this article;

(b) has refused or failed, or any of its principal officers has refused or failed, after notice, to produce any records of such organizations;

(c) is employing or about to employ, or there is employed or about to be employed, in any solicitation or collection of funds or other property for such organization, any device, scheme or artifice to defraud or for obtaining money or property by means of a false pretense, representation or promise;

(d) has made a material false statement in an application, registration or statement required to be filed pursuant to this article;

(e) has failed or is failing to apply the funds solicited from the public in a manner substantially consistent with its charitable purposes or the solicitation for charitable purposes or has engaged in repeated fraudulent or illegal activities, acts or conduct in connection with the solicitation for charitable purposes;

(f) violates any order or determination made by the secretary or the secretary's designee pursuant to the provisions of this article; or

(g) has used or intends to use false or materially misleading advertising or promotional material in connection with any solicitation for charitable purposes or with any commercial co-venture or fails to disclose the information required to be disclosed pursuant to Section 174-b of this article.

In connection with such proposed action the attorney general is authorized to take proof, issue subpoenas and administer oaths in the manner provided in the civil practice law and rules.

3. Upon a showing by the attorney general in an application for an injunction that any person engaged in the solicitation or collection of funds for charitable purposes, either as an individual or as a member of a copartnership, or as any officer of a corporation or as an agent for some other person, or copartnership or corporation, has been convicted in this state or elsewhere of a felony or of a misdemeanor involving the misappropriation, misapplication or misuse of the money or property of another, and who has not, subsequent to such conviction, received executive pardon therefor or a certificate of good conduct from the parole board, the Supreme Court, after a hearing, may enjoin such person from engaging in any solicitation or collection of funds for charitable purposes.

4. The attorney general may exercise the authority granted in this section against any charitable organization which operates under the guise or pretense of being an organization exempted by the provisions of Section 172-a of this article and is not in fact an organization entitled to such an exemption.

5. Whenever the attorney general shall have reason to believe that any professional fund raiser, fund-raising counsel, professional solicitor or commercial co-venturer is operating in violation of the provisions of this article, or has made any false statement in any application, registration or statement required to be filed pursuant to this article, or if any professional fund raiser, fund-raising counsel, or commercial co-venturer has refused or failed, after notice, to produce any records demanded of him, or there is employed or is about to be employed in any solicitation or collection of contributions for a charitable or religious organization any device, scheme or artifice to defraud or for obtaining money or property by means of any false pretense, representation or promise, in addition to any other action authorized by law, he may bring in the Supreme Court an action in the name, and on behalf, of the people of the state of New York against such professional fund raiser, fund-raising counsel, commercial co-venturer, professional solicitor, and any other person who has participated or is about to participate in such solicitation or collection by employing such device, scheme, artifice, false representation or promise, to enjoin such professional fund raiser, fund-raising counsel, commercial co-venturer, professional solicitor, or other person from continuing such solicitation or collection or engaging therein or doing any acts in furtherance thereof, or to cancel any registration statement previously filed with the secretary.

6. Whenever the attorney general has determined to commence an action under this article, he may present to any justice of the Supreme Court, before beginning such action, an application in writing for an order directing the person or persons mentioned in the application to appear before the justice of the Supreme Court or referee designated in such order and answer such questions as may be put to them or to any of them, or to produce such papers, documents and books concerning the practices to which the action which he has determined to bring relates, and it shall be the duty of the justice of the Supreme Court to whom such application for the order is made to grant such application. The application for such order made by the attorney general may simply show upon his information and belief that the testimony of such person or persons is material and necessary. The provisions of the civil practice law and rules relating to an application for an order for the examination of witnesses before the commencement of an action and the method of proceeding on such examination, shall not apply except as herein prescribed. The order shall be granted by the justice of the Supreme Court to whom the application

has been made with such preliminary injunction or stay as may appear to such justice to be proper and expedient and shall specify the time when and place where the witnesses are required to appear. The justice or referee may adjourn such examination from time to time and witnesses must attend accordingly. The testimony of each witness must be subscribed by him and all must be filed in the office of the clerk of the county in which such order for examination is filed. The order for such examination must be signed by the justice making it and service of a copy thereof with an endorsement by the attorney general signed by him or his deputy, to the effect that the person named therein is required to appear and be examined at the time and place and before the justice or referee specified in such endorsement, shall be sufficient notice for the attendance of witnesses. Such endorsement may contain a clause requiring such person to produce at such examination all books, papers and documents in his possession or under his control relating to the subject of such examination. The order shall be served upon the person named in the endorsement aforesaid by showing him the original order and delivering to and leaving with him at the same time a copy thereof, endorsed as above provided, and by paying or tendering to him the fee allowed by law to witnesses subpoenaed to attend trials of civil actions in any court of record in this state.

7. In addition to any other action authorized by law, the attorney general may bring an action or special proceeding in the Supreme Court on behalf of the secretary to recover any civil penalties assessed by the secretary.

8. Nothing contained in Section 177 of this article shall prevent, limit, restrict, impede or delay the attorney general from instituting, at any time, any action or proceeding authorized by the provisions of this article or any other appropriate law, as he may deem necessary.

§ 176. Advisory Counsel
(Omitted)

§ 177. Administration and Enforcement by Secretary of State.
1. The secretary shall make rules and regulations necessary for the administration of this article.

2. Upon a finding by the secretary that any person has committed or is committing a violation of subdivision 1, 2, 5, 6, 7 or 8 of Section 172-d of this article, or has failed or is failing to comply with Section 172-b of this article, the secretary may:

(a) revoke, suspend or deny a registration of a charitable organization or professional fund raiser or professional solicitor or fund-raising counsel or deny or revoke a claim of exemption or issue an order directing a charitable organization or professional fund raiser or professional solicitor or fund-raising counsel or commercial co-venturer to cease and desist specified fund-raising activities; and

(b) assess a civil penalty against the violator of not more than one thousand dollars for each act or omission constituting a violation and an additional penalty of not more than one hundred dollars for each day during which such violation continues. Prior to assessing a civil penalty, the secretary shall notify the violator in writing by certified mail to its last known business address that a civil penalty will be assessed pursuant to this section unless the violation is cured within thirty days of the date of the mailing of the notice.

3. The secretary shall, before denying, revoking or suspending any registration or exemption, or issuing a cease and desist order or assessing a civil penalty, notify the applicant or registrant in writing and provoke an opportunity for a hearing on a record in reference thereof in accordance with such rules as the secretary may promulgate to effectuate the purposes of this article. Such written notice may be served by personal delivery to the applicant or registrant or by registered or certified mail to its last known business address. Hearings must be requested within twenty days of receipt of notice from the secretary. Any hearing shall be held within thirty days of the receipt of the request by the secretary, at such time and place as the secretary shall prescribe. The secretary, or the secretary's designee, may issue subpoenas in accordance with the civil practice law and rules, compel the attendance of witnesses at the hearing, administer oaths, take proof and make determinations of relevant facts. The respondent may appear at the hearing and may cross-examine all witnesses and produce evidence on his or her behalf. The secretary or the secretary's designee shall not be bound by the rules of evidence during the conduct of the hearing. A final determination shall be made by the secretary or the secretary's designee within ten days of the conclusion of the hearing. The secretary shall serve a copy of such determination or order upon the registrant or applicant personally or by registered or certified mail at his or her last known business address.

4. The administrative remedies provided by this article shall not be applicable to any violation of this article which was the subject of any action or proceeding brought by the attorney general.

APPENDIX M
TAX-EXEMPT ORGANIZATIONS
SELECTED IRS REGULATIONS

§ 1.501(c)(3)-1 Organizations organized and operated for religious, charitable, scientific, testing for public safety, literary, or educational purposes, or for the prevention of cruelty to children or animals.

(a) *Organizational and operational tests.* (1) In order to be exempt as an organization described in section 501(c)(3), an organization must be both organized and operated exclusively for one or more of the purposes specified in such section. If an organization fails to meet either the organizational test or the operational test, it is not exempt.

(2) The term "exempt purpose or purposes," as used in this section, means any purpose or purposes specified in section 501(c)(3), as defined and elaborated in paragraph (d) of this section.

(b) *Organizational test* – (1) *In general.* (i) An organization is organized exclusively for one or more exempt purposes only if its articles of organization (referred to in this section as its "articles") as defined in subparagraph (2) of this paragraph:

(a) Limit the purposes of such organization to one or more exempt purposes; and

(b) Do not expressly empower the organization to engage, otherwise than as an insubstantial part of its activities, in activities which in themselves are not in furtherance of one or more exempt purposes.

(ii) In meeting the organizational test, the organization's purposes, as stated in its articles, may be as broad as, or more specific than, the purposes stated in section 501(c)(3). Therefore, an organization which, by the terms of its articles, is formed "for literary and scientific purposes within the meaning of section 501(c)(3) of the Code" shall, if it otherwise meets the requirements in this paragraph, be considered to have met the organizational test. Similarly, articles stating that the organization is created solely "to receive contributions and pay them over to organizations which are described in section 501(c)(3) and exempt from taxation under section 501(a)" are sufficient for purposes of the organizational test. Moreover, it is sufficient if the articles set forth the purpose of the organization to be the operation of a school for adult education and describe in detail the manner of the operation of such school. In addition, if the articles state that the organization is formed for "charitable purposes," such articles ordinarily shall be sufficient for purposes of the organizational test (see subparagraph (5) of this paragraph for rules relating to construction of terms).

(iii) An organization is not organized exclusively for one or more exempt purposes if its articles expressly empower it to carry on, otherwise than as an insubstantial part of its activities, activities which are not in furtherance of one or more exempt purposes, even though such organization is, by the terms of such articles, created for a purpose that is no broader than the purposes specified in section 501(c)(3). Thus, an organization that is empowered by its articles "to engage in a manufacturing business," or "to engage in the operation of a social club" does not meet the organizational test regardless of the fact that its articles may state that such organization is created "for charitable purposes within the meaning of section 501(c)(3) of the Code."

(iv) In no case shall an organization be considered to be organized exclusively for one or more exempt purposes, if, by the terms of its articles, the purposes for which such organization is created are broader than the purposes specified in section 501(c)(3). The fact that the actual operations of such an organization have been exclusively in furtherance of one or more exempt purposes shall not be sufficient to permit the organization to meet the organizational test. Similarly, such an organization will not meet the organizational test as a result of statements or other evidence that the members thereof intend to operate only in furtherance of one or more exempt purposes.

(v) An organization must, in order to establish its exemption, submit a detailed statement of its proposed activities with and as a part of its application for exemption (see paragraph (b) of § 1.501(a)-l).

(2) *Articles of organization.* For purposes of this section, the term "articles of organization" or "articles" includes the trust instrument, the corporate charter, the articles of association, or any other written instrument by which an organization is created.

(3) *Authorization of legislative or political activities.* An organization is not organized exclusively for one or more exempt purposes if its articles expressly empower it:

(i) To devote more than an insubstantial part of its activities to attempting to influence legislation by propaganda or otherwise; or

(ii) Directly or indirectly to participate in, or intervene in (including the publishing or distributing of statements), any political campaign on behalf of or in opposition to any candidate for public office; or

(iii) To have objectives and to engage in activities which characterize it as an "action" organization as defined in paragraph (c)(3) of this section. The terms used in subdivisions (i), (ii), and (iii) of this subparagraph shall have the meanings provided in paragraph (c)(3) of this section.

(4) *Distribution of assets on dissolution.* An organization is not organized exclusively for one or more exempt purposes unless its assets are dedicated to an exempt purpose. An organization's assets will be considered dedicated to an exempt purpose, for example, if, upon dissolution, such assets would, by reason of a provision in the organization's articles or by operation of law, be distributed for one or more exempt purposes, or to the Federal Government, or to a State or local government, for a public purpose, or would be distributed by a court to another organization to be used in such manner as in the judgment of the court will best accomplish the general purposes for which the dissolved organization was organized. However, an organization does not meet the organizational test if its articles or the law of the State in which it was created provides that its assets would, upon dissolution, be distributed to its members or shareholders.

(5) *Construction of terms.* The law of the State in which an organization is created shall be controlling in construing the terms of its articles. However, any organization which contends that such terms have under State law a different meaning from their generally accepted meaning must establish such special meaning by clear and convincing reference to relevant court decisions, opinions of the State attorney general, or other evidence of applicable State law.

(6) *Applicability of the organizational test.* [omitted]

(c) *Operational test –* (1) *Primary activities.* An organization will be regarded as "operated exclusively" for one or more exempt purposes only if it engages primarily in activities which accomplish one or more of such exempt purposes specified in section 501(c)(3). An organization will not be so regarded if more than an insubstantial part of its activities is not in furtherance of an exempt purpose.

(2) *Distribution of earnings.* An organization is not operated exclusively for one or more exempt purposes if its net earnings inure in whole or in part to the benefit of private shareholders or individuals. For the definition of the words "private shareholder or individual," see paragraph (c) of § 1.501(a)-1.

(3) *"Action" organizations.* (i) An organization is not operated exclusively for one or more exempt purposes if it is an "action" organization as defined in subdivision (ii), (iii), or (iv) of this subparagraph.

(ii) An organization is an "action" organization if a substantial part of its activities is attempting to influence legislation by propaganda or otherwise. For this purpose, an organization will be regarded as attempting to influence legislation if the organization:

(a) Contacts, or urges the public to contact, members of a legislative body for the purpose of proposing, supporting, or opposing legislation; or

(b) Advocates the adoption or rejection of legislation.

The term "legislation," as used in this subdivision, includes action by the Congress, by any State legislature, by any local council or similar governing body, or by the public in a referendum, initiative, constitutional amendment, or similar procedure. An organization will not fail to meet the operational test merely because it advocates, as an insubstantial part of its activities, the adoption or rejection of legislation.

(iii) An organization is an "action" organization if it participates or intervenes, directly or indirectly, in any political campaign on behalf of or in opposition to any candidate for public office.

The term "candidate for public office" means an individual who offers himself, or is proposed by others, as a contestant for an elective public office, whether such office be national, State, or local. Activities which constitute participation or intervention in a political campaign on behalf of or in opposition to a candidate include, but are not limited to, the publication or distribution of written or printed statements or the making of oral statements on behalf of or in opposition to such a candidate.

(iv) An organization is an "action" organization if it has the following two characteristics: (a) its main or primary objective or objectives (as distinguished from its incidental or secondary objectives) may be attained only by legislation or a defeat of proposed legislation; and (b) it advocates, or campaigns for, the attainment of such main or primary objective or objectives as distinguished from engaging in nonpartisan analysis, study, or research and making the results thereof available to the public. In determining whether an organization has such characteristics, all the surrounding facts and circumstances, including the articles and all activities of the organization, are to be considered.

(v) An "action" organization, described in subdivision (ii) or (iv) of this subparagraph, though it cannot qualify under section 501(c)(3), may nevertheless qualify as a social welfare organization under section 501(c)(4) if it meets the requirements set out in paragraph (a) of § 1.501(c)(4)-1.

(d) *Exempt purposes* – (1) *In general.* (i) An organization may be exempt as an organization described in section 501(c)(3) if it is organized and operated exclusively for one or more of the following purposes:

(a) Religious,	(e) Literary,
(b) Charitable,	(f) Educational, or
(c) Scientific,	(g) Prevention of cruelty to children or
(d) Testing for public safety,	animals.

(ii) An organization is not organized or operated exclusively for one or more of the purposes specified in subdivision (i) of this subparagraph unless it serves a public rather than a private interest. Thus, to meet the requirement of this subdivision, it is necessary for an organization to establish that it is not organized or operated for the benefit of private interests such as designated individuals, the creator or his family, shareholders of the organization, or persons controlled, directly or indirectly, by such private interests.

(iii) Since each of the purposes specified in subdivision (i) of this subparagraph is an exempt purpose in itself, an organization may be exempt if it is organized and operated exclusively for any one or more of such purposes. If, in fact, an organization is organized and operated exclusively for an exempt purpose or purposes, exemption will be granted to such an organization regardless of the purpose or purposes specified in its application for exemption. For example, if an organization claims exemption on the ground that it is "educational," exemption will not be denied if, in fact, it is "charitable."

(2) *Charitable defined.* The term "charitable" is used in section 501(c)(3) in its generally accepted legal sense and is, therefore, not to be construed as limited by the separate enumeration in section 501(c)(3) of other tax-exempt purposes which may fall within the broad outlines of "charity" as developed by judicial decisions. Such term includes: Relief of the poor and distressed or of the underprivileged; advancement of religion; advancement of education or science; erection or maintenance of public buildings, monuments, or works; lessening of the burdens of Government; and promotion of social welfare by organizations designed to accomplish any of the above purposes, or (i) to lessen neighborhood tensions; (ii) to eliminate prejudice and discrimination; (iii) to defend human and civil rights

secured by law; or (iv) to combat community deterioration and juvenile delinquency. The fact that an organization which is organized and operated for the relief of indigent persons may receive voluntary contributions from the persons intended to be relieved will not necessarily prevent such organization from being exempt as an organization organized and operated exclusively for charitable purposes. The fact that an organization, in carrying out its primary purpose, advocates social or civic changes or presents opinion on controversial issues with the intention of molding public opinion or creating public sentiment to an acceptance of its views does not preclude such organization from qualifying under section 501(c)(3) so long as it is not an "action" organization of any one of the types described in paragraph (c)(3) of this section.

(3) *Educational defined* – (i) *In general.* The term "educational," as used in section 501(c)(3), relates to:

(a) The instruction or training of the individual for the purpose of improving or developing his capabilities; or

(b) The instruction of the public on subjects useful to the individual and beneficial to the community.

An organization may be educational even though it advocates a particular position or viewpoint so long as it presents a sufficiently full and fair exposition of the pertinent facts as to permit an individual or the public to form an independent opinion or conclusion. On the other hand, an organization is not educational if its principal function is the mere presentation of unsupported opinion.

(ii) *Examples of educational organizations.* The following are examples of organizations which, if they otherwise meet the requirements of this section, are educational:

Example (1). An organization, such as a primary or secondary school, a college, or a professional or trade school, which has a regularly scheduled curriculum, a regular faculty, and a regularly enrolled body of students in attendance at a place where the educational activities are regularly carried on.

Example (2). An organization whose activities consist of presenting public discussion groups, forums, panels, lectures, or other similar programs. Such programs may be on radio or television.

Example (3). An organization which presents a course of instruction by means of correspondence or through the utilization of television or radio.

Example (4). Museums, zoos, planetariums, symphony orchestras, and other similar organizations.

(4) *Testing for public safety defined.* [omitted]

(5) *Scientific defined.* [omitted]

(e) *Organizations carrying on trade or business* – (1) *In general.* An organization may meet the requirements of section 501(c)(3) although it operates a trade or business as a substantial part of its activities if the operation of such trade or business is in furtherance of the organization's exempt purpose or purposes and if the organization is not organized or operated for the primary purpose of carrying on an unrelated trade or business, as defined in section 513. In determining the existence or nonexistence of such primary purpose, all the circumstances must be considered, including the size and extent of the trade or business and the size and extent of the activities which are in furtherance of one or more exempt purposes. An organization which is organized and operated for the primary purpose of carrying on an unrelated trade or business is not exempt under section 501(c)(3) even though it has certain religious purposes, its property is held in common, and its profits do not inure to the benefit of individual members of the organization. See, however, section 501(d) and § 1.501(d)-l, relating to religious and apostolic organizations.

(2) *Taxation of unrelated business income.* For provisions relating to the taxation of unrelated business income of certain organizations described in section 501(c)(3), see sections 511 to 515, inclusive, and the regulations thereunder.

(f) *Applicability of regulations in this section.* [omitted]

§ 1.501(c)(4)-1 Civic organizations and local associations of employees.
(a) *Civic organizations* – (1) *In general.* A civic league or organization may be exempt as an organization described in section 501(c)(4) if –

(i) It is not organized or operated for profit; and

(ii) It is operated exclusively for the promotion of social welfare.

(2) *Promotion of social welfare* – (i) *In general.* An organization is operated exclusively for the promotion of social welfare if it is primarily engaged in promoting in some way the common good and general welfare of the people of the community. An organization embraced within this section is one which is operated primarily for the purpose of bringing about civic betterments and social improvements. A "social welfare" organization will qualify for exemption as a charitable organization if it falls within the definition of "charitable" set forth in paragraph (d)(2) of § 1.501(c)(3)-1 and is not an "action" organization as set forth in paragraph (c)(3) of § 1.501(c)(3)-1.

(ii) *Political or social activities.* The promotion of social welfare does not include director or indirect participation or intervention in political campaigns on behalf of or in opposition to any candidate for public office. Nor is an organization operated primarily for the promotion of social welfare if its primary activity is operating a social club for the benefit, pleasure, or recreation of its members, or is carrying on a business with the general public in a manner similar to organizations which are operated for profit. See, however, section 501(c)(6) and § 1.501(c)(6)-l, relating to business leagues and similar organizations. A social welfare organization may qualify under section 501(c)(4) even though it is an "action" organization described in paragraph (c)(3)(ii) or (iv) of § 1.501(c)(3)-1 if it otherwise qualifies under this section.

(b) *Local associations of employees.* Local associations of employees described in section 501(c)(4) are expressly entitled to exemption under section 501(a). As conditions to exemption, it is required (1) that the membership of such an association be limited to the employees of a designated person or persons in a particular municipality, and (2) that the net earnings of the association be devoted exclusively to charitable, educational, or recreational purposes. The word "local" is defined in paragraph (b) of § 1.501(c)(12)-l. See paragraph (d) (2) and (3) of § 1.501(c)(3)-l with reference to the meaning of "charitable" and "educational" as used in this section.

APPENDIX N
BATF SELECTED PROVISIONS

Subpart A – Scope of Regulations

27 CFR § 6.1 General. The regulations in this part, issued pursuant to section 5 of the Federal Alcohol Administration Act (27 U.S.C. 205), specify practices which are prohibited by subsection (b) "Tiedhouse," and provide the exception to these prohibitions. This part does not attempt to enumerate all of the practices prohibited by section 5(b) of the Act. Nothing in this part shall operate to exempt any person from the requirements of any State law or regulation.

§ 6.2 Territorial extent. This part applies to the several States of the United States, the District of Columbia, and Puerto Rico.

§ 6.3 Application. (a) *General.* This part applies only to transactions between industry members and retailers. It does not apply to transactions between two industry members (for example, between a producer and a wholesaler), or to transactions between an industry member and a retailer wholly owned by that industry member.

(b) *Transaction involving State agencies.* The regulations in this part apply only to transactions between industry members and State agencies operating as retailers as defined in this part. The regulations do not apply to State agencies with regard to their wholesale dealings with retailers.

§ 6.4 Jurisdictional limits. (a) *General.* The regulations in this part apply where:

(1) The industry member induces a retailer to purchase distilled spirits, wine, or malt beverages from such industry member to the exclusion in whole or in part of products sold or offered for sale by other persons in interstate or foreign commerce; and

(2) If:

(i) The inducement is made in the course of interstate or foreign commerce; or

(ii) The industry member engages in the practice of using an inducement to such an extent as substantially to restrain or prevent transactions in interstate or foreign commerce in any such products; or

(iii) The direct effect of the inducement is to prevent, deter, hinder or restrict other persons from selling or offering for sale any such products to such retailer in interstate or foreign commerce.

(b) *Malt beverages.* In the case of malt beverages, this part applies to transactions between a retailer in any State and a brewer, importer, or wholesaler of malt beverages inside or outside such State only to the extent that the law of such State imposes requirements similar to the requirements of section 5(b) of the Federal Alcohol Administration Act (27 U.S.C. 205(b)), with respect to similar transactions between a retailer in such State and a brewer, importer, or wholesaler or malt beverage in such State, as the case may be.

Subpart B – Definitions

§ 6.11 Meaning of terms. As used in this part, unless the context otherwise requires, terms have the meanings given in this section. Any other term defined in the Federal Alcohol Administration Act and used in this part shall have the meaning assigned to it by that Act.

Act. The Federal Alcohol Administration Act.

Equipment. All functional items such as tap boxes, glassware, pouring racks, and similar items used in the conduct of a retailer's business.

Industry member. Any person engaged in business as a distiller, brewer, rectifier, blender, or other producer, or as an importer or wholesaler, of distilled spirits, wine or malt beverages, or as a bottler, or warehouseman and member does not include an agency of a State or political subdivision thereof, or an officer or employee of such agency.

Product. Distilled spirits, wine or malt beverages, as defined in the Federal Alcohol Administration Act.

Retailer. Any person engaged in the sale of distilled spirits, wine or malt beverages to consumers. A wholesaler who makes incidental retail sales representing less than five percent of the wholesaler's total sales volume for the preceding two-month period shall not be considered a retailer with respect to such incidental sales.

Retailer establishment. Any premises where distilled spirits, wine or malt beverages are sold or offered for sale to consumers, whether for consumption on or off the premises where sold.

Subpart C – Unlawful Inducements
General

§ 6.21 Application. Except as provided in Subpart D, it is unlawful for any industry member to induce, directly or indirectly, any retailer to purchase any products from the industry member to the exclusion, in whole or in part, of such products sold or offered for sale by other persons in interstate or foreign commerce by any of the following means:

(a) By acquiring or holding (after the expiration of any license held at the time the FAA Act was enacted) any interest in any license with respect to the premises of the retailer;

(b) By acquiring any interest in the real or personal property owned, occupied, or used by the retailer in the conduct of his business;

(c) By furnishing, giving, renting, lending, or selling to the retailer, any equipment, fixtures, signs, supplies, money, services or other thing of value, subject to the exceptions contained in Subpart D;

(d) By paying or crediting the retailer for any advertising, display, or distribution service;

(e) By guaranteeing any loan or the repayment of any financial obligation of the retailer;

(f) By extending to the retailer credit for a period in excess of the credit period usual and customary to the industry for the particular class of transactions as prescribed in § 6.65; or

(g) By requiring the retailer to take and dispose of a certain quota of any such products.

Interest in Retail License

§ 6.25 General. Industry members are prohibited from inducing the purchases of a retailer by acquiring or holding any interest in any license (State, county or municipal) with respect to the premises of a retailer.

§ 6.26 Indirect interest. Industry member interest in retail licenses includes any interest acquired by corporate officials, partners, employees or other representatives of the industry member. Any interest in a retail license acquired by a separate corporation in which the industry member or its officials hold ownership or are otherwise affiliated, is an interest in a retail license.

§ 6.27 Proprietary interest. (a) *Complete ownership.* Outright ownership of a retail business by an industry member is not prohibited.

(b) *Partial ownership.* Less than complete ownership of a retail business by an industry member constitutes an interest in a retail license within the meaning of the Act.

Furnishing Things of Value

§ 6.41 General. Subject to the exceptions listed in Subpart D, industry members are prohibited from inducing the purchases of a retailer by furnishing, giving, renting, lending or selling to the retailer any equipment, fixtures, signs, supplies, money, services or other thing of value.

§ 6.42 Indirect inducement through third party arrangements. The furnishing, giving, renting, lending or selling of equipment, fixtures, signs, supplies, money, services or other thing of value by an industry member to a third party, such as a retailer association or display company where the benefits resulting from such thing of value flow to individual retailers, is the indirect furnishing of a thing of value within the meaning of the Act. This section does not prohibit third parties from furnishing, giving, renting, lending or selling equipment, fixtures, signs, supplies, money, services or things of value to retailers which industry members may lawfully provide to retailers under Subpart D of this part.

§ 6.43 Sale of equipment. A transaction in which equipment is sold to a retailer by an industry member, except as provided in §§ 6.88 and 6.89, is the selling of equipment within the meaning of the Act regardless of how sold. Further, the negotiation by an industry member of a special price to a retailer for equipment from an equipment company is the furnishing of a thing of value within the meaning of the Act.

§ 6.44 Free warehousing. The furnishing of free warehousing by delaying delivery of distilled spirits, wine or malt beverages beyond the time that payment for the product is received, or if a retailer is purchasing on credit, delaying final delivery of products beyond the close of the period of time for which credit is lawfully extended, is the furnishing of a service or thing of value within the meaning of the Act.

§ 6.45 Assistance in acquiring license. Any assistance (financial, legal, administrative or influential) given the retailer by an industry member in the retailer's acquisition of the retailer's license is the furnishing of a service or thing of value within the meaning of the Act.

§ 6.46 Outside signs. (a) *Furnished to retailers.* The furnishing of outside signs to retailers by an industry member is the furnishing of a thing of value within the meaning of the Act.

(b) *Benefiting a retailer.* The placement by an industry member of a "billboard" or "spectacular" sign, advertising distilled spirits, wine or malt beverages, on the wall or roof of a building adjacent to or occupied by a retailer is the furnishing of a thing of value within the meaning of the Act if (1) the sign contains a panel identifying the retailer, or (2) the retailer is compensated, directly or indirectly (through a sign company), in conjunction with the placement of the sign.

§ 6.47 Item intended for consumers. Except as provided in §§ 6.87 and 6.93, the furnishing of things of value such as trading stamps, coupons, nonalcoholic mixers, pouring racks, and the like to retailers is the furnishing of a thing of value within the meaning of the Act regardless of whether the industry member intends for the items to be distributed free of charge to consumers.

Paying for Advertising, Display or Distribution Service

§ 6.51 General. Industry members are prohibited from inducing the purchases of a retailer by paying or crediting the retailer for any advertising, display or distribution service, whether or not the advertising, display or distribution service received is commensurate with the amount paid by the retailer.

§ 6.52 Cooperative advertising. An arrangement in which an industry member participates with a retailer in paying for an advertisement placed by the retailer constitutes paying the retailer for advertising within the meaning of the Act.

§ 6.53 Advertising in ballparks, racetracks and stadiums. The purchase, by an industry member, of advertising on signs, scoreboards, programs, scorecards and the like at ballparks, racetracks or stadiums, from the retail concessionaire constitutes paying the retailer for an advertising service within the meaning of the Act.

§ 6.54 Advertising in retailer publications. The purchase, by an industry member, of advertising in a retailer publication for distribution to consumers or the general public constitutes paying the retailer for advertising within the meaning of the Act.

§ 6.55 Display service. Industry member reimbursements to retailers for setting up product or other displays constitutes paying the retailer for rendering a display service within the meaning of the Act.

§ 6.56 Renting display space. A promotion whereby an industry member rents display space at a retail establishment constitutes paying the retailer for rendering a display service within the meaning of the Act.

Quota Sales

§ 6.71 Quota sales. An industry member is prohibited from inducing the purchases of a retailer by requiring a retailer to take and dispose of any quota of distilled spirits, wine or malt beverages.

§ 6.72 "Tie-in" sales. A requirement that a retailer purchase one product in order to purchase another is prohibited. This includes combination sales if one or more products may be purchased only in combination with other products and not individually. However, an industry member is not prohibited from selling at a special combination price, two or more kinds or brands of products to a retailer, provided (a) the retailer has the option of purchasing either product at the usual price, and (b) the retailer is not required to purchase any product he or she does not want.

Subpart D – Exceptions

§ 6.81 General. (a) *Application.* An industry member may furnish a retailer equipment, inside signs, supplies, services, or other thing of value, under the conditions and within the limitations prescribed by this subpart. The furnishing of these items or services may not be conditioned on the purchase of distilled spirits, wine or malt beverages.

(b) *Recordkeeping requirements.* Industry members shall keep and maintain records on the permit premises, for a three-year period, of all items furnished to retailers under §§ 6.83, 6.85, 6.88, 6.89, 6.90, 6,91, 6.96(a) and 6.100. Commercial records or invoices may be used to satisfy this recordkeeping requirement if all required information is shown. These records shall show:

(1) The name and address of the retailer receiving the item;

(2) The date furnished;

(3) The item furnished;

(4) The industry member's cost of the item furnished (determined by manufacturer's invoice price); and

(5) Charges to the retailer for any item.

§ 6.83 Product displays. (a) *General.* An industry member may furnish, give, rent, loan, or sell product displays to a retailer, subject to the limitations prescribed in paragraph (c) of this section.

(b) *Definition.* Product display means any wine racks, bins, barrels, casks, shelving and the like from which distilled spirits, wine or malt beverages are displayed and sold.

(c) *Conditions and limitations.* (1) The total value of all product displays furnished by an industry member under paragraph (a) of this section may not exceed $100 per brand in use at any one time in any one retail establishment. The value of a product display is the actual cost to the industry member who initially purchased it. Transportation and installation costs are excluded.

(2) Industry members may not pool or combine their dollar limitations in order to provide a retailer a product display valued in excess of $100 per brand.

(3) Product displays shall bear conspicuous and substantial advertising matter.

§ 6.85 Retailer advertising specialties. (a) *General.* An industry member may furnish, give, rent, loan, or sell retailer advertising specialties to a retailer if these items bear advertising matter and are primarily valuable to the retailer as point of sale advertising. These items include such things as trays, coasters, mats, menu cards, meal checks, paper napkins, foam scrapers, back bar mats, thermometers, clocks and calendars. An industry member may add the name or name and address of the retailer to the retailer advertising specialty.

(b) *Limitations.* (1) The total value of all retailer advertising specialties furnished by an industry member to a retailer may not exceed $50 per brand in any one calendar year per retail establishment. The value of a retailer advertising specialty is the actual cost of that item to the industry member who initially purchased it. Transportation and installation costs are excluded.

(2) Industry members may not pool or combine their dollar limitations in order to provide a retailer with retailer advertising specialties valued in excess of $50 per brand.

§ 6.87 Consumer advertising specialties. Consumer advertising specialties, such as ashtrays, bottle or can openers, corkscrews, shopping bags, matches, printed recipes, pamphlets, cards, leaflets, blotters, postcards and pencils, which bear advertising matter may be furnished, given or sold to a retailer for unconditional distribution by the retailer to the general public. The retailer may not be paid or credited in any manner directly or indirectly for this distribution service.

§ 6.88 Glassware. An industry member may sell glassware to a retailer if the glassware is sold at a price not less than the cost to the industry member who initially purchased it, and if the price is collected within 30 days of the date of sale.

§ 6.89 Tapping accessories. Tapping accessories, such as standards, faucets, rods, vents, taps, tap standards, hoses, washers, couplings, gas gauges, vent tongues, shanks and check valves, may be sold to a retailer and installed in the retailer's establishment if the tapping accessories are sold at a price not less than the cost to the industry member who initially purchased them, and if the price is collected within 30 days of the date of sale.

§ 6.90 Supplies. Carbon dioxide gas or ice may be sold to a retailer, if sold in accordance with the reasonable open market price in the locality where sold, and if the price is collected within 30 days of the date of sale.

§ 6.92 Newspaper cuts. Newspaper cuts, mats, or engraved blocks for use in retailers' advertisements may be furnished, given, rented, loaned or sold by an industry member to a retailer selling the industry member's products.

§ 6.95 Consumer tasting or sampling at retail establishments. An industry member may conduct tasting or sampling activities at a retail establishment. The industry member may purchase the products to be used from the retailer, may not purchase them from the retailer for more than the ordinary retail price.

§ 6.96 Consumer promotions. (a) *Coupons.* An industry member may furnish to consumers, coupons which are redeemable at a retail establishment under the following conditions:

(1) The coupons may not specify a particular retailer or group of retailers where such coupons can be redeemed.

(2) An industry member may reimburse a retailer for the face value of all coupons redeemed, and pay a retailer a usual and customary handling fee for the redemption of coupons.

(3) Payments for the redemption of coupons shall be made directly to the retail entity to reduce the cost of sales. An industry member may not pay officers, employees or representatives of retailers or wholesalers for the redemption of coupons.

(b) *Direct offerings.* Contest prizes, premium offers, refunds, and like items may be offered by industry members directly to consumers. Officers, employees and representatives of wholesalers or retailers are excluded from participation.

§ 6.98 Advertising service. The names and addresses of retailers selling the products of an industry member may be listed in an advertisement of that industry member, if:

(a) The advertisement does not also contain the retail price of the product; and

(b) The listing is the only reference to the retailer in the advertisement and is relatively inconspicuous in relation to the advertisement as a whole.

Pictures or illustrations of retail establishments and laudatory references to retailers in industry member advertisements are not hereby authorized.

APPENDIX O (1)
CALIFORNIA ALCOHOLIC BEVERAGE
CONTROL DEPARTMENT REGULATIONS

Rule 106(i)

(i) Contests (1) Contests sponsored by retail licensees. Without violating this rule, retail licensees may furnish prizes other than alcoholic beverages, to participants in competitive events held on the licensed premises, provided participation in such events shall not be conditioned on the purchase, sale or consumption of alcoholic beverages and provided that such contest or competitive event does not involve the consumption of alcoholic beverages.

2. Contests sponsored by suppliers. Without violating this rule, suppliers may sponsor contests, races, tournaments, and other similar activities on or off licensed premises. Sponsorships shall be only in the form of monetary payments to bona fide amateur or professional organizations established for the encouragement and promotion of the activities involved. Sponsorship shall be subject to the following conditions:

A. There shall be no requirement for the exclusive sale of the sponsor's products nor shall such products be sold exclusively at any such event.

B. No money or other thing of value other than approved advertising specialties shall be given by a sponsor to anyone other than the organizations conducting the contest.

C. Participants may be charged an entry fee, but entry shall not be conditioned upon the purchase of any of the sponsor's products.

APPENDIX O (2)
UTAH LIQUOR CONTROL COMMISSION
REGULATIONS

Reg. 96-1-7(i)

(i) No distiller, winery, brewer, rectifier or beer wholesaler shall sponsor or underwrite any athletic, theatrical, scholastic, artistic or scientific event, without first obtaining the permission of the Department. Permission shall be granted only upon a written description of the event and the type and scope of participation by the distiller, winery, brewer, rectifier or beer wholesaler. Permission shall not be granted if the event:

(a) Takes place on the premises of a retailer of light beer, Department licensee or permittee, Department liquor package agency, or any school, college, university or other educational institution;

(b) Involves any inducement to consume products by offering alcoholic products to the general public without charge;

(c) Involves the display of drinking scenes;

(d) Is conducted in such a manner as to unduly increase the consumption of alcoholic products.

Permission shall not be necessary for any advertisement otherwise complying with these Rules in bona fide programs or other literature incidental to the event.

APPENDIX P
CIGARETTE LABELING

15 U.S.C. § 1333. Labeling requirements; conspicuous statement

(a) Required warnings; packages; advertisements; billboards

(1) It shall be unlawful for any person to manufacture, package, or import for sale or distribution within the United States any cigarettes the package of which fails to bear, in accordance with the requirements of this section, one of the following labels:

SURGEON GENERAL'S WARNING: Smoking Causes Lung Cancer, Heart Disease, Emphysema, And May Complicate Pregnancy.

SURGEON GENERAL'S WARNING: Quitting Smoking Now Greatly Reduces Serious Risks to Your Health.

SURGEON GENERAL'S WARNING: Smoking By Pregnant Women May Result In Fetal Injury, Premature Birth, And Low Birth Weight.

SURGEON GENERAL'S WARNING: Cigarette Smoke Contains Carbon Monoxide.

(2) It shall be unlawful for any manufacturer or importer of cigarettes to advertise or cause to be advertised (other than through the use of outdoor billboards) within the United States any cigarette unless the advertising bears, in accordance with the requirements of this section, one of the following labels:

SURGEON GENERAL'S WARNING: Smoking Causes Lung Cancer, Heart Disease, Emphysema, And May Complicate Pregnancy.

SURGEON GENERAL'S WARNING: Quitting Smoking Now Greatly Reduces Serious Risks to Your Health.

SURGEON GENERAL'S WARNING: Smoking By Pregnant Women May Result In Fetal Injury, Premature Birth, And Low Birth Weight.

SURGEON GENERAL'S WARNING: Cigarette Smoke Contains Carbon Monoxide.

(3) It shall be unlawful for any manufacturer or importer of cigarettes to advertise or cause to be advertised within the United States through the use of outdoor billboards any cigarette unless the advertising bears, in accordance with the requirements of this section, one of the following labels:

SURGEON GENERAL'S WARNING: Smoking Causes Lung Cancer, Heart Disease, Emphysema, And May Complicate Pregnancy.

SURGEON GENERAL'S WARNING: Quitting Smoking Now Greatly Reduces Serious Risks to Your Health.

SURGEON GENERAL'S WARNING: Smoking By Pregnant Women May Result In Fetal Injury, Premature Birth, And Low Birth Weight.

SURGEON GENERAL'S WARNING: Cigarette Smoke Contains Carbon Monoxide.

(b) Conspicuous statement; label statement format; outdoor billboard statement format

(1) Each label statement required by paragraph (1) of subsection (a) of this section shall be located in the place label statements were placed on cigarette packages as of October 12, 1984. The phrase "Surgeon General's Warning" shall appear in capital letters and the size of all other letters in the label shall be the same as the size of such letters as of October 12, 1984. All the letters in the label shall appear in conspicuous and legible type in contrast by typography, layout, or color with all other printed material on the the package.

(2) The format of each label statement required by paragraph (2) of subsection (a) of this section shall be the format required for label statements in cigarette advertising as of October 12, 1984, except that the phrase "Surgeon General's Warning" shall appear in capital letters, the area of the rectangle enclosing the label shall be 50 per centum larger in size with a corresponding increase in the size of the type in the label, the width of the rule forming the border around the label shall be twice that in effect on October 12, 1984, and the label may be placed at a distance from the outer edge of the advertisement which is one-half the distance permitted on October 12, 1984. Each label statement shall appear in conspicuous and legible type in contrast by typography, layout, or color with all other printed material in the advertisement.

(3) The format and type style of each label statement required by paragraph (3) of subsection (a) of this section shall be the format and type style required in outdoor billboard advertising as of October 12, 1984. Each such label statement shall be printed in capital letters of the height of the tallest letter in a label statement on outdoor advertising of the same dimension on October 12, 1984. Each such label statement shall be enclosed by a black border which is located within the perimeter

of the format required in outdoor billboard advertising of the same dimension on October 12, 1984, and the width of which is twice the width of the vertical element of any letter in the label statement within the border.

(c) Rotation of label statement; plan; submission to Federal Trade Commission

(1) Except as provided in paragraph (2), the label statements specified in paragraphs (1), (2), and (3) of subsection (a) of this section shall be rotated by each manufacturer or importer of cigarettes quarterly in alternating sequence on packages of each brand of cigarettes manufactured by the manufacturer or importer and in the advertisements for each such brand of cigarettes in accordance with a plan submitted by the manufacturer or importer and approved by the Federal Trade Commission. The Federal Trade Commission shall approve a plan submitted by a manufacturer or importer of cigarettes which will provide the rotation required by this subsection and which assures that all of the labels required by paragraphs (1), (2), and (3) will be displayed by the manufacturer or importer at the same time.

(2)(A) A manufacturer or importer of cigarettes may apply to the Federal Trade Commission to have the label rotation described in subparagraph (C) apply with respect to a brand style of cigarettes manufactured or imported by such manufacturer or importer if –

(i) the number of cigarettes of such brand style sold in the fiscal year of the manufacturer or importer preceding the submission of the application is less than one-fourth of 1 percent of all the cigarettes sold in the United States in such year, and

(ii) more than one-half of the cigarettes manufactured or imported by such manufacturer or importer for sale in the United States are packaged into brand styles which meet the requirements of clause (i).

If an application is approved by the Commission, the label rotation described in subparagraph (C) shall apply with respect to the applicant during the one-year period beginning on the date of the application approval.

(B) An applicant under subparagraph (A) shall include in its application a plan under which the label statements specified in paragraph (1) of subsection (a) of this section will be rotated by the applicant manufacturer or importer in accordance with the label rotation described in subparagraph (C).

(C) Under the label rotation which a manufacturer or importer with an approved application may put into effect each of the labels specified in paragraph (1) of subsection (a) of this section shall appear on the packages of each brand style of cigarettes with respect to which the application was approved an equal number of times within the twelve-month period beginning on the date of the approval by the Commission of the application.

(d) Application; distributors; retailers

Subsection (a) of this section does not apply to a distributor or a retailer of cigarettes who does not manufacture, package, or import cigarettes for sale or distribution within the United States.

APPENDIX Q
TOBACCO PACKAGING

26 U.S.C. § 5723. Packages, marks, labels and notices

(a) Packages – All tobacco products and cigarette papers and tubes shall, before removal, be put up in such packages as the Secretary shall by regulation prescribe.

(b) Marks, labels and notices – Every package of tobacco products or cigarette papers or tubes shall, before removal, bear the marks, labels, and notices, if any, that the Secretary by regulation prescribes.

(c) Lottery features – No certificate, coupon, or other device purporting to be or to represent a ticket, chance, share, or an interest in, or dependent on, the event of a lottery shall be contained in, attached to, or stamped, marked, written, or printed on any package of tobacco products or cigarette papers or tubes.

(d) Indecent or immoral material prohibited – No indecent or immoral picture, print or representation shall be contained in, attached to, or stamped, marked written or printed on any package of tobacco products or cigarette papers or tubes.

(e) Exceptions – Tobacco products furnished by manufacturers of such products for use or consumption by their employees, or for experimental purposes, and tobacco products and cigarette papers and tubes transferred to the bonded premises of another manufacturer or export warehouse proprietor or released in bond from customs custody for delivery to a manufacturer of tobacco products or cigarette papers and tubes, may be exempted from subsections (a) and (b) in accordance with such regulations as the Secretary shall prescribe.

APPENDIX R (1)
ATLANTA OUTDOOR FESTIVALS ORDINANCE SELECTED PROVISIONS

AN ORDINANCE TO ESTABLISH A COMPREHENSIVE ADMINISTRATIVE PROCEDURE FOR THE GRANTING OF PERMITS TO HOLD OUTDOOR FESTIVALS IN THE CITY OF ATLANTA; TO PROVIDE FOR APPLICATION; REVIEW BY AFFECTED DEPARTMENTS; THE CLASSIFICATION, COORDINATION AND SCHEDULING OF SUCH EVENTS; TOGETHER WITH A FEE SCHEDULE FOR THE ISSUANCE OF SUCH PERMITS; AND AMENDING CERTAIN PROVISIONS OF THE ALCOHOLIC BEVERAGES LICENSING ORDINANCE AND STREET BANNERS ORDINANCE.

WHEREAS, outdoor festivals are important components in determining the quality of life in any urban environment; and

WHEREAS, an increasing number of individuals and organizations are expressing interest in sponsoring outdoor festivals throughout the City of Atlanta; and

WHEREAS, outdoor festivals not only contribute to the economy of the various businesses in the festival area but also provide revenues directly to the City; and

WHEREAS, outdoor festivals help promote the image of the City of Atlanta and increase the amount of cultural and entertainment available to residents of the metropolitan area; and

WHEREAS, outdoor festivals require coordination with the City of Atlanta as well as varying amounts of support services from certain City Departments; and

WHEREAS, Council has adopted an ordinance creating the position of Festivals Coordinator in the Department of Parks, Recreation & Cultural Affairs to facilitate the City's support of outdoor festivals; and

WHEREAS, it is desirable that persons and organizations wishing to produce outdoor festivals have available to them a procedure for permitting outdoor festivals and arranging for the provision of support services available from the City; and

WHEREAS, a uniform procedure for the issuance of necessary permits will facilitate the coordination of City support services and minimize administrative burdens.

THEREFORE, BE IT ORDAINED BY THE COUNCIL OF THE CITY OF ATLANTA:

Section I. That Part 10 of the Code of Ordinances of the City of Atlanta, Georgia, be, and the same is hereby amended by adding to said Part 10 a new Chapter 5, containing new code sections numbered 10-5001 through 10-5011, which new code sections shall read as follows:

"Chapter 5. Outdoor Festivals.
Section 10-5001. Title of Ordinance. This ordinance (Sections 10-5001 through 10-5011) shall be known and may be cited as the Atlanta Outdoor Festivals Ordinance of 1983.

"Section 10-5002. Scope of Ordinance. This ordinance is intended by Council to be the framework within which all outdoor festivals as defined in this ordinance held in the City of Atlanta are approved and regulated. It shall be unlawful for any person or organization to hold an outdoor festival as defined herein within the limits of the City of Atlanta without complying with the procedures set forth in this ordinance, provided that this ordinance shall not apply to a city-sponsored event, as defined herein.

"Section 10-5003. Definitions. As used in this ordinance the following definitions, and no other, shall apply to the following words:

Outdoor Festival: An outdoor public celebration or gathering which involves the use either of public parks or public streets and which includes entertainment, dancing, music, dramatic productions, art exhibition, parades, or the sale of merchandise, food or alcohol, or any combination of the foregoing; and which of necessity requires for its successful execution the provision and coordination of municipal services to a degree significantly over and above that which the City of Atlanta routinely provides under ordinary everyday circumstances. The definition of 'outdoor festival,' as used in this ordinance, does not include events which are solely parades, foot races, or political demonstrations, unless such parade, foot race, or political demonstration is proposed as an integral part of a larger 'outdoor festival,' as defined herein.

Application: A written request on forms supplied by the festivals coordinator which sets forth the information required to be provided by this ordinance.

Application Fee: The nonrefundable fee paid in connection with an application made pursuant to this ordinance.

Commissioner: Unless otherwise designated, the term "Commissioner" as used in this ordinance refers to the Commissioner of Parks, Recreation and Cultural Affairs.

Extra Personnel Hours: The total of the number of all hours worked by all city employees in the particular departments or areas under consideration for classification in connection with the production of the festival in question, to the extent that such hours exceed the total number of hours which would have been worked by those same city employees in the same location had the festival not taken place. Excluded from this definition are the personnel hours worked by the Festivals Coordinator or by a city employee designated to fulfill the function of Festival Coordinator on any particular occasion.

Permit Fee: The fee required to be paid pursuant to this ordinance for the issuance of a permit to hold a public festival.

Sanitation Bond: A bond conditioned upon good performance which shall be required by the Commissioner of any applicant who proposes to do the cleaning of streets or parks in connection with an approved festival.

Political Demonstration: A public gathering, procession or parade, the primary purpose of which is the exercise of the rights of assembly and free speech as guaranteed by the First Amendment to the Constitution of the United States. The fact that such an event may be advertised as a "festival" does not in and of itself bring such a demonstration within the scope of this ordinance.

Festivals Coordinator: The person employed by the City to carry out the functions of the ordinance which created the position of Festival Coordinator. In the event the position is vacant, the term as used in this ordinance shall apply to whomever the Mayor designates on a temporary basis to administer this ordinance.

City-Sponsored Event: A public event which is directly related to a recognized function of city government and which is in major part initiated, financed and executed by the City of Atlanta. It does not include events in which the City of Atlanta is merely listed as a co-sponsor if the City does not carry a major share of the burden of initiating, financing and executing the event.

"Section 10-5004. Entitlement to Permit. The Commissioner of the Department of Parks, Recreation & Cultural Affairs (hereinafter, "Commissioner") shall be charged with the responsibility of determining whether or not a particular applicant shall be entitled to an outdoor festival permit pursuant to this ordinance. In determining whether to grant or deny a particular permit application the Commissioner shall take into account the effect the proposed festival will have upon the environment and the public health and safety. The Commissioner shall also take into account the frequency with which such events are held and the convenience of the public in relation thereto. In any event, permits granted pursuant to this ordinance shall not authorize more than ten (10) calendar days of festivals for any particular applicant per calendar year. In addition to the criteria above, in making the decision whether to grant the permit, the Commissioner shall take into account the following considerations:

(1) Whether the history, if any, of the particular applicants, insofar as it can be determined, indicates their capability or incapability of executing the planned festival;

(2) Whether any inconveniences which may be suffered by the general public is outweighed by the potential benefit to the community as a whole;

(3) Whether budgetary considerations at the time of the application create such a heavy burden upon the city's financial resources that it would not be practical to hold the proposed festival at the time requested;

(4) Whether the holding of the festival as planned would create an undue burden upon the manpower resources of the city; and

(5) Whether the public safety would be compromised substantially.

"Section 10-5005. Application. Any person or organization desiring to hold an outdoor festival must make application for a permit to hold such event no later than sixty (60) days prior to the commencement of such event to the Festivals Coordinator. Such application shall be accompanied by a nonrefundable application fee of $10.00. The application must include the following information:

(1) The name of the festival and its purpose in general terms.

(2) The name(s) of the person(s) or organizations(s) sponsoring said festival, together with the addresses and telephone numbers of all such persons or organizations.

(3) The date or dates of the proposed festival.

(4) The specific location(s) within the City of Atlanta where such event or festival is being held.

(5) The number of persons estimated to be in attendance at such event or festival.

(6) Whether any street closings are requested, and, if so, which streets and when.

(7) Whether any beer, wine, or other spiritous beverages are expected to be present and/or sold for public consumption, together with a detailed proposal for any such sale, indicating among other things, who is expected to be the vendor or vendors, whether such vendor or vendors presently hold any type of license for on-premises consumption of alcoholic beverages, and stating the exact locations and times for such sales.

(8) Whether any temporary outdoor structures are proposed to be built, describing them in detail.

(9) Whether any signs or banners are proposed to be erected, giving details.

(10) Whether a parade is expected to be held in connection with such event, stating details, including the time, location and anticipated crowd.

(11) Whether entertainment will be involved, giving details as to nature, time and place.

(12) Whether there will be street vendors or peddlers involved, giving details, including specifically contracted or regularly licensed vendors and peddlers.

(13) Whether the applicant proposed either in whole or in part to be responsible for cleaning up the area used, specifying details.

(14) Whether the applicant proposed to hire security guards or off-duty policemen to assist in security and traffic control, giving details.

(15) Whether utility services such as electrical power or water will be required specifying amount and type.

(16) Whether electrical wiring shall be installed, specifying installation details.

"Section 10-5006. Review of Application. Upon receipt of the completed application and application fee the Festivals Coordinator shall forward copies of the application to the Departments of Law, Public Safety, Environment and Streets, and Parks, Recreation and Cultural Affairs and the Bureau of Buildings for review. The persons designated in each such department by their respective commissioners for such review shall review the application, endorse their comments thereon, and return the comments to the Festivals Coordinator within 10 working days from receipt. The comments so forwarded shall be retained with the file on such application.

"Section 10-5007. Classification and Approval. (a) After reviewing the comments of all the other departments and the Bureau of Buildings, the Commissioner shall then approve or reject the application for the permit. If the application is approved, the Commissioner in consultation with the heads of affected departments shall also impose any necessary restrictions or conditions to be observed in accordance with the public safety, environmental and administrative considerations involved in the particular application. Under no circumstances shall the Commissioner approve the permit if the applicant proposes to limit the use of public streets by pedestrians using said streets to move from location to location, or if the applicant proposes to limit the use of public parks when use of said parks by the general public shall not unreasonably disturb the activities of the planned festival. Nothing in this section shall be construed so as to prohibit the imposition of reasonable restrictions on the movement of the public which are necessary for the carrying out of the festival, *provided*, however, that said restriction shall not bar the admission of the public on the grounds of race, religion, sex or group affiliation.

Streets may be closed in connection with an outdoor festival at the discretion of the Commissioner, having due regard to the public safety and environmental effects of such closing, provided all reasonable steps are taken to minimize the adverse effect such closings have upon the public. In no event, however, shall Peachtree Street or Peachtree Road, or any portion thereof which lies within the City of Atlanta be closed by the Commissioner; authority for the closing of any portion of the Peachtree Corridor must be by specific resolution of the City Council. For classification purposes the Commissioner shall evaluate the application by the following criteria:

1. The anticipated amount of extra personnel which shall be required to be furnished by the City to accomplish the necessary public safety and sanitation components of the festival. By agreement, as endorsed upon the permit or in a separate contract, the applicant may furnish some of the personnel so required, and the anticipated personnel requirements for classification purposes shall be considered as reduced accordingly.

2. The type and amount of special, or technical, assistance required from City employees (other than the services of the Festival Coordinator, which shall not be considered);

3. The anticipated number of persons attending the event over the entire period of the festival;

4. Whether the organization(s) producing the festival are profit-making or nonprofit.

(b) The classes of outdoor festival permits shall be as follows:

Class A Permit: For a festival which will require between 300-500 extra personnel hours by city employees in the public safety and sanitation areas, or, more than (40) forty extra personnel hours from employees for technical assistance, or, in which the attendance shall be more than 25,000 persons over the entire time of the festival, which is provided by a profit-making organization.

Class B Permit: (i) For a festival which has the characteristics of a Class A Festival, but which is organized and executed by a nonprofit organization; or

(ii) For a festival which will require between 200-300 extra personnel hours in the public safety and sanitation fields, and less than 40 extra city personnel hours for technical assistance, and in which the attendance is anticipated to be less than _____ _____ _____ _____ of the festival, and which is provided by a profit-making organization.

Class C Permit: (i) For a festival which will require between 100-200 extra personnel hours by city employees in the public safety and sanitation areas and less than 40 extra city personnel hours for technical assistance, and in which the attendance is anticipated to be less than 25,000 persons over the entire period of the festival and which is provided by a profit-making organization; or

(ii) For a festival which has the characteristics of a Class B (ii) Festival, but which is organized and executed by a nonprofit organization.

Class D Permit: (i) For a festival which will require between 50-100 extra city personnel hours for public safety and sanitation; and less than 20 extra city personnel hours for technical assistance, and for which the anticipated attendance is less than 25,000 persons over the entire period of the festival.

(ii) For a festival which has the characteristics of a Class C (i) Festival, but which is organized and executed by a nonprofit organization.

Class E Permit: For a festival which will require less than 50 city personnel hours for public safety and sanitation; and less than 10 city personnel hours for technical assistance, and for which the anticipated attendance is less than 12,000 persons over the entire period of the festival.

"Section 10-5008. Issuance of Outdoor Festival Permit; and Bond Fees. If the Commissioner approves the issuance of the permit, as provided in Section 10-5007, the applicant may obtain such permit by agreeing to accept the classification and conditions imposed by the Commissioner and by paying the permit fee and sanitation bond fee if the applicant proposes to do the cleaning of streets and parks associated with the festival. Said fees shall be determined according to the following schedule:

Festival Permit Fees	*Sanitation Bond Fees*
a) Class A $2,000.00	250.00
b) Class B $1,000.00	150.00
c) Class C $ 750.00	125.00
d) Class D $ 250.00	75.00
e) Class E $ 50.00	55.00

Any festival requiring in excess of the agreed upon city personnel hours shall be charged a prorated fee in addition to the initial base rate. Upon satisfactory completion of the sanitation bond agreement the sanitation bond fee shall be refunded to the applicant.

"Section 10-5009. Other Permits. Nothing in this ordinance shall be construed as repealing other ordinances requiring separate applications for permits for specific portions of the proposed event or festival, such as permits, building or related permits, licenses to sell alcoholic beverages, or permits to sell in parks or on city streets. Those permits must be applied for separately in accordance with the laws or ordinances specifically governing those activities.

"Section 10-5010. Notification of Denial and Appeals. (a) Any applicant denied a permit to conduct a festival shall be notified in writing no later than 30 days prior to the proposed date of the event. Said notification shall state in specific terms the reasons for denial and the right of appeal, and shall be sent by registered mail to the applicant.

(b) Any aggrieved applicant shall be granted a hearing before the License Review Board provided said applicant shall make such request of the Commissioner in writing within (5) days of receipt of notification.

"Section 10-5011. Appeal Heard by License Review Board; Final Determination Made by Mayor. (a) Appeals from the determination of the Commissioner, as to the granting of a festival permit shall be made to the License Review Board. These appeals shall have priority and shall be heard at the next regular meeting of the Board.

(b) The hearing on such appeals shall be *de novo*. The Board shall hear evidence as to the manner by which the Commissioner evaluated the criteria set out in this ordinance and shall make a recommendation to the Mayor that the Commissioner's decision be sustained or reversed, in accordance with the Board's judgment as to whether the application meets the standards set out in this ordinance.

(c) In any event the Board immediately upon concluding its hearing shall cause to be written up their recommended decision together with the reasons therefor and shall forward this recommendation to the Mayor, who shall, no later than 5 days prior to the scheduled commencement of the festival in question, make the final decision in the matter on behalf of the City, and give notice thereof to affected parties."

APPENDIX R (2)
SAN FRANCISCO
EVENT ORDINANCE
SELECTED PROVISIONS

Resolution No. 14375

WHEREAS, Section 7.05 of the Park Code requires this Commission to adopt procedures for the filing and processing of applications for permits to engage in the activities set forth in Section 7.03; and

WHEREAS, Section 7.20 of the Park Code requires this Commission to adopt procedures for the appeal of the denial of an application for a permit to engage in the activities set forth in Section 7.03; and

WHEREAS, various provisions of the Park Code other than Section 7.03 require a permit to engage in certain activities without specifying the division responsible for issuing the permit or the appropriate appeal procedure; and

WHEREAS, the Commission recognizes that the right of citizens to hold assemblies is a treasured right in our society; and

WHEREAS, the Commission acknowledges that the use of park property for public assemblies is a privilege to be exercised by those who accept the attendant duty of protecting and preserving park property against damage and who agree to comply with all relevant laws; and

WHEREAS, the Commission finds that events involving 10,000 or more persons that are anticipated to extend more than one day pose police problems if such events are substantially likely to attract persons who will refuse to leave the park during the night, in violation of Park Code Section 3.13 (sleeping prohibited in the park at night) or who may use campers and other vehicles at night, in violation of Police Code Section 97 (use of vehicles for habitation at night in parks and on streets and public ways prohibited); and

WHEREAS, the Commission also finds that events held in grass areas involving 10,000 or more persons that extend more than one day are substantially likely to result in significant damage to the turf; and

WHEREAS, the Commission finds that Golden Gate Park was created to offer an alternative to the urban setting so that citizens would have available to them a serene, natural environment for their aesthetic, athletic and recreational enjoyment; and

WHEREAS, Golden Gate Park lands were constructed on shifting sand dunes and in most areas of Golden Gate Park there is only a two-inch layer of topsoil, and an unrestricted use of Golden Gate Park meadows by large crowds is substantially likely to cause damage to the fragile crust of soil and surrounding vegetation; and

WHEREAS, the Commission remains concerned that allowing an unrestricted number of events involving crowds of 25,000 or more in the Polo Field will result in a cumulative, long-term adverse impact upon the fragile soil and vegetation at the west end of Golden Gate Park; and

WHEREAS, the Commission reaffirms its objectives and policies for Golden Gate Park as set forth in its plan for Golden Gate Park, adopted pursuant to Resolution No. 11678 and amended pursuant to Resolution No. 14048, wherein, among other things the Commission states its policy that large gatherings may well be accommodated in San Francisco parks other than Golden Gate Park so as to balance the citywide recreational program and alleviate wear and tear on Golden Gate Park; and

WHEREAS, the Commission finds that the unrestricted and unregulated duration of amplified sound in Golden Gate Park has an adverse impact upon the surrounding neighbors' quiet enjoyment of their property and unreasonably interferes with their right of privacy; now, therefore, be it

RESOLVED, that this Commission does hereby adopt the policies and procedures stated herein for the issuance of permits for the use of park property; and be it

FURTHER RESOLVED, that the staff shall decide which park facility within the jurisdiction of this Commission is the most suitable facility to accommodate the interests of the permittee; provided, however, that staff shall in all cases consider the nature of the event, anticipated impact on the neighborhood, anticipated attendance, the policies and guidelines set forth in this resolution, the expertise and experience of the permittee in organizing the type of event proposed, and any other facts and circumstances that relate to any potentially adverse impact on the park property, the neighborhood or the public so long as such impacts are unrelated to the content of the event.

PARK CODE SECTION 7.03
PERMIT APPLICATIONS

A. Application Procedure

Except for permits for large events described below, and permits for the sale of food or distribution of free food, a written application for a permit to perform an activity listed in Section 7.03 shall be made to the Recreation and Park Department at least 15 days in advance, excluding Saturdays, Sundays and legal holidays, so that staff will have adequate time to process requests properly, meet with parties of interest, and coordinate with other affected public agencies as needed. A written application for a permit to perform an activity listed in Section 7.03 which is a large event with an expected attendance of at least 5,000 or for the sale or distribution of food shall be made to the Recreation and Park Department at least 30 days in advance, excluding Saturdays, Sundays and legal holidays, so that staff will have adequate time to schedule meetings with the permittee and other affected public agencies. The application shall include the following information:

(a) The name, address and telephone number of the applicant;

(b) The name(s) of all sponsoring, participating and/or performing groups;

(c) A description of the activity for which a permit is sought;

(d) The date, starting time, place and the estimated length of time of the event;

(e) The number of persons that are expected to be involved and the reasons for anticipating such a number;

(f) At least two preferred or desired locations;

(g) Plans or proposals, such as transit and transportation plan, detailing methodologies for minimizing traffic, litter, congestion and noise at the preferred or desired location and the surrounding areas that would be affected by the proposed event;

(h) Where the applicant is an individual, the signature of the applicant, and where the applicant is a person other than an individual, the signature, name, address, and telephone number of the individual executing the application on behalf of the applicant.

The various time requirements for advance application may be waived by the General Manager, upon request if she determines that the event or events giving rise to the permit application do not reasonably allow a person time to file a permit application within the required time or if an unusual event or combination of events renders such requirement an unreasonable restriction on the right of free speech. No permit application submitted more than 365 days before the proposed activity may be approved.

C. General

1. Permit applicants shall be advised by staff that any publicity issued by the applicant before a permit has issued is done at the applicant's own risk.

2. In order to insure that public enjoyment of park properties and the public comfort, convenience, safety and welfare are not disturbed and that public or private property is not damaged, staff may impose reasonable conditions on approval of permit applications, including but not limited to, the conditions that the applicant provide debris boxes, chemical toilet units, protective coverings, monitors, and security personnel (after staff consultation with the Police Department), and that the applicant permit staff to inspect stages, booths, platforms and other structures that might be erected.

3. Staff shall inform applicants of restrictions contained in City ordinances regulating the use of amplified sound, of the issuance of sound amplification permits by the Police Department, and of the fact that sound amplification ordinances are enforced by the Police Department.

4. Prior to issuing a permit, staff shall consult the Police Department, Municipal Railway, Fire Department, Health Department, Emergency Ambulance Service, Department of Public Works or other relevant agency if any aspect of a permit request requires action or permission from the agency. Staff may also consult the advice of experts in the community in evaluating which park facility is the most appropriate to accommodate the proposed event.

5. Staff may issue one-day permits for the sale of food products with approval of the General Manager and the Health Department. All food permits must be filed 30 days in advance of the event. Staff shall have permission to authorize the

serving or selling of alcoholic beverages for one-day permits with approval of the General Manager so long as the applicant has obtained the necessary approval from the Alcoholic Beverages Commission (ABC).

6. Permittee must secure proper Health Department Notice to Operate and if alcohol is involved a permit from ABC. The Recreation and Park Department letter of permit and the Health Department Notice to Operate must be visibly displayed on each booth or location.

7. Prior to issuing a permit, staff shall arrange a meeting of all public agencies involved in an event with the sponsors of the event if staff concludes the anticipated attendance is in excess of 5,000, or if some aspect of the event would require special services or permission from the affected public agencies which could not be arranged through normal permit procedures or by consultation with the agencies by telephone.

8. Staff shall process all permits without discrimination with regard to race, color, religion, ancestry, national origin, age, sex, political affiliation, sexual orientation, disability or on any other grounds prohibited by law, of those individuals or groups requesting such permits.

9. Material misrepresentations of fact in an application, in circumstances where the applicant reasonably knew or should have known the application did not contain the true facts, may be considered by the General Manager in determining whether the permit application should be denied or revoked because of the applicant's inability to be responsible for the use of park facilities in compliance with the Park Code and all applicable laws, rules and regulations.

If staff has reason to believe that advertising or publicity for an event for which an application is on file or permit has been issued describes or refers to the event in a manner which indicates that the event is different from that described in the letter of intent or application, staff may request the applicant or permittee to submit such advertising or publicity material. Staff shall examine the same for the purpose of determining whether there is reason to conclude that the application inaccurately or incompletely describes the planned event. If it so determines, in cases where the permit has not been granted, staff shall immediately notify applicant of the same and schedule a hearing before the General Manager to determine whether the applicant must modify its application.

In cases where the application has been granted, staff shall schedule a hearing before the General Manager for the purpose of revoking the issuance of the permit in light of the changed circumstances.

D. Performance Bonds

Staff shall require performance bonds pursuant to the following schedule in order to insure that property is restored and cleaned at the conclusion of the permitted activity:

Attendance	Amount Of Bond
100 – 1,000	$ 500
1,000 – 3,000	1,000
3,000 – 6,000	1,500
6,001 – 9,000	2,000
9,001 – 15,000	3,000
15,001 – 25,000	3,500
25,001 – 45,000	4,000
45,001 – 75,000	6,000
75,001 – Plus	$10,000

THE PERFORMANCE BOND SHALL BE IN THE FORM OF A CASHIER'S CHECK PAYABLE TO THE SAN FRANCISCO RECREATION AND PARK DEPARTMENT. The performance bond shall be returned after the event as soon as it is determined that every area of the park used in connection with the event has been cleaned and restored to the same or equivalent condition that existed immediately prior to the time permission to use the facility was granted. In no case shall the performance bond be returned before the property is returned to its original condition.

When an applicant for a permit to perform an activity which is protected by the First Amendment to the U.S. Constitution and for which a performance bond must be posted produces evidence that providing a cash performance bond would be impossible or so financially burdensome that it would preclude the applicant from using park property for the proposed activity, staff shall accept property in lieu of a cash performance bond so long as the property offered is of a type which will reasonably insure restoration and cleaning of the property to be used. If the applicant is unable to provide any such property in lieu of a bond or produces evidence that he or she is indigent, the General Manager may accept in its place written assurances that all necessary appropriate measures will be undertaken by applicant to protect park property against damage if the General Manager determines that the measures proposed by the applicant will be performed and will adequately protect the property.

If an applicant has used park property in the past pursuant to a permit and has caused damage or injury to property or failed to restore or clean the property at the conclusion of the permitted activity, staff may require the applicant to post a performance bond in an amount greater than that normally required, so long as the increased amount is reasonably related to the anticipated costs of restoring or cleaning the property. However, if an applicant who has damaged property or failed to restore or clean the property in the past has, since that occurrence, used park property pursuant to a permit and has left the property in good condition, the amounts normally required of applicants shall apply.

General Manager may waive or decrease the performance bond normally required if the applicant has a history of using park property pursuant to a permit and has consistently left the property used in good condition and no circumstances exist which indicate that the applicant might fail to restore the property after the proposed event.

E. Insurance Requirements

Insurance coverage of the type and amount described below shall be required for the following events where the sponsor is other than a governmental entity:

1. Any event involving groups of 1,000 or more persons;

2. Any event scheduled at night which takes place in whole or part outdoors unless (a) the number involved is so small given the type of activity involved and the location of the event that staff is able to determine that the risk of harm to persons or property is minimal or (b) the applicant or sponsor agrees to provide lighting of sufficient strength that staff is able to determine that the risk of harm to persons or property is minimal;

3. Any event involving animals;

4. Any event which involves large displays, machinery, or any large physical object which could come into physical contact with persons or property and cause injury;

5. Any race or marathon for which a permit is required pursuant to Article 7 of the Park Code;

6. Any festival except that festivals not providing food for sale or not having games which involve an element of risk do not require insurance.

The insurance requirements are as follows: Liability insurance covering all operations, including but not limited to the demised premises, personal injuries and injury to property for single limits of not less than $1,000,000 applying to bodily injuries (including death at any time resulting therefrom), and property damage or a combination of said injuries.

In addition, any event at which food is sold or given to persons other than those in one's own organized group must be covered by the following insurance: Food Products Liability of $1,000,000 when sale of food is contemplated as part of a requested permit. Conditions of sale as negotiated by the Business Office shall be subject to Commission approval.

The normal insurance coverage requirements shall not apply to applicants who propose to engage in an activity protected by the First Amendment of the U.S. Constitution when the applicant produces evidence that complying with those provisions is impossible or so financially burdensome that it would preclude the applicant from using park property for the proposed activity. However, in no event shall the requirement for food products liability coverage be waived when food is involved.

F. Hold Harmless Agreement
An applicant for any permit to engage in an activity for which a performance bond or insurance coverage is normally required shall also be required to sign an agreement to reimburse the Recreation and Park Department for any costs incurred by it in restoring damage to property caused by the action of the permittee, its officers, employees, or agents, or any person who was, or reasonably should have been, under the permittee's control, and to defend the City against, and indemnify and hold the City harmless from any liability to any person resulting from any damage or injury caused by the actions of the permittee, its officers, employees or agents, or any person who was or reasonably should have been, under the permittee's control and to defend the City against, and indemnify and hold the City harmless from any liability to any person resulting from any damage

or injury caused by the actions of the permittee, its officers, employees or agents, or any person who was or reasonably should have been under the permittee's control whenever the performance bond or insurance coverage is waived.

G. Appeal Procedure

(a) An applicant for a permit to perform acts described in Park Code 7.03 may appeal the denial of a permit application or revocation of a permit by filing with the Secretary of the Recreation and Park Commission a written request for a hearing. The request for a hearing shall state succinctly the grounds upon which it is asserted that the determination of the General Manager should be modified or reversed.

(b) Once an appeal has been filed, the Secretary shall place the matter on the agenda of the Parks and Planning Committee for its next regularly scheduled meeting and on the agenda of the Commission for its next regularly scheduled meeting.

(c) The Commission shall afford the applicant an opportunity for a hearing and may reverse, affirm or modify in any regard the determination of the General Manager concerning the denial of a permit application or revocation of a permit. When the Commission affirms the denial of a permit application or revocation of a permit, such a decision shall be based on one or more of the reasons listed in Section 7.07 of the Park Code.

(d) The Commission shall give the applicant written notice of its decision within 3 days after the hearing, Saturdays, Sundays, and legal holidays excluded. Such notice shall be mailed to the applicant at the address contained in the request for a hearing or, if none, in the permit application. The Secretary of the Commission shall keep a copy of the notice on file to be made available to the applicant upon request. When the Commission affirms the denial of the permit application or revocation of a permit or does not approve the permit application as originally made, it shall include within the written notice to the applicant the reasons for the decision and a specification of findings of fact on which the decision is based.

(e) A person whose permit application has been denied or permit revoked may file in a timely manner a request for an expedited appeal if the regular appeal procedure, set forth above, would deprive the person of a hearing before the

Commission prior to the date of the proposed activity for which a permit is sought and a postponement of the date of the proposed activity would prejudice the applicant.

(f) The Commission shall afford an expedited appeal by providing a hearing and a written notice of its decision within 72 hours of the time that the written request for a hearing is filed with the Secretary of the Commission. The written notice shall be filed with the Secretary of the Commission who shall give it to the applicant upon request. If the expiration of the 72-hour period does not fall during regular business hours of the Recreation and Park Department, the Commission shall, at the time of the hearing, arrange with the applicant a procedure for making the decision available within 72 hours.

(g) If a quorum of the Commission cannot be convened within the 72-hour period in order to provide an expedited appeal, the hearing and written notice of decision shall be provided by the General Manager. This duty shall be performed by the General Manager or, in the absence of the General Manager, by the Acting General Manager, and shall not be delegated.

(h) The determinations as to whether the request for an expedited appeal has been filed in a timely manner and whether postponement of the date of the proposed activity would prejudice the applicant shall be made by the General Manager and the decision of the General Manager on these issues shall be final. The General Manager shall not deny an applicant an expedited appeal without affording the applicant an opportunity to be heard on the issues described. This duty shall be performed by the General Manager or, in the absence of the General Manager, by the Acting General Manager, and shall not be delegated.

(i) All the procedures established for a regular appeal, other than those pertaining to time, are the same as to an expedited appeal, unless otherwise noted.

IV. Staff Review of Regulations
The Commission directs the General Manager and staff to continue to evaluate the viability of these regulations and to ascertain whether this scheme strikes the proper balance between the recreational, constitutional and property interests of San Franciscans heretofore mentioned and the Commission's substantial interest in preserving park property, limiting excessive noise and congestion and other police

problems that may result from activities on park property. The General Manager shall report to this Commission its findings as to this issue no later than the first and seventh Commission meetings of each calendar year.

APPROVED AS TO FORM: GEORGE AGNOST,
City Attorney

_____
Deputy City Attorney

5/15/86

GLOSSARY

Asterisk (*) indicates a definition taken in whole or in part from *Black's Law Dictionary*

Act of God – An unforeseen event uncontrollable by either party, such as a flood, fire, strike, war, government action, shortage of supply, illness of a key character or the like. Also called a *force majeure*.

Additional insured – Person(s) covered by an insurance policy in addition to the named insured; e.g., a person using another's automobile, which is covered by a liability policy containing a statutory omnibus clause, when the insured's permission is expressly or impliedly given for a particular use.*

AFTRA – American Federation of Television and Radio Artists; performers' union.

AF of M – American Federation of Musicians; union of performing and recording musicians.

ASCAP – American Society of Composers, Authors and Publishers; a collective organization that compensates writers and publishers of music for public performances of their works.

Appellate court – A court that reviews the decisions of lower courts. Trial level courts decide issues of fact; appellate courts review issues of law.

Bankruptcy – A federal procedure for the benefit and relief of creditors and their debtors in cases in which the debtors are unable or unwilling to pay their debts.

Barter – In syndication of television and radio programming, barter refers to the exchange of commercial time in lieu of an all-cash payment for rights to a program.

BATF – Bureau of Alcohol, Tobacco and Firearms in the U.S. Department of the Treasury.

BMI – Broadcast Music, Inc.; a collective organization that compensates writers and publishers of music for public performances of their works.

Boilerplate – Standard legal verbiage found in most contracts, covering routine matters of a housekeeping sort.

Bona fide – Good faith; integrity of dealing; honesty; sincerity.*

Clear – To clear a television station is to obtain its commitment to air a program.

Compulsory license – A license provided under the Copyright Revision Act of 1976. A compulsory license is available only to record a musical composition previously recorded or to include a phonorecord in a jukebox.

Consideration – The inducement to a contract; the cause, motive, price or impelling influence that induces a contracting party to enter into a contract; the reason or material cause of a contract; some right, interest, profit or benefit accruing to one party, or some forbearance, detriment, loss or responsibility given, suffered or undertaken by the other.*

Copyright – The bundle of rights granted by 17 U.S.C. § 106 to: (1) authorize copies of, (2) produce derivative works based on, (3) publicly perform, (4) publicly display or (5) initially publicly distribute copies of, a work fixed in a tangible medium of expression.

Defendant – The party in a lawsuit from whom redress is sought.

Downlink – The reception of a television signal from a satellite.

FCC – Federal Communications Commission, which regulates television and radio transmissions.

Force majeure – *See* Act of God.

GAAP – Generally accepted accounting principles.

Good faith – An intangible and abstract quality with no technical meaning or statutory definition, encompassing, among other things, an honest belief, the absence of malice and the absence of design to defraud or to seek an unconscionable advantage. An individual's personal good faith is a concept of his or her own mind and inner spirit and, therefore, may not conclusively be determined by his or her protestations alone.*

Goodwill – The good favor that the management of a business wins from the public; the fixed and favorable consideration of customers arising from established and well conducted business; the favorable consideration held by the purchasing public toward goods known to emanate from a particular source.*

Indemnify – To hold another harmless from liability or to restore the loss of a victim; one who indemnifies another reimburses the other party for its loss.

Indemnitee – The person who, in a contract of indemnity, is to be indemnified or protected by the other.*

Indemnitor – The person who is bound, by an indemnity contract, to indemnify or protect the other.*

Injunction – A court order that something shall not be done during the period of time specified in the order.

Make-good – A rebate or free time given to an advertiser to make up for deficiency in promised audience caused by a commercial interruption or program preemption or the like.

Mechanical rights – The right to reproduce the words and music of a copyrighted song in phonorecords or audiotapes.

Morals clause – A contract clause imposing standards of conduct on a key participant or employee.

Most-favored-nations clause – A contract clause that guarantees that a party has as good a deal as that offered to any other person.

Named insured – The person specifically designated in an insurance policy as the one protected; commonly, it is the person with whom the contract of insurance has been made.*

Pay-per-view – A method of broadcasting a program only to persons who have paid a fee to receive the signal of the specific program.

Payola – Commercial bribery for the inclusion of any commercial matter in a telecast or for the playing of a song on the radio. See 47 U.S.C. § 508 (Appendix H).

Plaintiff – The party initiating a lawsuit to seek legal redress for a wrong suffered or about to be suffered.

Public figure – For purposes of determining the standard to be applied in a defamation action, includes artists, athletes, businesspeople and persons who are famous or infamous because of who they are or what they have done.*

Rating system – A system for counting the number of viewers or listeners of a program on television, cable or radio.

Reasonable – Fair, proper, just, moderate, suitable under the circumstances.*

Release – The giving up of a right, claim, or privilege. Prior to entering an automobile race, the drivers execute releases in which they give up any right to sue the organizer of the race if they are hurt while participating.

Right of first refusal – Right to have first opportunity to purchase something, such as the right to sponsor an event, when those sponsorship rights became available; the right to meet the terms of any offer received for such sponsorship rights.

SAG – Screen Actors Guild; performers' union.

Secondary meaning – Wide public recognition of a descriptive mark as being associated with one source of goods or services.

Service mark – A trademark used in the sale or advertising of services rather than goods.

Summary judgment – A judgment rendered by a court, often before trial, when there are no facts in dispute.

Superstation – A broadcast station, such as WGN in Chicago, WTBS in Atlanta or WOR in New York, whose signal is carried by numerous cable television systems.

Synchronization – The recording of music with action in a visual medium.

Syndication – Arranging for a program to be shown on a variety of independent, unrelated television stations.

Title sponsor – The sponsor whose name is part of the name of the Event; examples include MAZDA GATOR BOWL; BENSON AND HEDGES COMMAND PERFORMANCE RIVER BLUES; OLD STYLE MARATHON/CHICAGO.

Tort – A civil wrong to a person, property or reputation.

Trademark – Generally speaking, a distinctive mark of authenticity, through which the products of particular manufacturers or the vendible commodities of particular merchants may be distinguished from those of others. It may consist in any symbol or in any form of words, letters or numbers.

UBIT – Unrelated business income tax. A federal tax on not-for-profit corporations.

Uplink – The transmission of a television signal to a communications satellite for distribution back to earth receiver stations.

BIBLIOGRAPHY

Basic Treatises/References in Relevant Areas of the Law and the Industry

Biederman and Berry, *Law and Business of the Entertainment Industries*, Auburn House Publishing Company (Dover, Mass.) (1987).

Farber, Donald C., Gen. Ed., *Entertainment Industry Contracts, Negotiation and Drafting Guide*, 4 vols., Matthew Bender (1987).

McCarthy, J. Thomas, *Trademarks and Unfair Competition* (2nd ed.), 2 vols., The Lawyer's Cooperative Publishing Co. (1984).

Nimmer, Melville, B., *Nimmer on Copyright*, 4 vols., Matthew Bender (1987).

Shemel, Sidney and Krasilovsky, M. William. *This Business of Music*, Billboard Publications, Inc. (1985).

Other

"The Merchandising Report," Charles W. Grimes & Gregory J. Battersby, exec. eds.; Penfair Communications, Inc. (Stamford, Conn.).

"Promo," Kerry E. Smith, editor and publisher; monthly, Smith Communications, Inc. (White Plains, N.Y.).

"Special Events Report," bi-monthly, International Events Group, Inc. (Chicago).

INDEX

ABOUT THE AUTHOR

Mary Hutchings Reed is a partner in the law firm of Winston & Strawn, Chicago, Illinois. She practices primarily advertising, trademark, copyright and entertainment law. In the sponsorship area, Mary has represented organizers of professional boxing matches, marathons and arts festivals, and has advised corporate sponsors of professional car races, concerts and other events. In addition to her law practice, Mary is Adjunct Professor of Law at Northwestern University School of Law, where she teaches entertainment law. She has also taught arts, entertainment and media law in the graduate school at Columbia College, Chicago, Illinois. She is a frequent writer and speaker on these topics, and is the author of *The Copyright Primer for Librarians and Educators* and a contributing editor of *Business Torts*. Mary earned her bachelor's and master's degrees in public policymaking and economics, respectively, at Brown University in 1973, and graduated from Yale Law School in 1976. From 1976 until 1989, Mary was associated with Sidley & Austin, Chicago, Illinois and was a partner there for six years.